ROCKY MOUNTAIN NATIONAL PARK

ERIN ENGLISH

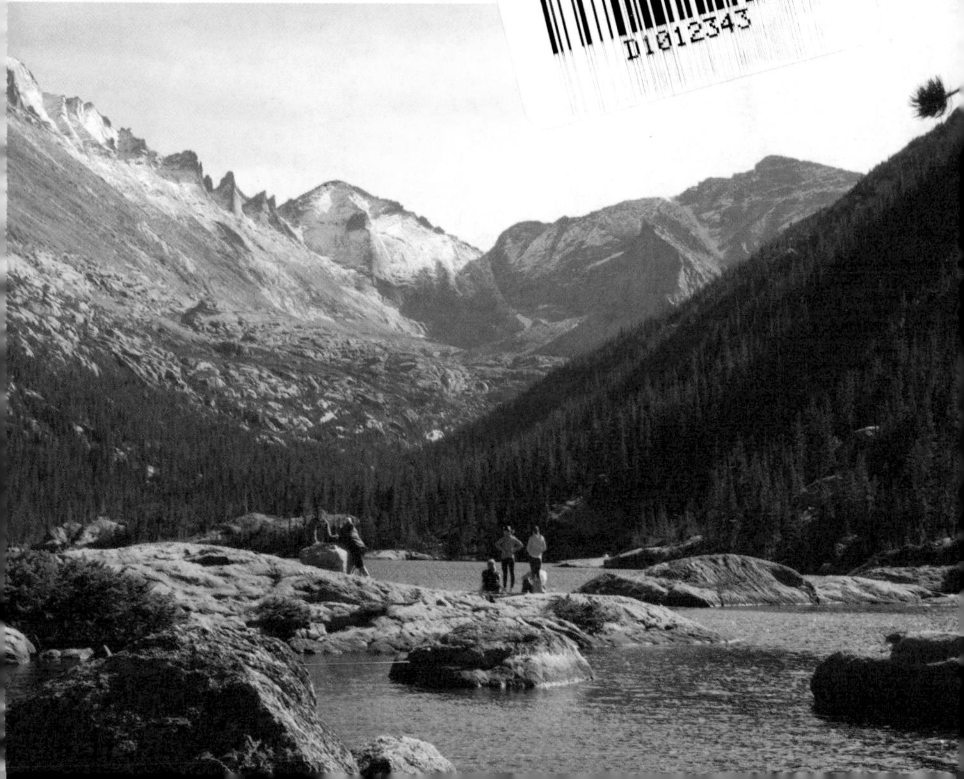

Comanche Peak
Wilderness Area
Neota
Wilderness
Area
14
Long Draw
Reservoir
Thunder Mtn
Mount Neota
Lulu Mtn
Flatiron Mtn
12,335ft
Hagues Peak
Mummy Mtn
Crystal
Lake
Desolation Peaks
12,949ft
Fairchild Mtn
Lawn
Lake
Mummy Range
Arapaho
National
Forest
Mount Richthofen
12,940ft
Lead Mtn
12,537ft
Specimen Mtn
12,489ft
Spectacle
Lakes
Ypsilon Lake
Mount
Tileston
Howard Mtn
12,810ft
Shipler
Mtn
Shipler's Park
Bighorn Mtn
Mount Cumulus
12,725ft
Never Summer Mountains
Rocky Mountains
Mount Nimbus
12,706ft
Mount Stratus
Baker Mtn
34
Forest Canyon
Deer Mountain
10,013ft
Mount Ida
12,880ft
Mount Julian
12,928ft
Rocky Mountain
National Park
CONTINENTAL DIVIDE
Never Summer
Wilderness
Area
Spruce Canyon
Nakai Peak
12,216ft
Gabletop Mtn
11,821ft
Knobtop Mtn
12,336ft
Ptarmigan Point
12,270ft
Flattop Mtn
12,362ft
Hallett Pk
12,599ft
Otis Pk
12,484ft
Glacier Gorge
Bowen Gulch
Protection
Area
Taylor Pk
13,143ft
Arapaho
National
Forest
Powell Pk
13,176ft
McHenrys Pk
13,242ft
Grand Lake
Grand
Lake
Longs Peak
14,259ft
Mount Meeker
13,911ft
Mount Alice
13,310ft
Shadow
Mountain
Lake
Arapaho Nat'l
Rec Area
Isolation Peak
13,118ft
Ogalalla Peak
13,138ft
© AVALON TRAVEL
Lake
Granby

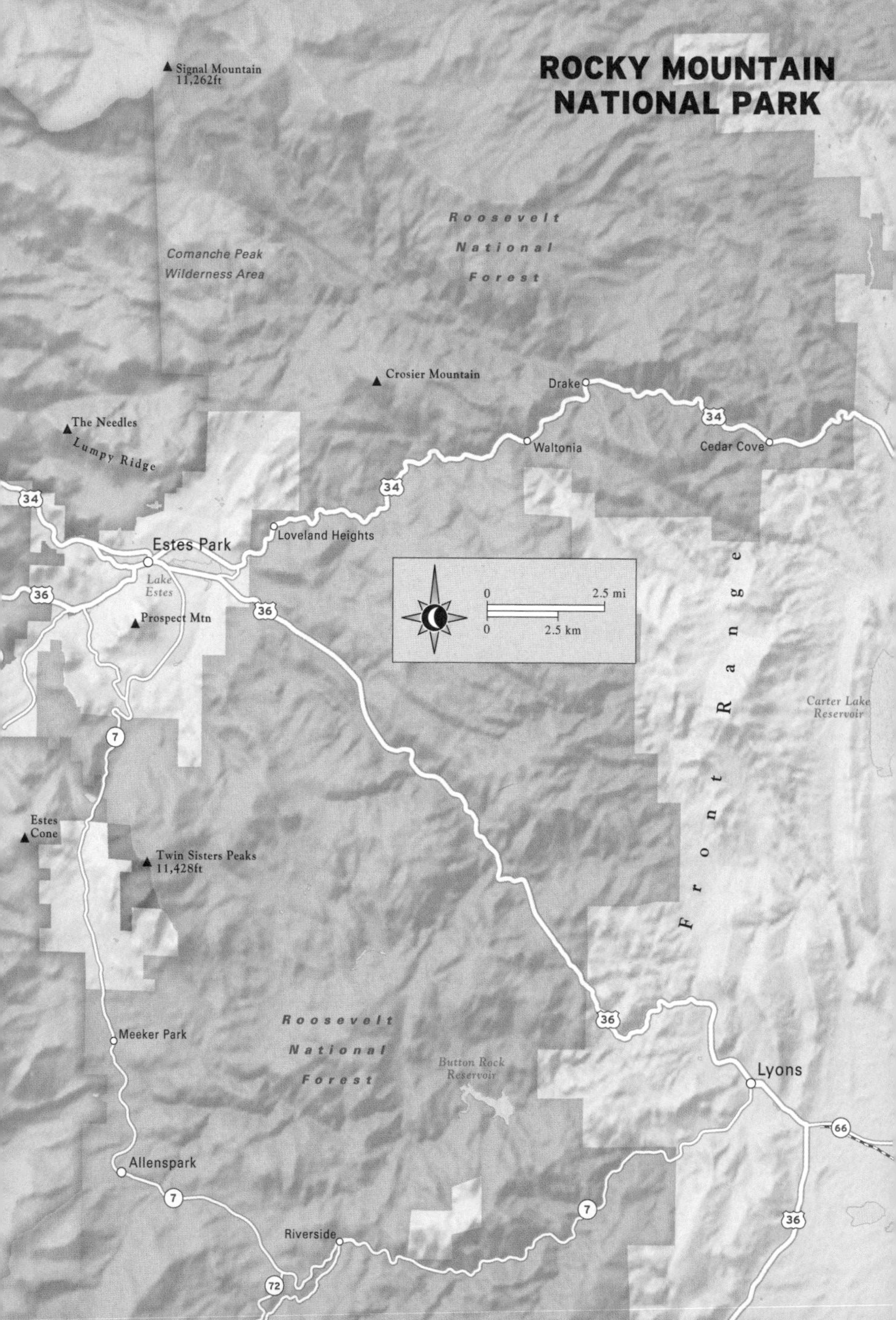
ROCKY MOUNTAIN NATIONAL PARK
Signal Mountain
11,262ft
Comanche Peak
Wilderness Area
Roosevelt
National
Forest
Crosier Mountain
Drake
34
Waltonia
Cedar Cove
The Needles
Lumpy Ridge
34
34
Loveland Heights
Estes Park
Lake
Estes
36
36
Prospect Mtn
0
2.5 mi
0
2.5 km
Front Range
Carter Lake
Reservoir
7
Estes
Cone
Twin Sisters Peaks
11,428ft
36
Roosevelt
National
Forest
Button Rock
Reservoir
Meeker Park
Lyons
66
Allenspark
7
7
36
Riverside
72

Contents

DISCOVER

Rocky Mountain National Park

Rocky Mountain National Park is a world of extremes. Within one hour, visitors can find themselves soaking up the sun under bluebird skies, then frantically piling on layers as a snow squall unapologetically sweeps through.

Massive landforms capped in brilliant white rise sharply from the valley floors, drawing your gaze ever upward. In the park's alpine tundra—above 11,000 feet in elevation—an ecosystem low to the ground is equally fascinating. Colorful, compact plants have adapted to harsh environs and are hardly ruffled, even in the presence of howling winds. Squeaky, beady-eyed pikas scurry about urgently, collecting and storing food.

Sensory delights wait around every corner: lakes glossy and lustrous, like shiny silver dollars; skin-tingling, cool sprays from tumbling waterfalls; butterscotch-scented ponderosa pine trees. The nature is intoxicating.

Clockwise from top left: an elk; Rocky Mountain columbine; a hammock at Glacier Basin Campground; fishing at Dream Lake; view of the Kawuneeche Valley; Lake of Glass.

The park's treasures are hardly secret. This designated wilderness area experiences an annual visitation of more than four million people. Visitors flock here for the scenic grandeur, watchable wildlife, and recreational opportunities. Spending time in this small cross-section of the 3,000-mile Rocky Mountain range nourishes the soul. You can't help but experience the present moment inside the park's boundaries.

The late U.S. President Woodrow Wilson formally established this protected region in 1915. The park, affectionately known as "Rocky," has enjoyed a remarkable 1st century.

Here's to another wild and wonderful 100 years.

Clockwise from top left: a horse at Moraine Park Stables; sparkling Fern Creek on the approach to Odessa Lake; authentic Native American wares at Eagle Plume's in Allenspark; glacial erratics along the Wild Basin Trail.

Planning Your Trip

Where to Go

Bear Lake and the East Side

Bear Lake is the most heavily visited region in the park and understandably so. Glacial cirques, wildflower-filled meadows, and sparkling lakes pack a scenic punch, and **Moraine Park** features one of the most picturesque mountain views in the entire park. **Bear Lake, Sprague Lake,** and **Alberta Falls** are easily accessible, family-friendly destinations, and many other scenic hiking trails beg to be explored. The area is home to three campgrounds, two visitor centers, the Moraine Park Discovery Center, and two horse stables. The gateway town of **Estes Park** is a short car ride away.

Longs Peak and Wild Basin

From many locations inside and outside of the park, visitors are able to see **Longs Peak** rising majestically from the earth, cresting at 14,259 feet. The most popular route to the top of this towering spectacle starts from the busy **Longs Peak Trailhead** on the east side. Climbers start their grueling 10- to 15-hour trek here in the early hours of the morning and often camp at the park's **Longs Peak Campground.** Shorter (yet still challenging) hiking trails in the vicinity lead to **Estes Cone** and **Chasm Lake.** A few miles up the road from the Longs Peak turnoff is **Lily Lake,** a great location for bird-watching and spotting wildflowers. **Wild Basin** is a paradise for hikers, who are richly rewarded with stunning views of gushing waterfalls and serene lakes.

Trail Ridge Road

On summer days, traffic rumbles along at a nearly constant pace on **Trail Ridge Road.** As the only

In every season, Lily Lake is a beauty to behold.

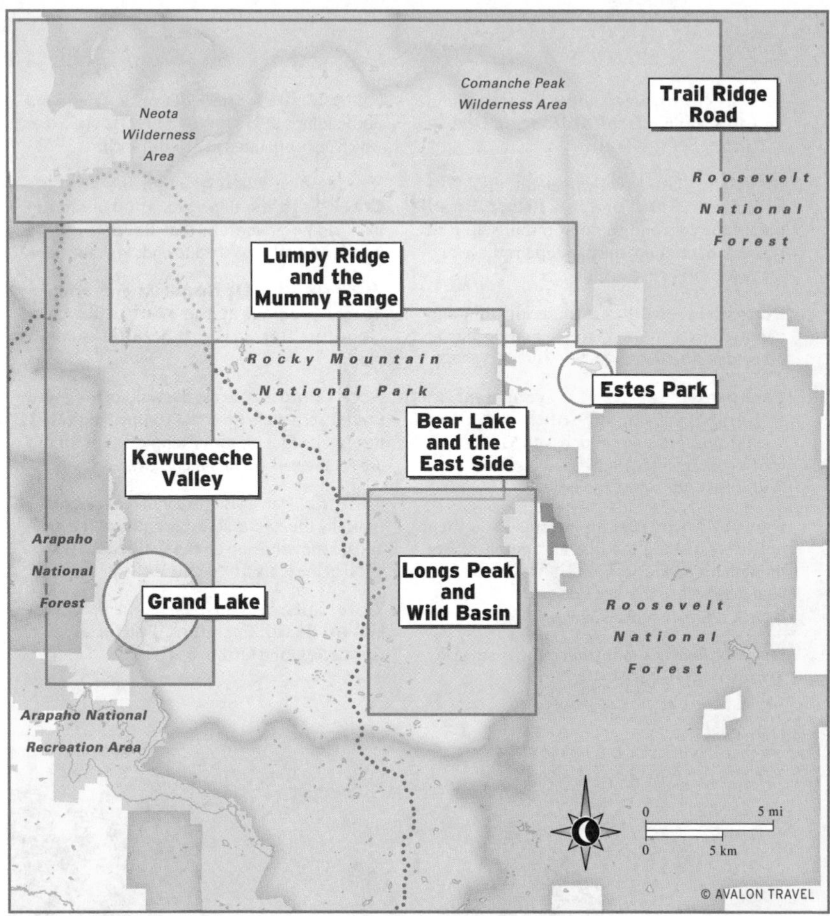

vehicle thoroughfare that spans the east and west sides of the park, this road is notable for being the highest continuous road in the U.S. **Milner Pass**—one of the many pullouts along the road—is the easiest place in the park to stand on the **Continental Divide.** Visitors are fascinated by the creatures and plants of the **alpine tundra,** and flock to the **Tundra Communities Trail** to get their fill. At 11,796 feet, the **Alpine Visitor Center** is a popular rest stop and the highest national park visitor center. **Old Fall River Road,** which intersects Trail Ridge Road at the visitor center, was the first road built in the park and is heavily traveled in the summer.

Kawuneeche Valley

Water and wide-open spaces are the main attractions in the **Kawuneeche Valley,** which—compared with the east side of the park—is less congested with people and therefore much quieter. The west side's many meadows are prime places to enjoy a moment of solitude and watch for wildlife, especially elk and moose. The legendary **Colorado River** snakes its way through the

If You're Looking for...

- **Backpacking:** Sleep under the stars along the park's portion of the **Continental Divide National Scenic Trail.**
- **Bicycling:** Take a two-wheeled tour of **Old Fall River Road** or **Trail Ridge Road** before the cars and summer throngs appear. Weather permitting, the park opens these two roads to bicycles in the spring.
- **Budget-Friendly:** Learn about flora and fauna, constellations, glaciers, and dozens of other topics in a **free, ranger-led program.**
- **Camping:** Get cozy in your tent at **Aspenglen Campground,** the park's second-smallest campground with 53 sites. The spot is convenient to Highways 34 and 36, which lead to east-side sights and trails.
- **Driving Tour:** Fuel up in Estes Park, then putter west along the first automobile route through the park, **Old Fall River Road.** Make your way back to the east side via **Trail Ridge Road,** one of America's Byways®.
- **Fishing:** Catch a brook trout or two in the **Big Thompson River.**
- **Historic Sites:** Check out rustic cabins and outbuildings at **Holzwarth Historic Site,** which once operated as a dude ranch.
- **Horseback Riding:** From the **Glacier Creek Stables,** depart for a 10-hour horseback riding adventure that travels over the **Continental Divide** and ends in Grand Lake.
- **Kid-Friendly Options:** Attend a Junior Ranger program at the **Junior Ranger Headquarters** in **Hidden Valley** (summer only).
- **Rock Climbing:** Scale the walls of the **Twin Owls,** accessible from the Lumpy Ridge Trailhead. Note that raptor-nesting closures for this area of the park occur March-July.
- **Solitude:** Plan a visit for January or February, typically the two quietest months of the year, and go snowshoeing on the **Colorado River Trail** in the **Kawuneeche Valley.**
- **Waterfalls:** Visit three outstanding gushers in **Wild Basin: Copeland Falls, Calypso Cascades,** and **Ouzel Falls.**

the Twin Owls

valley and is a big draw for fly-fishing aficionados. One campground, **Timber Creek,** can be found here, and two of the best family-friendly hikes in the park are located off Highway 34/ Trail Ridge Road: **Holzwarth Historic Site** and **Coyote Valley Trail.** Downtown **Grand Lake** is a few miles away from the **Kawuneeche Visitor Center.**

Lumpy Ridge and the Mummy Range

Hiking trails around **Lumpy Ridge** are usually the first to thaw out in the springtime, and lead to pretty destinations such as **Gem Lake** and **Bridal Veil Falls.** Lumpy Ridge is a rock climber's dream, and has many bumpy geologic features—with names like **Twin Owls** and **Pear Buttress**—to scale. Along the **Black Canyon Trail** and the greater **Lumpy Ridge Loop,** running is especially popular. In the **Mummy Range,** humans have blazed only a few trails to the area's lakes, which are located miles away from any form of civilization. **Mirror Lake** and **Little Yellowstone** are key attractions in the northwestern corner of the park. U.S. Forest Service campgrounds **Long Draw** and **Grandview**—located outside the park—accommodate overnight visitors to this remote region.

Gateways

On the east side of Rocky, **Estes Park** is the busiest gateway town, featuring many hotels, lodges, campgrounds, restaurants, and shops. Visitors destined for the national park are sometimes sidetracked here for days by all of the activities available, including an aerial tramway, golf, and boating on Lake Estes. On the west side, the town of **Grand Lake** is known for its namesake body of water, a quaint boardwalk lined with shops, and the **Rocky Mountain Repertory Theatre.** Lodging and dining options are also plentiful in Grand Lake. South of Grand Lake, in the **Arapaho National Recreation Area,** visitors enjoy boating, fishing, camping, and osprey viewing.

When to Go

High Season (mid-June-early Oct.)

In the summer, lakes sparkle in the sunshine, birds belt out tunes, colorful blooms carpet meadows, and torrents of water spill forth from waterfalls. Visitors are awestruck by the beauty of the park in the warm months. The full length of **Trail Ridge Road is open,** and **Old Fall River Road** typically **opens around the 4th of July.** The upshot about summer is that everyone else has the same idea as you to come at this glorious time of year. Parking lots can be crowded and the lines long to board the park's free shuttles. The trails are busy and vigilance is needed to snag a picnic table or a first-come, first-served campsite. To experience solitude on a summer hike, heed this advice: The earlier you go, the farther you go, and the higher you go, the fewer people you will see. A mass exodus of cars from the park usually occurs around 3pm-4pm every day in the summer, so sticking around on a clear evening to hike or sightsee has its advantages.

To enjoy a peaceful experience in the early fall, plan a **weekday visit** rather than a weekend getaway. Park administrators have conducted research that shows weekend visitation in September is 50 percent greater than visitation on weekdays. In the summer, mornings are often sunny, with afternoon thunderstorms typical. In the early fall, the daytime temperature ranges from warm to cool, and rain showers happen less frequently.

Mid-Season (early Oct.-Nov.)

Trails are still busy with hikers this time of year, and the **elk rut**—which starts in early September and lasts until mid-October—is a huge attraction for tourists. Shutterbugs delight in **foliage** that changes from verdant green to a brilliant palette of gold, red, and orange. Autumn unfolds on the west side of the park slightly earlier than on the east side. Sometime around mid-October, **Trail Ridge Road** and **the Alpine Visitor Center close** until the following summer season. **Old Fall River Road** closes after the first major snowstorm (usually earlier than Trail Ridge Rd.). Other features around the park **shut down** in stages after the summer rush, including the Junior Ranger Headquarters in Hidden Valley (Aug.); Longs Peak, Aspenglen, and Glacier Basin campgrounds (Sept.); the free shuttle bus system (mid-Oct.); and Timber Creek campground (Nov.) on the west side. **Moraine Park Campground** (year-round) regularly fills on fall weekends. In late October or November, when foot traffic is slowing, some business owners in Grand Lake and Estes Park temporarily shut their doors until the snowy season arrives. Pack a sweater, a warm hat, and snow clothes during this time of year; you might need them all.

Low Season (Dec.-mid-June)

There is no better season than winter in which to find peacefulness in Rocky. Visit during this time of year and you will find near-empty parking lots, quiet roads, trails with untracked snow, and wildlife still romping about. A handful of smaller roads are closed off—along with Trail Ridge Road and Old Fall River Road—but the main traffic arteries are open. Hidden Valley's **sledding hill** opens up for family fun, and ranger-led programs change focus to winter topics. Popular recreational activities include **cross-country skiing** and **snowshoeing.** In **Grand Lake,** some restaurants, businesses, and lodges stay closed all winter. In both gateway towns, numerous establishments **shut their doors briefly in early spring,** when trails have turned to slush and mud, and when business is consequently slow. On the plus side, at hotels that stay open year-round, lodging prices are often more reasonable in the off-season than they are in the busy season. **Pasque flowers** can make their first appearance as early as March, and numerous wild

Fall is an especially beautiful time to visit the park.

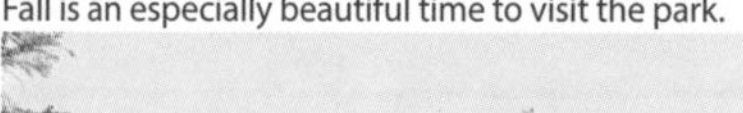

At the Alpine Visitor Center, hail and snow make a regular appearance.

animals emerge from hibernation about the same time. Around early May, visitation starts to pick up from a slow trickle to a steady stream, but it is still possible to sit in deep contemplation by a thawing river without being disturbed by anyone. Many people are eager to get on the trails at this point but are stymied by lingering snow and variable weather conditions. On Memorial Day, the barriers come down for the closed-off portion of **Trail Ridge Road,** barring any late-season snowstorms.

Be prepared for snow and cold temperatures in the winter; the west side of the park sees considerably more snow than the east side. In the spring, the weather can be sunny one day and snowing the next; your suitcase should contain short-sleeve shirts and a thick winter jacket as options.

Before You Go

Park Fees and Passes

A one-day pass for an automobile is **$20;** for a seven-day pass, the fee is **$30.** Individuals traveling by motorcycle or moped pay $20 for a one-day entrance pass and $25 for a seven-day pass. Bicyclists and pedestrians pay a $10 fee for a one-day visit and $15 for seven days of entry. Visitors can pay admission fees by cash, credit card, or check at park entrance stations (cash and credit card are preferred). An electronic payment option for one- and seven-day park passes is available online (www.nps.gov/romo).

A **Rocky Mountain National Park Annual Pass** costs **$60** and can be purchased in person at any entrance station or online (www.pay.gov). The pass grants one year of unlimited entry to the park for up to two people. Entrance station staff will ask you to present a photo ID every time you enter the park with your card.

An annual pass granting entry to both **Rocky Mountain National Park** and the **Arapaho National Recreation Area** runs **$70** and can be purchased at the park or from the **Sulphur Ranger District office** (9 Ten Mile Dr.) in Granby.

The **America the Beautiful Pass** series grants holders access to Rocky and to more than 2,000 federal recreation sites. The America the Beautiful National Parks and Federal Recreational Lands Annual Pass is $80 and the best deal for anyone planning to tour multiple national parks and/or monuments in one calendar year. Purchase your pass at any park entrance station or online at http://store.usgs.gov.

Each year, the park announces a short list of **Fee Free Days.** These days typically include Martin Luther King, Jr. Day in January; Presidents' Day in February; National Park Week weekends in April; the National Park Service's birthday in August; National Public Lands Day in September; and Veterans Day in November. However, special events during any given year can dictate a slightly different list.

Any individual 16 years of age and older who wishes to fish in the park must carry a valid **Colorado fishing license.** Permits can be obtained through the **Colorado Parks and Wildlife** (800/244-5613, www.cpw.state.co.us).

Entrance Stations

There are three main entrances to the park:

Beaver Meadows Entrance Station (Hwy. 36): This busy entrance station is located on the east side, 2.7 miles from downtown Estes Park, and is central to many park areas.

Fall River Entrance Station (Hwy. 34): Located on the east side, this entrance provides easy access to Trail Ridge Road (closed in winter), Old Fall River Road (closed in winter), and Aspenglen Campground.

Grand Lake Entrance Station (Hwy. 34): Located 1.8 miles north of Grand Lake, this station serves the Kawuneeche Valley on the west side of the park.

Reservations

There are no lodges inside the park. If you're here, you're camping. Estes Park (on the east side) and Grand Lake (on the west side) are your best bets for indoor accommodations.

Reservations (877/444-6777, www.recreation.gov) are accepted at **Aspenglen, Glacier Basin** (both summer only), and **Moraine Park Campgrounds** (open year-round) up to six months in advance. **Timber Creek** and **Longs Peak Campgrounds** (both summer only) are first-come, first-served. In late fall, winter, and early spring, **Moraine Park Campground** is first-come, first-served.

WILDERNESS CAMPING

Wilderness campers are required to carry a **wilderness permit,** which is acquired in person at one of the park's wilderness offices. In order to obtain a permit, first you need to **reserve your campsite.** For wilderness camping dates that fall May 1-October 31, reservations can be made online (www.pay.gov) or in person at a park wilderness office March 1-October 28. Campsite reservations must be made at least three days in advance, and a $26 Wilderness Administrative Fee must be paid for any reservation made for this time period.

For camping dates November 1-April 30, reservations can be made by phone (970/586-1242) or in person at a wilderness office October 1-April 30. On the east side of the park, a wilderness office is located next to the Beaver Meadows Visitor Center; on the west side of the park, a wilderness office is located inside the Kawuneeche Visitor Center. In the winter, it is also possible to self-register for backcountry camping at certain locations.

Rocky Mountain Vicinity Campgrounds

	Location	Price	Season	Amenities
Moraine Park Campground	Bear Lake/East Side	$18-26	year-round	tent and RV sites; shuttle stop
Glacier Basin Campground	Bear Lake/East Side	$26	late May-early Sept.	tent and RV sites; group sites; shuttle stop
Aspenglen Campground	Fall River	$26	late May-early Sept.	tent and RV sites
Longs Peak Campground	Longs Peak	$20	late May-Nov. 1	tent-only sites
Olive Ridge Campground (USFS)	Wild Basin	$14	late May-late Sept.	tent and RV sites
Meeker Park Overflow Campground (USFS)	Wild Basin	$11	mid-June-early Sept.	tent and RV sites
Timber Creek Campground	Kawuneechee Valley	$26	late May-early Nov.	tent and RV sites
Green Ridge Campground (USFS)	Arapaho National Recreation Area	$19-38	mid-May-late Sept.	tent and RV sites
Stillwater Campground (USFS)	Arapaho National Recreation Area	$22-44	May-Sept.	tent and RV sites
Willow Creek Campground (USFS)	Arapaho National Recreation Area	$19	late May-mid Oct.	tent and RV sites; group site ($75)
Sunset Point Campground (USFS)	Arapaho National Recreation Area	$22-44	May-Sept.	tent and RV sites
Arapaho Bay Campgrounds (USFS)	Arapaho National Recreation Area	$19-38	late May-mid-Oct.	tent and RV sites
Long Draw Campground (USFS)	Long Draw Road and Corral Creek	$16-32	July-mid Nov.	tent and RV sites
Grandview Campground (USFS)	Long Draw Road and Corral Creek	$16-32	July-mid Nov.	tent and RV sites

A double rainbow appears over Glacier Basin Campground.

In the Park

Visitor Centers

Two visitor centers serve the east side of the park: **Beaver Meadows Visitor Center** (1000 Hwy. 36, 970/586-1206) is the park's headquarters and the closest visitor center to downtown Estes Park, and **Fall River Visitor Center** (3450 Fall River Rd., 970/586-1206, www.rockymountaingateway.net) is 4 miles north of downtown Estes Park. The **Alpine Visitor Center** is located at the junction of Old Fall River Road and Trail Ridge Road inside Rocky. The west side is served by one information hub: the **Kawuneeche Visitor Center** (16018 Hwy. 34, 970/627-3471).

Where to Stay

In the early 20th century, numerous guest lodges graced Rocky Mountain National Park, but today, in-park accommodations are limited to the park's five campgrounds. For last-minute camping, try **Timber Creek** on the west side, which is always first-come, first-served (summer only). If all park campgrounds are full on the east side, consider one of the campgrounds or RV parks in Estes Park or along Highway 7 near Allenspark. I have routinely had good luck landing a site at first-come, first-served **Meeker Park Overflow Campground** (on the west side of Hwy. 7 at mile marker 11, 303/541-2500, http://fs.usda.gov, mid-June-early Sept., $11) when arriving in town early or mid-week. On the west side, you might also consider pitching your tent at one of the established campsites next to **Shadow Mountain Reservoir** or **Lake Granby.** Visitors can book a maximum of seven nights at park campgrounds June 1-Sept. 30 and an additional 14 nights during the rest of the year.

Estes Park offers more than 200 lodging options, including rustic cabins and charming bed-and-breakfasts, while Grand Lake features lodges, motels, inns, and cottages in a variety sufficient to suit most tastes.

Getting Around

In the **summer,** the best (and most eco-friendly) mode of transport on the east side is the park's **shuttle bus** system, which runs from late spring until early fall. This free service helps reduce traffic congestion at trailheads, and also enables hikers to arrange some great one-way hikes without having to shuttle their own vehicles. The park's shuttle service is only offered in the Bear Lake region.

The **Hiker Shuttle Express Route** (7:30am-8pm daily late June-mid-Sept., weekends only mid-Sept.-early Oct.) runs from the Estes Park Visitor Center and Beaver Meadows Visitor Center to the Park & Ride.

The **Bear Lake Route** (7am-7:30pm daily late May-early Oct.) takes passengers to the Park & Ride, Glacier Creek Stables, Bierstadt Lake Trailhead, the Glacier Gorge Trailhead, and Bear Lake.

The **Moraine Park Route** (7am-7:30pm daily late May-early Oct.) makes stops at the Park & Ride, Glacier Basin Campground, Glacier Creek Stables, Hollowell Park, Tuxedo Park, Moraine Park Discovery Center, Moraine Park Campground, Cub Lake Trailhead, and Fern Lake Bus Stop.

The only way to access the west side of the park is by private vehicle. **RVs** can travel on all park roads, with the exception of Old Fall River Road. RV travelers are also discouraged from driving on narrow Wild Basin Road.

Trail Ridge Road is generally open Memorial Day-mid-October (weather permitting), though it can stay open later in unseasonably warm years. **Old Fall River Road** is open July 4 until the first major snowstorm.

In the **winter,** the only option for going anywhere in the park is with a private vehicle.

The Best of Rocky Mountain National Park

Innumerable itineraries can be built around Rocky's beautiful sights, hikes, and scenic drives. This summer sojourn visits many of the park's attractions, while still leaving time for spontaneity and overnights at three of Rocky's campgrounds. Camping in the park is the catalyst for creating many indelible memories—from wildlife sightings to spectacular sunrises. If you can swing it, spend one or more nights within the park's boundaries; you will be duly rewarded. If not, book accommodations in Estes Park or Grand Lake instead.

Day 1

Enter the park at the Beaver Meadows Entrance Station. On the way, strike a pose at the official **Rocky Mountain National Park sign** on Highway 36, then orient yourself at the **Beaver Meadows Visitor Center.** Once inside the park, set up camp at **Moraine Park Campground,** where you have made reservations for two nights. Take the free shuttle to the **Glacier Gorge Trailhead** for a 1.6-mile round-trip hike to **Alberta Falls.**

Later in the afternoon, exit the park on Highway 36 to Marys Lake Road; then travel southeast on Marys Lake Road to Highway 7. Drive 4.7 miles south on Highway 7 for a tour at the **Enos Mills Cabin Museum** (reserve in advance). After the tour, drive 1.8 miles north to **Lily Lake** for a shoreline stroll. In the evening, return to the campground and attend a ranger-led program at the **Moraine Park Amphitheater.**

Day 2

Arrive at the **Bear Lake** parking lot early via the free park shuttle. Purchase a self-guided tour booklet for the **Bear Lake Nature Trail** and enjoy a walk around the lake (0.5 mile round-trip). Afterwards, hike to **Nymph Lake, Dream**

hiking in Glacier Gorge

Lake, and **Emerald Lake** on the **Emerald Lake Trail** (3.6 miles round-trip). After eating a sack lunch, return the way you came, or stop off at Dream Lake to fish for greenback cutthroat trout.

Catch a shuttle back down Bear Lake Road and head indoors at the **Moraine Park Discovery Center** to peruse the nature exhibits. On the way to the campground (take a shuttle; the road isn't designed for pedestrian traffic), keep your eyes out for deer, elk, and other **wildlife.** Treat yourself to an ice cream sandwich at the campground's firewood and **snack shack** (you've earned it!) and settle into your camp chair with a copy of *A Lady's Life in the Rocky Mountains* by Isabella L. Bird. After dinner, enjoy another ranger-led program at the **Moraine Park Amphitheater.**

Day 3

Pack up your things and drive 6.9 miles northwest to the turnoff for **Old Fall River Road.** First, check out the **Alluvial Fan;** then venture on to the 15-mph, one-way, dirt portion of Old Fall River Road to gaze at **Chasm Falls.** After an adventurous drive that culminates at the **Alpine Visitor Center,** grab a bite to eat at **Café in the Clouds.** Once refueled, take an invigorating hike (0.5 mile round-trip) up the **Alpine Ridge Trail.**

Continue driving west along **Trail Ridge Road,** stopping to check out **Medicine Bow Curve, Milner Pass,** and **Farview Curve.** Your final destination is **Timber Creek Campground,** where you will spend tonight and tomorrow night sleeping under the stars.

Day 4

Get an early start with some catch-and-release fly-fishing on the **Colorado River,** just steps away from the campground. Pack a lunch and a wildflower identification chart and drive south to the **East Inlet Trailhead,** keeping your eyes peeled for **moose** along the way. Check out **Adams Falls** (0.3 mile one-way), then continue hiking east as far as your legs will take you, looking out for flowers and wildlife.

Bighorn sheep are the official symbol of Rocky Mountain National Park.

Best in One Day

Emerald Lake hikers

7:00 AM

Enter Rocky at the **Beaver Meadows Entrance Station** and drive on Bear Lake Road to the **Bear Lake Trailhead.** Just a few minutes' walk from the parking lot, arrive at the banks of **Bear Lake.** Then, from the **Emerald Lake Trailhead** (accessed from the same parking lot), take a 3.6-mile round-trip hike to **Nymph, Dream, and Emerald Lakes** to see some of the best scenery in the park. Yes, this trail is popular, and yes, you should hike it, too.

10:30 AM

Heading back down **Bear Lake Road,** pop over to **Sprague Lake,** then continue north. From your car window, check out the gushing **Big Thompson River** on the left-hand side of the road; then take in spectacular meadow views as you round the bend to **Moraine Park.** Take Highway 36 to Highway 34, continuing north to the turnoff for **Old Fall River Road,** and stop at the **Alluvial Fan.** Then drive the scenic, one-way dirt portion of the road in about an hour.

12:30 PM

Park in the **Alpine Visitor Center** parking lot, eat lunch at **Café in the Clouds,** shop for a souvenir at the **Trail Ridge Store,** and check out tundra exhibits at the visitor center.

2:00 PM

Head east on **Trail Ridge Road** and get out at **Rock Cut** for a 0.6-mile round-trip hike on the **Tundra Communities Trail.** Next, pull over at the **Forest Canyon Overlook.** Toward the end of your drive, take in the views from **Rainbow Curve** and **Many Parks Curve.**

5:00 PM

Eat an early al fresco dinner at **a solitary picnic table** on the south side of the road leading to the **Moraine Park Campground,** and enjoy some quiet time. A good number of people leave the park by 4pm, so the park should look and feel less busy. Keep your eyes out for elk and other animals.

7:30 PM

Head to the **Moraine Park Amphitheater** to enjoy a ranger-led program.

9:00 PM

As you leave the park, step out of your car and cast your gaze upward at Rocky's darkening sky. Wish upon a shooting star that you will find yourself back in the park soon.

the view from Rainbow Curve

Post-hike, visit the small sandy beach at **Grand Lake.** Grab a slice of sunshine on the outdoor patio of **Pine Restaurant and Bar** and enjoy an early dinner. If it's Friday night, join a ranger for the Old Ranch Campfire at the **Holzwarth Historic Site** before snuggling up in your sleeping bag at Timber Creek Campground.

Day 5

Load up your car and head a few miles south to the **Coyote Valley Trailhead** for a short (1 mile round-trip) but pretty hike along the Colorado River. Drive back to the east side of the park on Trail Ridge Road and enjoy lunch at **Lake Irene**'s picnic area. Take an easy stroll out to the lake, then return to your vehicle and continue east on Trail Ridge Road. Once past the Alpine Visitor Center, step out at the **Gore Range Overlook** and **Lava Cliffs.** If there are no ominous clouds above, hike the **Tundra Communities Trail** (0.6 mile round-trip) and look for marmots and pikas scampering about near **Rock Cut.** Continue driving east, taking in the views at **Forest Canyon Overlook, Rainbow Curve,** and **Many Parks Curve.** Tonight, settle in at the campsite that you reserved in advance at **Aspenglen Campground.**

Day 6

From the Aspenglen Campground, drive 3.8 miles southwest on Highway 34 to Highway 36 and continue 2.8 miles southeast to Bear Lake Road. At nearly 6 miles along Bear Lake Road, take Sprague Lake Road to Sombrero Ranch's **Glacier Creek Stables** to check in for a two-hour guided horseback ride (reserve in advance). Afterward, take the one-minute drive from the stables over to **Sprague Lake** and enjoy a picnic lunch. Circle the lake on foot before driving back to your campsite at Aspenglen Campground. On the way, stop at **Sheep Lakes** to look for bighorns; they often visit this spot midday in the early summer to graze the mineral-rich soil.

In the late afternoon, stop in at the **Fall River Visitor Center** to pick out a memento from the **Rocky Mountain Conservancy Nature Store.** The money from your purchase will be used for future park improvements and programs. Cap off your day with a ranger-led program at the **Aspenglen Campground amphitheater.**

Family Fun

Shared experiences are one of the building blocks of a successful family vacation, and there are many opportunities for such moments while in Rocky. A few suggestions to get you started:

- Help your child earn a Junior Ranger badge through the **Junior Ranger Program.** Activity booklets can be picked up at any visitor center, and ranger-led Junior Ranger programs are held every day late June-late August at the **Junior Ranger Headquarters at Hidden Valley.**
- On a hot summer day, cool off your toes and make new friends at the **Alluvial Fan.** Mellow pools of water near the bottom of the fan—plus plenty of rocks to climb on—equals fun for kids. (Entering rushing water is a serious safety risk and much of the Alluvial Fan fits that description; **look for gentle waters only** and supervise children at all times.)
- Take an outing to **Bear Lake, Adams Falls,** or **Sprague Lake.** If you are visiting with babies or toddlers, don a carrier backpack and narrate the scenery as you go.
- Step back in time at the **Holzwarth Historic Site** and view artifacts from an old dude ranch. Bring marshmallows to roast for ranger-led evening programs held at this location.
- Check out educational displays, ponder relief maps, or shop for souvenirs at one of the park's visitor centers. View a short film about the park in the **Kawuneeche Visitor Center** or **Beaver Meadows Visitor Center** auditoriums.
- Travel by horseback around the park with your little one. Children as young as two can saddle up at Sombrero Ranch's **Glacier Creek Stables** or **Moraine Park Stables.**
- Sign up your child in advance for a **Rocky Mountain Conservancy Field Institute** (www.rmconservancy.org) program. Kid-class topics include photo journaling, geocaching, and "animal poop."
- Scramble up and over piles of boulders—found everywhere in the park—with your little one. Or watch real-life spider-men and spider-women climb the walls along **Lumpy Ridge.**

cooling off in a mellow pool of water at the Alluvial Fan

- Sleep under the stars at one of the park's five established campgrounds: **Timber Creek, Aspenglen, Moraine Park, Glacier Basin,** or **Longs Peak.** Watch and listen for wildlife activity at dusk and indulge in a gooey campfire treat. On summer evenings, head to one of the park's amphitheaters or auditoriums for a ranger-led program.
- In the winter, pack the car with saucers and sleds, and drive to **Hidden Valley sledding hill.** Or, with a pull-behind carrier, explore snow-packed trails on cross-country skis around **Wild Basin.**
- Go on a virtual treasure hunt with the **Across the Divide GeoTour,** a geocaching adventure that takes visitors to spots around Rocky, Estes Park, and Grand Lake.

Day 7

Finish your trip by packing up your campsite and heading north on Devils Gulch Road to the **Lumpy Ridge Trailhead** for one last hike. On the drive, observe the **Twin Owls** rock formation jutting out from the landscape. Hike to **Gem Lake** (3.2 miles round-trip) and enjoy lunch on the small beach. Cool off your feet in the water before returning the way you came, stopping off at **Paul Bunyan's Boot** to take some fun snaps.

Best Day Hikes

A mélange of easy-to-difficult hikes exists within the park's 355-mile trail system, which means that there is enough variety to satisfy the desires of both "never-ever" hikers and endurance athletes. Prime hiking season runs late June-October.

Fern Lake Trail

There is never a dull moment on this **9.5-mile one-way,** shuttle-aided hike, which starts at the Fern Lake Trailhead and ends at Bear Lake. Sights along the way include **Arch Rocks, The Pool, Fern Falls,** and **Fern Lake.** Little Matterhorn stands sentinel over pretty **Odessa Lake,** which is encountered at 4.8 miles.

Nymph, Dream, and Emerald Lakes

Many captivating natural features compete for your attention on the **3.6 miles round-trip** to **Emerald Lake:** wildflowers, giant boulders, and the gurgling waters of Tyndall Creek among them. **Nymph, Dream,** and **Emerald** are the most popular lakes in the park thanks to their relatively easy accessibility and first-class scenery.

Alberta Falls, The Loch, Lake of Glass, and Sky Pond

Travel **8.8 miles round-trip** through a classic, glacier-carved valley to visit a tumbling **waterfall** and three jaw-dropping **lakes.**

The Fern Lake Trail crosses over rock debris known as talus.

Escape the Crowds

If jam-packed shuttle buses and crowded visitor centers give you the heebie-jeebies, schedule your trip to Rocky sometime other than on a summer weekend. Here are some other suggestions for quiet time:

- Take a bike ride on **Old Fall River Road** or **Trail Ridge Road** in the spring. Both roads are usually open to bicycles in April; before you arrive, double-check with the park about exact dates.
- Explore the less-visited northwest end of the park. Hike on the **Mummy Pass Trail** and spend the night at **Desolation wilderness site** before trekking out to **Mirror Lake.**
- In August, drive up **Trail Ridge Road** after dark to view the annual **Perseid meteor shower.** Cozy up with a blanket on your tailgate or in a camp chair and watch meteors streak the sky.
- Snowshoe to the old mining town (and now ghost town) of **Lulu City.** In November, especially on a weekday, you might find yourself passing only Park Service vehicles on your drive through the **Kawuneeche Valley** to the **Colorado River Trailhead.**
- Have a sunrise breakfast by a scenic lake, such as **Dream Lake** or **Lily Lake.** Pack a portable meal and a hot beverage and plan to be at the trailhead before dawn.
- In the summer, join the 8am **Coffee with a Ranger program** at the Glacier Basin Campground amphitheater or Moraine Park Campground amphitheater. If evening ranger programs feel too busy for your taste, this is a more intimate opportunity to learn about the park and connect with park staff.
- During the elk rut in autumn, when everyone is clamoring over campsites at **Moraine Park Campground,** drive over Trail Ridge Road to the **Timber Creek Campground.** You are more likely to score a first-come, first-served spot here, and in all probability you will hear some elk bugling during your stay.
- On a clear morning, watch the sun rise at **Rainbow Curve.**

Lily Lake

Tundra Communities Trail

With a starting elevation of 12,110 feet and an ending elevation of 12,304 feet, this paved trail **above the tree line** might leave you breathless. Numerous interpretive signs along the **0.6-mile round-trip** trail feature fascinating tidbits about life on the tundra and complement the stunning views.

Ute Trail

Indigenous people used this trail as a transportation corridor as they hunted for deer, elk, sheep, and other mammals. Though this **6-mile one-way** hike requires a car shuttle, the views above tree line on a clear day are unparalleled. Consider the rocky trek 3,500 feet downhill to **Beaver Meadows** an adventure.

On the return from Chasm Lake, there is a great view of the Twin Sisters landslide.

Lily Lake

Lily Lake hums with life. Waterfowl, birds, butterflies, and wildflowers keep hikers' eyes and ears busy on this level, **0.8-mile round-trip** hike that is also **wheelchair-accessible.** Visit in the golden hour before sunset for an especially lovely stroll.

Chasm Lake

Of the many great vantage points of **Longs Peak** in the park, this **8.4-mile round-trip** hike provides one of the best. The trail winds upward through thick forest to krummholz, then tundra, eventually depositing hikers in front of a sparkling tarn. Longs' stunning east face is the backdrop to **Chasm Lake.**

Ouzel Falls

Along this **5.4-mile round-trip** hike, multiple water features delight visitors before reaching their final destination. Take in the glittering spray of **Copeland Falls** and **Calypso Cascades** before arriving at towering **Ouzel Falls.**

Granite Falls

Granite Falls is located along a section of the **Continental Divide National Scenic Trail** in the **Kawuneeche Valley.** On the **10.4-mile round-trip** journey to this mesmerizing waterfall, you will be wowed by the park's largest montane meadow.

Mirror Lake

Why is **Mirror Lake** so special? Solitude. Gain terrific views of the **Cache la Poudre River** near the start of the **12-mile round-trip hike.** Toward the end, you'll be treated to a ridiculous display of **wildflowers.**

Lumpy Ridge Loop

Granite domes, buttresses, and cliffs are the main eye-catchers on the **11-mile round-trip Lumpy Ridge Loop,** along with glistening **Gem Lake** and serene **MacGregor Ranch.**

Winter Adventures

Kids and kids-at-heart enjoy Hidden Valley's sledding hill.

Rocky is imbued with magic and spectacular stillness in the winter months. Come with the right gear and be prepared for winter-specific hazards, and you can almost have the park to yourself.

- **Classes:** Enroll in a winter photography class or avalanche awareness course with the Rocky Mountain Conservancy Field Institute, or sign up for an introduction to ice climbing course, taught by the Colorado Mountain School.
- **Camping:** Spend the night at Moraine Park Campground (open year-round) tucked into a sub-zero sleeping bag.
- **Cross-Country Skiing:** Click in to a pair of cross-country skis and explore the Tonahutu Creek Trail in the Kawuneeche Valley.
- **Full-Moon Walks:** Take a guided full-moon walk in the snow with a ranger, or join a ranger-led talk about animal adaptations in the winter.
- **Hiking:** Some east side trails at lower elevations might be only lightly covered with snow in the winter. Try the short, south-facing Nature Trail next to the Moraine Park Discovery Center.
- **Sledding:** Hidden Valley is home to the park's designated sledding and tubing hill.
- **Snowshoeing:** Stomp around Lily Lake on snowshoes and pause to sip from an insulated container of piping hot cocoa along the way.
- **Wildlife-Watching:** The bears may be hibernating, but there is still plenty of wildlife to be seen—from elk to Abert's squirrels. Be a winter detective and look for animal tracks that meander through the snow.
- **Winter Driving Tour:** Main park roads are regularly plowed in the winter, with the exception of Old Fall River Road and a portion of Trail Ridge Road. Enjoy crystalline scenery from the comfort of your vehicle.

Gaga for Glaciers

Along with massive geologic uplift, glaciers were instrumental in forming Rocky's dramatic landscape many thousands of years ago. This tour highlights some of the prominent glacial features of the park.

Day 1

Unload your camping gear at the **Glacier Basin Campground,** an area of the park that was long ago shaped by a massive valley glacier. Head to **Moraine Park** to view a few textbook examples of glacial moraines, both lateral and terminal. Stop in to the **Moraine Park Discovery Center** to view the center's glacier exhibits, then head upstairs to the large picture window for a view of Moraine Park's vast meadow. Continue north to see **Horseshoe Park,** which is framed by more moraines.

Late in the afternoon, if the weather is favorable, take a hike to **Cub Lake** to see some good examples of **glacial erratics**—large boulders that glaciers deposited in random places.

Day 2

First thing in the morning, ride the park shuttle from the Park & Ride to **Bear Lake** and take a good look at **Hallett Peak** in the background. Just to the viewer's right of Hallett Peak is **Tyndall Glacier,** one of six remaining glaciers in the park. Once at the lake, purchase the **Bear Lake Nature Trail** and learn more about glacial activity in this short and easy walking tour. In the afternoon, drive up **Old Fall River Road** to peer at some more examples of glacial erratics.

Stop at the **Café in the Clouds,** next to the **Alpine Visitor Center,** and grab a bite to eat. On your way back down to the east side, get out of the car at **Rainbow Curve** and gaze northwest from the viewing area at **Sundance Mountain,** a cirque that was shaped by a glacier.

Day 3

This morning, you'll drive south on Highway 7 to the **Longs Peak Entrance** and park at the **Longs Peak Trailhead.** Your destination today is **Chasm Lake,** which sits in a fabulous amphitheater (a glacier-formed cirque) below the east face of **Longs Peak.** After this strenuous 8.4-mile round-trip hike, relax at your campsite with s'mores and hot cocoa while watching the stars above.

Day 4

Set an early alarm to put on a sturdy pair of kicks and board the park shuttle to the **Glacier Gorge Trailhead.** The Glacier Gorge is a fantastic example of a U-shaped valley: a V-shaped river valley that was widened and molded into a *U* shape by glaciers. It's also one of the most popular destinations in the park (the parking lot fills by 6am in the summer). Hike through to **Alberta Falls** then continue on to **Mills Lake.**

Return to your campsite and pack up by noon in order to drive over **Trail Ridge Road.** Squeeze in a stop at the **Forest Canyon Overlook;** a 13-mile-long glacier once held court in this valley and shaped it into a *U.* Continue the scenic drive west to the glacier-formed **Kawuneeche Valley,** stopping at **Farview Curve** for a fantastic perspective of the green meadows below. Set up camp at **Timber Lake Campground** for your last night in the park.

glacial erratic

Bear Lake and the East Side

Look for ★ to find recommended sights, activities, dining, and lodging.

Highlights

★ **Beaver Meadows Visitor Center:** This National Historic Landmark was designed to blend in with the surrounding landscape (page 38).

★ **Moraine Park:** Visit one of the most idyllic meadows in the park (page 40).

★ **Elk Viewing:** Visit in September and October to watch the elk rut in Moraine Park, Horseshoe Park, or Upper Beaver Meadows (page 41).

★ **Fern Lake Trail:** This trail leads hikers past the Big Thompson River, Fern Falls, Fern Lake, Odessa Lake, and Lake Helene (page 47).

★ **Alberta Falls:** The perfect, family-friendly outing to see a beautiful waterfall (page 50).

★ **Sky Pond:** Enjoy an 8.8-mile hike that is replete with eye candy—three lakes and two waterfalls (page 52).

★ **Nymph, Dream, and Emerald Lakes:** Three very different, but equally attractive lakes await along this 1.8-mile path (page 54).

★ **Horseback Riding:** Make a new four-legged friend at one of the park's horse stables (page 57).

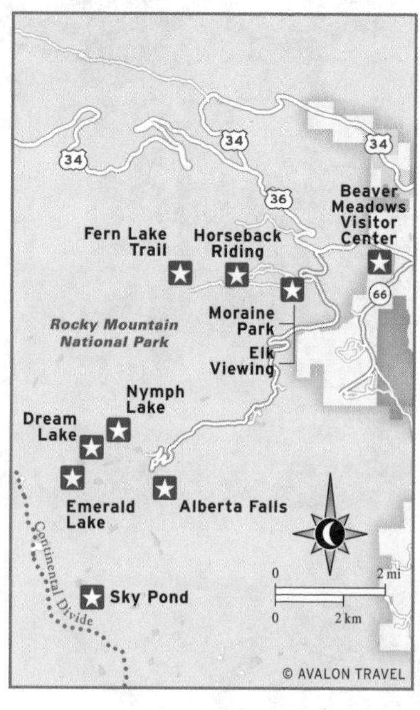

Home to several buildings and trails listed on the National Register of Historic Places, abundant wildlife, and stunning scenery, the Bear Lake region is a fantastic place to get acquainted with Rocky Mountain National Park.

Pretty paths in glacier-carved valleys are numerous, and the park's two horse stables are also located here. Moraine Park, Horseshoe Park, and Beaver Meadows are prime spots to see herds of elk and listen to them bugle during mating season. The Moraine Park Campground, situated in a lovely forest, is the largest campground in the park and the only one open year-round.

In the summer, the main parking lot to Bear Lake fills up by 8:30am or earlier, and for good reason. This area is the jumping off point to see some of the most stunning lakes in the park: Nymph, Dream, and Emerald, among them. Looming high over Bear Lake is the trio of Hallett Peak, Otis Peak, and Flattop Mountain—the most recognized peaks in the region. Popular activities in the area include hiking, sightseeing, photography, and picnicking.

PLANNING YOUR TIME

Rocky is a hiker's park, and the Bear Lake region has an especially large conglomeration of trails. If your primary agenda is to explore Rocky on foot, you could easily stay in this section of the park for **one week** and still have plenty of ground left to cover on a return visit. If, however, sightseeing is the main goal, just **2-3 days** in the area will suffice. A reasonable plan for exploring the park could include one day visiting Lumpy Ridge, one day along Trail Ridge Road, two days in the Bear Lake region, one day around Longs Peak, and one day in Wild Basin. For a **one-day excursion** to the Bear Lake area, essential stops include Bear Lake, Alberta Falls, Sprague Lake, and Moraine Park. In the summer especially, it is wise to use the park's free shuttle system and plan hikes for early in the morning or late in the afternoon when the area is less crowded.

Previous: Mount Chapin, Mount Chiquita, and Ypsilon Mountain, as seen from Deer Mountain; Dream Lake. **Above:** road cycling on the east side.

Bear Lake and the East Side

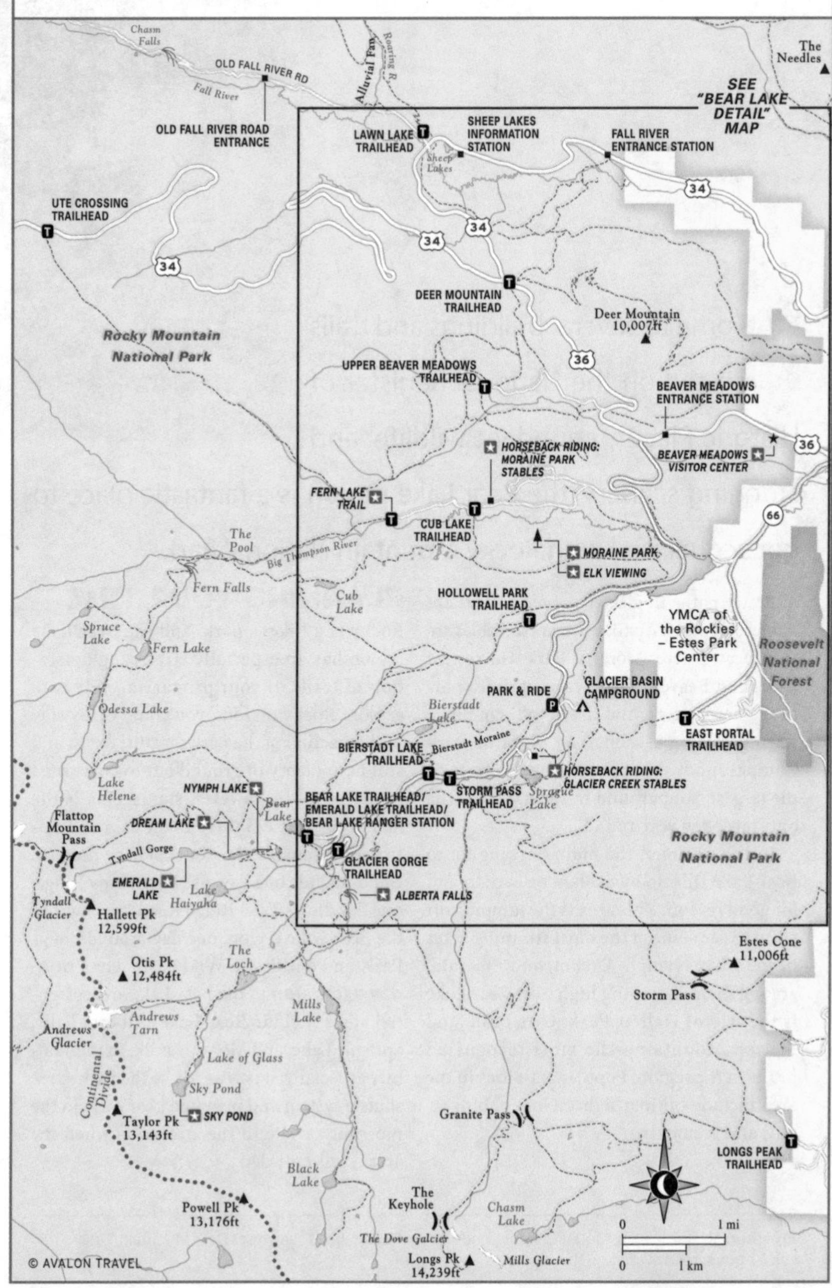

HISTORY

If only the ponderosa pines and Engelmann spruces could talk, what fascinating stories they could tell about the east side's earliest settlers. A complex tapestry of people has passed through and lived on this land over thousands of years, from Utes and Arapahos to homesteaders and tourism operators. In the last 100 years especially, the area has undergone tremendous change. In the late 1800s to early 1900s, Moraine Park—then known, for a brief time, as Willow Park—was home to the largest cluster of tourist lodges and cabins in the area outside of Estes Park—namely, the The Brinwood, Sprague's/Stead's Ranch, and Moraine Lodge. Hundreds of people recreated here and at the end of the day, enjoyed a roof over their heads at night. After the park was established, nearly all of the buildings at these guest ranches were purchased by the Park Service and demolished, to the chagrin of some and to the delight of others. Many mourned the loss of numerous historic structures, while preservationists were triumphant that the land would be returned to its natural state. Today, Moraine Park is a place to observe nature, recreate on horse or on foot, and stay overnight—though the latter activity now involves a tent or RV, not cozy quarters in a hotel.

Bear Lake, the nucleus of the region, has meant many things to many people. It served as a hunting spot for Native Americans, and was once home to a guest lodge and a sleep-away camp for youth. It even came close to being the site of a hydroelectric plant and dam in the early 1900s.

Humans have pressed many footprints into Rocky's land over the decades, particularly on the east side. But today, other than a handful of buildings and roads, the Bear Lake area is a scrupulously protected swath of wilderness.

Exploring the Park

ENTRANCE STATIONS

There are two main entrance stations to the east side of **Rocky Mountain National Park** (1000 U.S. Hwy. 36, Estes Park, 970/586-1206, www.nps.gov/romo, $20 per day per vehicle or motorcycle, $10 hikers and bikes; weekly passes available). The best way to bypass backed-up traffic at the entrance stations is to purchase a **Rocky Mountain National Park Annual Pass** ($60). Being a pass holder means you can use the Fast Pass lane when you enter at Beaver Meadows; simply swipe your card through a card reader to enter the gate. To see just how busy the park is, take a look at the Beaver Meadows or the Fall River Entrance Station webcams online (www.nps.gov/romo).

Booths at both the Beaver Meadow Entrance Station and the Fall River Entrance Station are staffed during the day with rangers who can offer itinerary suggestions, campground information, and tips for getting around. A park map and the Rocky Mountain National Park official newspaper are complimentary at each location.

Beaver Meadows Entrance Station

The closest access to Bear Lake is via the **Beaver Meadows Entrance Station** (Hwy. 36, open year-round). Beaver Meadows is the busiest entrance station in the park and can become quite congested with cars in the summer. The entrance station is staffed by rangers during peak daytime hours, but there are no services.

Fall River Entrance Station

Visitors interested in driving Old Fall River Road or Trail Ridge Road can enter via the **Fall River Entrance Station** (Hwy. 34, open year-round). The entrance station is staffed during the day, but there are no services.

Bear Lake

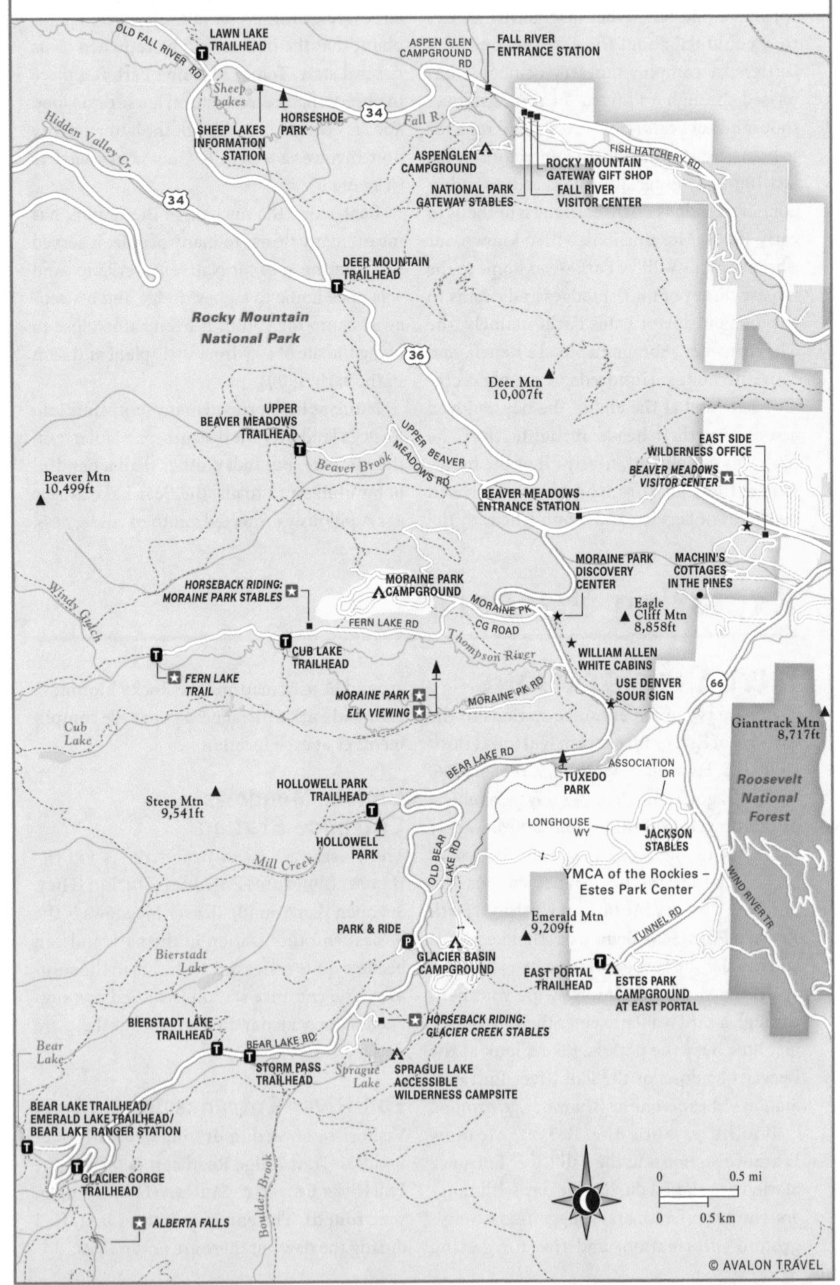
OLD FALL RIVER RD
LAWN LAKE TRAILHEAD
Sheep Lakes
SHEEP LAKES INFORMATION STATION
HORSESHOE PARK
34
Fall R.
Hidden Valley Cr.
ASPEN GLEN CAMPGROUND RD
FALL RIVER ENTRANCE STATION
ASPENGLEN CAMPGROUND
ROCKY MOUNTAIN GATEWAY GIFT SHOP
NATIONAL PARK GATEWAY STABLES
FALL RIVER VISITOR CENTER
FISH HATCHERY RD
DEER MOUNTAIN TRAILHEAD
Rocky Mountain National Park
36
Deer Mtn 10,007ft
UPPER BEAVER MEADOWS TRAILHEAD
UPPER BEAVER MEADOWS RD
Beaver Brook
Beaver Mtn 10,499ft
BEAVER MEADOWS ENTRANCE STATION
EAST SIDE WILDERNESS OFFICE
BEAVER MEADOWS VISITOR CENTER
MORAINE PARK DISCOVERY CENTER
MACHIN'S COTTAGES IN THE PINES
Windy Gulch
HORSEBACK RIDING: MORAINE PARK STABLES
MORAINE PARK CAMPGROUND
MORAINE PK CG ROAD
FERN LAKE RD
Eagle Cliff Mtn 8,858ft
Thompson River
CUB LAKE TRAILHEAD
FERN LAKE TRAIL
WILLIAM ALLEN WHITE CABINS
USE DENVER SOUR SIGN
66
MORAINE PARK
ELK VIEWING
MORAINE PK RD
Cub Lake
Giantrack Mtn 8,717ft
BEAR LAKE RD
ASSOCIATION DR
TUXEDO PARK
Roosevelt National Forest
Steep Mtn 9,541ft
HOLLOWELL PARK TRAILHEAD
HOLLOWELL PARK
OLD BEAR LAKE RD
LONGHOUSE WY
JACKSON STABLES
Mill Creek
YMCA of the Rockies – Estes Park Center
WIND RIVER TR
Emerald Mtn 9,209ft
PARK & RIDE
GLACIER BASIN CAMPGROUND
TUNNEL RD
EAST PORTAL TRAILHEAD
ESTES PARK CAMPGROUND AT EAST PORTAL
Bierstadt Lake
BIERSTADT LAKE TRAILHEAD
HORSEBACK RIDING: GLACIER CREEK STABLES
BEAR LAKE RD
Bear Lake
STORM PASS TRAILHEAD
Sprague Lake
SPRAGUE LAKE ACCESSIBLE WILDERNESS CAMPSITE
BEAR LAKE TRAILHEAD/ EMERALD LAKE TRAILHEAD/ BEAR LAKE RANGER STATION
GLACIER GORGE TRAILHEAD
Boulder Brook
ALBERTA FALLS
0 0.5 mi
0 0.5 km
© AVALON TRAVEL

East Portal Trailhead

The **East Portal Trailhead** (Hwy. 66, no entry fee) provides access to numerous features, including the Wind River Trail and Glacier Basin Campground. To get there from Estes Park, follow Highway 36 west to its intersection with Highway 66. Turn left and travel 3.3 miles southwest on Highway 66. The road ends in a circular drive. There is parking next to a small picnic area on the north side of the road (just before the circular drive) and along the roadside. An official RMNP trailhead sign is not visible from the road. Follow the wide dirt road just to the right of the sign for Estes Park Campground at East Portal. Directly ahead is a brown gate. Walk around the gate, and continue down the road toward the reservoir; cross over the reservoir and soon you will arrive at the official trailhead sign. The distance from the parking area to the trailhead sign is approximately 0.4 mile.

VISITOR CENTERS

Beaver Meadows Visitor Center

The **Beaver Meadows Visitor Center** (1000 Hwy. 36, 970/586-1206, www.nps.gov/romo, 8am-4:30pm daily mid-Oct.-mid-May, 8am-5pm daily mid-May-mid-June and early Sept.-mid-Oct., 8am-6pm daily mid-June-early Sept.) serves visitors to the east side of the park. Park rangers are on hand to offer hiking suggestions and maps, provide information about weather conditions, and otherwise give advice to travelers on a variety of matters relating to their visit. A short introductory film about the park can be viewed in a theater downstairs. Predictably, lines form at the ranger desks on summer weekends—especially in the morning—but move quickly. Restrooms and a gift shop are on-site.

Located in a small building next to the Beaver Meadows Visitor Center, the **East Side Wilderness Office** (970/586-1242, open daily, but hours vary seasonally) is an essential stop for anyone planning a backpacking trip in the park. Staff can inform you about wilderness trail conditions, campsites, water sources, weather, and more. Wilderness camping permits can be picked up at this location.

Fall River Visitor Center

The **Fall River Visitor Center** (3450 Fall River Rd., 970/586-1206, www.rockymountaingateway.net, 9am-4pm Fri.-Sat. mid-May, 9am-5pm daily late May-mid-Oct., limited hours Nov.-Dec.) has wildlife exhibits on

The Beaver Meadows Visitor Center is made of steel and moss rock.

the main level and a large downstairs area set aside for rotating exhibits and visitor activities. Park rangers are available to answer questions. Restrooms and a Rocky Mountain Conservancy Nature Store are on-site.

Moraine Park Discovery Center

In the summer, the **Moraine Park Discovery Center** (Bear Lake Rd., www.nps.gov/romo, 9am-4:30pm daily Memorial Day-Labor Day) serves as a third visitor center for the east side, with rangers available to field questions. The upstairs section of the center features exhibits, while souvenirs can be purchased from a Rocky Mountain Conservancy Nature Store. Check out the "What's Blooming in Moraine Park?" board for wildflower information. The center is 1.5 miles south of the Beaver Meadows Entrance.

ranger-led program at Sheep Lakes in the summer

Sheep Lakes Information Station

The **Sheep Lakes Information Station** (Hwy. 34 in Horseshoe Park, 9am-4:30pm daily mid-May-mid-Aug.) is 1.8 miles west of the Fall River Entrance next to the Sheep Lakes parking lot. Park staff and volunteers operate out of a kiosk and can answer visitors' questions about the area. A small amount of free park literature is available.

Bear Lake Ranger Station

At Bear Lake, rangers often stand outside of the small **ranger station** (open summer and fall) near the parking lot or trailhead entrance, greeting and assisting visitors. Park literature is available, including a guide for the Bear Lake Nature Trail ($2).

Park & Ride

The **Park & Ride** (Bear Lake Rd., across from Glacier Basin Campground) serves as the east side's transit center. Here you will find a small, staffed information booth as well as sheltered waiting areas for the park's three shuttles: the **Hiker Shuttle Express, Moraine Park Route,** and **Bear Lake Route.** Park staff is very visible and hands-on at this location. There is a restroom, informational signs about east side attractions, and parking for cars and RVs. Overnight parking is not allowed at the Park & Ride unless a permit has been obtained from one of the park's wilderness offices.

TOURS

Throughout the year the **Rocky Mountain Conservancy Field Institute** (1895 Fall River Rd., 970/586-0121, www.rmconservancy.org) offers a variety of hands-on courses in the park that take participants—both children and adults—to locations in the Bear Lake region. Topics include plants and wildflowers, wildlife, and environmental issues. While most classes are attached to specific calendar dates, there are a handful of on-demand course options, including geocaching, hiking, and fly-fishing, as well as winter bus tours.

Wildside 4x4 Tours (970/586-8687, www.wildside4x4.com, year-round) offers an Amazing Lower Valley Tour (4:30pm daily

May 1-Nov. 1, adults $65, children age 4-12 $45, children under 3 $35). This 3.5-hour sunset ride is designed as a sightseeing and photography tour; participants visit Horseshoe Park, Moraine Park, and Sprague Lake.

Yellow Wood Guiding (303/775-5484, www.ywguiding.com, year-round) specializes in hiking, nature, sightseeing, and photography tours. Hiking destinations include Glacier Gorge and lakes accessible from the Bear Lake Trailhead. The four-hour tours run $255 for 1-2 guests and $45 for each additional guest.

Thomas Mangan Photography (303/517-5325, www.thomasmangan.com) offers photo tours and instruction for up to three participants. The four-hour tour costs $210 for one person and $40 per each additional guest. There is also an eight-hour tour ($420 for one person, $80 per each additional guest).

The **Wildland Trekking** (800/715-4453, www.wildlandtrekking.com, $2,550 per person) Rockies Hiking Photography Tour includes visits to Bear Lake, Alberta Falls, and Sprague Lake, as well as Trail Ridge Road and west side attractions. Photography instruction, meals, transportation, and lodging are included in the five-day trip.

The **Estes Park Mountain Shop** (2050 Big Thompson Ave., Estes Park, 970/586-6548, www.estesparkmountainshop.com, 8am-9pm daily) offers guided hiking tours on the east side that run four, six, or eight hours in length. A four-hour tour for one person is $99; for two people the price is $119.

Kirks Mountain Adventures (230 E. Elkhorn Ave., Estes Park, 970/577-0790, www.kirksmountainadventures.com, 8am-5pm daily winter, 7am-8pm daily summer), a highly respected local outdoors shop, leads three-, six- and eight-hour hikes to waterfalls, lakes, and other natural attractions. A three-hour hike is $75 per person with a two-guest minimum (or $99 for one person).

A variety of hikes in the Bear Lake area are offered through The Stanley Hotel's **REI Basecamp at The Stanley Hotel** (333 Wonderview Ave., Estes Park, 970/577-4000, www.stanleyhotel.com, summer only, $65 for REI members, $65; $75 for non-members). Past destinations have included Lake Haiyaha and Mills Lake. Inquire about upcoming hikes at the large tent set up outside The Stanley Hotel, or check online for details.

Driving Tours

OLD FALL RIVER ROAD

This approximately **35-mile loop** drive travels through the montane, subalpine, and tundra ecosystems, giving visitors a taste of Rocky's great biodiversity. Plan this drive for **summer** or **fall,** when both Old Fall River Road and Trail Ridge Road are open. With no stops, the drive will take approximately **1.5 hours;** with stops, it can take a half-day. Vehicles over 25-feet long are not allowed on Old Fall River Road.

To start, depart from the **Beaver Meadows Entrance Station** and drive 3.1 miles northwest on Highway 36. Along this stretch of road, you'll have great views of Longs Peak and many other mountain peaks to your south. At **Deer Ridge Junction,** continue north on Highway 34, passing **Horseshoe Park** (4.7 mi). Take a left at the sign for Old Fall River Road (4.8 mi) and head west along **Endovalley Road.** The **Alluvial Fan** will soon be on your right (5.4 mi) and it is possible to get a good look at this natural feature without leaving your car. At 6.2 miles, you will reach the historic one-way section of **Old Fall River Road.** The next 9 miles offer great views, a fun driving experience (if your idea of fun is hairpin turns and narrow roads!), and at the height of summer, a chance to observe some beautiful wildflowers just beyond your bumpers.

At 7.7 miles into the tour, get out of your car and walk a short distance down to beautiful **Chasm Falls.** Around 8 miles, note the many large boulders alongside Old Fall River Road; these are called **glacial erratics.** At 10 miles, pass by gabions—rows of cages of rocks that help protect the road from landslides. You'll get your first look of the back of the Alpine Visitor Center and Trail Ridge Store at 12.1 miles; then at 13.9 miles, **Fall River Pass** comes into full view. Fifteen miles into the drive, Old Fall River Road meets with the **Alpine Visitor Center** parking lot at 11,796 feet elevation. Park if you can and take a half-hour to view the exhibits in the visitor center. Then exit the parking lot and head east on **Trail Ridge Road.** Along the way, take in the **Lava Cliffs** (17.2 mi), **Rock Cut** (19.2 mi), and the **Forest Canyon Overlook** (21.3 mi). Two other superb overlook areas still lay ahead: **Rainbow Curve** (24.1 mi) and **Many Parks Curve** (28.1 mi). Continue driving back to Deer Ridge Junction (32.1 mi) and then along Highway 36 to your starting point.

BEAR LAKE DRIVING TOUR

Most people use Bear Lake Road solely as a means of traveling to a trailhead, but this well-maintained thoroughfare can also be an enjoyable driving tour for visitors on a tight schedule. The road starts 0.2 mile west of the **Beaver Meadows Entrance Station** and is approximately **9.5 miles one-way** in length.

Near the start, get a good look at an **elk exclosure** (1.1 mi); this is an area fenced off from elk with the purpose of protecting vegetation that is vital to a variety of other wildlife. You will notice that the trees are dense in the exclosure, compared with its surroundings. Next, a fantastic view of **Moraine Park** unfolds (1.3 mi). A gushing section of the **Big Thompson River** (2 mi) is on the right-hand side of the road, which is even more impressive to look at on the return trip. After passing turnoffs for **Tuxedo Park, Hollowell Park,** and **Sprague Lake**—all stops worth making if you have the time—a very pretty view unfolds of **Hallett Peak** and **Flattop Mountain** (6.5 mi). Shortly after the **Bierstadt Lake Trailhead** (6.9 mi) the road narrows and steepens, and a sign alerts drivers that no roadside parking is allowed from this point to where the road dead-ends. Pass the **Glacier Gorge Trailhead** (8.5 mi) and finally, at 9.5 miles, arrive at the Bear Lake parking lot. At this point you should check out Bear Lake—if a parking spot is available—then return the way you came.

Sights

BEAVER MEADOWS AND MORAINE PARK

★ Beaver Meadows Visitor Center

Usually guests to a national park make a beeline for the front doors of a visitor center, eager to chat with a ranger or to purchase a souvenir. But in the case of the **Beaver Meadows Visitor Center** (1000 Hwy. 36, 970/586-1206, www.nps.gov/romo, 8am-4:30pm daily fall and winter, 8am-5pm daily spring, 8am-6pm daily summer) it is actually worth lingering for a while outside the entrance, taking in the structural details that make this building a National Historic Landmark. The center's architect, Thomas Casey, was an apprentice to the legendary Frank Lloyd Wright and utilized his "organic principles" throughout, building in harmony with the land. Primarily made of steel and sandstone, this boxy building's pastel colors came naturally with time through weathering. The building was completed in 1967 and received its National Historic Landmark designation in 2001. The visitor center now houses the park's administrative offices, a Rocky Mountain Conservancy Nature Store, an auditorium, and an information desk. Surprisingly, there are no large exhibits or displays in this center (the outside of the building is the main "exhibit"), but a relief map located downstairs is a great resource for getting oriented to the park's geologic features.

The Beaver Meadows Visitor Center is located on Highway 36, 1.2 miles east of the Beaver Meadows Entrance Station.

Moraine Park Discovery Center

In the early 1900s, homesteader Imogene Green MacPherson ran a bustling tourism operation, The Moraine Lodge, where the **Moraine Park Discovery Center** (Bear Lake Rd., 1.5 miles from the Beaver Meadows Entrance Station, 970/586-8842, 9am-4:30pm daily Memorial Day-Labor Day) is now located. For $45 a week, travelers enjoyed three meals a day, a place to stay, a horse to ride, and a variety of activities: tennis, hiking, and mule trips among them. It is hard to imagine, but at one time 40 buildings and tent-style dwellings were scattered about in this general vicinity. The Discovery Center building served as an office and the main gathering place for dances and other social events. In 1931, the National Park Service purchased the lodge, and nearly everything else was demolished.

Today, the two-story log structure that remains is a busy visitor center with interactive natural history exhibits and a small gift shop stocked with Rocky Mountain Conservancy items. The building, along with the adjacent Moraine Park Amphitheater, is listed on the National Register of Historic Places. A short, 0.6-mile family-friendly interpretive **Nature Trail** starts just outside the steps of the front entrance; a self-guided tour booklet for the trail can be purchased for $2. A park shuttle stop is located here and there is a reasonably sized parking lot. Upstairs, there is a large picture window for taking in the scenery of Moraine Park.

From the Beaver Meadows Entrance Station, travel west on Highway 36 for approximately 0.2 mile to Bear Lake Road. Turn left (south) on Bear Lake Road and drive 1.3 miles. The Moraine Park Discovery Center is on your left.

William Allen White Cabins

Writers and artists often remove themselves from all distractions as they craft a masterpiece. For the late Pulitzer Prize-winning writer and newspaper editor William Allen White (1868-1944), the natural palette and solitude of Rocky served as a perfect retreat. White summered in Rocky 1912-1943, and today his well-preserved home and outbuildings still stand about 300 yards from the Moraine Park Discovery Museum. Though White's wife was with him during these summer visits, he stole away often to a small dedicated writing studio to pen works short and long. He is perhaps best known for "What's the Matter with Kansas?" an editorial he wrote for *The Emporia Gazette*, the newspaper where he served as a longtime editor. White received his Pulitzer Prize for an editorial

Artist-in-Residence Program

Nature and creativity intersect in the park's long-running **Artist-In-Residence** program (www.nps.gov/romo), a special summertime opportunity for professional visual artists, storytellers, performing artists, photographers, writers, composers, and musicians. Just a handful of coveted spots exist for artists-in-residence, and positions must be applied for during the latter part of the prior year. Those who make the cut are offered temporary accommodations in Moraine Park's William Allen White Cabins in exchange for a piece of creative work that is donated to the park's permanent art collection. Pieces may be displayed in the Moraine Park Discovery Center, the park's other visitor centers, or at special events in the gateway towns. Artists also conduct several presentations about their craft to park visitors during their stay. This arrangement is a win-win for everyone involved; artists receive inspiration from the beauty of the park and have a dedicated, private space to work, and the resulting pieces serve to promote and highlight the park in a way that no brochure or newspaper advertisement ever could. Visitors, meanwhile, might be inspired to flex their own creative muscles after viewing, hearing, or experiencing the work of artists-in-residence.

entitled "To an Anxious Friend," the subject of which was free speech. He was also the author of numerous books. After White passed away, his cabins were still owned by family members until 1972 when the park purchased them. In 1973, they were the first location in Rocky to be added to the National Register of Historic Places.

Today, individuals who are accepted into the **Rocky Mountain National Park Artist-in-Residence Program** (www.nps.gov/romo) are allowed to stay in the fully furnished cabin for two-week increments in the summer. The general public is not allowed entry to the buildings—which include a main cabin, two sleeping cabins, a privy, and White's writing cabin—though they can be observed from Bear Lake Road.

From the Beaver Meadows Entrance Station, travel west on Highway 36 for 0.2 mile to Bear Lake Road. Turn left (south) on Bear Lake Road and drive 1.5 miles. The William Allen White Cabins can be viewed on your left.

★ Moraine Park

Moraine Park is considered by geologists to be one of the best exposures of glacial moraines in the Rocky Mountains. A moraine consists of natural materials that were put in place by the land-scouring action of a glacier. A handful of small glaciers at one point in time converged in the area of Moraine Park, and with impressive force, deposited voluminous mounds of rocks and dirt to the south, east, and north of the valley floor. The north and south moraines are lateral moraines—piles that form on the sides of the glacier—while the moraine at the foot of Eagle Cliff Mountain to the east is a terminal moraine—the spot where a glacier finally ceased its slide and melted away. Glaciers visited the area of Moraine Park more than once, retreating for the last time approximately 10,000 years ago.

In the present day, in any season, Moraine Park's expansive meadow is simply stunning. In the summer, Moraine Park is especially beautiful, with the **Big Thompson River** curling through its verdant grasses. In the fall, this is a prime place to watch **bull elk** battle each other for mating rights for eligible cows. Day trippers to this spot might choose to drive by the meadow, stop for a picnic lunch, book a horseback ride, or cast a line into the Big Thompson's waters. Not surprisingly, an overnight stay in the **Moraine Park Campground** offers great access to activities in Moraine Park.

Each fall, the leaves turn gold in Moraine Park.

To get to Moraine Park, travel west on Highway 36 for 0.2 mile to Bear Lake Road. Turn left (south) on Bear Lake Road and drive for 1.6 miles. There is a small parking lot and picnic table in this spot on the east end of Moraine Park. Another great spot for viewing Moraine Park is on Fern Lake Road, which travels along the north border of Moraine Park.

★ Elk Viewing

Everywhere you go, there they are: elk. Current estimates place the park's elk population at 200-600 and they are easier to spot—and surely more photographed—than any other mammal. In **mid-March** look for bull elk that have recently dropped their antlers (and if you see a rack sitting in a meadow, leave it be), only to immediately grow new ones. In **early summer,** keep an eye out for all-too-precious calves gallivanting on spindly legs. By far the biggest elk attraction of the year comes in early fall, when there is a nip to the air and the leaves are just beginning to turn. Elk mating season, also known as the **elk "rut,"** runs **September-mid-October,** and is a spectacle to be sure. Males fight one another to assert dominance and attract females, soak their bodies in their own urine, and wildly thrash around in trees and other foliage—often emerging with a disheveled tangle of branches and leaves wound around their antlers. A mixture of high-pitched whistles and grunts called "bugling" is the way bull elk ward off competition and express rampant sexual desire.

The elk rut generally takes place in **Moraine Park, Horseshoe Park, Upper Beaver Meadows,** and the **Kawuneeche Valley.** Park staff do not allow fishing and hiking in prime mating areas between the hours of 5pm and 7am to give these mammals space and ensure the safety of visitors. Be sure to observe posted signs of closures. No matter what time of the year, keep a distance of 25 yards or more from elk (and all wildlife, for that matter; for bears, a distance of 100 yards is recommended) when viewing or photographing them. The mammals may be accustomed to humans and their cameras and cars, but they will not stand for harassment from people. Death by goring or significant injuries can occur if visitors get too close to elk. I have seen many instances of elk getting cornered by people and cars, and it is a tense and scary situation. On one occasion, I witnessed a man stalking an elk in full camouflage—a not-okay move. Use a telephoto

Male elk clash antlers during the fall rut.

Big Thompson Flood of 1976

Locals talk a lot about the Colorado Flood of 2013 because it happened relatively recently, but you can still find old timers discussing a tragic tale of flooding that took place in 1976. The Big Thompson Flood of 1976 was the deadliest natural disaster in Colorado's history and took place in **Big Thompson Canyon,** from Estes Park to Loveland. Twelve inches of rain that fell in a four-hour time period caused the Big Thompson's water level to rise in a rapid and astounding fashion on the evening of July 31. Swollen and raging, the river tore through the canyon, ripping down anything and everything its path, including trees, cars, power lines, massive boulders, and debris. The terrifying 19-foot-high wall of water resembled a scene from a horror flick more than an actual river. In the end, 144 people lost their lives in the flood and 418 houses were decimated. Perhaps the flood might not have been so deadly if a special event weren't taking place that weekend; it was Colorado's centennial, and an estimated 2,500-4,000 people were happily recreating and camping in the canyon, oblivious to the horror that would strike. The rebuilding process was long, arduous, and expensive—costing $40 million. Highway 34 and nearby roads, as well as bridges, homes, and businesses were all affected. Those who remember the flood of 1976 will never forget.

camera lens for photos if possible, or simply be satisfied with the image you do capture, even if it is just a brown blurry speck. You will always have the story to tell even if you do not have the picture.

An outstanding place to view elk is a single picnic table that is located on the road heading to **Moraine Park Campground.** Families and groups of friends will gather at this spot in October to eat a meal and track elk with binoculars. Like all other picnicking spots, there are no reservations for this table, just snag it if you see it is free.

Of the many magical experiences to be had in Rocky, camping at Moraine Park Campground during the elk rut is one of them. I personally love drifting in and out of sleep all night while the elk bugle away nearby, but if you need a solid eight hours of Zs, consider bringing along a good set of earplugs.

Big Thompson River

The 78-mile-long **Big Thompson River** is life-giving in more ways than one. For starters, the river's lush riparian habitat plays host to numerous plants, insects, fish, birds, and mammals. Furthermore, the Big Thompson is part of a massive water collection and diversion system—called the Colorado-Big Thompson Project—that is critical to farms, ranch lands, and homes on the Front Range of Colorado. The river is most celebrated for being a fabulous spot to fish. The headwaters of the Big Thompson are in Forest Canyon south of Trail Ridge Road; there is no trail access to this spot. Instead, some of your best bets for fishing or admiring "The Big T"—as it is referred to by locals—are in **Moraine Park,** or along the **Fern Lake Trail.** In Moraine Park, the water fancifully winds through a vast meadow, at times branching off into streams and side channels. Along the Fern Lake Trail, the Big Thompson looks very different, its gushing waters are flanked by rocks and trees. Both settings are spectacular. Once outside the park, the Big Thompson continues east through the town of Estes Park before its waters join with Estes Lake. From there, the river travels on through the Big Thompson Canyon all the way to Loveland, where it eventually merges with the South Platte River.

Tuxedo Park

As the story goes, fancy dress-up parties were held in this area of the park around the 1920s and 1930s. Men and women affiliated with the nearby YMCA of the Rockies would don their formal attire—including tuxedos for men—and enjoy a picnic dinner in this area. Today, **Tuxedo Park** is still an enjoyable picnic spot, with tables situated along Glacier Creek. Though Tuxedo Park is not listed on the complimentary park map, the free park shuttle stops here in the busy season. There is also a small parking lot west of the shuttle stop, and a trail that is used by YMCA visitors.

From the Beaver Meadows Entrance Station, drive 0.2 mile west on Highway 36 to Bear Lake Road. Turn left (south) on Bear Lake Road and drive 2.5 miles to Tuxedo Park; both the shuttle stop and a parking lot will be on your left.

BEAR LAKE AREA

Hollowell Park

One of the more remarkable features of **Hollowell Park** is the view it provides of a nearby, massive, human-made scar on the earth. After stepping out of your vehicle at the parking lot and walking toward the trail-head sign, you will immediately notice it (provided it isn't winter): across the valley, on a steep mountainside, a wide and long trail carved out between a thick forest of Douglas fir. The trail is filled with aspen trees whose colors "pop" magnificently in the summer and especially in the fall. While pretty to view, it is important to note that humans ultimately damaged this swath of earth. In 1907, when the wheels were put in motion to build the historic Stanley Hotel in Estes Park, this area served as a busy logging trail for workers delivering wood from a sawmill to the site of the hotel. Officials expect that forest will eventually regrow in this path, but it could take decades. Fortunately, Hollowell Park has other fine attributes, including a **hiking trail** that provides access to several wilderness campsites and connects with other popular east-side hiking trails. The meadow itself is big and beautiful. There is also a nice, partially shaded **picnic area** at the trailhead. Hollowell Park was also once the site of a large Civilian Conservation Corps work camp.

To reach Hollowell Park from the Beaver Meadows Entrance Station, drive southwest on Highway 36 for 0.2 mile to the turnoff for Bear Lake Road. Turn left (south) on to Bear Lake Road and drive for 3.6 miles. Turn right (west) to access the Hollowell Park parking lot.

Bear Lake

So iconic is the destination of **Bear Lake** that one of the views from the shore looking up at Longs Peak is the featured artwork on the back of the Colorado state quarter. With the coin in hand, take a right at the **Bear Lake Trailhead** and stroll about a quarter of the way around the lake. Look up and compare the two; you will be seeing double. This mirror-like body of water that sits at 9,475 feet and is framed by peaks and trees is the stuff of classic Rocky Mountain beauty. That beauty didn't come easy though, and was in fact millions of years in the making, formed primarily by a massive uplift of the Earth's crust and glacial activity. Today, Bear Lake is fascinating to visit in all four seasons and incites natural curiosity in visitors of every age. A self-guided **nature trail** encircles the lake and is mostly wheelchair accessible, or you can simply find a bench or rock to sit on to take in the sights and sounds. This is also the jumping off point for a number of great hikes. Among them: Emerald Lake (1.8 mi one-way), Flattop Mountain (4.4 mi one-way), and Fern Lake (4.7 mi one-way).

As for seeing a bear here? It is possible, but not likely, considering how heavily this lake is visited and how bruins tend to make themselves scarce in the presence of groups. The name of the lake came about because the grandfather of one of the area's early homesteaders took a potshot at bear here with his rifle. It thereafter became known as "Grandpa's Bear Lake" or "Bear Lake."

To get to Bear Lake from the Beaver Meadows Entrance Station, take Highway 36 west for 0.2 mile to Bear Lake Road. Then drive approximately 9.5 miles southwest on Bear Lake Road to the parking lot (alternatively, ride the park's free shuttle bus here in the high season). Vault toilets are located next to the parking lot, and a spigot for filling water bottles is located near the ranger station. The best times to find solitude at the lake are early morning, late afternoon, on weekdays, and in the winter. Otherwise, expect to share this space with one or many other visitors.

Hallett Peak, Otis Peak, and Flattop Mountain

Of the three jutting landforms lined up along the Continental Divide, **Hallett Peak** is fawned over the most. It towers to the tune of 12,713 feet, with a distinctive, glacier-carved north face that can be easily admired from a variety of locations in the Bear Lake region, including Sprague Lake. Standing on the shore of the lake looking southwest, to the left of Hallett is **Otis Peak** (12,486 feet) and to the right, **Flattop Mountain** (12,324 feet). For many sightseers, these two mountains, while impressive in their own right, primarily enhance the unique shape and beauty of Hallett. The hiking crowd, though, has a special appreciation for Flattop Mountain. The only one of the three with its own dedicated **trail** to the top, Flattop's summit is reached from trails that originate on both the west and east sides of the park. The mountain receives a good amount of foot traffic because of its position along the **Continental Divide National Scenic Trail** (CDT).

Get a good look at Hallett Peak on the drive up Bear Lake Road (to the Bear Lake parking lot) or from Sprague Lake. To get to Sprague Lake from the Beaver Meadows Entrance, follow Highway 36 west for 0.2 mile to Bear Lake Road and continue six miles south to the Sprague Lake turnoff.

Recreation

One of the huge advantages of using Rocky's free **shuttle system** in the summer is it allows for one-way hikes in the Bear Lake area without having to arrange for a second car parked at your destination. Nowhere else in the park is that a possibility. As you take a look at east-side destinations on a map, you will notice a number of options for linking trails. It is best to plan ahead for a one-way, shuttle-aided hike, rather than make a spur-of-the-moment decision about a different route while out on the trail—especially if you've already communicated a specific itinerary to family or friends and they are expecting you back at a certain time.

At the Bear Lake Ranger Station, you can get a basic paper map of area trails, though it's best to carry a good topographic map as well.

HIKING

Beaver Meadows

UPPER BEAVER MEADOWS SHORT LOOP

Distance: 0.9 mile
Duration: 30 minutes
Elevation gain: 120 feet
Effort: easy
Trailhead: Beaver Meadows
Directions: Travel 0.7 mile west on Highway 36 from the Beaver Meadows Entrance Station; then travel west for approximately 1.5 miles on Upper Beaver Meadows Road.

Many east-side hikes are centered on an exciting destination—namely a peak, lake, or waterfall. On this short journey through the montane ecosystem, there is no big finish to hurry toward, which, quite frankly, is refreshing. The easy pace invites visitors to slow down and savor the crisp mountain air and expansive views. This is a great hike for spotting **wildlife**—such as elk and wild turkeys—and birders will tell you that this area offers some of the best bird-watching opportunities on the east side of the park. A former naturalist with the park who specializes in birds has spotted approximately 80 different bird species in the area of Upper Beaver Meadows, among them: the Western tanager, flycatchers, the green-tailed towhee, warblers, nuthatches, and crossbills.

Rocky's Peaks by the Numbers

Within Rocky's borders there are 124 named peaks, ranging from 8,789 feet in elevation (Twin Owls) to 14,259 (Longs). Nineteen of the 124 peaks are 13,000 feet or higher. Many Coloradans get the "Fourteener" bug and aspire to climb one or all of the 14,000-foot peaks in the state; there are 53 of them in total. While less popular than Fourteeners, Colorado's 637 Thirteeners also have an allure for weekend warriors. **Longs Peak,** the only Fourteener in the park, is the fifteenth-highest Fourteener in the state. There are also a handful of unnamed "peaks" in Rocky, which are often referred to simply by the elevation of the summit as it is shown on a trail map. The reason these summits do not have a name has to do with the way mountain summits are officially classified. In the eyes of a geographer, a peak is not genuinely a peak if it is in close proximity to another nearby summit. To get even more technical, an actual peak needs to have what is called "topographic prominence" and be 300 feet above any surrounding land mass to be recognized as its own mountain.

From the parking lot, cross over Beaver Brook on a **short log bridge** and advance a few dozen feet south to the **first trail marker.** Follow the arrow pointing north toward **Moraine Park,** taking a moment or two to check out the elk exclosure on your right—a fenced-in area that protects trees from grazing mammals and is part of the park's Elk and Vegetation Management Plan. Continue along a mostly flat stretch of gorgeous, grassy meadow with fantastic views of Longs Peak in the distance. At 0.3 mile from the trailhead, you will find yourself in an area shaded by ponderosa pine. Here there is a trail sign; take a right (west) toward **Trail Ridge Road.** Walk 0.2 mile to another sign, then take a right and travel north for another 0.4 mile back to the trailhead.

Bear Lake Area

HOLLOWELL PARK TO MILL CREEK BASIN

Distance: 3.4 miles round-trip
Duration: 2 hours
Elevation change: 610 feet
Effort: easy
Trailhead: Hollowell Park
Directions: From the Beaver Meadows Entrance Station, drive southwest on Highway 36 for 0.2 mile to Bear Lake Road. Turn left (south) on to Bear Lake Road and drive for 3.6 miles. Turn right (west) for Hollowell Park.

Year-round, the Hollowell Park Trailhead offers numerous options for hikers. This is a great spot for embarking on a not-so-challenging snowshoe or winter hike due to its gentle elevation gain. For the same reason, it is also a perfect hike for getting acclimated to the park in the first few days of a visit. With two **wilderness campsites** in Mill Basin less than 2 miles from the Hollowell Park parking lot, a satisfying overnight adventure for first-timer backpackers or families can start here. And, because the trail is served by the park shuttle and connects to so many other trails in the vicinity, a number of interesting longer hikes or backpacking trips can be initiated at the trailhead.

To start, park at the **Hollowell Park Trailhead** and step on to the flat dirt trail heading west. Walk along at an easy pace through the expansive meadow—perhaps humming a tune from *The Sound of Music* if you are so inclined. At 0.3 mile, you will see a sign for a horse trail to Moraine Park. Continue heading west, following the sign to **Mill Creek Basin.** At 0.5 mile, you will find yourself walking alongside Mill Creek. At 1 mile, a trail junction for Cub Lake and Mill Creek Basin appears. Head left (southwest) to Mill Creek Basin. Directly after the sign, you will walk across a **bridge** to get over Mill Creek. The trail gradually climbs higher through the trees before arriving at Mill Creek

The Beaver

At some point during your stay in Rocky, you will likely hear reference to "The Beaver" from a ranger, shuttle bus driver, or someone on the trails. It is the late author **James Michener** who gets credit for giving the already remarkable ridgeline of Longs Peak some mammalian attributes. In his 1974 best-selling novel *Centennial*—a mammoth book of historical fiction to commemorate the state of Colorado's 100th anniversary—the author makes reference to a beaver climbing up to Longs Peak. Indeed, if you look long and hard enough you will be able to see the beaver resemblance, too. Moraine Park, Beaver Meadows, and Horseshoe Park are all excellent locations to check out the eastern face of Longs. As you look up, examine the terrain that is found to the viewer's left of the actual summit. There's a thick paddle tail, rounded body, and a face looking directly up at the tip-top of the mountain.

Basin, a meadow blanketed with wildflowers in the summer. Two wilderness campsites, **Mill Creek Basin** and **Upper Mill Creek,** are in the vicinity. You can turn around at this point and head back the way you came, or do a loop hike by returning to the trailhead via the Mill Creek Trail to the north.

CUB LAKE

Distance: 4.6 miles round-trip
Duration: 2.5 hours
Elevation change: 540 feet
Effort: moderate
Trailhead: Cub Lake (see map p. 48)
Directions: From the Beaver Meadows Entrance Station, drive 0.2 mile west on Highway 36. Turn left (south) on to Bear Lake Road and drive for 1.2 miles to Moraine Park Road. Drive 0.5 mile west on Moraine Park Road until the road splits; stay left on Fern Lake Road for 1.2 miles to get to the Cub Lake Trailhead. Parking is limited.

In the summer, a lily pad-strewn lake is the reward at the end of this lovely hike, which starts at the northwest corner of Moraine Park. From the trailhead, walk over the **Big Thompson River** via a small **footbridge,** then travel south along relatively flat ground, enjoying views of Moraine Park to the left (east) while you can. At 0.5 mile you will leave Moraine Park behind, veering right (west) on the **Cub Lake Trail** through a section of large boulders to a set of **beaver ponds,** where the soothing serenade of frogs often fills the air. This is where you will start to really notice charred trees and tree stumps, a stark reminder of the **Fern Lake Fire.** The burn devastation becomes increasingly obvious winding up the mountain, but the scenery is no less beautiful. Keep your eyes peeled for wildlife as you continue west from the beaver ponds approximately 1.7 miles to Cub Lake. (Though it is relatively uncommon to see moose on the east side of the park, I was once treated to views of one quietly drinking and grazing in this stretch, just several hundred yards from the trail.) Several moderate switchbacks at the end will take you to your to final destination. The lake is a natural place to stop and lunch before turning around, but looking for shade is a lesson in futility; every tree ringing the lake was licked with flames. Heading back the way you came is one option. There are also numerous alternatives for connecting to other Bear Lake area trails. One popular loop option involves hiking approximately 0.9 mile farther west on the Cub Lake Trail, past the lake, to arrive at **The Pool.** From this point, head east on the Fern Lake Trail and back to the Cub Lake Trailhead.

SPRUCE LAKE

Distance: 7.6 miles round-trip
Duration: 4 hours
Elevation gain: 1,375 feet
Effort: moderate to strenuous
Trailhead: Fern Lake (see map p. 48)

Spruce Lake is an attractive spot for lunching, fishing, or camping overnight, and an appealing destination because it is generally less busy than other attractions in the region. Most people hiking on the Fern Lake Trail choose Fern Falls or Fern Lake as their turnaround point, and are less inclined to make a 1.6-mile detour to Spruce Lake. All the better for us solitude seekers.

To start, walk from your car or the Fern Lake shuttle parking lot to the **Fern Lake Trailhead.** Hike 1.2 miles to **Arch Rocks** (if it's summer, admire wildflowers along the way); then find a great view of the Big Thompson River at 1.4 miles. **The Pool**—a small feature of the Big Thompson River—is located at 1.7 miles from the trailhead. Immediately after crossing over a **footbridge** at The Pool, you will reach a trail junction. Continue west to **Fern Falls,** rather than east to Cub Lake and Mill Creek Basin. Fern Falls is another 1 mile away and a great place to rehydrate and consume an energy bar before forging on. Continue gaining elevation as you hike to the junction of Fern Lake and the Spruce Lake Unimproved Trail—you will have hiked 3.8 miles from the trailhead at this point. The **Spruce Lake Unimproved Trail** heads northwest for 0.8 mile to your destination. As you walk along, the trail gets rockier and you might run across some downed trees on the path, making the trail occasionally less clear. These short bursts of rockiness do not last long though, so if you don't find yourself on a distinct trail after several minutes of hiking, you might need to backtrack and regain your bearings. Some **cairns** have been placed on the path to mark the way. Before arriving at **Spruce Lake,** you will walk along a pretty stream that is resplendent with fish. Pay heed to signed area closures, which are in effect (mid-May-Sept.) to protect boreal toads, a state endangered species. Just a short walk from the lake's edge, find the **Spruce Lake wilderness campsite,** as well as a privy. The gorgeous lake is ringed with trees, with pointy and slightly off-kilter Castle Rock demanding your immediate attention. Hike back the way you came, stopping off at Fern Lake before heading east in the direction of the parking lot.

★ FERN LAKE TRAIL

Distance: 9 miles
Duration: 5 hours
Elevation gain: 2,540 feet
Effort: strenuous
Trailhead: Fern Lake (see map p. 48)

This **shuttle-aided hike** is one to add to your short list; it highlights numerous gorgeous water features in the park and is a satisfying workout. If you choose to drive, there is a parking lot next to the Fern Lake Trailhead and several small parking pullouts on the road to the trailhead. These spots often get snapped up quickly—by 8am in the summer—making the shuttle a more attractive option. The Moraine Park Shuttle takes hikers to the Fern Lake shuttle stop, which is a 0.8-mile walk from the trailhead.

The trail is lush and thick with foliage to begin, and then as you travel west, the landscape opens up, revealing mounds of talus spilled down the mountain on the right-hand side of the trail. A group of granite boulders called **Arch Rocks** appears at 1.2 miles from the trailhead. This is memorable landmark for me because of one particular hike, when several people headed in the other direction warned that there was a bear lingering "right next to the big rocks up ahead." My hiking companion and I also learned that the bear was sniffing around some bags left hanging on trees by several anglers (presumably containing food) just next to the trail, while they obliviously cast into the Big Thompson River below. Fortunately, the bear never materialized, but the next sight soon did, 0.5 mile later: **The Pool** is a small, swirling section of water at the junction of Fern and Spruce Creeks and The Big Thompson River. Continuing west, pass the **Old Forest Inn wilderness campsite,** which was named for a lodge that used to be located in this spot. **Fern Falls** appears roughly 0.9 mile after The Pool, and is an attractive and rather raucous waterfall. From the falls, continue 1.2 miles along on

Fern Lake Trail

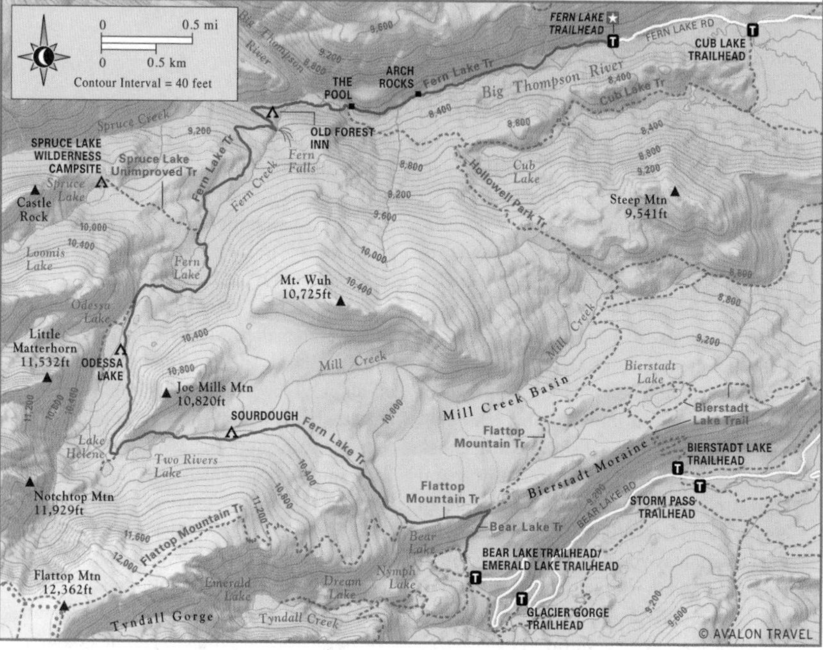

the trail to **Fern Lake** where you are also likely to see anglers waist-deep in the water in the summer. Cast your gaze upward to view Little Matterhorn—the mountain has a striking resemblance to the Matterhorn in the Swiss Alps.

The distance from Fern Lake to **Odessa Lake** is 1 mile, and the approach is one of my favorite stretches of trail in all of Rocky—a flat path that travels through a gorge and parallels Fern Creek all the way to Odessa Lake. At Odessa, you will gain an even better vantage point of Little Matterhorn. The next section of trail is from Odessa Lake to **Lake Helene,** which is not apparent from the trail. You will need to keep an eye out for an **unmarked social trail** on your right, where the Fern Lake Trail makes a sharp, hairpin turn. At that sharp bend, find the social trail; from here it is 0.1 mile to the lake. After backtracking on the social trail, you will now head east, still staying on the Fern Lake Trail for 1.9 miles. At this point, a trail junction appears for **Flattop Mountain.** Keep hiking east for approximately 0.4 mile to another trail junction for **Bear Lake.** Head south on the trail for 0.5 mile back to the parking lot. The **Bear Lake Shuttle** will take you to the **Park & Ride,** where you will need to catch the **Moraine Park Shuttle** back to the Fern Lake Bus Stop.

SPRAGUE LAKE

Distance: 0.8 mile one-way
Duration: 30 minutes
Elevation change: 20 feet
Effort: easy
Trailhead: Sprague Lake (see map p. 50)

The wide path encircling Sprague Lake is composed of flat, packed gravel and dirt, and one well-maintained wooden boardwalk at the start of hike. This trail is designated as

2012 Fern Lake Fire

The Fern Lake Fire is remarkable for many reasons, but mostly because it stubbornly and without apology burned everything in its path—even cold, snow-covered ground. No other fire in the park's history had ever been persistent enough to keep going in the snowy months. Trees burned, rocks were scorched, elk exclosure fences were torched, and one structure was lost in the blaze, which was started in Forest Canyon by an illegal campfire on October 9, 2012. The fire did plenty of damage during its onset, but was at its most ferocious a month and a half after the first sparks flew. Wild, howling winds pushed flames through Moraine Park and dangerously close to Estes Park on November 30 and in the early morning hours of December 1, 2012. In just over a half hour, the fire traveled an astonishing 3 miles, prompting emergency evacuations and a massive effort to keep the flames away from nearby homes and the YMCA of the Rockies-Estes Park Center. Though the fire was contained to some degree, it was far from over at that point, and kept on smoldering throughout the winter and following spring. Finally, nearly nine months after it started, fire officials went airborne to scrutinize the affected areas with infrared cameras. They declared the 3,500-acre fire to be officially over in June 2013. This human-started, preventable blaze caused exceptional strain on park resources and occurred outside of the typical fire season. It was also an especially scary blaze because it happened while Colorado was in a drought, and swept through vulnerable areas thick with dead and dying beetle-killed trees. Some experts say that without the overarching story of climate change, this fire never would have lasted as long as it did.

wheelchair and stroller accessible, and includes a spur trail roughly halfway around the lake to the only **wheelchair-friendly wilderness campsite** in Rocky.

An easy stroll from the parking lot immediately takes you to the marshy shores of the lake, and for some people it is enough to stop here and drink in the view. But continue on—there are plenty of other great vantage points along the trail, as well as interesting informational signs about **Abner Sprague,** who operated a guest lodge in this spot 1910-1940 (and created his namesake lake for guests to enjoy). Honking geese are often seen skimming the waters and there are plenty of benches to sit on and relax. People also enjoy fly-fishing here. Near the end of your journey, be sure to stop at a small wooden viewing platform on the north shore of the lake to peer up at the **Continental Divide.**

BIERSTADT LAKE

Distance: 2.6 miles round-trip
Duration: 1 hour, 15 minutes
Elevation gain: 556 feet
Effort: moderate
Trailhead: Bierstadt Lake (see map p. 50)

The body of water at the top of this hike may be gorgeous, but in the opinion of this author it is the views from the trail that are the real star attraction. Named after **Albert Bierstadt** (BEER-shtat) a German-born painter who heavily promoted Rocky Mountain National Park through his creative works, this destination is as popular as any other in the Bear Lake corridor. That said, in the summer, plan on taking a **shuttle to the trailhead,** as the parking lot is small and fills up early.

The path starts out in a pine forest and climbs immediately, switchbacking up **Bierstadt Moraine.** On a hot day the sun can beat down intensely, and you will come to appreciate areas of the trail pleasantly shaded by aspen. Early on, spectacular vistas of the Continental Divide unfold, along with a bird's eye view of the stream of cars traveling on Bear Lake Road below. The trail finally levels out at the top of the moraine before arriving at the lake. Several options unfold at this point. You can circle all the way around the lake on a 0.6-mile trail and head back the way you came; trek out to Bear Lake, head to the Park & Ride lot via the Bierstadt Moraine

Sprague Lake and Bierstadt Lake

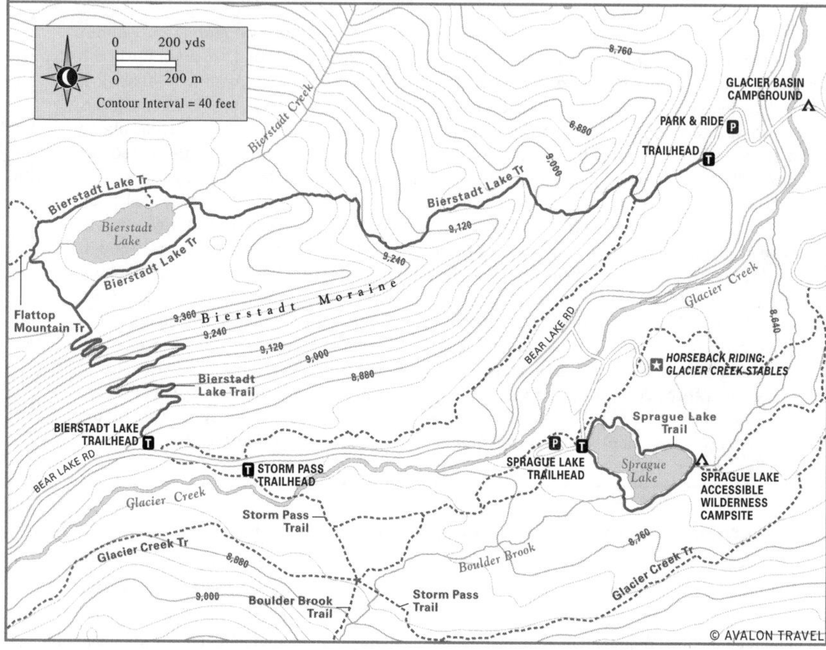

Trail; or hike to Hollowell Park. As you walk around **Bierstadt Lake,** you will notice that the shoreline is mostly filled in with sedge and impractical for sitting down, but there is one small beach that is suitable for enjoying a sack lunch.

★ ALBERTA FALLS

Distance: 1.6 miles round-trip
Duration: 45 minutes
Elevation gain: 160 feet
Effort: easy
Trailhead: Glacier Gorge (see map p. 53). Parking lot fills by 6am in the summer; taking the shuttle system is advised.

If you are on a mission to hike every trail in Glacier Gorge, you will witness more than once the dynamic, gushing waters of Alberta Falls; it is on the way to popular longer hikes such as Sky Pond, Mills Lake, and Black Lake. Alberta Falls is also an outstanding shorter hike on its own. The **Glacier Gorge Trailhead parking lot** routinely fills up by 6am (yes, you read that correctly) in the summer; therefore, it is ideal to arrive via the free **park shuttle.**

The **Glacier Gorge Trail** starts in a forested area that is especially pretty at the peak of fall when the aspens have turned brilliant yellow, and even in late fall when faded yellow leaves drop, then dust the trail. After approximately 0.2 mile of hiking you will reach a **trail junction** with one sign pointing to Bear Lake; follow the arrow clearly pointing left (south) to **Alberta Falls.** Continue along the trail at a gentle grade until you reach an impressive **overlook of Glacier Creek.** People sometimes pull out their map at this point, furrow their brow, and ask passersby, "Is *this* Alberta Falls?" No, the biggest reward is still ahead. Parallel the creek for another 0.2 mile and you will come to a **small wooden sign** identifying the falls and the beautiful cascade behind it. Alongside the water, find some wide slabs of

Abner Sprague, Trailblazer

Abner Sprague (1851-1943) is especially remembered for his entrepreneurial spirit and for his love of the Estes Valley. He was one of the area's first homesteaders, having snapped up a prime piece of land in Moraine Park in the late 1870s. He gave farming a try on his initial 160-acre parcel, but eventually switched gears and turned his property into a guest lodge. Over time, "Sprague's Ranch" was expanded in size and became a hot spot for tourists passing through. He and his wife, Alberta, provided visitors with meals, cabins in which to stay, and guided outings. Eventually his hotel was bought out by a business partner—J.D. Stead—and became known as "Stead's Ranch." The property, which grew over time to include a pool, a golf course, and dozens of buildings, held court in Moraine Park until the early 1960s.

Sprague's holdings eventually included two additional properties around Loch Vale and Mills Lake; he also opened up a hotel where **Sprague Lake** is located today. His namesake lake was one of two that he designed for the enjoyment of guests at Sprague's Lodge; the other lake no longer remains.

At one time a surveyor for Larimer County, Sprague named Moraine Park, Alberta Falls, and numerous other mountains and features around the park. When Rocky officially became a national park, Sprague went down in history as the first person to pay a park entrance fee. An avid outdoorsman, he hiked to the top of Longs Peak even at age 74. He was fiercely proud of being one of the region's first pioneers, and a lively account of his experiences and observations is detailed in *My Pioneer Life: The Memoirs of Abner E. Sprague*. The book is a must-read for those with curiosity about early settlement in the area.

Alberta Falls

rock that are great for taking in the view and eating a snack or lunch before heading back the way you came.

MILLS LAKE

Distance: 5.6 miles round-trip
Duration: 2.5-3 hours
Elevation gain: 700 feet
Effort: moderate
Trailhead: Glacier Gorge (see map p. 53). Parking lot fills by 6am in the summer; taking the shuttle system is advised.

It is hard not to have high expectations when hiking to Mills Lake. This subalpine body of water is named after the "father" of Rocky Mountain National Park, **Enos Mills,** so it has to be impressive, right? Indeed, the scenery does not disappoint—especially on a warm, cloudless fall afternoon, which is when I first experienced its beauty. The hike begins at the popular Glacier Gorge Trailhead where there is limited parking, so plan on taking the **park shuttle** if visiting in the summer.

To begin, take the **Glacier Gorge Trail** south for approximately 0.2 mile to a **trail**

junction with many options listed. Turn left (south) toward **Alberta Falls,** Mills Lake, and Loch Vale. In 0.9 mile after leaving Alberta Falls, the **trail splits** with the North Longs Peak Trail. Turn right (west) and follow the Glacier Gorge Trail south for another 0.5 mile. The vistas on this section of trail are gorgeous and the hiking is easy, even descending gradually at one point. You will reach another split in the trail. Head left for **Mills Lake,** which is now easily within reach—just 0.6 mile away. Walk through a pretty forested area, then cross over two **footbridges** before reaching a section of rock slabs marked by **cairns.** Once you have traveled over these rocks, views of Mills Lake unfold. It is worth plodding a little farther along the trail that skirts the left side of the lake to explore various rocky fingers extending into the water, and to access different vantage points of the surrounding mountains. From the lake, there are superb views in every direction, particularly of Longs Peak, Keyboard of the Winds, and Thatchtop Mountain. Return the way you came.

★ SKY POND

Distance: 9 miles round-trip
Duration: 6 hours
Elevation gain: 1,650 feet
Effort: strenuous
Trailhead: Glacier Gorge (see map p. 53). Parking lot fills by 6am in the summer; taking the shuttle system is advised.

Spectacular scenery awaits on the journey to Sky Pond, and adventurous souls will enjoy the final push toward the end of this hike, which includes a few fun minutes of rock scrambling.

Starting on the **Glacier Gorge Trail,** hike 0.8 mile to **Alberta Falls,** then continue along the path for 0.9 mile until the trail intersects with the **North Longs Peak Trail.** Continue right (west) toward **Mills Lake** and Loch Vale (Scottish for "lake valley"), and within a matter of minutes the landscape starts to dramatically open up. After a relatively flat section followed by a brief descent, the trail splits off again in 0.5 mile for Mills Lake/Black Lake and Loch Vale. Stay right (southwest) on the **Loch Vale Trail.** From here, the trail turns into a set of steeper switchbacks; heed the signs that say not to shortcut the trail. You will arrive at **The Loch** in roughly another 1.2 miles. As you wind around this stunningly gorgeous lake, there are plenty of nice spots to eat a snack or lunch, or go fishing. When you have had your fill, continue along on the Loch Vale trail to Sky Pond. After crossing **two small bridges,** hike past the trail split on your right for **Andrews Glacier Trail.** Here, the ground briefly becomes marshy, and multiple planks of wood have been set up to aid hikers across this sensitive area. Some steep rock steps finally plant you in the middle of a wide-open boulder field with great views in every direction. Continue hiking to a small **wooden sign** for Sky Pond that points to the right. But first, pause to admire the cascade of water that is **Timberline Falls,** just to the left of the sign. Your next move is the aforementioned scramble up a set of rocks, which is easier going up than going down—and made especially tricky because some of the rocks can be wet. If you can, especially on the way down, remove your backpack and hand it to someone below for better balance. At the top of the scramble is pretty **Lake of Glass.** Continue following **cairns** for another 0.2 mile along rocky terrain and you will reach your final destination, **Sky Pond,** at 10,900 feet. The cliffs surrounding this lake, including the jagged edges of The Sharkstooth, are the most impressive feature at the end of this memorable hike. Return the way you came.

BEAR LAKE NATURE TRAIL

Distance: 0.5 mile one-way
Duration: 20 minutes
Elevation gain: 20 feet
Effort: easy
Trailhead: Bear Lake (see map p. 53)

A fun way to learn about Rocky's landscape

Sky Pond, Emerald Lake, and Flattop Mountain

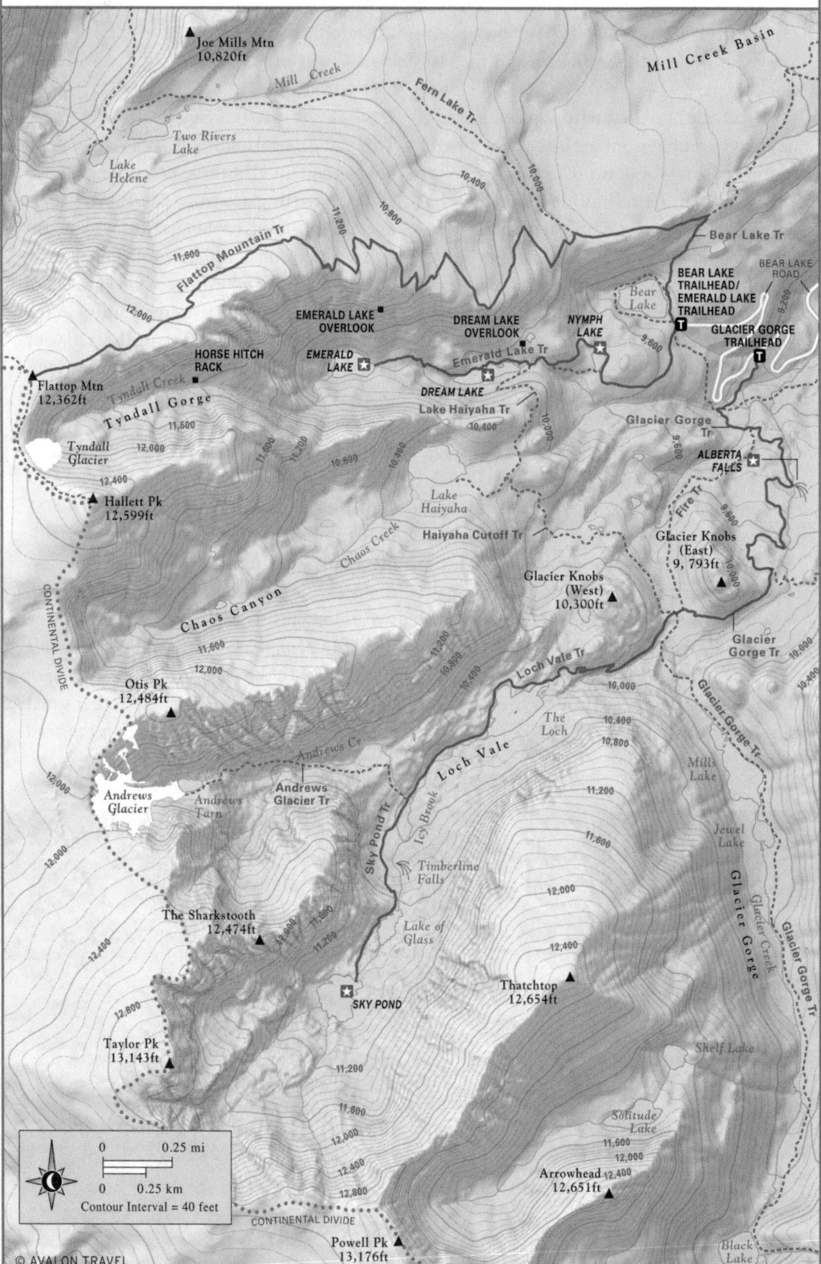

and history is by taking the **self-guided** Bear Lake Nature Trail tour, suitable for all ages. The corresponding booklet ($2) is sold at the **Bear Lake Ranger Station,** a self-serve kiosk near the trailhead, and the visitor centers.

Head counterclockwise around the lake and keep your eye out for **bear paw prints** mounted on wooden posts that correlate with facts in the self-guided tour booklet. Along the way, you will learn about natural phenomena such as "snow knees"—tree trunks that have been bent into a knee shape after being pummeled with sliding heavy snow year after year. For anyone who has wondered what the differences are among spruce, fir, and pine trees, an easy to follow tree identification method is outlined in the guide. The path is gorgeous to travel even without the self-guided tour materials, and most of the trail is level and **wheelchair accessible.** However, it would be difficult for a wheelchair user to completely circle the lake; around bear paw marker 22, the path heads downhill sharply and then goes uphill just as steeply. A sign at the start of the trail warns visitors of these changes. Numerous **benches** are situated around the lake and are great for relaxing.

★ NYMPH, DREAM, AND EMERALD LAKES

Distance: 3.6 miles round-trip
Duration: 2 hours
Elevation change: 605 feet
Effort: moderate
Trailhead: Emerald Lake (see map p.53)

This paradisiacal hike truly "has it all." In two hours you will visit three exceptional alpine lakes carved by glaciers. At nearly every turn, the scenery—from babbling streams to mountain peaks to boulders the size of semitrucks—is jaw-dropping and worthy of any number of superlatives. Wildflowers are plentiful in the summer, and as you travel along the trail your gaze is met by pristine beauty in all directions.

To start, park or take a shuttle to the Bear Lake Trailhead, and locate the **Emerald Lake Trailhead** sign. A wide, even trail gradually ascends west to the first of the three lakes—**Nymph Lake**—which is approximately 0.5 mile from the trailhead. In the summer, this glassy lake ringed with trees is cheerfully festooned with lily pads and their sun-colored, waxy blossoms. The lake was named after the pond lily, *Nymphaea polysepala.* Most people stop to take in the view at the first open spot on the south side, but there are other great vantage points as you continue up the trail

serene Nymph Lake

Tracking Snowfall

A good amount of white stuff dumps from the sky around Bear Lake each winter, and every inch of it is monitored using automated snow telemetry (SNOTEL) equipment. Walking out on the main path to Bear Lake from the parking lot, you will notice an interpretive sign for the SNOTEL on your left, and some unusual-looking equipment tucked back in the trees. The SNOTEL site has existed in this spot since 1979 and is managed by the **USDA Natural Resource Conservation Service.** Data tracked with the equipment appears in real time on the USDA's website (www.wcc.nrcs.usda.gov/snow). The USDA specifically logs how much precipitation has fallen at this location—including snow and rain—as well as the amount of water in the snow, air temperature, and total snow depth.

The USDA started observing snow levels back in the early 1900s in California, with the intention of predicting how much water the Sierra would produce in the spring. Today, just under 900 SNOTEL sites in the 13 western states primarily exist for the same purpose: figuring out how much runoff is going to come from snowpack in various regions each year. However, there are dozens of other reasons that agencies and individuals track this information. The Colorado Avalanche Information Center uses these data to help forecast avalanche risk. Backcountry skiers will look at snow depth reports and decide if conditions are optimal for getting some powder turns. River enthusiasts will plan out rafting trips with the data. All told, upward of 200 people per day check on Bear Lake's snow stats online for different purposes. There is not a walking path that will lead you close to the SNOTEL, and that's for a reason. The snowpack needs to remain untouched so the USDA's readings are as accurate as possible. So if you want to pack a snowball and toss it, do it elsewhere.

that are less busy—particularly a partially secluded bench on the north side of the lake. The next leg of the hike to **Dream Lake** is 0.6 mile and is another moderate climb uphill. On some steeper parts of the trail, steps are fashioned out of logs, and several small **wooden bridges** aid hikers during stream crossings. Immediately before you reach Dream Lake, there is a **junction** with the Lake Haiyaha Trail; continue traveling west on the Emerald Lake Trail. Dream Lake, with its blue-green waters, could easily be mistaken for Emerald Lake. This is one of the most photographed locations in the park and is especially picturesque at sunrise. (If your schedule allows it, try heading out to hike an hour before dawn to catch Hallett and Flattop Peaks awash in the blush tones of early morning light.) The last push from Dream Lake to **Emerald Lake** is 0.7 mile and passes through large rock outcroppings, with more steps to aid travelers uphill. Your final stop is a stunning body of water situated at 10,100 feet. A large group of rocks next to the lake fills with visitors lunching and relaxing on sunny days. You can also scramble over boulders on the viewer's right side of the lake to reach a more secluded spot. Return the way you came.

LAKE HAIYAHA

Distance: 4.2 miles round-trip
Duration: 2 hours
Elevation change: 745 feet
Effort: moderate
Trailhead: Emerald Lake (see map p. 53)

Many hikers travel along the Emerald Lake Trail with the plan of visiting Nymph, Dream, and Emerald Lakes and returning back to the parking lot. An alternative is to travel from Nymph Lake to Dream Lake, and from Dream Lake to Lake Haiyaha. This lake is considerably less crowded than the others and has incredible scenery. Those who have the time and energy can consider traveling to all four lakes (a visit to Bear Lake, next to the parking lot, would make five).

Start at the Emerald Lake Trailhead. After 0.6 mile of hiking west, arrive at **Nymph**

Lake. Continue another 0.5 mile west to **Dream Lake.** Upon arriving at Dream Lake, find a sign on the left-hand side of the trail for **Lake Haiyaha.** Climb through dense forest and head south along a ridgeline. At 1.3 miles from the trailhead, a grand vista appears, with Bear Lake and Nymph Lake looking particularly diminutive down below. As you hike this early stretch of the trail, take note of the rock work along the path. This trail is listed on the **National Register of Historic Places** because it is representative of the National Park Service's "naturalistic" design; the stonework is believed to be original, from the 1930s. Continue climbing another 0.4 mile until you reach a **trail junction** for The Loch and the Glacier Gorge parking areas; follow the trail southwest to Lake Haiyaha. On the final approach to the lake, the trail gets very rocky; small children might need assistance during this last stretch. The lake's edge is lined with large boulders, and visitors of all ages will need to use careful footing. From the lakeside, take in views of Otis Peak, Hallett Peak, and Chaos Canyon. The Canyon, which is filled with a jumble of giant boulders, is a popular spot for rock climbers.

FLATTOP MOUNTAIN

Distance: 8.8 miles round-trip
Duration: 5 to 5.5 hours
Elevation gain: 2,849 feet
Effort: very strenuous
Trailhead: Bear Lake (see map p. 53)

On a good weather day, you will be treated to impressive mountain views on the approach to—and on the summit of—Flattop Mountain. On a not-so-good day, a thick blanket of fog, a thunderstorm, or heavy precipitation might prevent you from attaining the summit. Plan to do this hike when the **weather forecast is fair/sunny,** and if conditions change once you are above the tree line—which they often do—do not be afraid to turn around. The **high elevation** can be an issue for people on this hike; if you are feeling signs and symptoms of altitude sickness, head down.

Flattop Mountain is located on the Continental Divide and is a popular destination in the summer. The summit can be hiked to from either side of the park.

To start, walk toward Bear Lake from the parking lot and head right on the **Bear Lake Trail.** After just a few minutes on the trail, you will arrive at a small sign for Flattop Mountain, then a large, **official trailhead sign.** Ascend on the path, which at the beginning, is lined with aspen trees and large boulders. About 0.5 mile from the trailhead, you will arrive at a **trail junction** for Mill Creek Basin. Take a left (head west) to continue on the **Flattop Mountain Trail.** Hike for 0.5 mile until reaching the junction for Odessa Lake, and continue west on the Flattop Mountain Trail. The trail ascends through forest, eventually arriving at the **Dream Lake Overlook** (1.7 mi from the start). Take in some water, a snack, and the views; then continue onward and upward. The terrain will slowly start to change, and gnarled trees called krummholz appear close to the tree line. As the trees disappear, **cairns** start to appear. These are some of the largest rock piles I have seen in the park, and they serve a good purpose, as it can be easy to get disoriented on the trail in low visibility conditions. At 3 miles from the trailhead, an **overlook** appears for Emerald Lake. Past the overlook, the path continues through alpine tundra. Keep your eyes out for ptarmigan on this stretch. In another 0.9 mile, you will arrive at a **horse hitch rack.** At this point, enjoy great views of Tyndall Glacier, one of the last remaining glaciers in the park. Hike another 0.5 mile and you will arrive at your destination. Hooray—you made it, and are now standing on the **Continental Divide** at a whopping 12,324 feet.

From here, you have several other options besides hiking back to the trailhead. If you have planned ahead (and have backpacking gear, a wilderness camping permit, and transportation on the west side of the park), you can take the Tonahutu Creek Trail or the North Inlet Trail over to the Kawuneeche Valley. You can also continue over to Hallett

What is a Social Trail?

Throughout the park, visitors will encounter what are known as **social trails.** These paths, well-worn by hiking boots, branch off from established park trails or roads. Unofficial trails get started because of a natural feature that is unreachable by the network of trails already created in the park. A social trail might take you to the shores of a lake, a bouldering problem, or a scenic viewpoint.

The park discourages the creation of social trails, and instead encourages people to travel in a dispersed fashion when hiking or walking off-trail—that is, space your group out over a wide area to avoid creating new trails. If you see the beginnings of a new social trail—such as matted down vegetation—consider taking a different route to get from point A to point B. Never take a social trail that cuts switchbacks on a mountain; doing so can lead to detrimental erosion.

Peak, which is located to the south. This option is located off established trails and the journey to the top is quite rocky. Choose your own adventure, depending on your stamina and experience level.

BACKPACKING

With its many connecting trails and numerous wilderness campsites, Bear Lake offers excellent backpacking opportunities. As you consult your map, consider not just out-and-back hikes, but loop hikes and shuttle-aided hikes.

The Bear Lake area is popular, so make wilderness campsite reservations well in advance through the **East Side Wilderness Office** (970/586-1242, open daily, but hours vary seasonally), located next to the Beaver Meadows Visitor Center. For backcountry camping dates that fall May 1-October 31, reservations can be made online (www.pay.gov) or in person at a wilderness office (not by phone) March 1-October 28. For camping dates November 1-April 30, reservations can be made by phone or in person October 1-April 30.

Although camping by Bear Lake or along the trail to Emerald Lake certainly sounds enticing, there are no wilderness sites available.

Continental Divide National Scenic Trail

A portion of the 3,100-mile long **Continental Divide National Scenic Trail (CDT)** makes a great destination for an overnight backpacking trip. From the Bear Lake Trailhead, hike to Flattop Mountain (4.4 mi one-way) which connects with the Tonahutu Creek Trail and the North Inlet Trail on the park's west side. Both trails are part of the CDT and lead to the Kawuneeche Valley. Along each trail are numerous wilderness campsites that may be reserved ahead. To complete the trip, you will need to arrange for a shuttle vehicle on the west side.

Sierra Club Outings (415/977-5522, www.sierraclub.org) offers a guided backpacking trip that travels from the east side to the west side: Across the Continental Divide in Rocky Mountain National Park (midsummer, $935). **Wildland Trekking** (800/715-4453, www.wildlandtrekking.com) also leads backpackers across the park on its Continental Divide Loop tour (multiple trips July-Sept., $1,240). Both tours meet in Estes Park.

Fern Lake Trail

A great spot for backpacking on the east side is on the **Fern Lake Trail.** My first backpacking trip in Rocky many years ago involved one night at **Spruce Lake** and a second night at **Fern Lake;** it was a winner. **Odessa Lake** and **Sourdough** wilderness sites are other fine spots to spend the night.

★ HORSEBACK RIDING

Inside the Park

One of the most pleasurable ways to

experience the landscape of Rocky is atop a horse. Two stables are found within the park boundaries, **Moraine Park Stables** (549 Fern Lake Rd., 970/586-2327, www.sombrero.com, mid-May-mid-Oct., $55-170) and **Glacier Creek Stables** (take Bear Lake Rd. almost 6 mi to the Sprague Lake turnoff, 970/586-3244, www.sombrero.com, late May-mid-Sept., $55-250). Both stables are operated by the same outfitter, Hi-Country Stables, Inc., and offer a similar high-quality riding experience to visitors. Guides are friendly, knowledgeable, and accommodating. The mellowest of rides is a two-hour saunter around Moraine Park, suitable for inexperienced riders and children as young as two (riding double with an adult). According to my guide on one ride, not just kids, but even grown-ups have actually been known to nod off briefly on this outing due to the gentle nap-inducing motion of the horses. For experienced riders, choose a 10-hour rugged adventure that leaves from Glacier Creek Stables and climbs up and over the Continental Divide to Grand Lake.

Reservations are recommended for all rides, particularly for larger groups. Wear long pants and sturdy athletic shoes or cowboy boots, and plan to bring your own snacks, lunch, and drinks. Rain slickers are provided and carried by guides. Helmets are also provided but not required. Overnight camping/pack trips are offered at both locations.

If you bring your own horse into Rocky, know that the following hiking trails are off-limits to horses: Bear Lake Nature Trail, Emerald Lake, Lake Haiyaha, Bierstadt Lake, Spruce Lake, Sky Pond, a portion of The Loch trail, and a portion of the trail between Mills Lake and Black Lake.

Those planning to overnight in the park with their horse should make arrangements with the wilderness office (970/586-1242; the east-side office is located next to the Beaver Meadows Visitor Center).

Outside the Park

Several liveries in Estes Park provide riding experiences in Rocky. **Jackson Stables** (2515 Tunnel Rd., 970/586-3341 ext. 1140, early Mar.-early Nov., $40-170) is located on the YMCA's property, though you do not have to stay at the YMCA in order to ride horses. Numerous guided rides are offered throughout the east side and run from an hour long to all day. **National Park Gateway Stables** (4600 Fall River Rd., 970/586-5269, www.skhorses.com, early May-early Oct., $55-170) guides two- to eight-hour rides to east-side locations, including Horseshoe Park and Deer Mountain. The stable's Dinner Ride ($45) includes two hours of evening riding and a discounted supper at the Trailhead Restaurant (located next to the stables) directly following the ride.

a scenic horseback ride through Beaver Meadows

FISHING

The east side has dozens of great spots to cast a line—some busier than others. The **Big Thompson River** in **Moraine Park** tends to be one of the more popular places to fish simply because it is so accessible from the main entrance. People also gravitate toward this spot because they can simultaneously catch trout in the river's undercut banks, gaze up at the surrounding peaks, and watch for wildlife—particularly elk—tromping through the meadow. At the risk of sounding trite, it all adds up to a scene that you might see in a Hollywood movie.

If you head north to the **Fall River** to fish, chances are, even at the height of summer, you will be able to find a nice secluded spot to yourself. One particularly nice place to get on the river is from a small parking lot off Highway 34, directly across from the turnoff to Old Fall River Road.

Different rules apply when it comes to Rocky's lakes, and it is imperative that you pick up the park's official fishing brochure before wetting a line. Some waters are catch-and-keep while others are catch-and-release. Bear Lake is completely off limits to fishing. Hiking in several miles to a high alpine lake, such as Mills Lake or The Loch, has its advantages: namely, a greater chance of solitude.

During the elk rut (Sept. 1-Oct. 31), sections of the Fall River or Big Thompson River are inaccessible 5pm-7am. The park restricts foot-traffic access to Horseshoe Park, Moraine Park, and Upper Beaver Meadows to give elk the space they need to mate.

Fishing Guides

Before I went out with a professional fishing guide for the first time, I will admit that I balked a little at the price. But now I am a true believer in these services and their value. A guide is a motivator, a tier of flies, and an encyclopedia of knowledge about specific rivers, streams, and lakes. A guide cheerfully untangles your line from a tree branch and teaches you the right way to army crawl along a river bank so as to not spook any fish with your shadow. No matter what your fish count is for the day, you will more than likely take away fun memories on a guided fishing trip.

Fishing guides see steady business on the east side of the park, and you can take your pick from a variety of outfitters. In Estes Park, there is **Kirks Fly Shop** (230 E. Elkhorn Ave., 970/577-0790, www.kirksflyshop.com, 7am-8pm daily summer, 8am-5pm daily winter), **Scot's Sporting Goods** (870 Moraine Ave., 970/586-2877, www.scotssportinggoods.com, 8am-8pm daily summer, 9am-5pm daily May and Sept-Oct.), **Estes Park Mountain Shop** (2050 Big Thompson Ave., 970/586-6548, www.estesparkmountainshop.com, 8am-9pm daily), and **Estes Angler** (970/586-2110 or 800/586-2110, www.estesangler.com, 9am-5pm daily). Numerous guiding services along the Front Range also offer trips to the park.

Two-, four-, or eight-hour trips are offered by guides, and some also offer two-hour evening hatch trips or overnight backpack, horseback, or llama pack trips. Pricing varies depending on whether you have one, two, or three individuals in your party, but can run anywhere from $120 for a four-hour trip for one to $450 for an eight-hour trip for three. Typically included in the price are your guide's expertise, gear (including waders, flies, rods, and reels), snacks and/or lunch, and transportation. A Colorado fishing license must be obtained separately. For gratuity, plan on shelling out between 15 to 20 percent of the trip cost.

Sasquatch Fly Fishing (970/586-3341 summer, 303/601-8617 winter, www.sasquatchflyfishing.com, 7:30am-4:30pm daily May., 7:30am-6pm daily June-Sept.), based out of the YMCA of the Rockies-Estes Park Center, offers prescheduled fly-fishing trips throughout the summer. Guides can also be hired for private outings ($120 for half day, $295 for full day).

BOATING

Boating isn't seen frequently in the park, but it can be done. Certain rules apply: mainly, no motorized watercraft are allowed on any body of water, and boats are prohibited on Bear Lake. Otherwise, visitors who have their own canoe or kayak and the ability to carry it to a lake are invited to do so. There are no boat rentals in the park and no boat docks. The easiest place to get afloat in the Bear Lake area is

Sprague Lake. Doing so requires hauling the boat a short distance from the parking lot to the water's edge. Those who fish may use float tubes on park waters.

BIKING

The glutes get a major workout on a bike ride up **Bear Lake Road.** From the intersection of Highway 36/Bear Lake Road, cyclists log around 1,500 feet of vertical climbing over the 9.5 miles (one-way) to Bear Lake parking lot. This popular ride is a beautiful one, especially the last 1.5 miles when great views of Otis Peak, Hallett Peak, and Flattop Mountain unfold. This road gets incredibly congested in the summer, so it's wise to start riding early in the morning to avoid traffic.

Cyclists also enjoy biking north on **Highway 36** (from the Beaver Meadows Entrance Station) to Trail Ridge Road. Rocky's roads do not have dedicated bike lanes, so cyclists need to be ever-vigilant for vehicles.

ROCK CLIMBING

The Bear Lake parking lot is consistently full in the summer because of the area's popularity with rock climbers, specifically those who like to boulder. Bouldering is conducted low to the ground without ropes; a thick mat called a crash pad is strategically placed just below a climber to cushion falls.

Lake Haiyaha is ground zero for bouldering in the Bear Lake region and attracts more members of the climbing community each year. Many of the folks you will see here are young, up-and-coming climbing talents from Denver, Boulder, and other Front Range towns. To get to this bouldering mecca, simply follow marked trails to Lake Haiyaha from the Bear Lake parking lot. Bouldering "problems"—as they are called—are found in Upper Chaos Canyon or Lower Chaos Canyon. Lower Chaos Canyon is accessed through a well-worn, obvious **social trail** that splits off to the right from the main trail as you approach the lake. Upper Chaos Canyon is accessed by walking along the Lake Haiyaha Trail until it peters out; afterward, forge uphill and west through the trees.

Get the scoop about specific bouldering problems from the **Estes Park Mountain Shop** (2050 Big Thompson Ave., Estes Park, 970/586-6548, www.estesparkmountainshop.com, 8am-9pm daily) or from a local climber. Other resources include **Mountain Project** (www.mountainproject.com) and Jamie Emerson's *Bouldering Rocky Mountain National Park & Mount Evans.*

Rangers in the park keep an eagle eye on negative human impact around Lake Haiyaha due to increased climbing activity. Travel lightly on the earth here, do not leave crash pads, and always pack out any trash.

GEOCACHING

A fun way to explore Rocky is through geocaching, a digital-age treasure hunt where Global Positioning System (GPS) waypoints lead participants to beautiful views, locations of geologic significance, and other rewards. The **Across the Divide GeoTour** takes visitors to spots in Rocky as well as Estes Park and Grand Lake. To get started, download a list of geocaches from the official geocaching website (www.geocaching.com). You will also need a GPS device or GPS app (www.geocaching.com) loaded to your smartphone for locating specific coordinates. More information can be obtained at the **Estes Park Visitor Center** (500 Big Thompson Ave., 970/577-9900, 9am-5pm Mon.-Sat., 10am-4pm Sun). The **Rocky Mountain Conservancy** (48 Alpine Cir., 970/586-0108, www.rmconservancy.org) also offers an introductory geocaching class for kids and parents in the summer.

WINTER SPORTS

Cross-Country Skiing and Snowshoeing

In the winter, a snowy fantasyland unfolds in Rocky, complete with frozen lakes and streams, pine boughs laced with icicles, and trails and meadows blanketed in snow. In the cold months, the Bear Lake corridor is best explored on cross-country skis or snowshoes. The mostly flat trails circling **Bear Lake** and **Sprague Lake** are especially popular spots for beginners; experienced skiers in good physical shape may choose from any of the park's longer, more challenging trails. **Estes Park Mountain Shop** (2050 Big Thompson Ave., 970/586-6548, www.estesparkmountainshop.com, 8am-9pm daily) has snowshoes ($5/day) and a cross-country ski package for rent (skis, boots, and poles, $15/day). **Kirks Mountain Adventures** (230 E. Elkhorn Ave., 970/577-0790, www.kirksmountainadventures.com, 8am-5pm daily winter, $6/day) rents snowshoes.

The **Rocky Mountain Conservancy** (48 Alpine Circle, 970/586-0108, www.rmconservancy.org), Estes Park Mountain Shop, and Kirks Mountain Adventures offer guided tours. **Apex Ex** (303/731-6160, www.apexex.com, $275) hosts a snowshoe and fondue outing that departs from the Bear Lake Trailhead and includes a feast of hot, cheesy goodness and warm-you-to-the-bones apple cider.

While Rocky's trails are well-marked, getting discombobulated in the woods is entirely possible, particularly after new snow has fallen. Lakes and waterways can also be hazardous to cross. Do not expect every body of water to be a solid—and therefore sturdy underfoot—mass of ice. Check with the visitor center about potential avalanche danger on trails, and consult the weather forecast before any outing. The park provides a winter trail map for Bear Lake that is helpful in conjunction with a topographical map, and indicates areas of particular concern for avalanche danger. Dress in warm layers, and come ready for moisture with waterproof boots and gaiters. A map and compass and/or a GPS unit are essential; make sure you know in advance how to use these navigational tools.

Backcountry Skiing

Hidden Valley (off Trail Ridge Rd.) is the most popular area to backcountry ski, but powder hounds seek out stashes in the Bear Lake corridor as well. Popular spots to carve turns near Bear Lake include **Tyndall Gorge** and the **Lake Haiyaha** drainage. Only experienced backcountry skiers should venture into the park with the right gear, a day-of consideration of avalanche danger via the **Colorado Avalanche Information Center** (www.avalanche.state.co.us), good maps, and navigation skills. For the most complete guide to backcountry skiing in the park, grab a copy of Mark Kelly's *Backcountry Skiing and Ski Mountaineering in Rocky Mountain National Park*—it is an outstanding primer on the sport.

Entertainment and Shopping

RANGER PROGRAMS

People pay good money to have private guides show them all over the park, but the best teachers are the ones that do not cost a cent. Rocky's rangers know the park inside and out and are brimming with knowledge they are eager to share. The best way to learn about **ranger-led programs** is to browse listings in the free park newspaper (www.nps.gov/romo), which is distributed at entrance stations and is also online. Programs are held at the visitor centers and on park trails. In the summer, rangers host programs most evenings at park amphitheaters, with topics ranging from beavers to tundra. A great way to start off a summer day is by heading over to the Moraine Park Campground or Glacier Basin Campground amphitheater for **Coffee with a Ranger,** to talk with a ranger (and fellow visitors) about resource issues affecting the park. This program is an hour long and takes place several days a week; check the newspaper for details.

Discovery Days (Moraine Park Discovery

Center, 12:30pm-4:30pm Tues. and 9am-4:30pm Wed. late June-early Aug.) is an educational program featuring interactive exhibits, quickie craft projects, learning stations, and ranger-led activities for kids of all ages. Topics differ, but are typically centered on ecology and geology themes. No reservations are needed, and activities are free of charge; just drop by and stay as little or as long as you like.

Discovery Hikes (9:30am Thurs.-Tues. late June-late Aug.) are ranger-led family-friendly hikes. On Saturday, an additional hike takes place at 2pm. Hikes depart from the Moraine Park Discovery Center; expect to be out for 1-1.5 hours.

Free ranger-led snowshoe walks are a fun way to become introduced to the sport. The **Snowshoe Ecology Walk** (12:30pm Wed., Sat., and Sun. Jan.-mid-Mar.) lasts two hours; participants must provide their own snowshoes. **Reservations** (970/586-1223, 8am-4pm daily) must be made no more than seven days in advance.

Stargazing

Countless hours are invested in maintaining Rocky's landscape. A lesser-known aspect of park management is monitoring and preserving the natural nighttime "lightscape" for the benefit of humans and nocturnal animals. It takes work to maintain a memorable night sky and park officials place great importance on this aspect of the park experience. Visitors who hail from areas heavily affected by light pollution are often taken aback by the dazzling display above.

For a great stargazing experience, bundle up after the sun dips behind the mountains and head to **Upper Beaver Meadows.** Cast your gaze heavenward with the naked eye, or use a telescope, binoculars, or star binoculars for a better view. During the summer, several different ranger-led astronomy programs are offered in conjunction with the **Estes Park Memorial Observatory** (1500 Manford Ave., 970/586-5668, www.angelsabove.org); check the park newspaper or the observatory website for dates and times. The observatory also has a "clear sky chart" for Upper Beaver Meadows linked to its homepage; the chart and other charts like it are used by professional astronomers and can be helpful in deciding whether to swap sleep for stargazing on any given night.

Free **ranger-led astronomy programs** in the summer include Party with the Stars, Astronomy in the Park, and Stories Behind the Moon and Stars. In mid-summer, a three-day Rocky Mountain National Park Night Sky Festival takes place, and includes speakers, night sky viewings, and special programs.

Especially popular with visitors are ranger-led full moon walks, which usually last 1-1.5 hours; spots must be reserved in advance. Dates, times, and locations vary monthly.

SHOPPING

The Beaver Meadows Visitor Center, Moraine Park Discovery Center, and Fall River Visitor Center each contain a **Rocky Mountain Conservancy Nature Store** (www.rmconservancy.org), with a small selection of clothing, toys, games, books, and maps for sale. A portion of the proceeds from each sale is funneled back into park projects. The gift shops share the same business hours as the visitor centers.

Next to the Fall River Visitor Center, the **Rocky Mountain Gateway Gift Shop** (3450 Fall River Rd., 970/577-0043, www.rockymountaingateway.net, 9am-5pm daily) is stocked with jewelry, garden items, furniture, kitchen supplies, and souvenirs.

Camping

There are no overnight lodging options in Rocky Mountain National Park. Campgrounds provide the only place to stay. **Reservations** (877/444-6777, www.recreation.gov) are accepted for the following campgrounds. Visitors are limited to seven nights in any area of the park June 1-September 30.

In Estes Park, accommodations of every type, including campgrounds, RV parks, hotels, and lodges, are in close proximity to the Fall River Entrance Station and Beaver Meadows Entrance Station.

INSIDE THE PARK

Moraine Park Campground

Moraine Park Campground (Bear Lake Rd., 2.5 miles from the Beaver Meadows Entrance Station, late May-late Sept., $26; late Sept.-late May, $18) is the busiest campground in the park, with 244 spots to pitch your tent or park your RV. This is also the only park campground **open year-round,** with 77 spots available on a first-come, first-served basis in the winter. Most sites are pleasantly shaded under a canopy of trees, and include a fire pit with grate, picnic table, and tent or parking pads. Bear boxes are scattered throughout each of the four loops and must be shared. The campground affords easy access to the Moraine Park Stables, Moraine Park Discovery Center, several hiking trails, ranger-led evening programs at the outdoor amphitheater, and the park's **shuttle system.** In high season, amenities include water; dishwashing stations; firewood and ice sales; trash, recycling, and propane canister disposal; a dump station; vault toilets, solar shower stalls (bring your own solar shower bag); and restrooms. In the off-season, water in Moraine Park Campground is shut off. The RV and trailer length limit is 40 feet. Four campsites—A39, A40, A41, and A42—are wheelchair-accessible.

Glacier Basin Campground

The effects of pine beetle infestation are obvious in **Glacier Basin Campground** (Bear Lake Rd., 6 mi south from the Beaver Meadows Entrance Station, late May-early Sept., $26) where the trees have been wiped out in the campground's C, D, and group loops. There is a lack of shade in these areas, and stumbling over tree stumps is a common occurrence. Regardless, this is a fine place to sleep under the stars, with many amenities for a pleasant park stay. One hundred fifty sites are available for tent campers and RVs. The RV trailer and length limit is 35 feet. For seeing major east-side sights, the convenience factor at Glacier Basin is huge: a **shuttle stop** is located at the campsite entrance, and the **Park & Ride** is across Bear Lake Road. Be careful of traffic when walking over to the Park & Ride, since there is no crosswalk. On the east side of the campground, a hiking trail leads to Sprague Lake, Storm Pass, and other destinations. Each campsite features a picnic table, fire pit with grate, and graded tent or parking pads. Bear boxes are shared. On summer evenings, a line forms at a shack near the front entrance where ice cream, firewood, and ice are sold. Ranger-led programs take place in the amphitheater most nights. Help yourself to a book or leave a nature-themed book at the Little Free Library box near the ranger station.

There are 13 tent-only **group sites** (late May-early Sept., $4 per person, per night) at the Glacier Basin Campground. Even if you are not camping with a large party, it can be fun to stroll by this section of the campground on an evening walk and observe camping logistics handled on a large scale: tents lined up in a row, and food served assembly-line style from large metal pots atop propane stoves. Trees were removed in this section because of the pine beetle infestation, so in general this is a camping area with less privacy. Sites are categorized as small (9-15 people), medium

Private Inholdings

Private inholdings, or privately owned properties within the park boundaries, have existed since the park was established. In 1926, there were a staggering 16,659 acres under private ownership in the park; about 7 percent of Rocky's total acreage. In 1965, that number had been whittled down to just 2,300 acres. By that time, the park had acquired many lodges and homes and removed them.

Today, there are approximately 50 privately owned parcels of land still in the park, totaling 365 acres. Mostly, these are small seasonal cabins that have been passed down from family member to family member and are used a few weeks out of every year. On the south edge of Moraine Park, for example, you might notice several privately owned homes, as well as a solitary, forlorn-looking chimney of a cabin that burned to the ground during the Fern Lake Fire in 2013. Generally, private properties in the park are fairly obscured. Visitors are asked to be respectful of private homes in the park.

Just one privately owned lodge remains on the eastern edge of the park near Eagle Cliff Mountain: **Machin's Cottages in the Pines** (970/586-4276, www.machinscottages.com). The property has served guests since 1946. Cascade Cottages, which operated for many decades on 40 acres of land just inside the Fall River Entrance Station, was the last inholding of a significant size to be acquired by the park. Its final season of operation was in 2016. The Rocky Mountain Conservancy follows the park's private properties closely, and whenever one becomes available, will work with willing sellers on a possible purchase.

(16-25 people), and large (26-40 people), and are ideal for any type of group—from family reunions to scout troops. There are no RV parking spots in this section, and most tents must be pitched in the grass.

Aspenglen Campground

Aspenglen Campground (from the Fall River Entrance Station, drive west on Hwy. 34 to the turnoff for the campground; late May-late Sept., $26) isn't as close to Bear Lake attractions as Moraine Park Campground and Glacier Basin Campground are, but is still an excellent jumping-off point for area sights and trails. On the flipside, with only 53 sites, the campground has a much more private feel than the other two. Amenities include firewood sales, restrooms, an amphitheater, water, trash disposal, and recycling. Most sites have partial shade and include a tent pad, fire pit with grate, and a grill. Aspenglen is unique for having dedicated food storage boxes at every campsite. This campground is not served by the park's shuttle system. The RV and trailer length limit is 30 feet.

Sprague Lake Accessible Wilderness Campsite

Sprague Lake is home to the one wheelchair-accessible wilderness campsite in the park. Up to 12 people—including five wheelchair users—may use this area for a maximum of three nights. At least one person in the party must use a wheelchair. **Reservations** can be made through the wilderness office (located next to the Beaver Meadows Visitor Center, 970/586-1242). As with all other wilderness campsites, a Wilderness Administrative Fee of $26 is charged May 1-October 31.

To get there, travel to Sprague Lake, which is located off Bear Lake Road. From the southwest side of the lake, take the level path for approximately 0.5 mile to a short spur trail. The spur trail is about 120 yards long and dead-ends at the campsite, which is equipped with accessible picnic tables, two large tent pads, a bear box, a storage locker for non-food items, and an accessible vault toilet. Water must be collected from the lake's inlet and purified. The site also features a charcoal grill and fire pit; wood must be carried in. This is the only campsite located at Sprague Lake, affording its users a good deal of privacy.

OUTSIDE THE PARK

Just 0.5 mile from the Beaver Meadows Visitor Center, campers can pitch a tent at the **Elk Meadow Lodge & RV Resort** (1665 Hwy. 66, 970/586-5342, www.elkmeadowrv.com, May 1-early Oct., $39-125). There are 36 tent-only campsites that may be reserved, as well as cabins, teepees, and 169 spots designated for RV use. Amenities include showers, restrooms, a swimming pool, and laundry facilities. One pet is allowed per campsite.

Estes Park Campground at East Portal (3420 Tunnel Rd., 970/586-4188, www.evrpd.com, May 15-early Oct., $30-45) is located adjacent to the East Portal Trailhead and includes 68 sites. Four sites have full hook-ups; 37 sites have water and electric; 27 sites are tent-only. The maximum limit for RVs is 24 feet. Amenities include a playground, water, showers, restrooms, a dump station, and ice/firewood for sale.

Food

INSIDE THE PARK

Rocky's one restaurant is **Café in the Clouds** (Fall River Pass, at the junction of Trail Ridge Rd. and Old Fall River Rd., www.trailridgegiftstore.com, 10am-4:30pm daily late May-late June and late Aug.-mid-Oct.; 9am-5:30pm late June-late Aug., $6-10). The café serves typical lunch fare—burgers, hotdogs, chili, and soup—and a variety of snacks are available for purchase. For day-trippers to the Bear Lake area, a more reasonable option is to travel to Estes Park for lunch or dinner or pack ahead for a picnic rather than travel up Trail Ridge Road just for a bite to eat.

Picnicking

Brown bagging-it types and gourmands alike find picnicking a delightful way to spend a few hours in the park. The largest picnicking spots in the Bear Lake area are at **Hollowell Park, Upper Beaver Meadows,** and **Sprague Lake.** There are also picnic tables at the Park & Ride, Beaver Meadows Visitor Center, and at a several locations near Moraine Park. One of the best places to snag a table is at **Sprague Lake.** In addition to having standard picnic tables, each of Sprague Lake's 27 spots has its own grill/fire pit. **Tuxedo Park** also has lovely streamside picnicking spots. Campsites in the park are off-limits for day use Memorial Day Weekend-September 30. Portable camp stoves and charcoal grills may be used at picnic sites.

Transportation and Services

DRIVING

Estes Park is the gateway town for Bear Lake and the park's east side. From the junction of Highway 36 and Highway 34 in downtown Estes Park, Highway 36 leads 4 miles west to the **Beaver Meadows Entrance Station,** while Highway 34 continues 4.9 miles northwest to the **Fall River Entrance Station.** Both Highway 36 and Highway 34 are open year-round and well-maintained. The roads are plowed in the winter months and chains are not required, but it is wise to have all-season tires or snow tires on your vehicle in the winter.

In the summer, the **Estes Park shuttle** (late June-early Sept., free) transports passengers throughout town and to the park's Beaver Meadows Visitor Center.

In the fall, when watching the elk rut is popular, signs regarding parking and elk viewing are posted along key roadways. During the rest of the year, use only designated pullouts on park roads to view wildlife. Under no circumstances should your car be parked on vegetation.

For emergency roadside service, contact **Bob's Towing and Repair** (800 Dunraven St., Estes Park, 970/586-3122, 8am-5pm Mon.-Sat.) or **Up Top Towing** (875 Moraine Ave., Estes Park, 970/586-4248, open 24/7).

Parking

On a summer morning, the trade-off of lingering over coffee is giving up the luxury of parking next to a trailhead around Bear Lake. The Glacier Gorge Trailhead parking lot regularly fills by 6am, while the Bear Lake Trailhead parking lot often fills by 8:30am. The Park & Ride can be full by 10:30am. An electronic sign on Bear Lake Road lets visitors know when the Bear Lake parking lot and/or Park & Ride lot is full.

The park will **temporarily close access** to Bear Lake Road when parking lots are full. If you arrive mid- to late-morning in the summer, you could get turned back on the road just past the Moraine Discovery Center. To avoid this scenario, arrive early or late, or plan to use the park's free shuttle system.

Parking lots are located at Beaver Meadows Visitor Center, Moraine Park Discovery Center, Tuxedo Park, Hollowell Park, Park & Ride, Sprague Lake, Bierstadt/Storm Pass Trailheads, Glacier Gorge Trailhead, Bear Lake Trailhead, Cub Lake Trailhead, Fern Lake Trailhead, Upper Beaver Meadows Trailhead, Deer Mountain Trailhead, Horseshoe Park, Sheep Lakes, Alluvial Fan, and Fall River Visitor Center.

RVs

Roads on the park's east side are RV accessible, though drivers should use extra caution on Bear Lake Road south of the Park & Ride; this section is narrow and windy. Moraine Park Campground and Glacier Basin Campground have the nearest dump stations. There are a handful of RV parking spaces at the Beaver Meadows Visitor Center and Fall River Visitor Center; however, there are no RV parking spots at trailheads.

SHUTTLES

A convenient **park shuttle system** (summer only, free) ensures that visitors to the Bear Lake area can still hike any trail, even when trailhead parking lots are brimming. The **Hiker Shuttle Express** (7:30am-8pm daily June-Sept., Sat.-Sun. Sept.-Oct.) provides transport to and from the Estes Park Visitor Center to the Park & Ride, with a stop at the Beaver Meadows Visitor Center. Travelers do not need shuttle reservations or tickets, but a park pass is required.

The **Park & Ride** (Bear Lake Rd., across from Glacier Basin Campground) is the east side's transit hub and provides access to all park shuttles. A long line of people often forms by mid-morning for the **Bear Lake Route** (7am-7:30pm daily late May-Oct.). In the late afternoon, the Bear Lake shuttle can be so jam-packed that visitors waiting to get on at the Glacier Gorge and Bierstadt Trailheads can't board. Be patient—shuttle drivers are doing their best to accommodate passengers and you will eventually get a ride.

If the Park & Ride lot is full in the morning (which often happens during the summer), you may be able to find a parking spot at the Moraine Park Discovery Center and ride the **Moraine Park Route** shuttle (7am-7:30pm daily late May-Oct.) from there. But be careful where you park—some spots are reserved for 1-2-hour parking only. Otherwise, you might need to head out of the park to leave your car at the Beaver Meadows Visitor Center or, in a worst-case scenario, backtrack to the Estes Park Visitor Center and take the Hiker Shuttle Express route in. Consider the time involved with this plan; the best option might be to find other activities to do in Estes Park and plan for an earlier start the following day.

Where Can I Find...?

- **Bank/ATM:** You will need to venture outside of the park to replenish your wallet. Several banks are located in downtown Estes Park.
- **Emergencies:** Call 911 or the park's dispatch center (970/586-1203). Seek help at the Estes Park Medical Center (555 Prospect Ave., 970/586-2317, www.epmedcenter.com, open 24/7) or Timberline Medical (131 Stanley Ave., 970/586-2343, 8am-5pm Mon.-Fri.).
- **Firewood and Ice:** Firewood, kindling, lighter fluid, charcoal, and ice are available at the Moraine Park Campground, Glacier Basin Campground, and Aspenglen Campground on summer evenings. Firewood cannot be collected anywhere in the park.
- **Gas:** There are no gas stations on the east side of the park; however, there are numerous places to fill up in Estes Park. It is best to start the day with a full tank.
- **Internet Access:** For a digital fix, bring your electronic device to the Beaver Meadows Visitor Center to gain access to the park's free Wi-Fi.
- **Newspaper:** The free park newspaper is available at entrance stations, visitor centers, and online. Estes Park's two newspapers include the *Estes Park News* and the *Estes Park Trail Gazette*, and can be picked up at locations in town.
- **Phones:** A pay phone is located at the Moraine Park Campground. Emergency phones are at Glacier Basin Campground, the Park & Ride, Aspenglen Campground, and the Bear Lake Trailhead.
- **Restrooms:** Toilets are located at the Bear Lake Trailhead, Sprague Lake, Fern Lake Bus Stop, Park & Ride, Moraine Park Discovery Center, Beaver Meadows Visitor Center, Moraine Park Campground, and Glacier Basin Campground. Some bathrooms have flush toilets, while others are basic vault toilets.
- **Showers:** At the Moraine Park Campground Solar Shower Facility (in the A loop), there are two shower stalls where campers and park guests can string up their own water-filled bag on a height-adjustable pulley and wash off the grit and grime. This is the only shower facility in the park.

Longs Peak and Wild Basin

There are 124 named mountain peaks in the park—but only one towers more than 14,000 feet into the air.

Longs Peak is considered one of the trickiest of Colorado's "Fourteeners" to summit; to avoid preventable tragedies, the park has emphasized the word "climb" rather than "hike" in its Peak-related literature. For those who do not wish to get up close and personal with Longs, gentler hikes are available in this area. Three miles north of the Longs Peak Trailhead is Lily Lake, a delightful spot for picnicking, bird-watching, and relaxing.

While the masses head to Bear Lake, visitors to Wild Basin are treated to fantastic lake and waterfall views with a greater sense of solitude. Less traveled than other areas of the park, this region still shows scars from a massive fire in 1978 that devastated the area. Hiking and fishing are the most prevalent summer activities in Wild Basin. In the winter, this is a favorite location for day-tripping snowshoers.

PLANNING YOUR TIME

For a portion of visitors, exploring the Longs Peak area consists of driving up from the Front Range in an evening, **camping, climbing** to the summit of Longs Peak during the early morning hours and the next day, and driving home that evening. If you plan to stay in the area longer than 24 hours and bagging (slang for completing a peak hike) Longs isn't your primary goal, then several other options are worth considering. One is to stay multiple nights at the park's **Longs Peak Campground** (which is first-come, first-served), or at a nearby **lodge** or campground along **Highway 7.** Then spend **2-3 days hiking** around Longs Peak, and 2-4 days exploring the trails of Wild Basin. Longs Peak and Wild Basin can also play a role in a more expanded 7-10 day itinerary that includes the Bear Lake region, Trail Ridge Road, and Lumpy Ridge. Short on time? A single day of sightseeing in the area should include a visit to **Lily Lake** and the short hike to **Copeland Falls** from the Wild Basin Trailhead.

HISTORY

Longs Peak was discovered in 1820 by Stephen Harriman Long, an army officer who conducted a series of exploratory trips around the country at the request of Secretary of War John G. Calhoun. On that particular

Previous: the Keyhole; Lower Copeland Falls in late spring. **Above:** golden banner in bloom.

Look for ★ to find recommended sights, activities, dining, and lodging.

Highlights

★ **Lily Lake:** Keep an eye out for ducks and muskrats as you stroll around this tranquil lake (page 76).

★ **The Baldpate Inn:** Add your own key to the world's largest key collection on display here (page 76).

★ **Longs Peak:** Everywhere you go, there it is—the highest peak in Rocky is seen from all over the park. It is climbed by thousands each year (page 77).

★ **Enos Mills Cabin Museum:** Visit the first home of the father of Rocky Mountain National Park and enjoy great views of Longs Peak from the "front yard" (page 77).

★ **Twin Sisters Western Summit:** On a clear day, the scenery from the summit is simply magnificent (page 80).

★ **Chasm Lake:** This hike has the hallmarks of a true mountaineering adventure but isn't as long—or as hard—as Longs Peak (page 82).

★ **Calypso Cascades:** Cool off in the fine mist offered up by this fabulous series of waterfalls (page 84).

★ **Ouzel Falls:** Pack a brown bag lunch and hike out to this gorgeous spill of water for a great half-day outing (page 85).

★ **Sandbeach Lake:** Treats await at the end of this trail, including soft places to sit and one stunner of a lake (page 86).

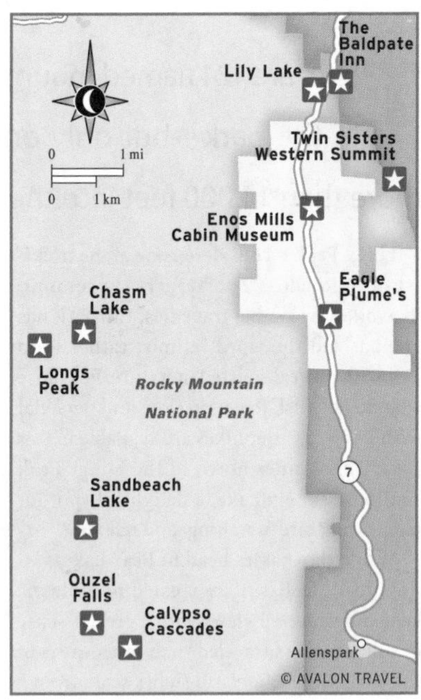

★ **Eagle Plume's:** Ogle remarkably intact Native American relics in a 1,000-piece collection of items from all over North America (page 98).

Longs Peak and Wild Basin

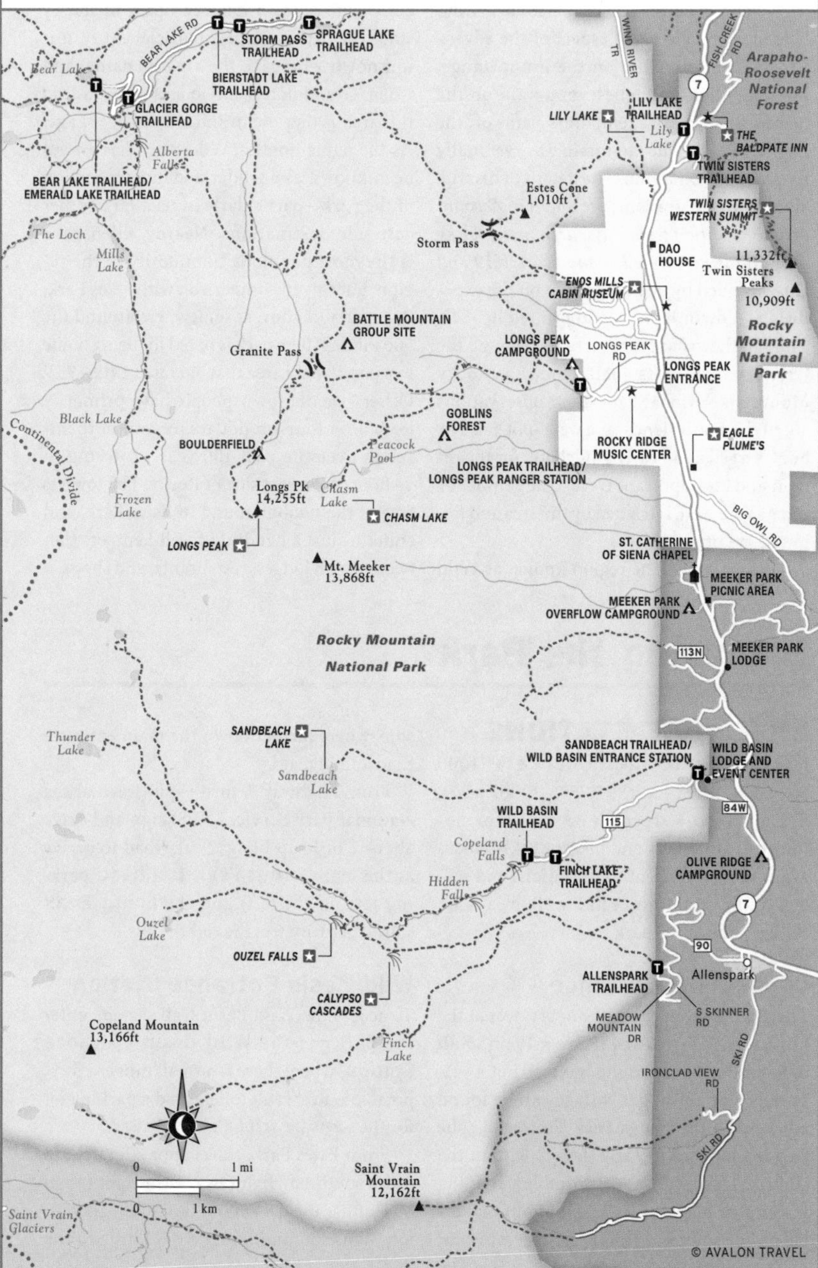

surveying trip, known as the Stephen H. Long Expedition, he had 22 men in tow—including volunteers and military personnel—who helped chronicle every aspect of the adventure. While traveling on the Front Range, Long spotted the highest mountain on the horizon and gave it a temporary name of "the Highest Peak." The mountain was eventually renamed to honor him. The details of his trip, along with illustrations, are found in *Account of an Expedition from Pittsburgh to the Rocky Mountains Performed in the Years 1819 and '20,* compiled by one of the men on the expedition—Edwin James—and printed in 1823. Though the group never actually entered the territory that is designated today as Rocky Mountain National Park, their observations about the nearby landscape were spot-on. The book served as an early guidebook for the region and an important travel companion for others who were intrigued by the area and followed in Long's path.

Farther south, the region known as Wild Basin has perhaps a less-storied past than other east-side locations. Though this glacier-formed basin has been part of Rocky since the park became an official entity, it is unknown who gave the area its name, and when. Grand hotels and lodges never graced this area as they did in and around Bear Lake. As the name implies, Wild Basin has always been known as a wilder and quieter section of the park—particularly in relation to other east-side destinations. Nearby Allenspark is the most populous community in the region, but tiny in comparison with Estes Park; its population hovers somewhere around the 500 mark. Allenspark is noted for being home to a popular ski area that operated 1919-1952. Otherwise, its townspeople have primarily leaned on tourism dollars to sustain themselves over the past 100 years, catering to visitors of the east side of Rocky. The town is free of the hubbub found in Estes Park, and contains just a handful of well-kept, off-the-beaten-path lodges, restaurants, and shops.

Exploring the Park

ENTRANCE STATIONS

Rocky Mountain National Park (1000 Hwy. 36, Estes Park, 970/586-1206, www.nps.gov/romo, $20 per day per vehicle or motorcycle, $10 hikers and bikes; weekly passes available) has two entrance stations and several trailhead entrances lining Highway 7 on the east side of the park.

Longs Peak Entrance

There are no ranger booths or services at the **Longs Peak Entrance** (Hwy. 7, 10 mi south of Estes Park, year-round, no fee), but a seasonally staffed ranger cottage can be found adjacent to the Longs Peak Trailhead. The parking lot can fill early (before 8am in the summer), especially with climbers arriving in the wee hours of the morning to make a bid for the summit. Otherwise, expect to park somewhere farther down the main entrance road and hike up.

From Highway 7, turn right (west) at the National Park Service (NPS) sign and drive about 1 mile up Longs Peak Road to arrive at the main **Longs Peak Trailhead** parking lot (on the left) and the **Longs Peak Campground** (on the right).

Wild Basin Entrance Station

To access the Wild Basin trail system, enter the park via the **Wild Basin Entrance Station**, where there is a small ranger kiosk, potable water, vault toilets, and a parking lot for the **Sandbeach Lake Trailhead.**

From Estes Park, travel approximately 13 miles south on Highway 7. Turn right (west) on County Road 84 (Wild Basin Rd.) and follow signs for approximately 0.4 mile to the

The Many Shades of Gray and Green

The standard National Park Service uniform today is a gray shirt, green pants, a hat, and a badge. If you see one of these folks in the park, you will quickly note that they are a park ranger. But did you know that numerous levels of specialization for rangers exist? Among them are interpretive ranger, protection ranger, wilderness ranger, and climbing ranger. Each type of ranger has very different responsibilities in the park, from teaching about flora and fauna (interpretive ranger) to conducting law enforcement (protection ranger).

One of the most adventurous jobs is that of **climbing ranger.** These employees spend much of their time hiking and climbing around the park, and are a regular presence around Longs Peak in the busy months (note that their backcountry uniform might consist of black pants instead of green, and they might don a high-visibility yellow shirt if the situation calls for it). Climbing rangers are constantly assessing trail and rock conditions and assembling detailed reports so that visitors have the most up-to-date information possible before they head out on a climb. Climbing rangers also participate in Search-and-Rescue (SAR) and Emergency-Medical-Service (EMS) activities. If you stop by the **Longs Peak Ranger Station** and receive valuable information about a hike or climb, it is likely that a climbing ranger was recently traveling along the route.

entrance. Once inside the park, County Road 84 continues for another 2 miles. Along the way you will find a small parking area for the **Finch Lake Trailhead** and several areas to pull off for parking leading up to the **Wild Basin Trailhead**. The road dead-ends at the Wild Basin Trailhead, where there is a parking lot, vault toilets, and the **Wild Basin Ranger Station** (staffed in summer only).

ALLENSPARK TRAILHEAD

The **Allenspark Trailhead** is a second option for those who want to hike **Wild Basin**'s trails. From Estes Park, travel approximately 21 miles south on Highway 7 to the turnoff (on the right) for Allenspark. Drive south for less than 0.1 mile on Highway 7 into the community of Allenspark before turning right (west) onto County Road 90. Drive 1.3 miles on County Road 90 (also marked as S. Skinner Rd.) to Meadow Mountain Drive, and turn right; in about 500 feet you will arrive at the small dirt parking area and trailhead. There are no services here and no park fees are required. The Allenspark Trail connects with the Finch Lake Trail and the Calypso Cascades Trail.

VISITOR CENTERS

Longs Peak Ranger Station

During the busy season, the **Longs Peak Ranger Station** (end of Longs Peak Rd. next to Longs Peak Trailhead, closed in winter) is staffed during daytime hours and features several historical displays, including a fantastic collection of old-style climbing equipment. Books, rain ponchos, and a handful of souvenir items are available for purchase. Consult with the ranger on hand about weather, trail conditions, hikes, and climbs.

Wild Basin Ranger Station

The **Wild Basin Ranger Station** (8am-4:30pm daily summer only), is a small cabin located next to the Wild Basin Trailhead parking lot. Listed on the National Register of Historic Places, the cabin was built in 1932, and with painted logs and a wood shingle roof, is considered an excellent example of National Park Service "rustic architecture." There is a small information desk in the cabin, some leaflets free for the taking, a few small displays on the walls, and merchandise for sale (water, sunscreen, rain ponchos, bear canisters, and other essentials; cash only).

TOURS

Longs Peak

CLIMBING

For nearly 30 years, the **Colorado Mountain School** (CMS, 341 Moraine Ave., Estes Park, 800/836-4008, www.coloradomountainschool.com, 8am-5pm Mon.-Fri.) was the only guide service with a permit to lead technical climbs in the park. Park regulations changed several years ago, allowing more outfitters to obtain technical guiding permits. The general consensus remains that CMS guides have the most extensive experience in and knowledge of the park, because they carried those exclusive permits for so long. CMS guides trips up Longs Peak on the Keyhole Route and numerous other routes. For one person, a non-technical climb runs $425 for one day; a technical climb costs $500. For two people, the cost is $300 for non-technical and $385 for technical; for three individuals it is $275 for non-technical and $360 for technical. The minimum price for one person climbing The Diamond is $600; for two people, the price is $450. Meals are not included. Out-of-town visitors may stay in CMS's hostel-style, 16-bed lodge in Estes Park for an additional $30 per night.

Kent Mountain Adventure Center (Estes Park, 970/586-5990, www.kmaconline.com, $300 pp, $450 for 2 people) guides climbers up the Keyhole Route as well as a handful of other technical routes on Longs.

Local guide service **Estes Park Mountain Shop** (2050 Big Thompson Ave., Estes Park, 970/586-6548, www.estesparkmountainshop.com, 8am-9pm daily, $399 for 1 person, $429 for 2 people, $459 for 3 people) offers one-day guided adventures to Longs Peak. The hiking day starts at 2am and generally runs 10-14 hours. Lunch and beverages are included.

Kirks Mountain Adventures (230 E. Elkhorn Ave., Estes Park, 970/577-0790, www.kirksmountainadventures.com, 7am-8pm daily summer, 8am-5pm daily winter) is a local guide service offering one- and two-day excursions to the peak. The one-day trip ($400 pp, $80 each additional guest) includes breakfast, lunch, and transportation, while the two-day trip ($390 pp per day; $195 pp per day with 2-person minimum) includes meals, backpacking equipment, transportation, and wilderness camping at the Longs Peak Boulderfield.

Guide service **Apex Ex** (303/731-6160, www.apexex.com, July 1-Oct. 31) leads one- and two-day trips up to Longs Peak. The service operates out of Golden, Colorado, but guides meet clients in the field at the Longs Peak Trailhead. Lunch is included for one-day trips ($375 pp, $299 pp for 2-3 people), and camping fees, meals and camping gear are provided for two-day adventures ($699 pp, $375 pp for 2 or more). Apex Ex will also guide individuals or groups.

HIKING

Estes Park Mountain Shop (2050 Big Thompson Ave., Estes Park, 970/586-6548, www.estesparkmountainshop.com, 8am-9pm daily) and **Kirks Mountain Adventures** (230 E. Elkhorn Ave., Estes Park, 970/577-0790, www.kirksmountainadventures.com, 7am-8pm daily summer, 8am-5pm daily winter) offer guided day hikes in the Longs Peak area. **Wildland Trekking** (800/715-4453, www.wildlandtrekking.com) guides numerous hiking trips around the park, including a day hike to Chasm Lake (6-8 hours, $215 pp for 2 people). **REI Basecamp at The Stanley Hotel** (333 Wonderview Ave., Estes Park, 970/577-4000, www.stanleyhotel.com, summer only) offers guided hikes on the east side, including one to Chasm Lake (8 hours, $85).

Driving Tour

HIGHWAY 7

Looking at a map of Rocky, you will quickly see that a driving tour through the belly of the lower east side of the park is not a possibility. In fact, your only vehicle entry point in this region is the several miles of Wild Basin Road leading to the Wild Basin Trailhead. That said, you can still drive close to the border of the park on Highway 7. Given the choice between arriving at Rocky via Highway 36 or

Tip Your Guide

Tips are not necessary or expected if you are hiking or engaging in another activity with a park ranger. However, if you climb, hike, fish, horseback ride, or take a vehicle tour with a **commercial guide service,** it is best to be ready with various increments of cash in your wallet for a gratuity. Most people have an idea in the back of their mind that they should tip their guide, and might note when they are booking a trip online that "gratuity not included" is mentioned in the trip description, but nevertheless find themselves unprepared when it is time for handshakes and thank-yous.

A tip should run anywhere between 10 and 20 percent of the total bill, depending on the level of service rendered. To decide on a tip amount, think about every aspect of your trip: safety, the condition and organization of trip supplies, food and drink, timeliness, whether or not your guide was personable, and if the guide handled situations with calm, ease, and professionalism. Tipping shows appreciation and also gives commercial guides valuable feedback about the services they are providing. There are **no ATMs in the park,** so plan to withdraw cash in Estes Park or another nearby town.

Highway 7, I take Highway 7 from Lyons almost every time. The road is generally less busy than Highway 36 and parallels pretty St. Vrain Creek for the first chunk of the drive. Numerous points of interest can be seen just off the highway.

From Highway 7 at Allenspark, head north, passing **Wild Basin Road** (2.1 miles). At 3.3 miles, take a quick peek at **Mount Meeker.** (There is a scenic viewpoint sign here, but no real pullout for stopping, so your viewing time will be brief.) The **St. Catherine of Siena Chapel** is on the left at 4.1 miles; you can get out and walk around at this sight if you wish. Stop in to **Eagle Plume's** for some shopping at 5.2 miles, then check out a memorial plaque on the right side of the road at 6.7 miles for Rocky Mountain National Park (RMNP) founder **Enos Mills.** If you get out of your car and look across the meadow, you can see Enos's one-room historic cabin peeking through the trees. Looking north at this spot, you will also gain a great view of Estes Cone up ahead. Continue driving north to the **Longs Peak Viewing Area** at around 6.9 miles and stop to admire both Mount Meeker and Longs. At **Lily Lake** (8.5 miles), a stroll around the lake or a picnic lunch is practically mandatory before returning to your vehicle. To wrap up the tour, turn right (east) off of Highway 7 at 8.7 miles to check out the historic **The Baldpate Inn.** If you are simply driving past all the sights on this tour, the whole journey will take no more than 20 minutes; if you choose to stop at each sight along the way, the trip could occupy 1-2 hours of your day.

From The Baldpate, continue driving north along Highway 7 into Estes Park, then cut over to the Beaver Meadows Entrance Station via Marys Lake Road, or return the way you came. From the Baldpate Inn, it is approximately 7.8 miles (via Marys Lake Road) to the Beaver Meadows Entrance Station.

Sights

★ LILY LAKE

At 9,000 feet, Lily is situated at an invisible midline for two ecosystems: subalpine and montane. Fragrant ponderosa pines are abundant on the north side of lake, while the south is characterized by wetlands that are attractive to birds and resplendent with wildflowers in the summer. Industrious muskrats are delightful to watch in the water—they swim to and from small dams and are easy to miss if you aren't looking for them. On a clear day, three nearby peaks are visible from various spots on the trail: Estes Cone, Mount Meeker, and Longs Peak.

The 0.8-mile trail circling Lily Lake is short and flat, and you can zip around it in under an hour if you were so inclined. But it is completely worthwhile to slow down and savor this lovely spot and even spend an entire morning or afternoon here. The wide gravel trail is one of four **wheelchair-accessible paths** in the park, and great for families with children and individuals with limited mobility. It's possible to extend your walk 0.4 mile by taking the Lily Ridge Trail (not wheelchair accessible), accessed on the north side of the lake. Restrooms are located at the trailhead.

The **Lily Lake Trailhead** is a fee-free area of the park, providing access to Lily Lake and the Estes Cone. From the junction of Highway 7 and Highway 36 in Estes Park, drive 6.3 miles south on Highway 7 to the lake. There are two parking lots, one directly next to the lake and one on the other side of Highway 7. There is a designated crosswalk here, but be cautious when crossing as traffic can move fast. Vault toilets can be found at the parking lot closest to the lake.

★ THE BALDPATE INN

Through clever marketing, early homesteaders Gordon and Ethel Mace and Gordon's two brothers, Charles and Stuart, created a sense of intrigue around their lodge, **The Baldpate Inn** (4900 Hwy. 7, Estes Park, 970/586-6151, www.baldpateinn.com, Memorial Day-Columbus Day; closed in winter) that has held strong for more than a century. When the family was building their hotel and trying to come up with a name, they took inspiration

The key room at The Baldpate Inn contains thousands of keys from all over the world.

from a popular early 1900s mystery romance novel: *The Seven Keys of Baldpate* by Earl Derr Biggers. The story revolves around seven travelers who visit the inn in the winter, each believing that they possess the only key to the front door. Ironically, there is no key or keyhole for the front door to the actual Baldpate Inn, though keys have been used to advertise the hotel since its inception. Originally, guests were given a souvenir key to keep after their stay, until it became too expensive a gimmick for the owners to keep up. That is when guests started bringing their own keys and leaving them at the inn.

Today, the best reason to visit The Baldpate is to see the **world's largest key collection,** numbering 30,000-40,000 keys. An entire room is filled floor to ceiling with keys that come from all over the globe. Among them are a key from Buckingham Palace, a key from a submarine, a key from Mozart's wine cellar, and an ancient key from Tibet. The dining room also houses a fantastic collection of autographed photographs of celebrities. Outside, a small amphitheater is used for performances in the summer months. Though not nearly as famous for its ghosts as The Stanley, those fascinated with paranormal activity will love knowing that The Baldpate is considered "enchanted," with original owner Ethel Mace reportedly having an eternal presence on the property. The structure is historically significant (it is listed on the National Register of Historic Places) because it is the only remaining example of rustic Western Stick style architecture that remains in Estes Park. Note in particular the building's gabled and dormered roof with overhanging eaves, and the board-and-batten and log exterior. Even if you know nothing about architecture, the place just looks rustic, especially with its balcony made out of nubby wood posts.

There is no charge to visit the main lobby, key room, and grounds of the inn, although the innkeeper will tell you with a smile that the first visit to the key room is free, but the next time "you owe a key." Do make a point to visit the inn when your stomach is growling—you will no doubt find that the **dining room**'s array of soups, salads, pies, and baked goods smell too good to pass up.

The turnoff for the Baldpate Inn is located across from Lily Lake on Highway 7, approximately 7 miles south of Estes Park. A sign directs visitors east on Fish Creek Road to the inn, a brief 0.2-mile drive.

★ LONGS PEAK

Longs Peak looks more awesome than fearsome when viewed from Highway 7. For many visitors, viewing the peak from the car is enough. Thousands of tales could be told about this 14,259-foot behemoth that is the 16th highest Fourteener in the Rocky Mountain range. It has tempted many adventurers since the late 1800s and still carries an air of mystery and intrigue for people to this day. While its features have been endlessly photographed, videoed, and displayed online for the world to see, images are no substitute for being on top of the real thing—experiencing breathlessness, traversing a treeless landscape, or (possibly) enduring howling, unrelenting winds. As I have stood in this particular pullout many times admiring Longs, I find myself thinking less about the physical characteristics of the mountain and more about the people who are clambering over it that particular day. I put a little positive vibe out to the universe that everyone arrives back at the trailhead safely.

The Longs Peak Viewing Area pullout is located near mile marker 8 on Highway 7, about 9 miles south of Estes Park.

★ ENOS MILLS CABIN MUSEUM

Enos Mills wore many hats in his full life, including those of author, naturalist, guide, and lodge owner. However, he is most recognized for his role in lobbying the U.S. Congress to officially create Rocky Mountain National Park. "The Father of Rocky Mountain National Park," or "Colorado's John Muir," as he is often referred to, moved to Colorado from Kansas as a sickly teenager—with hopes that

Rocky Mountain Jim and Isabella Lucy Bird

Any "good girl" who has ever fallen for a "bad boy" will appreciate the story of Isabella Lucy Bird and Jim Nugent.

English-born Isabella Lucy Bird was the daughter of a reverend who made an epic journey of hundreds of miles on horseback through Colorado to Rocky Mountain National Park. In her travels she met Jim Nugent, a local trapper with a wild past. Described by Bird as strikingly handsome, Nugent, who was better known as "Rocky Mountain Jim," or simply "Mountain Jim," was in fact grotesquely disfigured on one side of his face from being mauled by a grizzly bear. No matter—his bad boy personality apparently won over Bird anyway.

Though this proper Victorian lady's relationship with Jim isn't completely clear, it is evident from her writings that Bird had great affection for Jim, and him for her. Historians suspect that there was a dalliance or even a real romance brewing between the two. At one time she wrote, "He is a man who any woman might love but no sane woman would marry." Bird and Jim summited **Longs Peak** together, and her account of doing so is well chronicled in *A Lady's Life in the Rocky Mountains,* a compilation of letters she wrote to her sister Henrietta about her adventures in the West.

Bird and Nugent ultimately parted ways and Bird eventually ended up marrying another man. She continued to be an avid traveler until her death at age 72. Rocky Mountain Jim suffered a dramatic death less than a year after he met with Bird that might or might not have had to do with a dispute over land or his interest in another man's teenage daughter; accounts of this event vary. He was shot in the head and perished three months after the fact.

the rarified air of Colorado would improve his health. After a short time spent in the town of Greeley, Colorado, he lived by himself in the warm months in a one-room cabin that he built over the course of two summers. His humble first home, the **Enos Mills Cabin Museum** (6760 Hwy. 7, Estes Park, www.enosmills.com, 970/586-4706, year-round by appointment only, $20 pp), still stands today and is operated as a museum by granddaughter and great-granddaughter team, Elizabeth and Eryn Mills. The twosome carries on his legacy by leading tours of Enos's cabin—a National Historic Landmark—and by keeping as many of his nature books in circulation as possible. The cabin itself isn't as remarkable as the passion his family has for telling his life story. Great-granddaughter Eryn leads most of the tours, which are customized based on visitors' interests. Photographs and articles hung on the walls of the cabin serve as talking points. By the time you leave, you will be filled with knowledge about this fascinating activist and nature-lover who climbed Longs Peak more than 300 times before his passing and who once kept two grizzly cubs named Johnny and Jenny as pets.

Parking for the cabin is at the Longs Peak Viewing Area on Highway 7 (located just south of mile marker 8); visitors who have made advance reservations are then escorted onto the property. No restrooms are available and no pets are allowed—dogs or grizzlies.

CHAPEL ON THE ROCK

St. Catherine of Siena Chapel (10758 Hwy. 7, Allenspark, 970/586-8111, www.campstmalo.org, 10am-4pm daily), known as the Chapel on the Rock, rises castlelike from a large rock outcropping with Mount Meeker as a stunning backdrop. Catholic Monsignor Joseph Bosetti was the visionary behind this beautiful stone chapel. In 1916 Monsignor Bosetti set about looking for the impact site of a falling star and came across the rocks upon which his chapel stands. He was inspired by the Bible passage, "Upon this rock I will build my church" (Matt. 16.18), to build a house of worship here, but ran into many stumbling blocks in his quest to do so. After much perseverance, he finally debuted his chapel in 1936. A boys' camp called Camp St. Malo was run at this location for many years, and then it became a destination for religious retreats. But fire gutted most of the chapel's conference center in 2011. Then the chapel experienced a double whammy, with a landslide caused by the Colorado Flood of 2013 further damaging the building and grounds. Remarkably, the main chapel was unaffected.

Today, visitors are welcome to stop by and investigate the grounds on their way to Rocky. Inside the chapel, a small, framed sign on the wall displays words of inspiration from Monsignor Bosetti that resonate with even the religiously unaffiliated: "There is no such thing as too much mountaineering, just as there is no such thing as too much virtue."

From the junction of Highway 36 and Highway 7 in Estes Park, drive 10.8 miles south on Highway 7.

MOUNT MEEKER

The two highest peaks in the park, Longs Peak and **Mount Meeker,** sit next to each other and their names are often uttered in the same breath. Early on, the pair of peaks was dubbed *Les Deux Oreilles* (The Two Ears) by French fur trappers who spotted them from far away on Colorado's plains. Today, they are often referenced simply as "Meeker and Longs." These peaks have a shared history of geological uplift and are part of the same massif, or group of mountains, in the southeast section of the park. Mount Meeker sits at 13,911 feet and was named after Nathan Meeker, founder of the town of Greeley, a town some 50 miles or so from the east side of the park. Though Meeker was highly respected by many, the history books will tell you that not everyone who knew Nathan Meeker liked him. He was deemed the key responsible party for the last major Indian uprising in America, and was killed during what is now known as the Meeker Massacre.

No dedicated trail to the top of Meeker exists, but climbers can follow several commonly traveled routes to the summit. The most popular route starts at the **East Longs Peak Trailhead** and leads to the "The Loft," which is the saddle between Longs Peak and Mount Meeker. The climb, which has some exposure, is mostly Class Two with a small Class Three section. Otherwise, for non-climbers, this mountain is simply impressive to look at, with its long sloping ridges and massive faces.

Mount Meeker can best be viewed from Meeker Park along Highway 7.

COPELAND LAKE

A mountain, a moraine, a waterfall, and this lake are all named after John B. Copeland, an early homesteader to the area. Copeland had a skirmish with the law over this body of water, which started out as a small spring-fed pond. Copeland considerably enlarged the lake by constructing a ditch that diverted water from the North St. Vrain Creek (acceptable). He then stocked the lake with fish without securing a license from the Colorado State Game and Fish Department (unacceptable). The department also filed a lawsuit against Copeland for not submitting the required license fees; he eventually paid up. Even though he was not the most cooperative fellow, various features in the park were still named after him for historical purposes.

Today, **Copeland Lake** is often just glanced at by Wild Basin visitors. Positioned along the main road to Wild Basin's popular trailheads, it receives day-use from anglers who have decent luck catching brook trout and rainbow trout.

Copeland Lake is located 14 miles south of Estes Park. From Highway 7, turn west onto Wild Basin Road and continue 0.5 mile to the lake and the Wild Basin Entrance Station. Two small parking areas are located alongside the lake.

Recreation

HIKING

Lily Lake Area

★ TWIN SISTERS WESTERN SUMMIT

Distance: 7.4 miles
Duration: 4.25 hours
Elevation gain: 2,253 feet
Effort: strenuous
Trailhead: Twin Sisters (see map p. 80)
Directions: Across from Lily Lake on Highway 7, access a well-signed 0.4-mile dirt road to the Twin Sisters Trailhead. Park along the roadside.

Simply outstanding views await at the top of this challenging hike that travels through Rocky and the Roosevelt National Forest. From the end of the dirt road, travel roughly 400 feet to the Twin Sisters Trailhead sign. Hike up the trail through forest until you are 1 mile from the trailhead; at this point there is a break in the trees and you will get your first good glimpse of Longs Peak to the west. No need to pause too long at this spot, though, as there will be opportunities to see Longs along other parts of the trail. Continue ascending, and at 1.2 miles from the trailhead, you will arrive at the site of a huge **landslide** that was the result of a devastating flood that affected Rocky and surrounding areas in 2013. The trail crosses directly over the slide, affording a good look at the damage. At 1.3 miles, the trail turns into a **social trail** (due to the flood damage) and is harder to follow. Look for cairns and broken branches/logs that have been positioned along the trail that guide

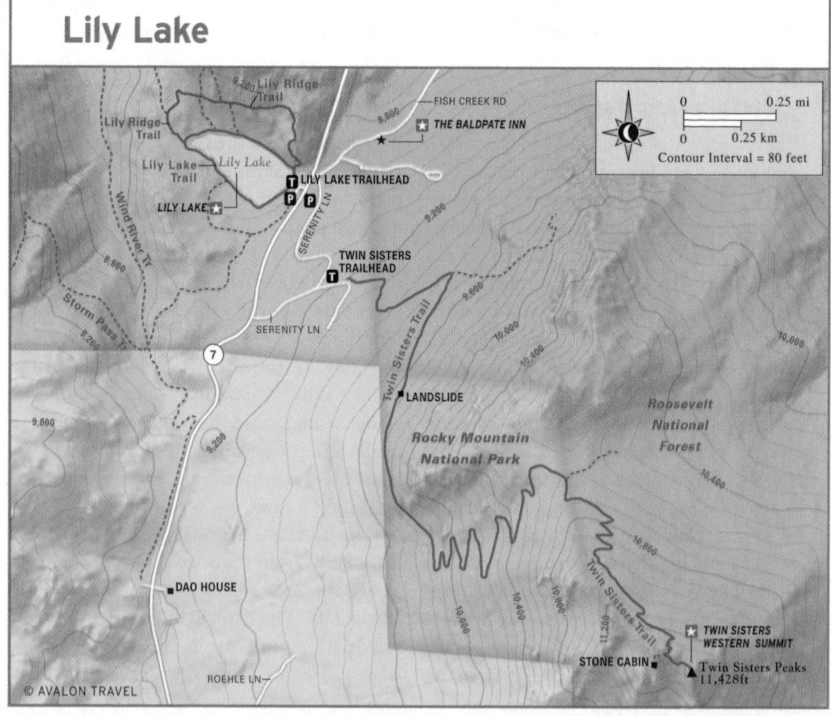

Colorado Flood of 2013

For eight days in September of 2013, widespread flooding along Colorado's Front Range caused significant damage in and around Rocky. Up to 17 inches of rain fell in some counties. Ten people were killed, 18,000 people were forced to evacuate their homes, and some major roadways were temporarily impassible. Millions of state and federal dollars were paid out to assist people affected by the event. In Rocky, trails were affected, bridges were destroyed, and major damage occurred in the area of the Alluvial Fan and Old Fall River Road. At the **Twin Sisters,** a massive landslide occurred; it wasn't the only one in the park, but certainly one of the most visible. Rocky, though, was not affected by the flood nearly as much as Estes Park, Lyons, Glen Haven, and Boulder. The rebuilding and recovery efforts in these communities were huge (and are still ongoing). The flood still feel very fresh in the minds of Estes Park residents, and if you chat up people in town, they can share many stories of their community's resiliency in the face of a natural disaster.

hikers rather steeply uphill to connect with the original trail. At approximately 1.7 miles, you will be back in action on the main trail.

Continue steadily ascending through the forest until you reach a **scree field** at approximately 3.2 miles from the trailhead and 0.5 mile from the summit. Before you proceed, take a moment to **assess current weather conditions.** There are still a few trees dotting the landscape ahead, but mostly the terrain is exposed and not a place you want to be in a thunderstorm. Wind your way up the rocky path to a saddle between the two summits. Here you will find a **stone cabin** that is listed on the National Register of Historic Places. The cabin used to serve as a housing facility for employees stationed at a fire lookout tower on the western summit. The fire lookout tower has long since been removed, though you will still find some metal clamps on the rocks that are remnants of that structure. Continue following the trail to the top of the **western summit** and find a good rock to sit on (there are many). If the skies are clear, you'll have a particularly fantastic view of Longs Peak and Mount Meeker. Your options from here are to head back down to the saddle and follow cairns over to the less-visited eastern summit, or return the way you came.

The **Twin Sisters Trailhead** is located off Highway 7. From the junction of Highway 7 and Highway 36 in Estes Park, drive 6.3 miles south on Highway 7. On the east side of the highway, there is a parking lot and sign directing visitors to the Twin Sisters Trailhead. Drive 0.4 mile east on a dirt road to the parking area. This is a fee-free entrance to the park; there are no services.

ESTES CONE

Distance: 6.8 miles round-trip
Duration: 3.5 hours
Elevation gain: 2,066 feet
Effort: strenuous
Trailhead: Lily Lake

Many more people make their way to Estes Cone via the Longs Peak Trailhead than the Lily Lake Trailhead, presumably because the route via Lily Lake is slightly longer and has more elevation gain. You'll likely be rewarded with a fair amount of solitude on this trail because it is less traveled. In the summer, though, you will need to **arrive to the trailhead early,** as the two Lily Lake parking lots fill up quickly with visitors to the lake.

To start, identify a small wood trail marker for the **Storm Pass Trail** next to the Lily Lake Trailhead sign; walk for 0.2 mile along a paved trail until you reach another **trail sign** on your left for Storm Pass. Continue along a wide dirt road for less than 0.1 mile to yet another **trail marker,** and you will now be on the **main trail.** In early summer, you are likely to spot purple fringe wildflowers blooming along the first section of trail. The trail descends for approximately 0.7 mile to a junction of three paths; here, you will need to cross over Aspen Brook via a large wooden **footbridge** to stay on the main trail. The trail ascends through forest and then, at 1.1 miles from the trailhead, you gain a view of the Twin Sisters **landslide** on your right-hand side. Continue climbing, sometimes on rock steps, until you reach the **Estes Cone trail turnoff.** Before making the final push to the top of Estes Cone, people commonly stop to rest or have a snack at the trail junction. The trail to the summit is 0.7 mile, but it is not an easy one. The path, which is marked with **cairns,** is very steep and challenging. Trekking poles are helpful for this section, both heading up and coming down. To get to the top of the mountain, some easy scrambling is involved. Return the way you came.

Longs Peak Area

EUGENIA MINE

Distance: 2.8 miles round-trip
Duration: 2 hours
Elevation gain: 503 feet
Effort: moderate
Trailhead: Longs Peak (see map p. 83)

In the late 1800s, people flocked to the Longs Peak area in the hope of striking it rich. At one point, 19 mines were located in what was the Longs Peak Mining District, but the Eugenia Mine is the only spot where any real artifacts remain. There isn't a whole lot in the way of eye-popping scenery on this hike, but history buffs will enjoy poking around the old mining site, perhaps imagining what activities miners engaged in while in pursuit of valuable ore. Unfortunately, those who worked here never made a profit.

Start by heading northwest on the **East Longs Peak Trail** through a dense swath of forest. At 0.5 mile, bear right at the sign for **Eugenia Mine.** From here, it is another 0.9 mile of gentle hiking to the site of the mine. Just before reaching the remains of a log structure and the Eugenia Mine sign, there are two easy **footbridges** that cross over gurgling Inn Brook. At the official site, the most remarkable evidence of mining activity is a pile of old mine tailings and an old rusty steam boiler. Return the way you came.

★ CHASM LAKE

Distance: 8.4 miles round-trip
Duration: 5.5 hours
Elevation gain: 2,380 feet
Effort: strenuous
Trailhead: Longs Peak (see map p. 83)

Chasm Lake is a fantastic destination for those who want to get up close and personal with Longs Peak without being literally on top of it. This backcountry adventure is not nearly as technical or as physically exhausting as summiting Longs Peak, but it can still be difficult—especially if attempted in winter, spring, or early summer.

Begin by heading west on the **East Longs Peak Trail.** The path ascends through a forest, and at 0.5 mile there is an option to head right (north) to Eugenia Mine and Estes Cone; stay to the left to continue west to **Chasm Lake.** The trail gets a bit steeper, still climbing through trees, and eventually you will parallel Alpine Brook on your left-hand side. Continue west on a now rockier path, passing the **Goblins Forest wilderness campsite,** which is around 0.7 mile from the Eugenia Mine trail junction. A series of switchbacks is next, followed by a **bridge crossing** at Alpine Brook. Immediately after the bridge, signs appear warning visitors about fragile tundra and lightning hazards. The landscape starts transitioning from subalpine to alpine shortly after these signs, and the "diamond" face of Longs Peak soon comes into a view—a welcome change from slogging through forest.

As you continue on the trail, take a minute to turn around—behind you is a great view of a massive landslide on the Twin Sisters peaks that was a result of the **Colorado Flood of 2013.** Pass the sign for the **Battle Mountain wilderness campsite** and continue traveling west, on the north side of Mills Moraine, to **Chasm Junction.** At Chasm Junction, you are now 0.8 mile from your destination and approximately 3.4 miles from the trailhead. This is a fine **turnaround point** if your

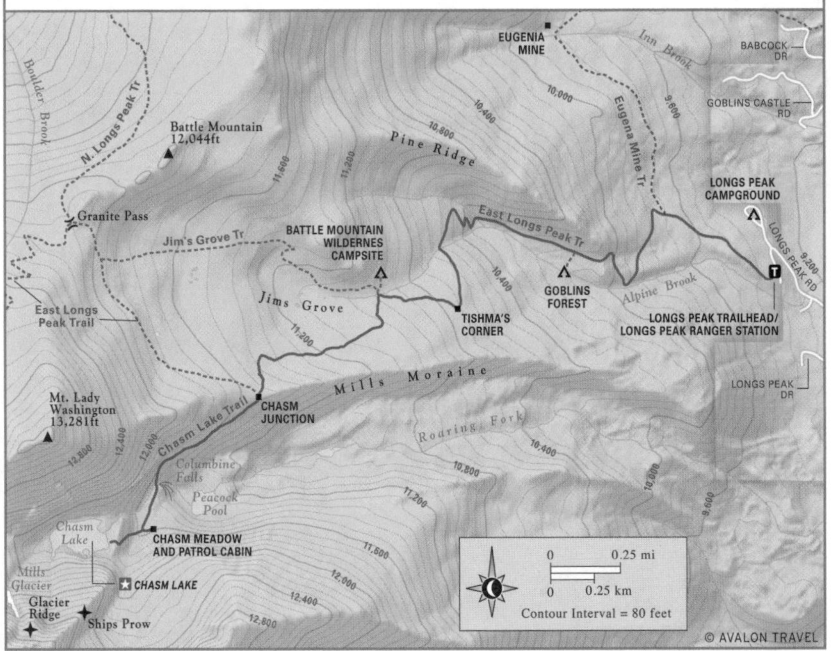

energy is wearing thin or if weather conditions do not seem right for forging on.

After Chasm Junction, the hike along **Chasm Lake Trail** can become technically difficult and dangerous if you aren't hiking in the sweet spot of **July-mid-September.** A snowfield can be present along the trail, and an **ice axe** and **crampons** are recommended (and are often not optional) if you plan to hike this route outside of the summer season. If you were to make a misstep, you could slide 100 feet down a 45-degree snow slope into a pile of boulders. Some people find that the trail is not as difficult if the snow is slushy and soft. But, if you continue hiking, stay a while at Chasm Lake and hike out when the sun has slipped behind the clouds; otherwise, the slush can harden back into ice and become increasingly more difficult to travel on. If foot travel is going well along this section, take a moment to pause and admire Peacock Pool below, a small but beautiful alpine lake located southeast of the trail. Continue for approximately 0.6 mile to **Chasm Meadows,** where there is an open-air toilet and a small **patrol cabin.** Then get set for a couple hundred feet (5-10 minutes) of **rock scrambling** to the end. The trail is not well-defined at this point, though cairns are placed along the way. The trail ends about 15 feet above Chasm Lake. Here you will be challenged with the question of what is more stunning, the lake or the massive diamond-shaped wall of Longs Peak rising above it. For most people, there is no clear answer. Return the way you came.

Wild Basin

COPELAND FALLS

Distance: 0.6 mile round-trip
Duration: 30 minutes
Elevation gain: 15 feet
Effort: easy
Trailhead: Wild Basin (see map p. 84)

Copeland Falls is a perfect hike for families

Calypso Cascades

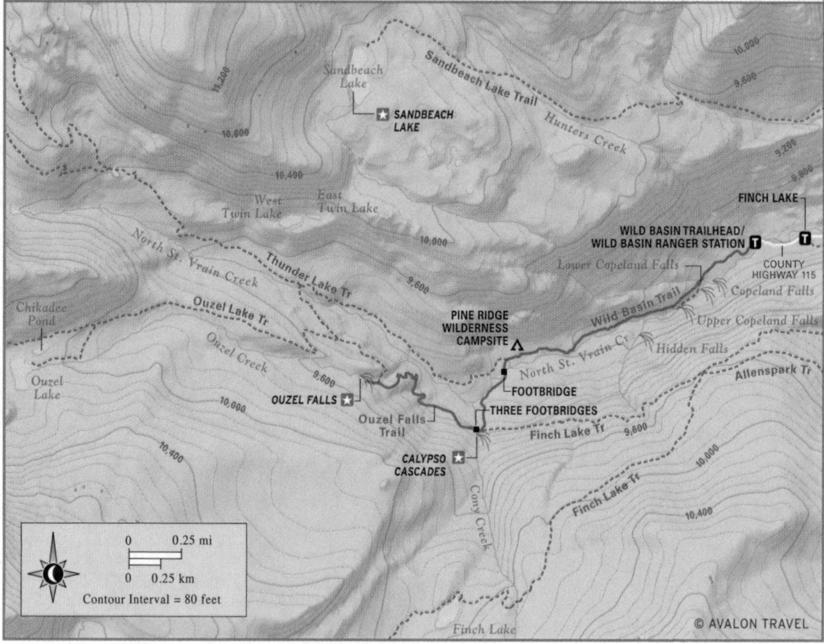

with wee ones and those on a tight schedule. This waterfall is a teaser for bigger attractions farther along the trail, but it is also great as a standalone outing. To start, head over Hunters Creek on the wooden **footbridge** at the start of the **Wild Basin Trail** and head west. The dirt path is wide and makes a gradual ascent. Lush foliage is found on both sides of the trail. In 0.3 mile, you will reach a sign with arrows pointing to the lower falls and upper falls. Take the **spur trail** to the lower falls. This is not a tall waterfall by any means, but it is plenty picturesque. There is space along the water's edge for painting with an easel and canvas, or just plopping down for a snack. To visit the upper falls, keep following the spur trail southwest for a hundred yards or so. **Copeland Falls** from its upper vantage point appears bigger and gushier. A few large rock slabs at this spot are perfect for relaxing and sunning. Once you have had your fill, return the way you came on the spur trail, or head north on a short path to get on the Wild Basin Trail earlier (bypassing the lower falls on your way back to the trailhead). There are signs in the area warning visitors about swift water; keep a safe distance from the falls as you view them and keep an eagle eye on kiddos.

★ CALYPSO CASCADES

Distance: 3.6 miles round-trip
Duration: 1.5 hours
Elevation gain: 700 feet
Effort: easy to moderate
Trailhead: Wild Basin (see map p. 84)

With an abundance of water along the trail, Calypso Cascades is great destination for a warm summer day. Depart from the Wild Basin trailhead and hike 0.3 mile to **Copeland Falls.** Continue west along the trail, climbing through the forest and stepping over seeps of water on the trail as you go. As you hike, you will see several glacial **erratics** on the side of the trail. These extra-large

Ouzel Lake Fire

Until the human-ignited Fern Lake Fire swept through Rocky in late 2012 and early 2013, the Ouzel Lake Fire was the biggest blaze on the park's record books. Lightning struck a tree near **Ouzel Lake** on August 9, 1978, causing the fire. The blaze not only impacted the land, it also had a lasting effect on Rocky's formal fire management plan. In its early stages, officials were keen to let this wildfire run its course in a natural way, rather than suppress the flames. For weeks, the park monitored the fire's path and growth, which was fine until strong winds caused the fire to spread in a manner that incited fear in people living near Rocky's eastern border. Their fear was not unfounded. After a first attempt to contain the blaze was unsuccessful, flames came so close to hopping over into nearby Allenspark that on September 15, 500 firefighters were summoned to extinguish the fire before lives or homes were sacrificed. All told, flames touched 1,050 acres of land in Wild Basin.

The Ouzel Lake Fire served as a talking point for park officials long after the last spark was stamped out, as they weighed the advantages and disadvantages of allowing a naturally caused fire to burn so close to private property. Today, stands of dead trees in various areas of **Wild Basin** serve as reminders of this fast-moving fire; it will take decades for full re-vegetation to occur.

boulders look like they were haphazardly dumped onto the earth by some great force, and indeed they were—the force was a long-forgotten glacier. The trail starts to gradually ascend, and **rock steps** have been placed in this section for easier hiking. Continue until you reach a sign for the **Pine Ridge wilderness campsite** at 1.4 miles from the trailhead. A few dozen paces farther west, you'll see a sign for four additional wilderness campsites and the **Calypso Cascades.** Turn left (south) at this junction; your destination is now 0.4 mile away. A wooden **footbridge** presents itself right after the sign, and a massive amount of water is tumbling around below. This unnamed feature is so impressive, you might think you have arrived at the Cascades already, even though the trail sign has told you otherwise. Cross the bridge and continue on the trail. Depending on the time of year and water flow, water might be covering a part of the steps in a section of trail just after the footbridge. If that is the case, take great care in negotiating the slippery rocks and turn around if it just doesn't feel right to cross. Otherwise, continue along the last part of the trail to the Cascades. At your destination, you will find **three long footbridges.** Admire the Cascades from every angle you wish along the bridges, again taking care any time you find yourself within close proximity to rushing water. Return to the trailhead, or if you are still bursting with energy and have enough food and water for a longer hike, head west to **Ouzel Falls** (0.9 mile).

★ OUZEL FALLS

Distance: 5.4 miles round-trip
Duration: 3 hours
Elevation gain: 950 feet
Effort: moderate
Trailhead: Wild Basin (see map p. 84)

On Rocky's trails, I have heard some of the same questions time and again from visitors. The top two: "How much farther?" and "Is it worth it?" For the latter question, I always answer "yes," unless some sort of weather issue or obstacle along the trail makes going on dangerous. Everything in the park is worth your time, though some features are more memorable than others; Ouzel Falls is among them. This waterfall is tall (50 feet), bold, and wonderfully raucous. The father of Rocky, Enos Mills, was particularly fond of Ouzel Creek—the waterway on which Ouzel Falls is located—and gave it its name. Ouzel Falls and Ouzel Lake were named after the creek. (The ouzel, also known as the Water Dipper, is a type of bird that is seen in the creek and is known for vigorously plunging its body into the water as it gathers food.)

To get to the waterfall, hike west on the

Sandbeach Lake

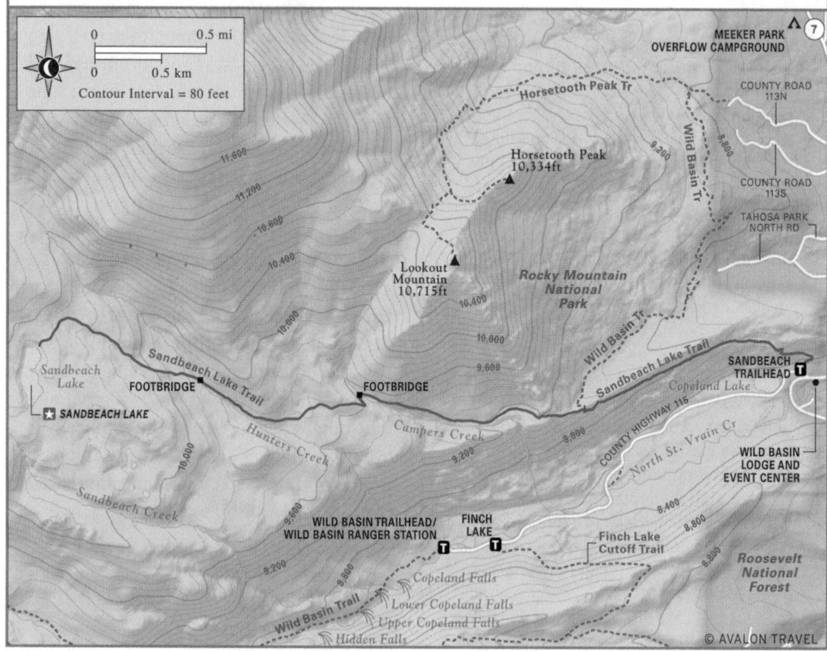

Wild Basin Trail, along the way enjoying **Copeland Falls** (0.3 mi) and **Calypso Cascades** (1.8 mi). After arriving at Calypso Cascades, continue hiking an additional 0.9 mile west to reach the falls. Wind your way up through the forest at a moderate grade until you arrive at a wooden **footbridge** for viewing. Stay for a snack or lunch, then return the way you came.

★ SANDBEACH LAKE

Distance: 9 miles round-trip
Duration: 4.5 hours
Elevation gain: 1,971 feet
Effort: moderate to strenuous
Trailhead: Sandbeach Lake, located next to the Wild Basin Entrance Station (see map p. 86)

The hike to Sandbeach Lake isn't over-the-top spectacular in terms of scenery—it is mostly a shaded journey through a thick forest—but the gem at the end is truly beautiful. While you will have made significant elevation gain by the time you reach the lake, the trail is fairly forgiving—it is never relentlessly uphill, has decent shade, and includes some completely flat sections that come as a welcome break. A pretty display of aspen trees mixed with lodgepole and ponderosa pines is an early treat after you jump on the trail. Also in the first leg, a great view of the North St. Vrain Creek winding through lush greenery unfolds to the southeast.

The trail **splits** at 1.4 miles, and if you traveled north toward Meeker Park, you would arrive at Lookout Mountain. Instead, continue straight (west) to **Sandbeach Lake.** In the next several miles, you will wind through the forest, passing four different **wilderness campsites** along the way, and cross Campers Creek and Hunters Creek on **wooden footbridges.** The trail becomes rather steep after Hunters Creek, but the hard work is over before long—your final destination is 0.6 mile away. Upon arrival, the

Sandbeach Lake

landscape opens up dramatically. On a sunny day, the warm sand smells, indeed, "beachy." Your first inclination might be to plop down on the beach, but there is more to see. Walk out to the lake's edge and turn around to see an exceptional view of Mount Meeker, Pagoda Peak, Keyboard of the Winds, and Longs Peak. From here, you might choose to wade in the water, relax on the beach, or meander along an easy path that encircles the lake. For a great lunch spot, take the path clockwise and stop at a small but obvious rocky peninsula. An additional **wilderness campsite** is located at the lake. Return the way you came.

BACKPACKING

Backpacking in the Longs Peak area is often a means to an end for people—the end being the summit of Longs. Breaking up one of the park's most grueling climbs into a two-day affair makes the journey more manageable for some. The **Boulderfield's wilderness campsites** are closest to the summit and the most popular with climbers. Climbers also choose to spend the night at the **Battle Mountain Group site** and **Goblins Forest wilderness site**. All three wilderness sites usually book up months in advance, so hop to it early if you think you want to split up the climb with an overnighter.

From the Longs Peak Trailhead, you can also backpack over to Bear Lake attractions, or venture northeast to the East Portal Trailhead. Both of these options require a car shuttle.

A number of satisfying out-and-back backpacking trip options exist in the **Wild Basin** area. Wilderness campsites are tucked in along the trails—particularly on the **Sandbeach Lake Trail** and **Wild Basin Trail**—and next to lakes such as Finch, Pear, Ouzel, and Thunder. As with Longs Peak, the earlier you book, the better.

For backcountry camping dates May 1-October 31, reservations can be made online (www.pay.gov) or in person at a wilderness office (not by phone) March 1-October 28. For camping dates November 1-April 30, reservations can be made by phone or in person October 1-April 30. The closest wilderness office to the Longs Peak/Wild Basin region is the **East Side Wilderness Office** (970/586-1242), located next to the Beaver Meadows Visitor Center.

CLIMBING

For the intermediate to expert rock climber, Longs Peak is something akin to Shangri-La.

There are hundreds of technical climbs available on Longs itself and on features nearby. On a Saturday in late summer, there are typically two- to three-dozen climbing parties in the cirque. No special permits are necessary for climbers using the area for the day only, though a bivouac permit is required for parties conducting multiday climbs.

Mountain Project (www.mountainproject.com) is a great online spot for getting virtually acquainted with any climb in the area. Locally, the **Colorado Mountain School** (341 Moraine Ave., Estes Park, 800/836-4008, www.coloradomountainschool.com) is an outstanding resource for climbing information; the school also offers guided ice climbing in the winter.

Guide service **Apex Ex** (303/731-6160, www.apexex.com, 9am-5pm daily July 1-Oct. 31) doesn't have a storefront that is open to the public. Climbing trips are booked over the phone or online; participants meet at trailheads or other locations in Estes Park.

The Keyhole Route on Longs Peak, which starts out as a hike and ends as a climb, is the most talked-about climb of them all.

Longs Peak: Keyhole Route

Distance: 15 miles round-trip
Duration: 10-15 hours
Elevation gain: 5,000 feet
Effort: very strenuous
Trailhead: Longs Peak (see map p. 90)

The Keyhole Route is the most popular route to the summit of Longs Peak and attempted by thousands of people each year. The route is so named for a large notch in the ridgeline that extends off the north side of Longs Peak. It is considered the least difficult path to the top. But—and this is a big "but"—just because it is the most popular does not preclude climber injury or death. Every year people get into serious trouble on this grand peak. The weather is a major factor that will determine the success of a climb, but even on a bluebird day, climbers can encounter terrain slicked with ice or find themselves headed in the wrong direction because of a slow-melting snowfield that has obscured the trail. Fatigue, dehydration, and altitude can all affect hiker judgment. Prepare in every way possible, and even then, expect that there will be points along the trail that require you to reevaluate your ability to complete the journey.

All warnings aside, hundreds of people successfully complete this climb each year. If you finish—and even if you don't—you will be rewarded in more ways than one for all of your effort.

WHEN TO GO

Longs Peak sees the most foot traffic **June-September.** The climbing season gains momentum at a slightly different time each year, depending on the amount of snowfall the previous winter, and on how long the snow sticks to the mountain. June-August, afternoon monsoon thunderstorms are typical in Rocky. **Late August-early September** there is comparatively less afternoon rain, and a high-pressure weather system predominates. This short window is considered **the most ideal time to attempt Longs.** Also, at this point in the summer season, most of the snow from the previous winter should have melted off. However, the tradeoff for nice weather during the day is that temperatures start dipping below freezing at night. This translates to areas of thin ice forming on the route, making for slick conditions.

The estimated time to complete the 15-mile round-trip Keyhole Route is usually **10-15 hours.** It might sound counterintuitive to hike in the dark, but the safest time to **start the trek** is **1am-3am.** An early start time and a headlamp packed with fresh batteries are essential, as you will want to **be on your way down** from the peak at or **before noon,** when foul weather can start to develop. Many people aim to **arrive at the Keyhole around sunrise.**

If possible, schedule your Longs Peak trip for a **weekday,** when the trails are less crowded.

EAST LONGS PEAK TRAILHEAD

The most important stop on the first leg of your journey is the information kiosk just in front of the **Longs Peak Ranger Station.** Shine your headlamp on the **weather report** and current **climbing conditions** and make your first decision of the day—whether to go. The park also posts a **Longs Peak Conditions Report** on its website and strives to keep the information as updated as possible; it's best to start keeping an eye on the weather a few days out.

Just next to the ranger station, jump on the **East Longs Peak Trail,** then wind steadily uphill through forest for 0.5-mile until you reach your first **junction** with Eugenia Mine and Storm Pass. Continue to follow signs heading straight (west) to Longs Peak and Chasm Lake. Your climb continues through dense forest and you will encounter switchbacks on the way. The trail plateaus just before you hit the wilderness campsite of **Goblins Forest** and then stays fairly level for the next 0.5-mile before turning into switchbacks again. The next landmark is a footbridge that is called **Lightning Bridge** by some, because it comes right before a sign warning individuals about lightning danger just ahead. The bridge crosses Alpine Brook, a seasonal creek that rages at the beginning of the climbing season, and mellows considerably as the summer unfolds.

TISHMA'S CORNER

After the bridge, the trail makes a huge switchback, first heading south and then northwest. The switchback, located just below tree line is informally known as **Tishma's Corner;** it is named after Walter Tishma, a local man (now deceased) who climbed Longs more than 100 times in his life. While this is still a maintained trail, Tishma's Corner is a spot where winter and early season hikers can get discombobulated. Snow hangs on longer on this section of trail, and hikers on many occasions have accidentally dropped down into nearby basins off-trail and become lost. Suffice it to say, **keep a close eye on your map and route in this section** if there is snow.

At this point, you will notice that the landscape is quickly changing. The trees are becoming stouter, the terrain rockier. You are in the transition zone between subalpine and alpine and will soon be entirely above the tree line. After several sets of switchbacks, a sign for the **Battle Mountain wilderness campsite** appears. Head straight (west)

the large, flat summit of Longs Peak

Longs Peak

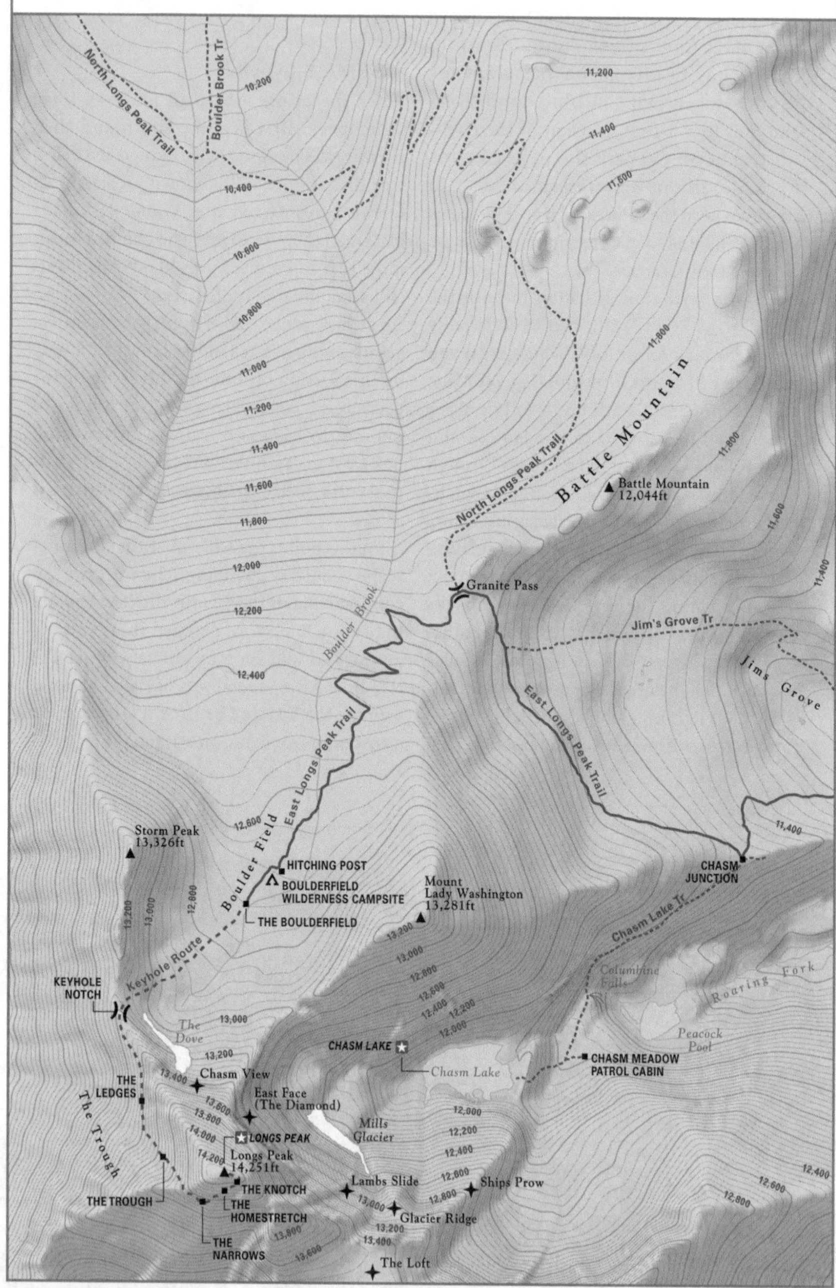
North Longs Peak Trail
Boulder Brook Tr
Battle Mountain
Battle Mountain
12,044ft
Granite Pass
Jim's Grove Tr
Jims Grove
Boulder Brook
East Longs Peak Trail
East Longs Peak Trail
Boulder Field
Storm Peak
13,326ft
HITCHING POST
BOULDERFIELD
WILDERNESS CAMPSITE
THE BOULDERFIELD
Mount
Lady Washington
13,281ft
CHASM
JUNCTION
Chasm Lake Tr
Keyhole Route
KEYHOLE
NOTCH
Columbine
Falls
Roaring Fork
The
Dove
CHASM LAKE
Peacock
Pool
CHASM MEADOW
PATROL CABIN
Chasm Lake
Chasm View
THE
LEDGES
The Trough
East Face
(The Diamond)
Mills
Glacier
LONGS PEAK
Longs Peak
14,251ft
Lambs Slide
Ships Prow
THE KNOTCH
THE TROUGH
THE
HOMESTRETCH
Glacier Ridge
THE
NARROWS
The Loft

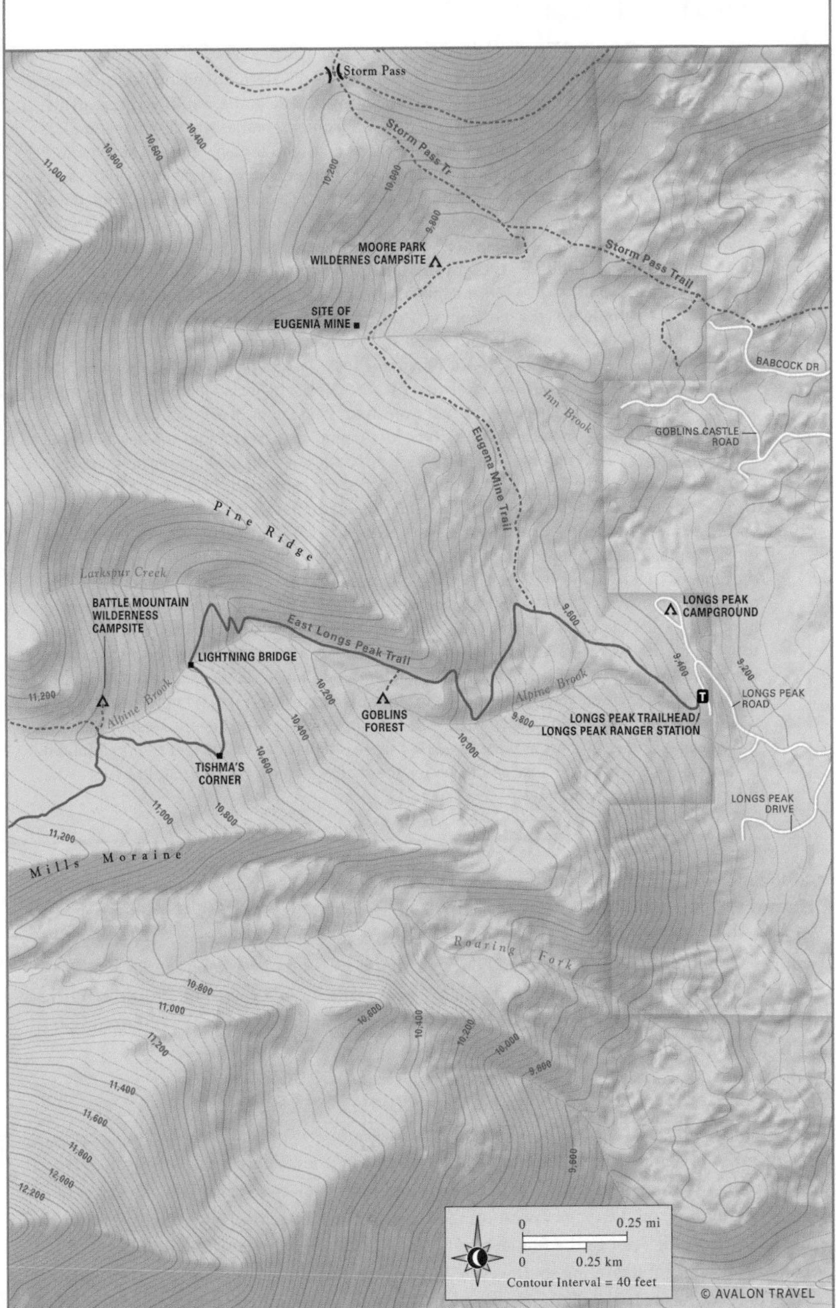
Storm Pass
Storm Pass Tr
Storm Pass Trail
MOORE PARK
WILDERNES CAMPSITE
SITE OF
EUGENIA MINE
BABCOCK DR
Inn Brook
Eugena Mine Trail
GOBLINS CASTLE
ROAD
Pine Ridge
Larkspur Creek
BATTLE MOUNTAIN
WILDERNESS
CAMPSITE
LIGHTNING BRIDGE
East Longs Peak Trail
LONGS PEAK
CAMPGROUND
Alpine Brook
GOBLINS
FOREST
LONGS PEAK TRAILHEAD/
LONGS PEAK RANGER STATION
LONGS PEAK
ROAD
TISHMA'S
CORNER
LONGS PEAK
DRIVE
Mills Moraine
Roaring Fork
0
0.25 mi
0
0.25 km
Contour Interval = 40 feet
© AVALON TRAVEL

Firsts on Longs Peak

Long before wicking fabric, GPS, hydration backpacks, and waterproof hiking boots existed, Rocky's early pioneers climbed the park's mountains with little in the way of accouterments. What they did have in common with their modern-day contemporaries was determination. It is speculated that Native Americans may have summited Longs, and certainly, the first documented party of seven hikers to stand atop Longs's flat peak had ample amounts of both grit and courage.

Professor **John Wesley Powell** (who had the better part of one arm missing from a war injury), five science students, and the editor of the *Rocky Mountain News*, **W. L. Byers,** triumphantly achieved the summit on August 23, 1868. That first summit was followed by many other climbs, and numerous other firsts on the mountain. Among them were the first ascent by a woman (**Addie Alexander,** 1871) and the first ascent of The Diamond (**David Rearick** and **Robert Kamps,** 1960). Estes Park born-and-raised **Tommy Caldwell** is noted for making the first Class 5.13 ascent on The Diamond, called "The Honeymoon Is Over" (2001) and, along with climbing partner **Joe Mills,** free climbing the first Class 5.14 route on The Diamond, the "Dunn-Westbay." In 2011, Estes Park local **Lisa Foster** (author of *Rocky Mountain National Park: The Complete Hiking Guide*) became the first woman to climb Longs in every month of the year. **Andy Anderson** has the fastest known time for running up to the summit and back: 1:56:46.

On January 12, 1925, mountaineer **Agnes Vaille** set out with a hiking partner, **Walter Kiener,** to become the first woman to ascend the East Face of Longs Peak during the winter. To date, no one had achieved this lofty goal, and she was bound and determined to be the first. Vaille had attempted three wintertime ascents previously without success. The pair summited on that brutally cold January day, but an exhausted Vaille slipped and fell on the descent. During the time that her partner left to seek help, Vaille, exposed to cold and wind, perished on the side of the mountain. Would a basic shelter have saved her life? It is impossible to know, but following her death, Vaille's father had a small shelter built just below the Keyhole. The structure is unusual: cylindrical with a conical roof, and made out of stone and concrete. The Denver architects who conceived the shelter fancied an Italian-influenced design. A simple plaque on the shelter acknowledges Vaille and one of the men who attempted to rescue her that fateful day. Rangers have no means for tracking how often anyone actually uses this tiny shelter to rest or wait out the weather. Some climbers are reassured that there is a place at 13,200 feet to find refuge if unfavorable circumstances arise. In the winter, the shelter—which has two window cuts and a door frame—fills up with snow.

following the sign that says **Longs Peak Summit**. You are now 4 miles from the peak. Shortly after leaving this signpost, you will get your first good look at the east face of Longs. Continue along the trail until you reach **Chasm Junction** (3.3 mi from the trailhead; 4 mi from the peak).

CHASM JUNCTION

At **Chasm Junction,** there is a toilet, and a small meadow where hikers tend to briefly congregate, hydrate, and refuel. When you are ready to forge on, head northwest on the **East Longs Peak Trail** to the Boulderfield/ Longs Peak summit (traveling southwest will take you to Chasm Lake). For 0.8 mile, the trail slowly ascends and skirts the east side of Mount Lady Washington until it reaches **Granite Pass.** Follow the trail marker left (southwest) and travel along a series of switchbacks which leads you to the **Boulderfield.** You are now 6 miles from the trailhead.

THE BOULDERFIELD TO THE KEYHOLE

Once you arrive at the **Boulderfield,** expect to find big views, perhaps a ptarmigan or two, and lots of rocky terrain. You can say goodbye to maintained trail once you have traveled about halfway through the Boulderfield to Rocky's established **wilderness campsites.** Next to the Boulderfield's horse **hitching**

post and privy, there is a sign for the Keyhole Route. **Cairns** mark the way thereafter. This vast valley of rocks, ranging in size from small talus to boxcar-sized boulders, is where the trickier part of the journey begins. Spending the night at the Boulderfield is the best option for hikers who want to break up their journey into two days. However, know that these nine wilderness campsites are in high demand and must be **reserved well in advance** through the wilderness office (970/586-1242). Finding **water to filter** is usually not difficult in the Boulderfield and within a few hundred yards of the established campsites.

In general, the Boulderfield is a slow, gradual uphill stretch. At any point, rocks can wobble and teeter underfoot; twisting your ankle is a real possibility. As you approach the Keyhole, there is some **Class Two** climbing involved. The rocks become bigger and you will use your hands in some parts to gain upward momentum. While there is no doubt as to where you are headed—the large notch in the rock up ahead—navigating the path of least resistance to your destination will take some thought and consideration. The **Keyhole,** a long ridge that extends off the north side of Longs Peak, is a game changer. From here on out, the pace of the trek changes, and exposure presents itself, much to the chagrin of acrophobics. Swift, unforgiving gusts of wind combined with steep drop-offs make this a **turnaround point** for many travelers. One of the many reasons to exercise good caution in this spot is that the rocks here may be covered in veriglass—thin layers of ice. If you choose to continue and walk through the Keyhole, a heady view of Glacier Gorge a few thousand feet below opens up. **Yellow and red bull's-eyes** painted on rocks from here to the summit prove helpful for many hikers, but do not imply safety and should not be followed to the end if unforeseen hazards present themselves along the way. The bull's eyes are also not always apparent if there is snow on the route.

Many people turn back for the parking lot at the Keyhole; either they never planned to summit in the first place or they decide that pressing on isn't wise. Making it to the Keyhole alone is without question a huge accomplishment. If you take pause at the Keyhole and wonder if you should go on, consider this: the Keyhole is the **halfway point in your journey** to the peak. Even though the summit is only a mile or so away as the crow flies, you should expect it to take just

Boulderfield Shelter Cabin

Rocky is often touted for having the highest continuous paved road in the United States (Trail Ridge Road) and the highest visitor center (Alpine Visitor Center) in all of the national parks. What was at one time considered the highest hotel in the world was located in the Boulderfield. From 1927 to 1935, the Boulderfield Shelter Cabin operated as a high elevation (12,750 feet) shelter and restaurant for peak baggers, and was universally known as the **Boulderfield Hotel.** The park's superintendent at the time, Roger Toll, was the impetus behind creating the shelter after his cousin, Agnes Vaille, perished on the side of the mountain during a peak descent. Consisting of one room and a loft, this rather crude space had no electricity and no running water. The first floor of the 14x18-foot building contained a bunk bed and a stove. People otherwise splayed out on mattresses in the loft. The team that built the shelter struggled to create a roof that could withstand the mighty winds tearing through the Boulderfield, and eventually fashioned a removable roof that came down each winter. The property also featured a horse barn and a working telephone. For nine years the hotel operated—and was heavily used—until it fell into a state of disrepair and was demolished. *Ripley's Believe it or Not!* acknowledged the cabin before it disappeared from the landscape.

as long to reach the top as it did to get to this point. So, if it took you four hours to get to the Keyhole, it will likely take you four more hours to get to the top because of the increasingly difficult terrain ahead.

As you poke your body on the other side of the Keyhole, the next challenge ahead is the **Ledges.**

THE LEDGES

In this next section, you will navigate across a series of slabbed **rock ledges.** The trail is relatively flat, but the terrain drops off steeply to the west. This is historically a **problematic spot** for climbers, and not a place you want to slip or trip. You will encounter a piece of rebar sticking out from the rocks and some steps chiseled into the rock. While the sight of the rebar provides some climbers with a feeling of extra security, know that the metal is surprisingly slick from polishing by thousands of boots, so serious caution is necessary. The slipperiness is not unlike the feeling of marble. You will use all four limbs to navigate this section; a **bottleneck of climbers** waiting for their turn is common.

THE TROUGH

The **trough** is an approximately 0.3-mile long gully, a scree-filled couloir. This is another spot where people assess their strength and might decide to turn around. Though the summit is close, there is somewhere around **1,000 vertical feet to climb** in the trough, and the presence of loose rocks is maddening. Don't be surprised if you hear an expletive or three in this spot (or blurt one out yourself). Follow the **bull's eyes,** but always be aware of who is above and below you. Make a point to not climb directly under another person, or you might find pebbles and rocks raining down on you.

THE NARROWS

The **narrows** is a stretch of rock that is a little less than the width of a sidewalk, which sounds relatively tame if it weren't for some serious exposure on the right-hand side. At this point you are at the **technical crux** of the route. There is a **large boulder** in this section that gives people some serious pause. Climbers usually end up doing an awkward step-around between the wall and the rock. Be aware that this spot becomes **bottlenecked** with people; it is basically one in, one out. After the narrows, it is time to press on to the homestretch.

the narrows

THE HOMESTRETCH

The last section past the narrows is appropriately named the **homestretch.** It is several hundred feet of **Class Two** slabs to the top. The rocks tend to be a little wet, and slicker than regular wet rock, because so many people have climbed them. Climbers usually find this spot much more challenging going down than coming up.

THE SUMMIT

The top of Longs is magnificent because of its spectacular views and its size. The **summit** is wide and flat, the size of several football fields. On a clear day, you can see Wyoming

The Diamond

On the east face of Longs, a diamond-shaped granite headwall serves as the mountain's most recognizable—and most photographed—feature. In the climbing community, the headwall is referred to as "**The Diamond,**" or "D1." After many challenging routes up Longs were attempted and conquered in the late 19th century and early 20th century, climbers still yearned for more. They wanted to scale The Diamond, the largest, most intimidating face on the mountain. Starting in 1954, climbers asked permission from the National Park Service to scale the wall, only to receive "no" in response. The National Park Service's hesitation had to do with the overall danger of the climb, and with their concern about staging a successful rescue if something were to go awry. Finally, in 1960, officials implemented a new policy that allowed access to this sheer rock wall, with eager climbers required to complete applications before their attempt. Two men from California, **David Rearick** and **Robert Kamps,** were granted the first go at the climb, and complete it they did, in 52 hours. Others soon followed.

Today, The Diamond remains ever popular for climbers, an ultimate challenge within the boundaries of Rocky. Along with two other climbing routes in Rocky, authors Steve Roper and Allen Steck include The Diamond in their book, *Fifty Classic Climbs in North America.* Zealous climbers use the authors' book as a bucket list. The most popular way to climb The Diamond is via "The Casual Route," which includes about seven pitches of traditional climbing.

to the north, Pikes Peak to the south, Grays and Torreys peaks to the west, and the sprawl of Denver to the east. One hundred or more people could fit in this spot. While it is feasible to find yourself alone at the top, you should expect to have company, especially if you are climbing in high season. People have been known to lug some interesting items to the top—juggling balls and violins among them. Some people settle in to cook up a celebratory sausage on their camp stove before heading down. At the minimum, it's a great idea to swig some water, have a snack, and sign the **summit register** to make your achievement official. A note about the loo: there are **no toilets** at the top of Longs Peak. Plan to use the toilets at the Boulderfield and save your personal business for places other than the mountaintop.

HEADING DOWN

Though climbers are often awash with relief at having made it to the top, it is still **7.5 miles back to the car,** and down-climbing from the peak to the Boulderfield is where accidents can and do happen. Stay focused, stay hydrated, and keep on keeping on until you are back where you started.

FISHING

The majority of people come to the Longs Peak area for hiking, climbing, and camping, but there are some who want to check out the fishing scene as well. There is really just one option off the Longs Peak Trailhead: **Peacock Pool,** which is a great spot to catch a brook trout.

The options open up more as you head farther south to Wild Basin. The **North St. Vrain Creek** has a healthy population of brooks and browns, with the occasional cutthroat. From the Wild Basin Entrance Station to the Wild Basin Trailhead is a great area to fish the North St. Vrain. Ouzel Lake and Ouzel Creek fish well for brook trout, and Thunder Lake is well populated by cutthroats. At **Copeland Lake,** you can find both brook trout and rainbow trout.

Kirks Mountain Adventures (230 E. Elkhorn Ave., Estes Park, 970/577-0790, www.kirksmountainadventures.com, 7am-8pm daily summer, 8am-5pm daily winter, $195 for 4 hrs., $290 for 8 hrs.) and **Estes Park Mountain Shop** (2050 Big Thompson Ave., Estes Park, 970/586-6548, www.estesparkmountainshop.com, 8am-9pm daily, $120 for 4 hrs., $220 for 8 hrs.) offer guided fly-fishing trips on the east side of Rocky.

The Complicated Story of Greenback Cutthroat Trout

Any time a species is down-listed by the U.S. Fish and Wildlife Service from "endangered" to "threatened," it is considered a huge success story. That is exactly what happened with Greenback Cutthroat Trout, a species of fish that was once believed to be extinct in Colorado in the 1930s. The cause of their disappearance was linked to hybridization—the mating of Greenbacks with other trout, which created an impure species—and because this fairly docile fish was pushed out by more aggressive brook and brown trout. Several small populations of the native fish were discovered and carefully, over many years, reintroduced in the park. In 1978, the fish was reclassified as "threatened" and there was even talk of delisting Greenback Cutthroat Trout altogether.

The story, however, doesn't end there. In 2007, a group of biologists released research indicating that native Greenback Cutthroat Trout had been misidentified. This discovery was quite stunning and a huge setback for those involved with the species' recovery. Additional research followed, and in 2012, biologists concluded that just one population of pure Greenback Cutthroat Trout remained, and the location of the fish was not in Rocky. Today, fish in the park are still referred to as Greenback Cutthroat Trout, even though they are of a different lineage than the fish originally classified as endangered. As well, Rocky still manages these populations as though they are endangered. In waters deemed fishable by the park, visitors who hold a valid Colorado fishing license are welcome to catch Greenback Cutthroat Trout, but they, without exception, must be released.

In 2014, Greenbacks staged a disappearing act from **Lily Lake**—which was previously one of the most popular places to view and catch the fish. Several theories exist as to why this occurred. Some people have speculated that the Colorado Flood of 2013 caused fish to tumble over the top of the lake's dam, never to be seen again. Because fish could have hung out at the bottom of the lake to avoid getting washed out, this scenario is unlikely. A more plausible cause is that physical changes made to the dam on the outlet of Lily Lake in 2012 resulted in disappearing fish. It is believed that fish now only enter the stream for spawning in the spring, and head downstream thereafter.

HORSEBACK RIDING

An option for people who do not want to hike or climb the entire way to Longs Peak is to travel one leg of the trip on horseback with **Sombrero Ranches** (970/577-6818, www.sombrero.com, $180) the day before or day of a peak ascent. This specialty trip requires advance reservations; the outfitter will guide riders and their gear up to Chasm Lake or a different spot along the route to the top. Riders can then climb under their own power for the rest of the way to the summit and depart on their own timeline. Sombrero does not have a stable next to Longs Peak, but will deliver horses to the trailhead from its Estes Park location.

Meeker Park Lodge's (11733 Hwy. 7, Allenspark, 303/747-2266, www.meekerparklodge.com, daily Memorial Day-Labor Day) livery offers horseback rides around Longs Peak and Wild Basin in the summer, ranging from one-hour ($40) to all-day ($170). Destinations include Chasm Lake, Thunder Lake, and Sandbeach Lake and reservations are recommended.

WINTER SPORTS

Snowshoeing and Cross-Country Skiing

Snowshoeing is a consistently popular wintertime activity in Wild Basin, and to a lesser extent, so is cross-country skiing. On the area's lower trails, avalanche hazards are considered minimal. However, it is prudent to call the main line for the park (970/586-1206) ahead of a visit to check on snow conditions and to download a winter-specific trail map for Wild Basin from the park website (www.nps.gov/romo). Often, it is enough for families with small children and first-timers to take a jaunt along the one-mile section of unplowed road from **Wild Basin's winter trailhead** to the summer trailhead (though sometimes, repeatedly blowing snow might mean that part of your hike is in the snow, part in the dirt). Many, though, venture farther to Copeland Falls, Calypso Cascades, or beyond. Come prepared with the right equipment and clothing, a map, navigation skills, food, water, and emergency supplies.

Sleigh Rides

Dao House (6120 Hwy. 7, Estes Park, 970/586-4094, www.daohouse.com, $30 adults, $20 children) has an edge when it comes to one highly sought-after wintertime activity: sleigh rides. No other business in the area offers sleigh rides, and the hotel receives many more requests for rides than they can provide. One year, between Christmas and New Year's Day, they turned down a whopping 600 requests for sleigh rides because they were so booked up. When enough snow has fallen, the lodge's on-site Belgian draft horses pull people around on a sleigh, with jingling bells and the promise of hot cocoa by a blazing fire pit making for an altogether festive experience. The rides take place on the Dao House property, which has great views of Longs Peak. Make **reservations** in advance (stables@daohouse.com, 970/577-3448).

Dao House also offers one-hour to all-day horseback rides into the park; locations include Eugenia Mine, The Boulderfield, Lily Lake, and Estes Cone.

Ice Climbing

Ice climbing is a popular activity on the east side. **Hidden Falls** is a favorite spot of climbers, and is accessed from the Wild Basin Winter Trailhead. The falls consist of a huge column of ice that stands approximately 75 feet from top to bottom. The winter trail to the falls, which runs along the south side of North St. Vrain Creek, is usually packed out in the snow. There is no maintained trail to the falls, which are located about 0.25 mile past Copeland Falls (GPS coordinates: 40.2015, -105.5755).

Entertainment and Shopping

In the summer, check the park's newspaper for **ranger-led programs** at Lily Lake; there are usually several options offered, from hiking to photography. No regular programs are offered in the Longs Peak or Wild Basin regions.

The **Rocky Mountain Conservancy's Field Institute** (RMC, 1895 Fall River Rd., Estes Park, 970/586-0121, www.rmconservancy.org) course catalog changes each year, but is always worth consulting for programs specific to the Wild Basin area. RMC has offered "Hike with a Naturalist" opportunities around Wild Basin in the past to destinations such as remote Pear Lake.

ENTERTAINMENT

Rocky Ridge Music Center (465 Longs Peak Rd., Estes Park, 970/586-4031, www.rockyridge.org) holds music concerts—mostly of the classical variety—throughout the summer at its concert hall and at several other locations in Estes Park. The center operates as a residential music camp for adults and youth, and is recognized as one of the oldest summer music programs in the United States. A concert series called "Music in the Mountains" requires tickets ($25 general admission, $20 seniors and children 12 and under), though a number of free student performances are also open to the public. For local history buffs, there is added interest in attending a concert at the concert hall: the property and buildings once comprised a long-running lodge frequented by Longs Peak climbers and tourists: the **Hewes-Kirkwood Inn.** Poet-novelist Charles Edwin Hewes operated the inn for four decades before it eventually closed. The music center has existed since 1942. Purchase tickets for events by phone, online, at the center's box office, or at the door.

The music center is located along the road to Longs Peak Trailhead and campground, approximately 10 miles south of Estes Park along Highway 7 (turn west onto Longs Peak Rd.).

SHOPPING

A small quantity of park souvenirs and hiking essentials are sold at the **Longs Peak Ranger Station** (closed in the winter), located at the end of Longs Peak Road next to the Longs Peak Trailhead.

★ Eagle Plume's

Eagle Plume's (9853 Hwy. 7, Allenspark, 303/747-2861, www.eagleplume.com, 10am-5pm daily late Apr.-Oct., winter hours vary) was originally a teahouse and antiques shop when it first opened in 1917; the business eventually morphed into a highly regarded American Indian arts-and-crafts trading post. Exquisitely handcrafted pieces of jewelry, textiles, and baskets have always held appeal for tourists, but it is the enduring spirit of longtime owner Charles Eagle Plume, who passed in 1992, that makes this a spot worth visiting. Charles danced for customers, told wild tales, and regularly wore an Indian headdress to work. Young patrons received a complimentary feather from Charles, a tradition that is still carried on today. Family members who now run the shop say they have "seen" or "heard" the ghost of Charles over the years, and every September hold a small event called "Toast the Ghost," where old-timers share memories of a well-loved man. Charles's vast collection of authentic Native American items is displayed in cases and on the walls; it is a fascinating mini-museum within the store.

Accommodations

All lodging accommodations are located outside the park. There are a number of places to rent in the vicinity of Longs Peak and Wild Basin. It is worth perusing www.vrbo.com or www.airbnb.com for privately owned homes and cabins.

HIGHWAY 7

The first word that comes to mind walking in the front door of **The Baldpate Inn** (4900 Hwy. 7, Estes Park, 970/586-6151, www.baldpateinn.com, Memorial Day-early Oct., closed in winter, $130) is comfort. The dining room smells of homemade pie and baked goods coming fresh out of the oven. The warmth and crackle from the large stone lobby fireplace beckons you to plop down on a couch and relax. A library brimming with books and another giant stone fireplace could easily suck you in for an entire afternoon. This is a place to leave the cares of the world behind. There are 12 guest rooms upstairs in the main lodge, as well as four cabins and the standalone Baldpate homestead located on-site. Each inn bed is topped with a quilt lovingly handcrafted by the owner; rooms are quaint, with old-fashioned washbasins, and frilly curtains framing the windows. Because this is a century-old structure, be prepared to embrace the inn's quirks, like an upstairs floor that has major speed bumps. Also, be aware that most of the inn's guest rooms have a shared bathroom. The inn operates as a bed-and-breakfast, with a hearty three-course breakfast served up to guests. Lily Lake is located right across Highway 7.

There is nothing fancy about **Meeker Park Lodge**'s (11733 Hwy. 7, Allenspark, Estes

Park, 303/747-2266, www.meekerparklodge.com, Memorial Day-Labor Day, $118) cabins, simply appointed with thin bedspreads and kitchen countertops reminiscent of the 1970s. Sturdy, no-frills furniture decorates the living rooms. You might even detect a faint, musty smell upon entering your quarters, but the scent is not at all unpleasant; it evokes a feeling of stepping back in time. Lodge rooms are a budget-friendly option and offered with a shared bath ($66) or private bath ($85). At the main lodge, there is a common area with a piano, fireplace, puzzles and games, and reading material. Additional amenities include a gift shop, a small store, and laundry facilities. Breakfast is available to guests ($7.50 pp).

Wild Basin Lodge and Event Center (1130 County Road 84 West, Allenspark, 303/747-2274, www.wildbasinlodge.com, lodge rooms $190, suites, $265) is in a prime location just outside the Wild Basin Entrance Station. Chances are good that if you drive by the lodge June-October, a sign noting that a private event is in progress will greet you before you make it anywhere near the front door. This facility is first and foremost a wedding venue, and hundreds of events are booked each year. However, it is possible to book a lodge room when it is not the peak of summer. Room pricing and other lodging details are not listed online; you can call the main lodge number to inquire about openings. Three beautifully appointed lodge rooms and two suites can be reserved.

Dao House (6120 Hwy. 7, Estes Park, 970/586-4094, www.daohouse.com, $219), which is owned by a Daoist priest, has activities and services that you will not find at any other lodging option in the area, including spiritual counseling, martial arts instruction, Daoist lectures, and Chinese medicine treatments. The main lodge building smells like incense and herbs, and in the lobby seating area, you'll find a giant 50-pound Himalayan salt lamp (which reportedly has healing benefits). A small oxygen bar is located off the main lobby. Accommodations are simple and clean; the overall vibe here is one of peacefulness. Continental breakfast is included. Dao House was greatly affected by the Colorado Flood of 2013, and you can still see markings several feet up on the front door from flood water and debris.

ALLENSPARK

At the **Allenspark Lodge B&B** (184 Hwy. 7, Allenspark, 303/747-2552, www.allensparklodgebnb.com, $105-150), owners Bill and

Meeker Park Lodge's cabins are tucked into the aspens.

Juanita have created a great haven for visitors looking to get away from it all. This old log building constructed in the 1930s is relaxing, quiet, and an especially nice retreat for couples. Only those 14 years and older may stay at the lodge. Six of the simply furnished lodge rooms have a shared bath, while six include a private bath. There is also one private apartment with its own kitchen. Breakfast is hot and hearty.

While promoting a meat-free and raw foods lifestyle is Cathy and Cory Osban's specialty at **Sunshine Mountain Lodge** (18078 Hwy. 7, Allenspark, 303/747-2840, www.sunshinemtlodge.com, $105-135), the couple welcomes visitors with any dietary preference and won't bat an eye if animal products are brought on-site. This pet-friendly property is located halfway between the towns of Lyons and Estes Park, and is 5 miles away from the park's Wild Basin Entrance Station. Six cabins built in the 1940s have low-slung ceilings and no-frills furnishings, and a funky second bedroom in cabins 1, 2, and 3 is just large enough to hold a twin bed. A bunkroom upstairs from the main lodge is great for kids or larger groups. Outside, find horseshoes, volleyball, a hot tub, hammocks, picnic tables, and a fire pit. The Osbans' obsession with the carrot is apparent in a communal kitchen where root vegetable decor dominates, and they will happily juice up a bunch on request. In the fall, the couple prepares breakfast for guests on the weekends.

Camping

INSIDE THE PARK

Longs Peak Campground

It's possible to get lucky and score a site at the **Longs Peak Campground** (Longs Peak Rd., www.nps.gov/romo, late May-Nov. 1, $20), but have a plan B in your back pocket because there are only 26 spots available. Only tents are allowed at this first-come, first-served campground. This is the best possible location to spend the night before making a bid for the summit of Longs, and often you'll find fellow campers tucked into their tents as early as 8pm. If you aren't heading up to the peak and have plans to sleep in, be aware that you could be awakened at 1am by an alarm buzzing or someone stumbling around in the dark packing up their gear. On the north end of the campground, visitors commonly hear children playing at a summer camp that is located next to the Longs Peak Campground. This is the most rustic of the park's five campgrounds, with only vault toilets and no sinks for dishwashing. There is potable water, as well as trash and recycling bins. Firewood is sold at the campground entrance. Sites include a tent pad, picnic table, and fire pit. Bear boxes are shared.

To get to the campground from Estes Park, take Highway 7 south for 9 miles, then drive 1 mile west on Longs Peak Road. Some people consider sleeping in their cars or "stealth" camping in the Longs Peak parking lot, but get caught by a ranger and you might be told to leave, or worse, get fined; then your peak-bagging day would start with some really bad mojo. Signs prominently displayed in the area indicate that camping is prohibited.

OUTSIDE THE PARK

Olive Ridge Campground

When NPS campgrounds on the east side are bursting at the seams, the National Forest Service's **Olive Ridge Campground** (mile marker 14, west side of Hwy. 7, 877/444-6777, www.recreation.gov, late May-late Sept. $14 per vehicle, $4 for each additional car) is a great place to score a site. The campground is ideally located for visitors who want to explore Wild Basin (approximately 1 mile north) and is convenient to the Longs Peak Trailhead

(5.5 mi north). The park's Beaver Meadows Entrance Station is a 15-20 minute drive from Olive Ridge Campground. Half of the sites are reservable and the other half are first-come, first-served. Thirty sites are designated for tents only, while 26 spots are designed for RVs. Sites include a tent pad, grill, fire pit, and picnic table. Firewood is sold here and vault toilets are available. No water is available at this campground.

Meeker Park Overflow Campground

Bears like to poke their noses around **Meeker Park Overflow Campground** (mile marker 11, west side of Hwy. 7, www.fs.usda.gov, 303/541-2500, mid-June-early Sept., $11), which is hardly a surprise considering how busy this spot gets—and the fact that there are no bear-proof storage containers. But for frugal travelers, the price is right and the 29 campsites outfitted with picnic tables and fire pits are shady and attractive. RVs and trailers are welcome, but roads leading around the campground are fairly narrow, making travel difficult for larger vehicles. All sites are first-come, first-served. Firewood is available for sale and portable toilets are on the grounds; there is no water. The sign for the campground is easy to drive by without noticing; keep an eye out for the Forest Picnic Ground sign on the east side of the highway, then turn west across the highway into the campground. This spot usually fills up by midday Friday or earlier in high season. Nonetheless, it's a great option for last-minute travelers. Early to mid-week, the campground can be surprisingly empty.

Dispersed Camping

Free dispersed camping can be found east of the park in the **Roosevelt National Forest** (www.fs.fed.us). Heading south on Highway 7, pass the entrance to Longs Peak and look for Big Owl Road (located on the left side of the highway, shortly after crossing into Boulder County). Cabin Creek Road, which also has dispersed camping, is farther south and ultimately connects with Big Owl Road. These camping areas have seen so much human impact over the years that calling them "overrun" is putting it nicely. You will do yourself and the land a big favor by reserving a different campsite or hotel in advance. However, if you find yourself driving around at 11pm without a place to sleep, it is good to know that Roosevelt National Forest is an option.

Camping is also possible along Ski Road in the Roosevelt National Forest near Allenspark, but be aware that a four-wheel drive/high-clearance vehicle is necessary to reach most sites.

Food

INSIDE THE PARK

Picnicking

One of the most delightful places to picnic on the east side of the park is at **Lily Lake.** There are just four first-come, first-served tables at this location, so interested parties must swoop in before prime dining hours to secure a spot—they are very popular. There is also a **group picnic area** (970/586-1206, $300) at Lily Lake available by reservation only; call the park's main line for more information. Twelve picnic tables are located in this spot.

A handful of tables are available for picnicking near the **Longs Peak Trailhead.** Another option is to look for a vacant table at the Longs Peak Campground, but only outside of peak camping times. Park rules state that you cannot picnic at the campground from the Friday before Memorial Day through September.

In Wild Basin, picnic tables are located at the **Wild Basin Trailhead** and at various spots along Wild Basin Road. A medium-size picnic area, located west of Copeland Lake, includes one wheelchair-accessible picnic site and vault toilets.

OUTSIDE THE PARK

Highway 7

The one-room grocery store at **Meeker Park Lodge** (11733 Hwy. 7, Allenspark, 303/747-2266, www.meekerparklodge.com, 8am-5pm daily, Memorial Day-Labor Day) is well-stocked with essentials like firewood, ice, canned goods, milk, and ice cream. A selection of produce is available and a large barrel holds peanuts that can be bought by the pound. This is the only store serving the Longs Peak and Wild Basin areas.

One of the most whimsical displays for a salad bar is at **The Baldpate Inn Dining Room** (4900 Hwy. 7, Estes Park, 970/586-6151, www.baldpateinn.com, 11:30am-8pm daily Memorial Day-Labor Day; 11:30am-4pm Tues.-Sun. Sept.-Oct.; closed in winter; $16): lettuce, salad toppings, and fruit/veggie salads are chilled on ice in a deep, free-standing bathtub. The dining room also serves freshly made soup, rolls, muffins, and cornbread, as well as heavenly homemade pies in a variety of flavors ($6.75 per slice). Together, the all-you-can-eat soup and salad buffet comprise the Baldpate Inn Dining Room's sole menu offerings. The space feels cozy and casual, with an old piano tucked into one corner, lace window treatments, and kerosene lamps set atop wooden tables.

Meeker Park Picnic Area (east side of Hwy. 7 at mile marker 11, 6am-10pm, free) is a convenient place to eat lunch along Highway 7, where food and restaurant options are scant. The picnic area has eight tables, each with its own grill, that are first-come first served. Vault toilets are available and pets must be leashed.

Allenspark

★ **Meadow Mountain Cafe**'s (441 Business Hwy. 7, Allenspark, Estes Park, 303/747-2541, 7:30am-2pm Weds.-Mon., closed Tues., $4-12) homemade wheat bread is a customer favorite, and it is not hard to see why. It's nubby and rustic, subtly sweetened with molasses, and sliced thick. The bread accompanies every egg dish and plays a starring role in most of the restaurant's sandwiches. Small and cozy, the café has just one room inside—heated by a woodstove in the winter—and a covered deck out front. Decorations mostly consist of owner Roxanne "Rocky" St. John's funky salt-and-pepper shaker collection. The vibe at Mountain Meadow is earthy and casual, and on one visit, I observed something I have never seen at any restaurant before or since: a patron sharing a milkshake with his pet parrot. Roughly 75 percent of patrons in the summer are tourists, but in the winter you will rub elbows mostly with locals and residents from the Boulder area.

The scene is undeniably set for romance at **The Fawn Brook Inn** (357 Business Hwy. 7, Allenspark, 303/747-2556, www.fawnbrookinn.com, 5pm-8pm Wed.-Sat., noon-2pm and 5pm-8pm Sun. in summer; 5pm-8pm Fri.-Sun. in winter, $42-60) and not just after dark. Even on a bright Sunday morning you might find smartly dressed couples sitting on this five-star restaurant's front patio, holding hands and speaking in soft tones to each other while hummingbirds flit to and fro. The patio is a lush and pretty haven with flowers, potted plants, and trees. Inside, there is also an air of enchantment—a beautifully appointed dining room with rich wood flooring is housed by log walls that have been standing since 1927. For a major splurge, order the Beef Wellington for two ($168), which includes black truffle-infused mousse de foie gras. While the inn actually used to function as a hunting lodge, today this building is a restaurant only and not a place to stay overnight.

Transportation and Services

DRIVING

Estes Park is the gateway town for Longs Peak and Wild Basin. From downtown Estes Park to Lily Lake, it is a 6.3-mile drive south down Highway 7. Longs Peak Road (which takes you to the Longs Peak Trailhead) is approximately 10 miles south of Estes Park, while the Wild Basin Entrance Station is approximately 13 miles south.

Highway 7 is the main access road for Lily Lake Trailhead, Twin Sisters Trailhead, Longs Peak Trailhead, and Wild Basin Trailhead. While it is certainly a fun road to drive, and it is not uncommon to see people tackling the curves in race-car mode, posted speed limits should be observed for obvious reasons. Be especially aware of heavy foot traffic around Lily Lake. At night, keep an eye out for wildlife crossing the road.

From Highway 7, **Longs Peak Road** heads west. During the summer and fall, visitors often end up parking alongside the main road and walking uphill to get to the trailhead, so be aware of pedestrian traffic. Longs Peak Road is plowed in the winter.

In Wild Basin, **Wild Basin Road** is plowed to the winter trailhead parking area, which is 1 mile east of the summer trailhead. Though chains are not required in the winter and early spring around Longs Peak/Wild Basin, it is never a bad idea to be prepared for snow, slush, and ice, with winter or all-season tires on your car.

For emergency service or towing, call

Where Can I Find...?

- **Cell Service:** Cell coverage is nonexistent along Highway 7, from Lily Lake south to the town of Lyons.
- **Emergencies:** Use emergency phones located at the Longs Peak Ranger Station and the Wild Basin Trailhead.
- **Firewood:** In the summer, firewood can be purchased at Longs Peak Campground and Meeker Park Lodge (11733 Hwy. 7, Allenspark, 303/747-2266, www.meekerparklodge.com, 8am-5pm daily in summer).
- **Gas:** The closest service stations to Longs Peak and Wild Basin are found in Estes Park or Lyons.
- **Laundry and Showers:** Meeker Park Lodge (11733 Hwy. 7, Allenspark, 303/747-2266, www.meekerparklodge.com, 8am-5pm daily in summer) has public showers ($3 pp) and laundry facilities.
- **Restrooms:** Toilets are located at Lily Lake, Longs Peak Trailhead, Longs Peak Campground, the Wild Basin Entrance Station, Wild Basin Trailhead, and at the picnic area west of Copeland Lake.
- **Water:** In the summer, bottled water is sold at the Wild Basin Ranger Station; a potable water spigot is also available. Water is seasonally available at the Longs Peak Trailhead and Longs Peak Campground. If you are driving in via Allenspark, fill up containers for free at Crystal Spring (look for a small signed wooden shelter on Hwy. 7, across from The Fawn Brook Inn; open seasonally).

Bob's Towing and Repair (800 Dunraven St., Estes Park, 970/586-3122, 8am-5pm Mon.-Sat.) or **Up Top Towing** (875 Moraine Ave., Estes Park, 970/586-4248, open 24/7).

Parking

Parking is located at the Longs Peak Trailhead, Sandbeach Lake Trailhead, Finch Lake Trailhead, the picnic area next to Copeland Lake in Wild Basin, Wild Basin Trailhead, and Lily Lake Trailhead. Along Wild Basin Road, there are also a few random parking spots available for one or two cars only. Inevitably, there are more visitors than parking spots in the summer season. If **Wild Basin Road** becomes overly congested with cars and all parking spaces are full, rangers **temporarily block off access** to the road. To avoid getting turned away at the Wild Basin winter parking area, arrive early or late in the day, or on a weekday, when the road is less crowded.

The **Longs Peak parking lot** can be full early in the morning. Parking along the side of the mile-long road leading up to Longs Peak Trailhead is acceptable if every space in the trailhead parking lot is occupied. Day hikers cannot park in the campground.

RV parking is not available at Longs Peak or Lily Lake. Visitors with RVs are advised to not travel on narrow Wild Basin Road.

Trail Ridge Road

Look for ★ to find recommended sights, activities, dining, and lodging.

Highlights

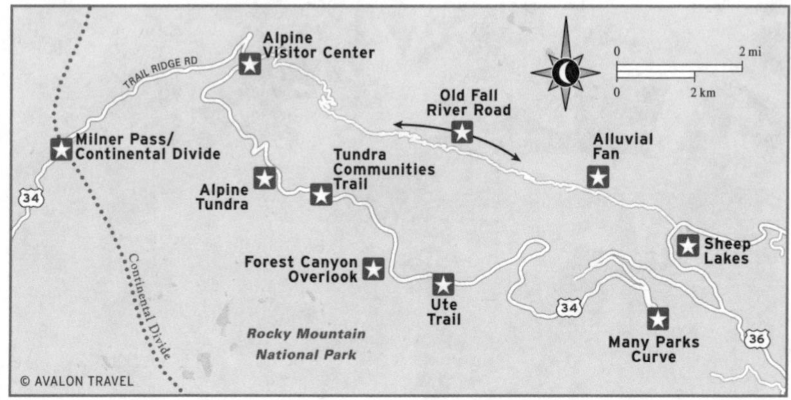

★ **Alluvial Fan:** On a summer day, this spot is a great place to dip your toes in the water or simply bask in the sunshine (page 113).

★ **Sheep Lakes:** Swing by these lakes in the warmer months and you might spot a bighorn sheep, the official mammal of Rocky (page 113).

★ **Old Fall River Road:** Take an enjoyable "Sunday drive" on this road any summer day (page 114).

★ **Many Parks Curve:** Stop at this scenic viewpoint year-round on Trail Ridge Road (page 119).

★ **Forest Canyon Overlook:** Check out a multitude of mountaintops, a spire, and a gorge from this easy-to-access viewing area (page 120).

★ **Alpine Tundra:** Drive up Trail Ridge Road above 11,000 feet, where only the hardiest plants and animals survive (page 122).

★ **Alpine Visitor Center:** Shop, rest, or check out tundra-themed exhibits at the highest visitor center in the United States (page 122).

★ **Milner Pass/Continental Divide:** You can literally straddle the Continental Divide at this location (page 124).

★ **Ute Trail:** Set your camera to "panorama" and get ready for awesome 360-degree views of Rocky (page 128).

★ **Tundra Communities Trail:** Feel like you are on top of the world during this short alpine tundra hike (page 129).

It is hard to fathom the blood, sweat, and tears that went into building this 48-mile road that crests at 12,183 feet in elevation.

Trail Ridge Road is the highest continuous paved road in the United States, and an 11-mile stretch is entirely above the tree line. It goes without saying that the views—though dizzying at times—are extraordinary. Not just a scenic drive, this road provides access to hikes and the highest visitor center in all of the national parks. White-knuckled drivers—or anyone, for that matter—can opt to comfortably experience Trail Ridge Road via a guided tour.

Old Fall River Road has historical significance as the first road built in the park. First opened in 1920, it is scenic, narrow, and curvy. This region was one of the hardest hit by a 100-year flood that occurred in and around Rocky in 2013, and the road was closed for nearly two years while $4 million in repairs were made. Today, any remaining signs of a natural disaster are largely undetectable to the average visitor. People happily motor along uphill at a slow speed on the dirt-and-gravel road, sightseeing and relishing a brief respite from everyday life. Along the 9-mile route you will find prime spots for fishing, a waterfall, trails, and great views.

PLANNING YOUR TIME

Trail Ridge Road typically opens to automobile traffic by **Memorial Day** and is drivable until mid- to **late October.** Snow determines whether the road will open on time and if it stays open later in the fall (unseasonably warm weather in 2016 meant it remained open until mid-Nov.). If Trail Ridge Road is an absolute must-see, schedule your trip to Rocky around a **June-September** timeframe. Snow can cause temporary road closures for Trail Ridge Road and Old Fall River Road even in the summer months; always check the park's road status report (www.nps.gov/romo).

The window of time for visiting **Old Fall River Road** is even shorter than Trail Ridge Road; the road usually opens around **July 4** and stays open until the first significant snowfall. If maintenance must be performed on the road, it can close earlier.

One full day on Trail Ridge Road and

Previous: wildflowers on the tundra; the Tundra Communities Trail. **Above:** cairns, unofficial trail markers.

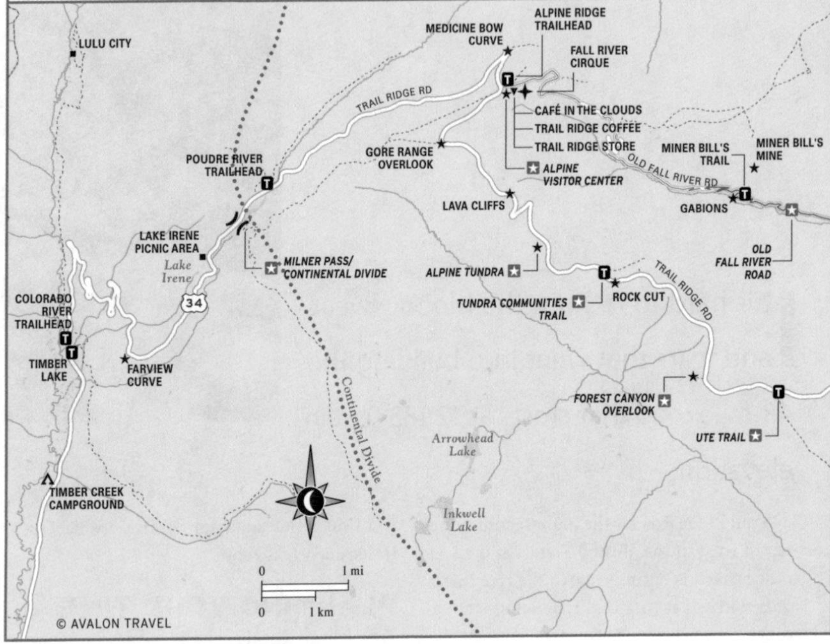

Old Fall River Road is often enough to satisfy the curiosity of visitors on a tight time schedule. But if the idea of exploring the tundra sounds enthralling, a longer, multi-day itinerary can easily be developed. Keep in mind that there are no overnight accommodations on or near Trail Ridge Road, with the exception of Timber Creek Campground in the Kawuneeche Valley and several hike-to wilderness campsites.

Exploring the Park

ENTRANCE STATIONS

Three entrance stations provide access to this region of **Rocky Mountain National Park** (1000 U.S. Hwy. 36, Estes Park, 970/586-1206, www.nps.gov/romo, $20/day per vehicle or motorcycle, $10 hikers and bikes, weekly passes available). The park newspaper and free park map are distributed at entrance stations and visitor centers. Self-guided tour booklets ($2) for Old Fall River Road and Trail Ridge Road are sold at the visitor centers.

Fall River Entrance Station

On the east side of the park is the **Fall River Entrance Station** (Hwy. 34, year-round), located approximately 4 miles north of downtown Estes Park. Inside the park, Highway 34 is also known as Trail Ridge Road and continues west to the Grand Lake Entrance Station. The Fall River Entrance Station consists of ranger booths only; there are no services or amenities.

From the entrance station, Old Fall River

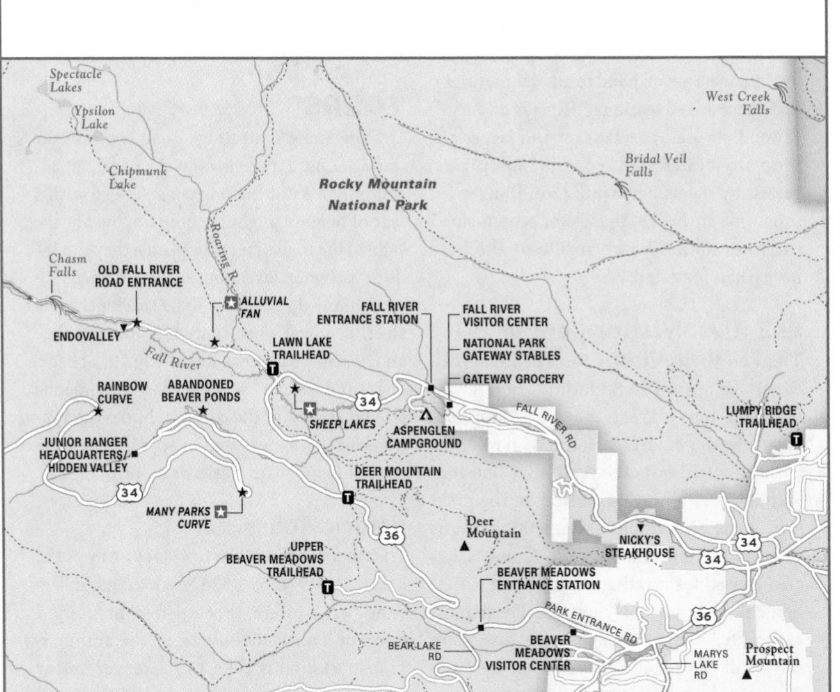

Road is located 2 miles west along Highway 34; turn right (northwest) onto paved Endovalley Road. The traffic is two-way from Horseshoe Park to Endovalley for approximately 1.8 miles until the signed entrance to one-way Old Fall River Road.

Beaver Meadows Entrance Station

The **Beaver Meadows Entrance Station** (Hwy. 36, open year-round) is west of Estes Park. Though Beaver Meadows is the busiest entrance station in the park, there are no services.

From the entrance station, Trail Ridge Road is accessed 3 miles north on Highway 36. At Deer Ridge Junction turn left (west) on Highway 34/Trail Ridge Road. To reach Old Fall River Road, continue north on Highway 36 for another 1.8 miles until arriving at the turnoff for Old Fall River Road.

Grand Lake Entrance Station

Grand Lake Entrance Station (Hwy. 34, year-round) is the west side entrance for Trail Ridge Road. Immediately upon entering the park, you will follow Trail Ridge Road north through the Kawuneeche Valley. The Grand Lake Entrance Station does not feature any amenities.

Because Old Fall River Road is a one-way road traveling east to west, the only way to get there from the Grand Lake Entrance Station is to drive approximately 37 miles east on Trail Ridge Road to the Deer Ridge Junction (Hwy. 36/34) on the east side. From Deer Ridge Junction, head north on Highway 34 for 1.7 miles to the turnoff for Old Fall River Road (on the left).

VISITOR CENTERS

Alpine Visitor Center

The **Alpine Visitor Center** (Trail Ridge Rd.

and Old Fall River Rd., 970/586-1206, 9am-5pm daily summer, 10:30am-4:30pm daily spring and fall) serves Trail Ridge Road visitors. Rangers are on hand to answer questions, and there are educational displays and a gift shop to peruse. A restaurant and larger gift shop are located in a separate building accessed by the same parking lot. Ranger-led programs are held at the visitor center; check the information board inside or the park newspaper for details.

Fall River Visitor Center

The **Fall River Visitor Center** (3450 Fall River Rd., www.rockymountaingateway.net, 9am-4pm Fri.-Sat. mid-May, 9am-5pm daily late May-mid-Oct.; limited hours Nov.-Dec.) is located east of the Fall River Entrance Station on Highway 34. Inside on the main level, there are exhibits about wildlife, a gift shop, and an information desk. A downstairs area is used for rotating exhibits and activities. An additional gift shop and a restaurant are located in the same complex, and there is a small playground for children ages 2-5. Ranger-led programs are held at the visitor center.

Beaver Meadows Visitor Center

The **Beaver Meadows Visitor Center** (1000 Hwy. 36, 970/586-1206, www.nps.gov/romo, 8am-4:30pm daily mid-Oct-mid-May, 8am-5pm daily mid-May-mid-June, 8am-6pm daily mid-June-early Sept., 8am-5pm daily early Sept.-mid-Oct.) houses a small theater, a Rocky Mountain Conservancy Store, and an information desk staffed with rangers. Ranger-led programs meet at this location.

Kawuneeche Visitor Center

The **Kawuneeche Visitor Center** (16018 Hwy. 34, 970/627-3471, www.nps.gov/romo, 8am-5pm daily summer, 8am-4:30pm daily fall, winter, and spring) is the only visitor center on the west side of the park. The building contains educational displays, a theater for park films, a gift shop, and an information desk. There is also a **wilderness office** for obtaining overnight camping permits. Ranger-led programs are held at this location.

TOURS

Driving along Trail Ridge Road is one of the most unique experiences in the park, but admittedly it's not for everyone. Those with a fear of heights might become unglued at the sight of the road's steep drop-offs; they can induce vertigo in just about anyone. Other visitors simply do not want to be stuck behind a steering wheel when there is so much to see and do. Guided tours allow visitors to sit back, relax, and take in the scenery while someone else takes care of the driving. Make reservations for these tours well in advance, as spots can get snapped up weeks or months ahead.

Vehicle Tours

The **Rocky Mountain Conservancy Field Institute** (970/586-3262, www.rmconservancy.org) offers three different guided tours of Trail Ridge Road in the summer. Transportation is via a 14-passenger bus or 12-passenger van; fees include lunch and admission to the park. On each of the Field Institute's tours, an educator provides commentary about area sights. Stops along the way offer ample opportunity for limb-stretching and photo-taking. All tours start and end at the **Fall River Visitor Center** (3450 Fall River Rd., www.rockymountaingateway.net). Pack for all weather conditions. Tours include:

- Grand Lake Safari: An Educational Adventure by Bus (8:30am-4:30pm Tues. June-Aug., $95 adults, $55 children 12 and under) takes passengers the full length of Trail Ridge Road with a turn-around point at Grand Lake.
- Journey to the Top! A Trail Ridge Road Bus Adventure (9am-3:30pm Wed.-Thurs. June-Labor Day, $75 adults, $45 children 12 and under) goes as far as the Alpine Visitor Center before heading back.
- Sunset Safari: An Educational Adventure by Bus (6pm-10pm Fri. June-Labor Day,

$50 adults, $25 children 12 and under) takes passengers to Rock Cut to view the evening colors.

In the winter, visitors can create a customized sightseeing itinerary that includes a trip along the open portion of Trail Ridge Road (as far as Many Parks Curve). Inquire about the On-Demand: Winter Time Wonders Bus Tour ($250 up to 4 adults, $50 additional adult, $25 additional child age 12 and under) when you call.

Yellow Wood Guiding's (tours@ywguiding.com, www.ywguiding.com, $180-510) tours include transportation in a luxury SUV with a panoramic moonroof. Owner Jared Gricoskie is available to run private tours for up to four guests daily throughout the park, including on Trail Ridge Road (when it is open). His customizable tours range from photography to hiking to sightseeing. Water and snacks are included; park admission must be paid separately. Outings last 3.5-8 hours.

Wild Side 4x4 Tours (970/586-8687, www.wildside4x4.com, $55 adults, $34 children) SUVs turn heads because they are so unique. Open-air tours are offered in customized 4x4 vehicles with giant window panels that flip out and up. This family-owned business offers a Top of the World Tour (9am-12:30pm or 1pm-4:30pm) that takes passengers up Old Fall River Road and back on Trail Ridge Road. The emphasis of the 3.5-hour tour is photography. Snacks and water are included; park admission is not included. Tours are offered when Trail Ridge Road and Old Fall River Road are open.

Bicycle Tours

New Venture Cycling (970/231-2736, www.newventurecycling.com, June-Oct.) offers three different bike tours for participants age 12 and older. On the 29-mile Trail Ridge East tour (7:30am-11:30am, $80), riders whiz down Trail Ridge Road, stopping at several viewpoints, and enjoying an alfresco lunch in Horseshoe Park. Bikes, helmets, water, and snacks are included in the price; park admission is not included.

The Trail Ridge West tour (7:30am-2:30pm, $125) is a full-day, 23-mile endeavor due to the drive time from Estes Park to the start point (Gore Range Overlook) plus the drive from the Grand Lake Entrance Station back to Estes Park. Tours include multiple stops along Highway 34/Trail Ridge Road, including a midday meal at the Holzwarth Historic Site. The Old Fall River Road tour (7:30am-11:30am, $80) is 17 miles in length, and is offered when the park allows bicycle access to Old Fall River Road (usually spring and/or fall).

Photography Tours

For instruction on night sky photography, consider signing up for a Digital Night Landscape Photography Workshop with **Glenn Randall Photography** (303/499-3009, www.glennrandall.com, June or Aug., $395). Participants head up Trail Ridge Road after dusk and learn how to take stunning shots of the Milky Way. These workshops sell out well in advance.

Hiking Tours

Wildland Trekking (800/715-4453, www.wildlandtrekking.com) offers several guided day hikes that embark from trailheads on Old Fall River Road and Trail Ridge Road. Destinations include Mount Chiquita and Mount Ida. Rates vary depending on group size; for a party of two, a day hike runs $215 per person.

Driving Tour

Trail Ridge Road stretches 48 miles from the Grand Lake Entrance Station on the west side of the park to the Fall River Entrance Station on the east side. **Old Fall River Road** is located north of Trail Ridge Road; traffic runs one-way (east to west) for 9 miles. Each road has its own unique flavor, and both should be explored during a visit to the region.

Most people enter the park at the Beaver Meadows Entrance Station or Fall River Entrance Station where they drive **west** on **Old Fall River Road,** stop at the Alpine

Trail Ridge Road's Stone Walls

At various spots along Trail Ridge Road, neat, attractive stacks of stones serve as guard walls. **The Civilian Conservation Corps** (CCC)—crews of young men that worked all over the park in the early 1930s to improve trail and road systems—created these masonry walls. In other national parks throughout the country, you can find similar stonework that has been attributed to CCC workers. These laborers were typically physically fit but unskilled, and were directed in their work by professional stonemasons. After many decades, some of the rockwork inevitably crumbled and fell into a state of disrepair, prompting the park service to rehabilitate the walls in recent years. The process is a painstaking one—the walls are carefully taken apart, and each rock is numbered so workers can keep track of the order in which they were originally laid. The walls are then rebuilt exactly the way they were found.

repairing Trail Ridge Road's walls

Visitor Center, and then head back **east** on **Trail Ridge Road.** This drive can take **2-4 hours,** depending on the stops. While there are many sights to see along this abbreviated driving tour, a better plan is to get an early start and explore the full length of Trail Ridge Road. The same recommendation holds true for visitors coming from the west side via the Grand Lake Entrance Station—drive the entire 48 miles (one-way) if you can. Plan to set aside **one full day** to drive Trail Ridge Road in its entirety. You will want to stop at a number of sights and possibly spend some time in Grand Lake or Estes Park. Plan your driving tour for early or late on a **weekday** rather than the weekend to avoid traffic.

Many of the sights along Trail Ridge Road are just a short distance walk from your vehicle, so much can be accomplished in one day. On the **must-see list** are Milner Pass/The Continental Divide, the Alpine Visitor Center, the Tundra Communities Trail, Forest Canyon Overlook, and Many Parks Curve.

Strapped for time? If you can only pop out of your car to see one sight on Old Fall River Road, make it **Chasm Falls.** On Trail Ridge Road, take the time to walk up and down the **Tundra Communities Trail;** you'll be glad you did.

Two excellent self-guided tour booklets are available at Rocky's visitor centers, the *Guide to Trail Ridge Road* and the *Guide to Old Fall River Road* ($2 each). The Trail Ridge Road guide features write-ups about 12 sights that correlate with numbered signs along the road. The Old Fall River Road self-guided tour is organized by mileage and can be easily followed by resetting your trip odometer at the start of the one-way road. Both guides are published by the Rocky Mountain Conservancy.

Sights

FALL RIVER AREA

★ Alluvial Fan

In 1982, a ruptured dam forever changed the landscape of the park and created a massive deposit of debris that is now a major attraction for visitors. The Lawn Lake Dam was 79 years old when it burst and sent 29 million gallons of water down the Roaring River, through Horseshoe Park, and into Estes Park. Three lives were lost in the flood and many tons of boulders, trees, gravel, and sand were swept downhill before settling in this spot in a fan-shape. Needless to say, plants and animals were markedly affected. This section of the park was mercilessly pummeled a second time by natural forces during the Colorado Flood of 2013. A new wave of debris and sediment piled on top of the first, causing devastation to the area. A half-buried sign at the West Alluvial Fan parking lot is a reminder of that devastation.

Today, an altogether different-looking **Alluvial Fan** is as popular as ever. People enjoy lounging on the rocks and dipping their toes in areas of shallow water. A two-mile out-and-back **trail** provides a great vantage point for **Horseshoe Falls,** a cascade that tumbles over the damaged area. Two parking lots, the East Alluvial Fan Parking Lot and West Alluvial Fan Parking Lot, provide visitors access to the fan.

From the Beaver Meadows Entrance Station, drive northwest on Highway 36. At Deer Ridge Junction, continue north on Highway 34. Take a left at the sign for Old Fall River Road and head west along Endovalley Road. The Alluvial Fan will be on your right, approximately 5.4 miles from your starting point.

★ Sheep Lakes

Nothing stops traffic in the park more than a herd of elk in a meadow . . . except maybe a herd of bighorn sheep crossing Highway 34 to visit **Sheep Lakes.** In the spring and early summer, bighorns regularly trek down from higher elevations to visit this spot just a few miles in from the Fall River Entrance Station. The area is a natural mineral lick, with soils rich in sodium, iron, zinc, and

When the Lawn Lake Dam broke in 1982, debris swept along by water created the Alluvial Fan.

magnesium—nutrients that are depleted in sheep during the long winter months and during pregnancy. In small groups or sometimes solo, bighorns will descend from a nearby ridge and travel over the highway to lick minerals around the lake before returning to their home base.

Bighorns are especially unique for having their own volunteer support staff in the park called the Bighorn Brigade. In the past, researchers have studied the sheep's travel over busy Highway 34, and concluded that crossing guards were needed to ensure safe and successful visits to the lake. As you pass by the lakes, do not stop your vehicle, follow any directions given by crossing guards, park only in the **Sheep Lakes parking lot,** and observe these interesting creatures from a distance.

Typically, sheep only visit the area once or twice a day for a few hours at a time, between the hours of 9am and 3pm—but don't hold them to any particular schedule. Mid-June, precious lambs make an appearance. Check in with the Sheep Lakes Information Station next to the parking lot to get the latest scoop.

From the Fall River Entrance Station, drive 1.9 miles west on Highway 34 to the Sheep Lakes parking lot.

Horseshoe Park

The western corner of **Horseshoe Park** is where the official dedication ceremony of Rocky was held on September 4, 1915. That choice may have, in part, been dictated by the need to accommodate the large group assembled on that day, but probably more so by the beauty of this particular area of the park. Fall River cuts a path through this expansive, glacier-carved meadow, which is a great place to view the Mummy Range to the north.

Today, this park framed by moraines is devoid of buildings, but at one time a large lodge was located here called the Horseshoe Inn. The multistoried lodge, which could accommodate more than 100 guests, operated from 1907 until 1931 when it was purchased by the park and eventually demolished.

Two varieties of four-legged mammals are among the main reasons people love to visit Horseshoe Park today. **Elk** meander through this montane meadow year-round, and in the fall, this is a great spot to view the animals' mating rituals. In the summer, **bighorn sheep** have a proclivity for hanging out at Sheep Lakes, located on the northern edge of Horseshoe Park. Little Horseshoe Park, which sits south of the "main" Horseshoe Park, was once a tent city that housed hundreds of workers from the Civilian Conservation Corps (CCC).

From the Fall River Entrance Station, drive west for 1.9 miles on Highway 34 to the parking lot for Sheep Lakes; there are good views of Horseshoe Park from this location. There is also a pullout for Horseshoe Park at 2.3 miles west on Highway 34, a parking lot for West Horseshoe Park at 2.7 miles from the entrance station, and another parking lot located 3.4 miles from the entrance.

★ OLD FALL RIVER ROAD

There is a fantastic black-and-white photograph from 1926 of a tourist caravan puttering along **Old Fall River Road.** Men and women clad in coats and hats are beaming at the camera as their convertible Pierce-Arrow touring cars wind their way up to higher elevations. The road appears relatively dry, but bright white snow piled many feet high on both sides starkly contrasts with the group's line of black cars. What a thrill it must have been back then to travel on the park's first automobile route. Until Old Fall River Road was built, anyone who wanted to get up and over the Continental Divide had to do so on foot or horseback. Before early settlers arrived, Native Americans used a unique type of dog sled called a travois to carry heavy loads over the Continental Divide. While the dogs surely made the trip less burdensome, there's no denying the physical exertion required to traverse these mountains.

The building of Old Fall River Road actually predates the opening of Rocky, with workers first putting tools to earth in July 1913. The

Civilian Conservation Corps

A conservation program initiated by then-President Franklin D. Roosevelt while our nation was in the throes of economic depression vastly improved Rocky's visitor experience and facilities. The Civilian Conservation Corps, better known by its acronym—the CCC—rapidly went from idea to reality in a matter of weeks after President Roosevelt took office. The idea was to provide work experience and a paycheck to young men age 18-25 that may have otherwise wallowed in unemployment, and at the same time, improve and conserve U.S. lands. Rocky was home to five CCC camps over nearly a decade (1933-1942).

The first in the park—and the first to pop up west of the Mississippi River, for that matter—was located in **Horseshoe Park.** Living quarters for laborers resembled an Army camp, with basic cots for sleeping, sheltered by canvas tents. Workers were outfitted in matching uniforms. They worked full days and were permitted recreation and leisure time in the evenings. The list of contributions the CCC made to Rocky is long and quite astounding. Laborers built and maintained miles of trails in the park, constructed footbridges, sprayed and chopped down beetle-infested trees (yes, it was a problem back in the 1930s, too), planted hundreds of trees, built amphitheaters, improved campgrounds, and transformed the Moraine Park Discovery Center from a guest lodge into a museum. They fought fires, installed utility lines under Trail Ridge Road, and were even enlisted to help with Search and Rescue (SAR) operations. Though the CCC was eventually dissolved during World War II, historians reflect on so many positive outcomes from the development of this young labor force. It built men's self-esteem, gave them job skills, and improved our nation's public lands. The CCC served as an important model for all government workforce conservation programs that followed it.

plan was to create a road that would stretch from Grand Lake to Estes Park. The road would follow old Arapaho trails across the Continental Divide. Initially, state penitentiary workers were enlisted to build the road, and they lived in a cluster of cabins and tents nearby. After a year or so, contract workers from Larimer and Grand Counties took over. Progress was painfully slow, not because of the abilities of the work crew, but due to politics and conflicts between project leaders. When all was said and done, the road finally opened in September 1920.

Back then, Old Fall River Road was a more rough-and-tumble version of Trail Ridge Road. It featured steep grades, mud holes, and more than a dozen switchbacks that were difficult for cars to navigate. Add to this the fact that the road accommodated traffic going in both directions, and you had yourself an adventure. Visibility around certain corners was poor, and visitors were advised to beep their horn liberally when approaching sharp turns. There are stories of people backing up especially steep sections of the road, because their vehicles were more powerful when run in reverse. Sometimes cars couldn't make it up the steep parts at all. Other cars got stuck in snowbanks. The area was prone to avalanches. The risks were many.

The road served its purpose for a time, but only several years after its completion park officials were already envisioning an even better route across the Divide. Trail Ridge Road, completed in 1932, incorporated some of the original Old Fall River Road, but was wider and featured many improvements over the old route. The unused stretch of Old Fall River Road was off-limits to visitors until 1968, when it reopened. Today, Old Fall River Road consists of 9 miles of dirt road.

Start the Drive

Old Fall River Road is a **narrow, 15-mph** road traveling **one-way** from **east to west.** The road **opens July 4** and **closes at first snowfall** (closed through winter). From the **Fall River Entrance Station,** drive 2 miles

Driving Old Fall River Road is an unforgettable experience.

west along Highway 34 and turn right (northwest) onto Endovalley Road. (The road is not marked as Endovalley Road, though this is the name used by park staff. Instead, look for a road sign at this junction for Old Fall River Road and the Endovalley Picnic Area.) Endovalley Road is paved and the traffic is two-way from Horseshoe Park to Endovalley for approximately 1.8 miles until the clearly marked entrance to one-way Old Fall River Road. To reach Old Fall River Road from the **Beaver Meadows Entrance Station,** drive 3 miles north on Highway 36 to Deer Ridge Junction. Then take Highway 34 for 1.7 miles to the turnoff for Old Fall River Road.

Bring along a sweater and jacket. For every 1,000 feet in elevation gain, the temperature on average decreases by 3.6°F, and the air pressure also drops by 1 inch of mercury. When air is less dense, it is generally colder.

For example, if you take a morning hike on Lumpy Ridge and in the trailhead parking lot the temperature is 70°F, you will be at one of the lower points of the park at 7,852 feet in elevation. If you then drive all the way to the top of Trail Ridge Road to 12,183 feet in elevation, the temperature could be 55°F or even cooler. I have witnessed a temperature drop of more than 20 degrees just from Deer Ridge Junction to the Forest Canyon Overlook.

Chasm Falls

MILE 1.4

A short, downhill path leads to this picturesque waterfall, located 1.4 miles from the start of Old Fall River Road. **Chasm Falls** is one of the most elegant waterfalls in the park, spilling roughly 25 feet down between two narrow walls of granite and swirling into a pretty froth before rejoining Fall River. There is a fenced viewing platform at the bottom of the trail, or visitors can clamber down a set of rocks for a slightly different perspective. A sign at the start of the trail warns hikers of swiftly moving water at the falls, and wading or playing in the dangerous water. In the Chasm Falls parking area, there are only spots for about 15 vehicles. If you arrive mid-morning or midday, you might miss your chance to see the falls if those spaces are all full. **Arrive in the early morning** or **later in the day** for the best chance to secure a parking space.

Miner Bill

At around 3 miles along Old Fall River Road, it is possible to take an adventurous trek up the side of **Mt. Chapin** to the spot of an old mine. **William Currence,** better known as "Miner Bill," sought gold in these parts, but was never successful in extracting any ore. He constructed several oddly shaped cabins for himself along Old Fall River Road, which he called the Snowshoe Cabin and the Hackmandy, and was at one point kicked out of the park for not obtaining the proper permits to build.

Bill was known to be eccentric and a rule bender. He illegally constructed fencing on Old Fall River Road and charged tourists to drive along the road and camp, acts that resulted in his arrest. Currence's cabins were removed in the 1950s, but his small mine and random historical artifacts remain on the side of the mountain.

Getting to the mine involves some route-finding: Park at the pullout nearest to mile marker 3 (40.424613, -105.702944). A few yards past the sign is a small clearing where Miner Bill's cabins use to be. From this point, the route-finding begins; you will need to head straight up the side of Mt. Chapin and look for a faded trail that was created by Bill himself. (The park does not maintain the trail, so it's easy to lose your way.) As you trek, your main order of business is to get near **Currence Spire,** an impressive, slender rock formation that was named after Mr. Currence. The mine is located no more than 0.25 mile northwest of the spire (40.428814, -105.701007). All that is left is a small tunnel in the granite that is not very tall or very deep.

In addition to the mine, hikers may find old artifacts from Bill's mining days, such as logs with old nails and hinges attached. The hike is not very long, but trudging up the steep mountainside is slow-going; those who want to attempt the trek should allow at least **three hours** to get to the mine and back. Bring along a hiking partner and a map, compass, and/or GPS unit.

Gabions
MILE 3.8

In an effort to protect Old Fall River Road and the surrounding landscape from erosion and slides, the park relies on an age-old civil engineering method: the use of **gabions** (French for "big cage"). At 3.8 miles, you won't miss what appear to be long staircases erected on the side of road. The "stairs" are made up of many individual wire cages filled with rocks that are secured together to form a retaining wall. The park first installed gabions in 1967. Up until that point, laborers had spent many spring seasons conducting extensive repairs on the road; they ultimately closed the road for a period after a major landslide in 1953. The gabions provide relief from some of the undesirable side effects of spring runoff, and effectively hold back sodden soil. The history of gabions dates back thousands of years with an earlier, more natural version (willow baskets instead of wire) once used on the banks of the Nile River. In the present day, they are used for erosion control, flood control, and even to create architectural interest around a home.

Fall River Cirque
MILE 8.5

On the last leg of the drive, the landscape opens up to reveal a stunning cirque. Glacial-formed **Fall River Cirque** is the headwaters for the Fall River. There are no remnants of actual glaciers here, but snow tends to collect and stick around in this bowl-like formation for the better part of the year. The **Alpine Visitor Center** (Trail Ridge Rd. and Old Fall River Rd., 970/586-1206, 9am-5pm daily summer, 10:30am-4:30pm daily spring and fall) is perched on the rim of the cirque at Fall River Pass and is the end point for your drive along Old Fall River Road.

TRAIL RIDGE ROAD

It must have been demoralizing for those who built Old Fall River Road to learn that a

What's in a Name?

A story lies behind every named feature in Rocky. Some place-names come from the time of early homesteaders, such as **Sprague Lake** in the Bear Lake region, named for homesteader Albert Sprague. Other spots, like the **Ute Trail** on Trail Ridge Road, were named by native peoples or derived from Ute or Arapaho words. In the early 1900s, Arapaho elders spent several weeks traveling throughout Rocky on horseback with members of the Colorado Mountain Club recounting old tales and providing names of features that had been passed along from their predecessors. Today, several dozen park features carry names of Native American origin.

Trail Ridge Road's numerous pullouts and scenic viewpoints have great names, and you might think that park officials sat around for days or weeks mulling over lists of possible descriptors. However, although bureaucracy was involved in other aspects of the planning and construction of the road, naming was not one of them. Naming these viewpoints was a completely last-minute affair. It was only the night before the road's opening that two early park naturalists took this task upon themselves, driving along the road and arbitrarily coming up with good descriptors for sights. Though conjured up rather hastily, the road's monikers stuck and were used from there on out.

new-and-improved thoroughfare was being envisioned just a few years after the route was completed. But Old Fall River Road was far from perfect and posed numerous safety issues; action needed to be taken. In part, the Good Roads Movement helped to transform the idea of **Trail Ridge Road** into a reality. This political movement of the late 1800s and early 1900s was originally launched so that better roads across the United States would be built for both social and economic reasons. The Good Roads Movement put pressure on the government to create a national network of roads and preceded the National Highway System. While Old Fall River Road was built by the state of Colorado, Larimer County, and Grand County, Trail Ridge Road was a federally funded and supported endeavor.

As planners envisioned Trail Ridge Road, they thought of it not just as a way to get from point A to point B, but as a drive that would showcase some of the area's most significant natural attractions. The chosen route would travel east to west just south of Old Fall River Road, roughly following the Native Americans' Ute Trail, which still exists as a hiking trail along Trail Ridge Road. Some nonnegotiables for the road: it needed to be wider than Old Fall River Road and it needed to be paved to allow smoother, safer automobile travel. Construction began on the road in 1929. Workers were subjected to sometimes miserable conditions: cold temperatures, precipitation, wind, and thin air. In 1932, the road was completed and opened to traffic. Travelers delighted in the road's splendid scenery and were pleased to note that travel was much less harsh than on Old Fall River Road.

Today this "wonder" road, as it was sometimes referred to back in the day, is traveled by hundreds of thousands of visitors each year and is a highlight of any park visit.

Start the Drive

Trail Ridge Road typically opens by **Memorial Day** and is drivable until **mid-late October.** However, the higher portions of the **two-lane road** can close at any time due to snow. There are a couple of options to get on Trail Ridge Road (Hwy. 34) from the east side of the park. From the Beaver Meadows Entrance Station, drive north 3 miles to the junction of Highway 34 and Highway 36—known as Deer Ridge Junction—and turn west to get on Trail Ridge Road. Alternatively, you can get on Trail Ridge Road immediately after entering via the Fall

River Entrance Station. The starting point for this driving tour is Deer Ridge Junction.

Abandoned Beaver Ponds

MILE 1.8

Beavers closed up shop at this location some time ago, but it's still a wonderful spot for a short stroll or a picnic lunch. A boardwalk leads out to a seating area, where you can view Hidden Valley Creek meandering through lush vegetation. You will not see any cute, orange-toothed dam-builders at this location, though it is suspected that they might return someday to rebuild. In the meantime, other wildlife are frequent visitors to these wetlands; one evening at sundown I discovered a moose there, snuggled up in the grass, minding its own business.

The **Beaver Ponds** are marked on the park's map, but there is no sign along the road. Keep an eye out for a pullout on the right (north) side of the road. You'll see the start of the boardwalk not far from the curb.

Hidden Valley

MILE 2.4

Of the lodges and buildings that have been part of Rocky's past, many have been demolished or removed but still remain in people's memories. Perhaps no other park feature is more mourned than **Hidden Valley Ski Resort,** which operated from 1955 until 1991. Consisting of a ski hill, a toboggan run, an ice-skating rink, and a lodge, Hidden Valley was a full-fledged resort, even if it was small at just 1,200 acres.

Two different families ran the resort before the Estes Park Recreation District took over in later years. The National Park Service was initially supportive of the resort, but the writing was on the wall in 1976 when a National Park Service (NPS) master plan revealed that "some removal of facilities are in order." The rationale for the eventual closure was that a busy developed area such as ski resort was in direct conflict with the goals of a national park. It took another decade and a half for the lifts to stop running for good.

Proponents of Hidden Valley say that the resort provided strong benefits: a healthy outlet for physical activity for both kids and adults, and a tourism draw and social hub for Estes Park and Rocky in the winter. Indeed, archival photos from the resort during this time period show a ski hill swarming with skiers grinning from ear to ear. Locals fiercely loved their home mountain.

There are still plenty of folks around town who can recall the resort's heyday, and their stories are often tinged with sadness. Documentarian Brian Brown captures this element of loss well in his 2013 documentary, *Ski Hidden Valley Estes Park*. Though backcountry skiing is still an option at Hidden Valley, the lack of lifts and groomed trails means that many novice to intermediate skiers either don't ski here at all or drive to Eldora Mountain Resort in the town of Nederland (roughly an hour away from Estes Park) to engage in the sport.

When the weather is warm, Hidden Valley is generally busy with two kinds of visitors: young children taking part in activities at the **Junior Ranger Headquarters,** located in a small building next to the parking lot, and picnickers. There is a short 0.5-mile **interpretive trail** that starts behind Hidden Valley's buildings and makes a loop around Hidden Valley Creek. Eleven **picnic tables** are up for grabs. In the winter, Hidden Valley is busy with the **sledding** set and backcountry skiers.

★ Many Parks Curve

MILE 4

At **Many Parks Curve,** visitors gain a great view of numerous parks, or wide mountain meadows, within the boundaries of Rocky. Upper Beaver Meadows, Horseshoe Park, Moraine Park, and a portion of Endovalley are visible from this overlook, as well as the lengthy moraines that rise up next to these lush meadows. A long boardwalk along the bend in the road invites visitors to leave their cars and gaze over the wide expanse of land below. There is also a small rocky outcropping next to the boardwalk that people enjoy scrambling up to take photos. When winter comes, this is as high on Trail Ridge Road as visitors can go on the east side of the park before having to turn around.

Rainbow Curve

MILE 8

The prospect of traveling up Trail Ridge Road is thrilling for some, anxiety inducing for others. This stop offers a happy medium for those whose nerves are rattled by steep drop-offs and absent guardrails. At 10,829 feet in elevation, **Rainbow Curve** offers dramatic views, but the road is mostly tame (until just past this parking lot). Many folks who are apprehensive about Trail Ridge Road choose this as a **turnaround point,** but leave feeling satisfied that they were still able to see something remarkable. Sometimes that is a showy rainbow appearing to the east; other times it is a group of bighorn sheep gathering in Horseshoe Park below. This is a particularly great vantage point for checking out the Alluvial Fan at the north end of Horseshoe Park. Look to the west and you will see Sundance Mountain, which has an easily visible glacial cirque on its east face.

★ Forest Canyon Overlook

MILE 10.9

With stunning peaks all around, the last thing you might think to do at the **Forest Canyon Overlook** is look down near your feet—but make a point to anyway. A geologic phenomenon called "patterned ground" is noticeable just beyond the edges of this viewpoint's easy paved trail and is the result of a continual freezing and thawing cycle found only in locations above tree line. The shapes you see are rock fragments thrust above the soil into interesting patterns. A pathway of roughly 600 feet will take you to the overlook, an attractive rock wall perched atop a knoll that provides a nice semi-shelter on windy days. Views of glacier-formed Forest Canyon are spectacular. An interpretive sign will help you identify specific landmarks, including pointy Hayden Spire rising above Hayden Gorge, and broad Terra Tomah Mountain. In the rocks around the base of the overlook, marmot sightings are all but guaranteed. Take care to stay on the

Perch on the platform at Many Parks Curve and take in the views.

Forest Canyon Overlook

walking path, since this location is designated as a **Tundra Protection Area.**

Rock Cut

MILE 12.8

As if constructing a thoroughfare above the tree line weren't difficult enough, one rocky outcropping posed a significant challenge to construction workers during the process of building Trail Ridge Road. Using a large amount of explosives, workers had to clear enough rock in this location so that cars would be able to pass through. This was one of—if not the most—difficult sections of the road to prepare before it opened to automobile traffic in 1932 because of the heavy labor involved and the ever-variable weather conditions above the tree line. Laborers also went to great lengths to protect the surrounding landscape during blasting operations, constructing crude barricades out of wood. Any rocks that went flying beyond these barriers had to be collected and returned to the work site.

Rock Cut is mostly a feature to be admired as you drive through it; it also looks impressive from points on Trail Ridge Road. The Rock Cut parking lot is used primarily by those exploring the **Tundra Communities Trail.** Good **wildlife viewing** (elk and bighorn sheep) is possible from the side of the road opposite the trailhead. If you look southwest from this location on clear day, you can spot a series of appealing tiered lakes in the distance called **Gorge Lakes.** There are no official trails to these bodies of water that sit high on rock benches. (To get to this section of the park you need a map, good route-finding abilities, technical skills, and stamina.) For most people, it is enjoyable enough to view the landscape from Trail Ridge Road.

Another important feature at this location is a small, fenced-off plot of land on the other side of the sidewalk at Rock Cut (next to the restrooms) that was used by the late alpine botanist Beatrice Willard to study the tundra. Willard was the co-author of a groundbreaking book published in 1972 called *The Land Above the Trees;* she significantly influenced how the park has managed and protected its tundra over the years. A second, similar tundra study area is found at the **Forest Canyon Overlook.** Both sites were added to the National Register of Historic Places in 2007.

Lava Cliffs

MILE 15

A common misconception is that the **Lava Cliffs** were once the site of an active volcano. Not so. Experts have determined that this unique rock formation is actually the result of volcanic activity that occurred farther west in the Never Summer Mountains more than 20 million years ago. The cliffs are made up of volcanic ash that flowed from afar, settled, and hardened into rock. This feature is usually a fairly brief stop for tourists, avid **bird-watchers** being the exception. Cavity-nesting birds such as swallows love the many nooks and crannies of the cliffs and are often spotted here.

★ Alpine Tundra

Tundra is an ecosystem in the park that starts at 11,000-11,500 feet in elevation. Rocky is noted for having the largest expanse of tundra in the lower 48 states, with about one-third of the park located above the tree line. About **11 miles of Trail Ridge Road** are entirely above the tree line: On the east side of the park, the alpine tundra starts approximately **0.5 mile west of Rainbow Curve;** on the west side of the park, the trees disappear approximately **1.5 miles east of Milner Pass.**

The tundra is fascinating to explore from an ecological perspective, but it also evokes a range of emotions. Standing out in the wailing wind being pelted by tiny balls of hail, you might feel invigorated, fearful, humbled, speechless, or renewed. Being on the tundra is like arriving on another planet that is untamed, seemingly desolate, unforgiving, and strangely beautiful all at once.

Renowned scientist Beatrice Willard advises in her book *Land Above the Trees: A Guide to American Alpine Tundra* to get down low while above the tree line—crouch or plant yourself on all fours, even—to fully appreciate the unique selection of plants and organisms that have adapted to survive in Rocky's harsh weather. While the tundra is big and showy in one sense, its vegetation—which includes sedges, grasses, cushion plants, and lichen—is small and low to the ground. Even flowers are often dwarfed, with stems and leaves smaller than those you will find on plants at lower elevations. Only a select group of mammals can survive at high elevation, and have it in their constitution to withstand conditions considered harsh for humans. Pikas, for example, find shelter in rock piles, and with great fortitude collect food for months in the summer in anticipation of a long and tough winter ahead. When the snow comes, they burrow underground and patiently wait out months of cold temperatures until the grasses grow and they can gather nourishment once again.

Above the tree line, I often feel tremendous gratitude for the basics: food, water, and shelter. See if you feel the same.

TUNDRA PROTECTION AREAS

While tundra vegetation can stand up to remarkably harsh weather conditions, it has a tough time regenerating when disturbed by humans. Around some of Trail Ridge Road's most popular trails and viewpoints, adverse impacts have been noted in spots where many thousands of people have stepped off the pavement or trail. These areas are now designated Tundra Protection Areas by the park, and officials are keeping a close eye on how and when the vegetation and soil return to a natural, healthy state.

Tundra Protection Areas are located near the **Forest Canyon Overlook, Rock Cut, Gore Range Overlook, Alpine Visitor Center,** the **Tundra Communities Trail,** and the **Alpine Ridge Trail.** On all other parts of the tundra that are not designated Tundra Protection Areas, tread gently on the earth, and walk in a dispersed manner—not single file or in a tightly knit pack.

Gore Range Overlook
MILE 16

On a clear day, the main attraction at this stop are eye-popping views of nearby and faraway peaks, including the Gore Range and the Never Summer Mountains. The Gore Range is a 60-mile stretch of impressive, jutting peaks located approximately 50 miles southwest of the park. Just under a mile southeast of the overlook is the highest point on Trail Ridge Road at 12,183 feet. The **Gore Range Overlook** is still very high at 12,018 feet. There are no big signs at the overlook, just a small interpretive sign. Simply pull over at the parking area located between the Alpine Visitor Center and the Lava Cliffs, get out, and enjoy the scenery.

★ Alpine Visitor Center
MILE 16.9

The highest national park visitor center in the country is the **Alpine Visitor Center** (Trail

Ridge Rd. and Old Fall River Rd., 970/586-1206, 9am-5pm daily summer, 10:30am-4:30pm daily spring and fall), positioned on Fall River Pass at a head-spinning 11,796 feet above sea level. The concept of the national park visitor center was born in the mid-1950s. From 1955 to 1966, architects designed and built nearly 100 visitor centers as part of a federally sponsored national parks improvement program called Mission 66. The Alpine Visitor Center was the first Mission 66 visitor center in the park (preceding The Beaver Meadows Visitor Center and Kawuneeche Visitor Center by two and three years respectively). Construction started on this building in May 1963 and its doors first opened to guests in June 1965 as part of Rocky's 50th anniversary celebration.

The structure is designed to withstand extreme weather conditions that are typical at this elevation. Heavy logs crisscross the roof to prevent shingles from flying off in high winds. A diesel generator is the sole source of power for the center, and sewage must be hauled down the road daily during the summer. In the winter, the building is unused for around seven months.

For travelers along Trail Ridge Road, this building is a welcome sight when wild winds blow or snow flurries start tumbling out of the sky. Inside are restrooms, a Rocky Mountain Conservancy gift store, educational displays, and large picture windows with stunning views of the headwaters of the Fall River, Ypsilon, Chiquita, and Chapin Mountains, and numerous other landmarks. Rangers field many altitude-related questions, and are a great resource if you suspect you are feeling adverse effects from the thin air. They are also vigilant about tracking weather conditions and will warn visitors if lightning and thunder are imminent in the area.

The **Trail Ridge Store** (www.trailridgegiftstore.com) and the **Café in the Clouds** (9am-5:30pm daily late June-Aug., 10am-4:30pm daily late May-June and late Aug.-mid-Oct.) are located just steps away in a separate building. A short but steep hike up the Alpine Ridge Trail, aka "Huffer's Hill," begins next to the parking lot and is worth the heavy breathing involved. Visitors are rewarded with outstanding views of the surrounding mountains at the top.

Medicine Bow Curve

MILE 17.3

From the **Medicine Bow Curve** pullout on a clear day, some of the peaks of the 100-mile-long Medicine Bow Mountain Range are visible in the distance some 20 miles away.

The Snogo Snow Plow and Snow Removal

Every winter, the closed-off portion of Trail Ridge Road is encased in 20 feet (give or take) of snow. When the road first opened in 1932, a robust piece of machinery called the **Snogo Snow Plow** was used to remove all the white stuff in the spring. It continued to be the main source of snow removal until 1952, when it was given by Rocky Mountain National Park to the Town of Estes Park. In 1979, when the machine was no longer operational, it was returned to the park and for some time was put on display for visitors. There are few, if any, other Snogo Snow Plows left in the United States, and Rocky's made it onto the National Register of Historic Places as a "structure" with historical significance in the areas of transportation and engineering. Today the plow is still in the park; however, it is not on display.

Today snow removal on the road is still a mammoth task, and must, at times, feel like a Sisyphean feat for workers. Crews on the east and west sides of the park scoop and blow snow with heavy machinery for around six weeks, starting in mid-April. But eventually there is payoff: the plows meet in the middle, high atop Trail Ridge Road, and the job is complete. Crews work to have Trail Ridge Road open by Memorial Day, but an especially wet winter can mean a delayed opening.

(Wyoming is 35 miles away as the crow flies.) This stop also provides an excellent vantage point of the Cache la Poudre River. On the right side of the road (from the east) and before the number 9 sign—which corresponds to one of the stops in the park's self-guided Trail Ridge Road tour booklet—is what appears to be a park trail. This is a **social trail** that runs for about 100 yards and then peters out, but is a great place to spot ptarmigan and check out tundra flowers.

Poudre Lake and Cache la Poudre River

MILE 20.6

It is rare to hear a Coloradan refer to the **Cache la Poudre River** using proper French pronunciation. To most, it is simply known as "The Pooder." Likewise, its headwaters—Poudre Lake—also tend to be mispronounced. The full French name of the river translated means "hiding place for the powder" and was named by French trappers who, in 1836, were caught in a snowstorm and buried some of their items next to the river. Gunpowder was among their supplies. The following spring, they successfully retrieved their belongings, and the name was thereafter known as Cache la Poudre.

Poudre Lake is located at Milner Pass, just a short walk from the official Milner Pass/Continental Divide sign. From the lake, water narrows into the Cache la Poudre River, which flows east of the Continental Divide for 125 miles to the Great Plains. At times difficult to follow, a hiking trail follows the river and can be accessed north of Trail Ridge Road across from the lake (there is no trailhead sign, just the start of a path), or off of the Corral Creek Trail in the northeast corner of the park. In 1986, the Cache la Poudre River was designated a Wild and Scenic River. It is thoroughly enjoyed by recreationists, particularly boaters in areas outside of Rocky. At Poudre Lake, the primary source of recreation is **fishing.** Many visitors enjoy strolling over to this grass-ringed lake after taking an obligatory photo in front of the Milner Pass/Continental Divide sign.

wildflowers blooming on the Continental Divide

★ Milner Pass/ Continental Divide

MILE 21

At 10,759 feet elevation sits the **Milner Pass/Continental Divide** sign. The Continental Divide runs north to south the length of the park, but this is one of only two places in Rocky where you can slip out of your car and instantly stand on top of the Divide (the other spot is La Poudre Pass in the northwest corner of the park).

The Continental Divide creates two distinct drainages for snowmelt: one side drains into the Pacific Ocean and one side drains into the Atlantic Ocean. If you were to throw water over your left shoulder and then your right, theoretically that water would end up in two different oceans.

If you are inspired for a short hike along the Divide, jump on the trail at **Poudre Lake** and follow it 4 miles to Mt. Ida. This highly exposed hike should only be attempted in good weather, as some of the trail is rocky and challenging to follow.

Farview Curve

MILE 23.1

When the pine beetle epidemic was at its worst in the Kawuneeche Valley, people would pull over at this stop and shed tears over how ravaged the trees were. Photos from 2008 reveal a startling landscape of trees tinged in rust-red—a forest clearly not in optimal health. Today, the scenery is considerably more attractive. Now the focus lies on the **Kawuneeche Valley** below, which includes the Colorado River snaking its way through the valley's vibrant green meadows. Shift your gaze west and you will see two additional features of note: the Never Summer Mountains and the **Grand Ditch.** You might first mistake the Grand Ditch for a road carved into the mountainside, but it is actually a long canal used to divert snowmelt from the west side of the park to the east side.

NEVER SUMMER MOUNTAINS

The **Never Summer Mountains** are not frosted with a thick layer of snow year-round, as their name implies, but you can often see patches of white on the range's ridges and saddles in early August or later. Storms can hit this 10-mile-long range from the west, and snow subsequently dumps on the tops and east sides of the mountains. The east side of the mountains receive less solar radiation, since the sun is in the south during the hottest parts of the day, so snow naturally clings to these heights longer. Each of the range's peaks tops 12,000 feet; the tallest is Howard Mountain at 12,810 feet. Four of the range's 17 peaks were named after types of clouds: Mount Cumulus, Mount Stratus, Mount Nimbus, and Mount Cirrus. From various spots on Trail Ridge Road—particularly at the **Farview Curve** pullout—it is possible to get a great look of these peaks rising up to meet puffs of white in the sky.

To the west and south of the mountains is the **Never Summer Wilderness,** 21,090 acres of remote backcountry that does not get nearly as much publicity and fanfare as Rocky, but is enjoyed by many outdoor enthusiasts. From within Rocky, entry into the Never Summer Wilderness is possible via the **Bowen/Baker Trailhead.** In the winter, few people venture into the Never Summers; the main months of activity here are **July-September.** The Never Summers set themselves apart from all other mountains in the area, having been a volcanic hotbed of activity millions of years ago.

Recreation

Trails around Old Fall River Road and Trail Ridge Road offer extraordinary views and unforgettable experiences. Preparation is key before setting out on these hikes. Have a contingency plan ready for **wind, cold, thunderstorms, hail,** and **snow.** You'll need to be on-point with **hydration** even if you don't feel especially thirsty, which is often the case at high elevation. As you explore, pay close attention to Tundra Protection Area signs around Trail Ridge Road.

HIKING

Fall River Area

YPSILON LAKE

Distance: 8.4 miles round-trip
Duration: 5 hours
Elevation gain: 2,100 feet
Effort: moderate to strenuous
Trailhead: Lawn Lake on Endovalley Road (see map p. 126)

From the trailhead, start ascending northwest on the **Lawn Lake Trail.** As you get higher in elevation, great views unfold of Hidden

Ypsilon Lake

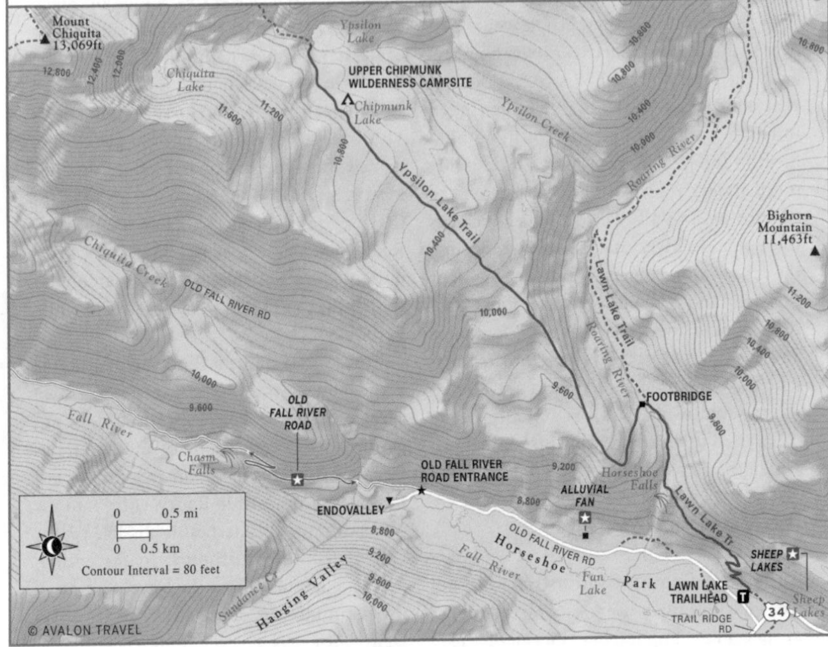

Valley, the Alluvial Fan, Trail Ridge Road, and Horseshoe Park. At approximately 1 mile, you'll get a good look at some of the damage caused by the **Lawn Lake Flood of 1982.** When a dam at Lawn Lake failed spectacularly, 29 million gallons of water rushed down into the valley, killing three people and causing major devastation in the park. Decades later, there is still a major scar on the earth in this location.

At 1.4 miles, a trail junction appears. Continue hiking northwest to Ypsilon Lake on the **Ypsilon Lake Trail.** Several minutes later, you will arrive at a **footbridge,** which crosses over the Roaring River. For several years this bridge was missing—the result of another natural disaster, the Colorado Flood of 2013. Suffice it to say, Ypsilon Lake Trail and the Lawn Lake Trail have sustained more damage than most other paths in the park over the years. For the next 2.4 miles, you will plod along through dense forest. Shortly before arriving at **Chipmunk Lake** (10,636 feet), the trail descends. This marshy lake—which is more of a pond than a lake—is unexpectedly delightful, and with Ypsilon Mountain rising majestically in the background, you might feel inclined to take some photos. A *Y* shape on the mountain is visible from the lake; this deeply cut couloir is the reason the mountain was named Ypsilon (the Greek word for the letter Y). A sign for **Upper Chipmunk wilderness campsite** appears shortly after; then you will descend for approximately 0.4 mile to **Ypsilon Lake** (10,522 feet). Take some time to admire the inflow of water to Ypsilon Lake, which is a captivating waterfall. Or, travel along a social trail that follows the edge of the lake before returning the way you came.

Always carry a detailed topographic map on hikes; this is important for safety reasons, and so you know what features to expect along a trail. Chipmunk Lake is not listed on the free park map, or on the trailhead sign. Because

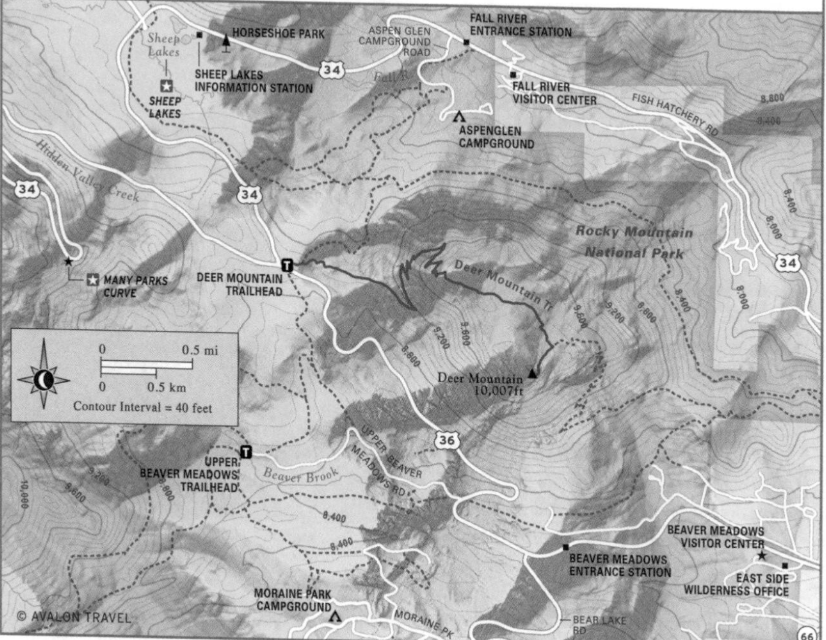

of this, some people mistake Chipmunk Lake for Ypsilon Lake, and never arrive at their intended destination.

DEER MOUNTAIN

Distance: 6.2 miles round-trip
Duration: 3 hours
Elevation gain: 1,083 feet
Effort: moderate
Trailhead: Deer Mountain, located at Deer Ridge Junction, at the intersection of Highways 34 and 36 (see map p. 127). Park along the side of the road.

The trek to the top of Deer Mountain is not excessively long or extremely steep; though more than one hiker has been guilty of cutting the trail's many switchbacks to shorten the journey. Do not be similarly tempted. Erosion, which is both unsightly and causes damage to vegetation and soil, is the main negative consequence of hiking straight up or down the mountain off-trail.

Almost immediately after jumping on the **Deer Mountain Trail,** you will see a sign with two choices: Aspenglen Campground or Deer Mountain Summit. Follow the **North Deer Mountain Trail** straight (southeast) to the summit. As you head up through a grassy open landscape dotted with trees, you will notice something that isn't typical on most of Rocky's trails: traffic noise from Highway 36 down below. It is not obnoxious though, and quickly becomes unnoticeable as you forge on up the mountain. Through the forest you will climb, switchback after switchback, for the first 2.2 miles or so. Then the trail flattens and surprisingly descends for roughly another 0.7 mile. At this point, a **spur trail** for the summit will appear; turn right (southwest) on the spur trail. The last 0.2-mile stretch is the steepest section of the trail but goes by quickly. You will finally arrive at a large, relatively flat summit with spectacular views. From the top you can see where Estes Park, Lake Estes, Moraine Park, the park entrance,

Glacier Basin Campground, and the YMCA of the Rockies are in relation to each other. There is not a summit register tucked into the rocks here, but you can snap a photo of the **USGS summit marker** as proof of your journey. You can return the way you came, or choose to circumnavigate the mountain on the Deer Mountain Trail and North Deer Mountain Trail. The circumnavigation option is 10.8 miles (round-trip) of hiking and should be planned for in advance.

on the Ute Trail

Trail Ridge Road

★ UTE TRAIL

Distance: 6 miles one-way
Duration: 4 hours
Elevation change: 3,500 feet
Effort: strenuous
Trailhead: Ute Trail, 1 mile east of Forest Canyon Overlook (see map p. 129)
Directions: From the Fall River Entrance Station, drive 14 miles west on Trail Ridge Road (Hwy. 34). There is not a traditional trailhead marker at this trailhead, just an interpretive sign. For this hike, a second vehicle parked at the Beaver Meadows Trailhead is necessary.

The sign at the start of the trail indicates that Ute and Arapaho tribes once traversed Trail Ridge Road and surrounding mountains in moccasins, a fact that might have you repeatedly shaking your head in wonder as you hike down 3,500 feet in elevation to Beaver Meadows in (hopefully) much sturdier shoes. Most people are content to hike an hour or so on the mellower first part of the trail and turn around, but if you choose to do the whole thing, you will be rewarded with solitude and a real thigh-burner of a workout. An even more strenuous way to do the hike is by starting at the Beaver Meadows Trailhead and ending on Trail Ridge Road.

From the **Ute Trail** interpretive sign, head uphill on a single-file-only trail carved into the tundra. On a clear day, unobstructed views of blue sky meeting with mountaintops are immediately magnificent. The trail eventually makes a gradual descent, passing by a large rock outcropping named **Tombstone Ridge** at around 1.5 miles. There are no surprises on the trail—just more great views for another 0.5 mile or so—until you descend to **Timberline Pass.** The pass is not specifically identified on the trail but is listed on topographical maps. At this point, the tundra turns to tree line and the trail becomes rocky and steep; it is time to bust out the **trekking poles** to save your knees. Not surprisingly, this is when most people **turn around.**

As you continue, the slog to the bottom feels relentless at times. The trail is often marked with **cairns** and travels through thick, wild forest for roughly 2 miles until finally opening up at **Ute Meadow,** a wilderness stock campsite for llamas. Continue hiking until you reach a **trailhead marker** with two possible paths arriving at the **Beaver Meadows Trailhead;** one is 3.5 miles and the other is 1.5 miles (I chose the latter). As you get closer to the end of your journey and find yourself in Beaver Meadows, the landscape becomes much softer and prettier and the parking lot is a welcome sight.

The Ute Trail is a path that indigenous

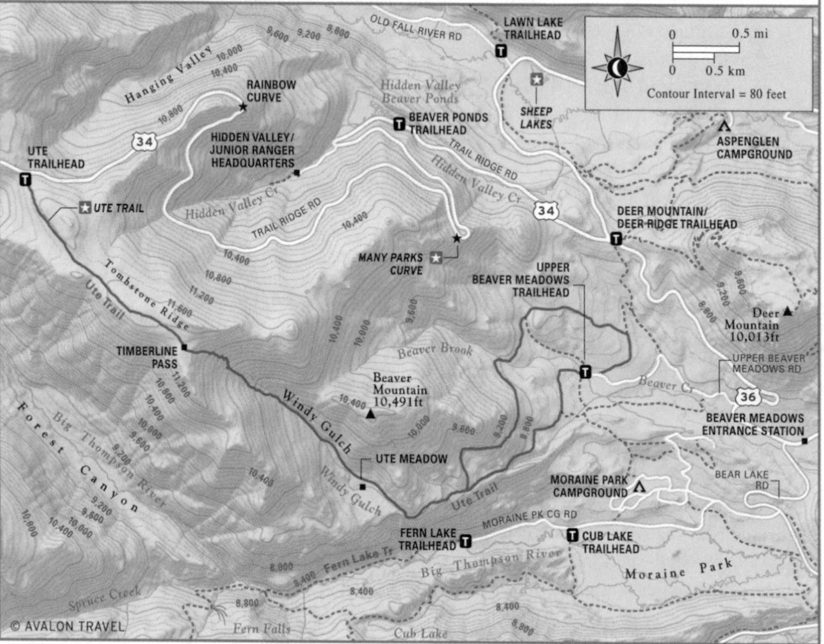

people used long ago to travel over the Continental Divide from Estes Park to Grand Lake. On maps, the trail is typically shown as two separate unconnected trails, labeled varyingly as Ute Trail, Ute Trail West and Ute Trail East, or Ute Crossing. If you wish to hike the entire 16.8-mile trail from Beaver Meadows to Farview Curve, you can, though it can be difficult to follow as the path becomes indistinct in more than one place. In addition to the Ute Trail hike, the other popular leg of the trail (sometimes referred to as Ute Trail West) runs from Milner Pass to the Alpine Visitor Center (4 mi).

★ TUNDRA COMMUNITIES TRAIL

Distance: 0.6 mile round-trip
Duration: 30 minutes
Elevation gain: 260 feet
Effort: easy
Trailhead: Rock Cut on Trail Ridge Road

A stroll on this paved trail can feel like exploring a different planet, with its wide-open, treeless landscape. While the tundra might seem stark and desolate, **interpretive signs** along the path tell a different story: one of vibrancy and life. Here you will find a rock garden community that supports various insects and animals, hardy flowers, marmots scurrying around, and white-tailed ptarmigans going about their business.

The trail climbs moderately to start, but levels out in roughly 0.25 mile. Be sure take a **spur trail** on your right to a set of unique mushroom-shaped rocks jutting from the earth. Points of interest on both sides of the main trail include sweeping views of mountains, cushion plants, and wildlife such as pikas. At the end of the hike, scramble up a section of rocks to find a peak finder and **plaque** dedicated to Roger Toll who served as superintendent of the park in the 1920s.

Apply sunscreen, pack layers, and gauge current weather conditions before starting out. If there are dark clouds present or moving in, choose another activity until the skies clear; finding shelter here in a lightning storm is next to impossible. Restrooms are located next to the parking lot.

While this trail is paved, it is not listed as an official wheelchair-accessible hike in park literature. The path isn't level, and there are some uneven spots/potholes to negotiate. However, some or all of the trail could be explored using a wheelchair, depending on the comfort level of the visitor.

ALPINE RIDGE TRAIL

Distance: 0.5 mile round-trip
Duration: 30 minutes
Elevation gain: 209 feet
Effort: easy to moderate
Trailhead: Alpine Ridge Trail, next to the Alpine Visitor Center

Bodies stream up and down this tundra trail, located near the **Alpine Visitor Center,** all day long. From the parking lot it might appear to be a relatively easy climb, but keep in mind the lofty starting elevation of 11,796 feet. This trail is often referred to informally as Heart Attack Hill or **Huffer's Hill** for reasons that quickly become obvious when making your way up. Even those in decent physical shape can find themselves laboring for breath after a few minutes of exertion.

The trailhead is located next to the Trail Ridge Store and Café building. The trail starts off paved, but eventually alternates between **pavement** and **steps** the remainder of the way. Though you might find yourself occupied with counting the seemingly endless amount of steps (as I did), make sure to divert your attention off-trail to look for blooming tundra flowers. A small circular paved **viewing area** is at the top; from here you can view snow-capped peaks in every direction. Take your picture next to the "Elevation 12,005 Feet Above Sea Level" sign and return to the parking lot the way you came. Give anyone who is huffing along in the other direction a few words of encouragement.

Huffer's Hill

LAKE IRENE

Distance: 0.8 mile round-trip
Duration: 30 minutes
Elevation gain: 60 feet
Effort: easy
Trailhead: Lake Irene Picnic Area, west of Milner Pass

Even though it is easy to reach, Lake Irene is never a mob scene in the same way that other easily accessible lakes (like Sprague and Bear) can be. To get here, head southwest on the **well-defined path** and descend through an attractive grassy meadow that is dotted with wildflowers in the summer. The lake quickly comes into view and you can choose to circle around either way on the mostly level trail.

To extend your journey a little farther, hike south to a marked **overlook.** You will find a peaceful view: a lush green meadow, trees, and mountains. Many people head to Lake Irene with fishing pole in-hand, but are disappointed to find that there are no fish in this body of water. However, **picnicking** is a fine activity, as there is a nice wooden bench situated lakeside and a wonderful set of shaded picnic benches located just steps from Lake Irene's parking lot.

BACKPACKING

A handful of options exist for backpacking in this region, though none are geared toward beginners. The **Chapin Creek wilderness site** is located north of the Chapin Creek Trail, but getting there is tricky, as a section of trail is unmaintained and difficult to follow. A challenging cross-country trek from the Ute Trail near Milner Pass is also required to get to **Little Rock Lake wilderness site,** which is located near Gorge Lakes. **Ute Meadow wilderness site,** found along the Ute Trail, is a pleasant place to spend the night, but is a llama-only campsite.

All backpacking reservations must be made through one of the park's two wilderness offices (970/586-1242). The **East Side Wilderness Office** is located adjacent to the Beaver Meadows Visitor Center, while the **West Side Wilderness Office** is located in the Kawuneeche Visitor Center. For backcountry camping dates that fall May 1-Oct. 31, reservations can be made online (www.pay.gov) or in-person (not by phone) March 1-October 28.

BIKING

In the spring and late fall, Trail Ridge Road and Old Fall River Road are **closed to automobile traffic** and usually—at the park's discretion—**open to bicycles.** Road closures differ each year, depending on snowfall. For road information, view the park's road status report online (www.nps.gov/romo), call the **Trail Ridge Road Information Line** (970/586-1222), or call the park directly for information (970/586-1206). Otherwise, **bicycles are not allowed on Old Fall River Road during the summer season.**

Trail Ridge Road

A driving tour on America's highest continuous paved road is one thrill, a bicycling tour is altogether another. Using leg-power alone to get up and over Trail Ridge Road is a challenge met by many cyclists each summer, who delight in the thoroughfare's spectacular views and enjoy a guaranteed endorphin-producing workout.

The most popular biking routes are from the **Beaver Meadows Entrance Station** to the Alpine Visitor Center and back (40 miles round-trip, 5 hours) and from the Beaver Meadows Entrance Station to the Grand Lake Entrance Station and back (79 miles round-trip, 7-8 hours). On the west side, cyclists often begin at the **Grand Lake Entrance Station,** ride to the Alpine Visitor Center, and then return to their starting point (40 miles round-trip, 5 hours).

There are many things to be mindful of while cycling on the road: first and foremost are the cars that are sharing this relatively narrow space. There is **no dedicated bike lane** on the road, making it critical that cyclists ride single file, dress in high visibility clothing, and wear a helmet. With a good portion of Trail Ridge Road lying above the tree line, weather factors must also be evaluated. If rain starts dumping, the closest shelter is the Alpine Visitor Center or a stranger's vehicle. Thick fog sometimes appears along high sections of the road, creating a potentially hazardous situation. The effects of high elevation on stamina and performance should be also considered.

HORSEBACK RIDING

Horseback rides around the Fall River area are offered by **National Park Gateway Stables** (Hwy. 34, 970/586-5269, www.skhorses.com, open Memorial Day-Oct. 1, closed in winter, $55-175 pp), between the Fall River Visitor Center and the Fall River Entrance Station. Destinations include Endovalley, Horseshoe Park, and Lawn Lake. Reservations are strongly recommended and are required for rides four hours or longer.

FISHING

Fly-fishing is popular in the vicinity of Trail Ridge Road and Old Fall River Road. **Fall**

River sees its fair share of fish, and people particularly enjoy positioning themselves along the water in **Horseshoe Park** and **Endovalley** (Hwy. 34 and Endovalley Rd.). Past Endovalley, access to the Fall River becomes more difficult and the river doesn't fish as well.

Another popular spot to fish is the **Roaring River** at the Alluvial Fan (Endovalley Rd.). **Poudre Lake** (Trail Ridge Rd.) on the west side is superb for catch-and-release fishing. In order to cast a line, individuals 16 years and older must carry a current Colorado Fishing License. Licenses are available in Grand Lake and Estes Park, and can be purchased through **Colorado Parks & Wildlife** (800/244-5613, www.wildlife.state.co.us). Review the park's fishing regulations ahead of any outing.

WINTER SPORTS

Backcountry Skiing

Hidden Valley (along Trail Ridge Rd.) was once a bona fide ski resort and the terrain is still conducive for backcountry skiing. While many trails are still obvious, they are not groomed or managed for avalanche danger. Backcountry ski gear is essential, including skis with "skins" (grippy strips of material that attach to the bottom of skis and allow a person to ascend a slope) and an avalanche beacon, probe, shovel, and a partner. First-timers should tag along with someone who has prior experience and knowledge.

If you want to do as the locals do, "skin" up Main Vein or Lift Line (not labeled as such; ask a local to point you in the right direction) in the morning for a nice burst of cardio. For late-day outings, come prepared with a headlamp, and a backup headlamp or fresh batteries stowed in your pack, along with other supplies for spending a night out in case of emergency. Mark Kelly's *Backcountry Skiing and Ski Mountaineering: Rocky Mountain National Park* is a great resource for backcountry skiers.

Sledding

Fast and fun is the best way to describe the sledding hill at the **Hidden Valley Snow Play Area** (along Trail Ridge Rd.). Bring your own tube, sled, or saucer to this spot and experience pure exhilaration (and maybe a touch of fear) as you barrel down this moderately pitched sledding hill and fall in a giggling heap at the bottom. Hike up to the top and repeat. Follow it up with a good old-fashioned snowball fight and some snow angels and you have the makings of a memorable wintery morning or afternoon in the park. There is no additional charge to use the hill beyond the park entrance fee.

The snow play area isn't risk-free. Backcountry skiers regularly cross the bottom of the sledding hill, and the first person I watched sled here ended her day of fun due to a wrist injury. In a light snow year, the hill can be patchy or even dry so call the park (970/586-1206) for snow conditions. There is a restroom and a warming room staffed with an attendant on weekends and holidays.

Entertainment and Shopping

RANGER PROGRAMS

Junior Ranger Headquarters

During the height of summer (late June-mid-Aug.), **Hidden Valley** becomes headquarters for all things Junior Ranger. Fun and educational programs for kids are held daily (10am, 11:30am, 1pm, 2:30pm) at this location and outside on nearby picnic benches. Programs are 30 minutes long; a parent or guardian must be present for the duration of the program. Advance sign-ups are not necessary and programs are free of charge. Children who have completed a Junior Ranger booklet obtained elsewhere in the park can also get "sworn in' and receive a badge.

Ranger-Led Programs

Ranger-led programs regularly take place at the **Alpine Visitor Center** (Trail Ridge Rd. and Old Fall River Rd., 970/586-1206, 9am-5pm daily summer, 10:30am-4:30pm daily spring and fall). Topics run the gamut from geology to lightning. Guided tundra hikes are also offered. Special twilight nature programs on Trail Ridge Road require day-of reservations. Otherwise, programs are free of charge and do not require reservations unless otherwise noted.

In the summer, ranger-led programs are held regularly at the **Fall River Visitor Center** (3450 Fall River Rd., 9am-5pm daily late May-mid-Oct.), the amphitheater at the Timber Creek Campground (Hwy. 34, 10 mi north of Grand Lake), and the **Kawuneeche Visitor Center** (16018 Hwy. 34, 970/627-3471, 8am-5pm daily summer). The schedule changes every summer; check the park newspaper for details.

STARGAZING

By day, **Trail Ridge Road** is busy with sightseers and hikers; by night, sky watchers and night photographers head above the tree line for unobstructed views. On a clear evening, stars pop beautifully against the onyx sky. Provided there is no wind, the tundra is peaceful but for animal murmurings and the occasional car driving by. Any of the established **parking lots** or **pullouts** along the road will do as a stopping point for stargazing.

A bright and beautiful nighttime show unfolds mid-July-late August: the annual Perseid meteor shower. Hundreds of meteors streak the night sky during this event, which culminates in early August (check www.nasa.gov for peak viewing dates). The best time to watch the Perseids is between midnight and dawn; the best way to watch is flat on your back and with no sense of urgency (it can take awhile for your eyes to adjust to the darkness, and for the dazzlers to appear). Trail Ridge Road is one of many places in the park people flock to during the Perseids.

The Alpine Visitor Center is unstaffed in the evening, so you will be on your own in case an emergency arises. The nighttime temperature on Trail Ridge Road can be considerably cooler than at the park entrances—possibly a difference of double digits. Bring plenty of layers, as well as a camp chair, food and refreshments, and a headlamp or flashlight.

SHOPPING

Every visitor center features a moderately sized selection of books and souvenirs for sale. But die-hard shoppers who have done their research head for the **Trail Ridge Store** (Trail Ridge Rd. and Old Fall River Rd., www.trailridgegiftstore.com, 9am-6pm daily May-Sept. 3; 10am-5pm daily Sept. 4-Oct. 13, weather permitting). An impressive amount of high-quality goods packs this space, including Native American jewelry, apparel, books, jams, note cards, and small items for the home.

A large selection of wares is available for purchase at the privately owned **Rocky Mountain Gateway Gift Shop** (3450 Fall

River Rd., 970/577-0043, www.rockymountaingateway.net, 8am-8pm daily summer, 8am-6pm daily winter) located in the same complex as the Fall River Visitor Center, though the quality is not what you will find at the Trail Ridge Store. Shop here for Christmas decorations, Native American jewelry, pottery, wind chimes, walking sticks, and more.

Camping

INSIDE THE PARK

Camping is the only form of overnight accommodation. The nearest hotels, lodges, and inns are in Grand Lake or Estes Park, both of which serve as a fine home base for Trail Ridge Road. If you plan to stay in Estes Park and extensively explore Trail Ridge Road, look for lodging options along Fall River Road (Hwy. 34), where numerous lodges and cabins put visitors close to the Fall River Entrance Station.

Aspenglen Campground

On the east side of the park, **Aspenglen Campground** (Hwy. 34 west of the Fall River Entrance Station, 877/444-6777, www.recreation.gov, late May-late Sept., $26) affords easy access to Old Fall River Road and Trail Ridge Road. Fifty-three sights can be reserved, including two wheelchair-accessible sites. RVs are allowed in the B and C loops, but generators may only be used in the C loop. Six tent sites are hike-in only. Amenities include tent pads, grills and grates, water, restrooms, and firewood for sale. This is an especially popular campsite in the park, so book your stay well in advance. Reservations for Aspenglen can be made up to six months ahead of a visit.

Timber Creek Campground

Timber Creek Campground (Hwy. 34, 10 mi north of Grand Lake, www.nps.gov/romo, late May-early Nov., $26) is located off Trail Ridge Road on the west side of the park. This is a convenient jumping-off point for visitors who want to explore extensively above the tree line. The campground contains 98 tent and RV sites, which are available on a first-come, first-served basis. Amenities include restrooms, an amphitheater, tent pads with grill and fire rings, and bear-proof storage lockers. There is also a ranger station and emergency phone at the campground entrance.

Food

INSIDE THE PARK

When inclement weather swiftly moves in on Trail Ridge Road, **Café in the Clouds** (Trail Ridge Rd. and Old Fall River Rd., www.trailridgegiftstore.com, 10am-4:30pm daily late May-June and late Aug.-mid-Oct., 9am-5:30pm daily late June-Aug., $6-10) provides a welcome refuge from the elements. Sandwiches, soups, and salads are served here cafeteria-style, and hot drinks are whipped up steps away at the **Trail Ridge Coffee Bar.** Snag a table by a window if you can—the views are spectacular. Plenty of grab-and-go items (fruit, yogurt, cookies, and snacks) are great for picnics or to stow in your car.

Picnicking

Endovalley is the largest picnic area in the park with 32 spots, and is exceptionally lovely. Families often come here for the whole day to enjoy a birthday party or other celebration. There is a sign at the entrance that states

Visitors to the Endovalley picnic area cool off in Fall River.

"no camping," and it is easy to see why someone would be tempted; each shady and private spot, complete with fire grill/grate, feels like it is made for an overnight adventure. In fact, this area actually was once a park campground from the late 1920s to the 1970s. After eating lunch or dinner, wander over to Fall River to fish or simply enjoy the scenery.

Additional picnic tables are found at the West Alluvial Fan, Rainbow Curve, Hidden Valley, and Lake Irene. All locations are first-come, first-served.

OUTSIDE THE PARK

Nicky's Steakhouse (1350 Fall River Rd., 970/586-5376, www.nickyssteakhouse.com, 11am-9pm daily year-round, $30-50) has been around since 1967 and is ideally situated for visitors staying along Fall River Road (Hwy. 34). Multiple seating areas cater to different types of diners: The casual garden room is great for families, the lounge is perfect for date night, and the Cattleman's Steakhouse is ideal for formal occasions. Outside, a large deck overlooking the Fall River is the most popular place to eat in the summer. The lounge is my favorite spot: large, backlit, stained-glass pieces created by a local artist are situated above the bar and chianti bottles drained by guests dangle from the ceiling. The menu is very meat focused, with prime rib the most popular entrée. The lounge features live entertainment on Friday and Saturday nights.

Within strolling distance of the Fall River Visitor Center, the **Gateway Grocery** (3450 Fall River Rd., 970/577-0043, 8am-7pm daily late May-Labor Day) is stocked with sundries and camp supplies. At the ice cream counter, indulge in a cone or milkshake.

Transportation and Services

For road information, inquire at an entrance station, visit the nearest visitor center, or call the Trail Ridge Road Recorded Information Line (970/586-1222) or Colorado Department of Transportation Road Conditions (877/315-7623).

TRAIL RIDGE ROAD

Both Estes Park and Grand Lake provide access to Trail Ridge Road. From the junction of Highway 34 and Highway 36 in downtown Estes Park, it is 4.9 miles west to the Fall River Entrance Station. From the junction of Highway 34 and County Road 278 in Grand Lake, it is a 1.8-mile drive north to the Grand Lake Entrance Station.

On Trail Ridge Road, it is critical that **drivers use only designated pullouts** and parking lots, and avoid making sudden stops to view wildlife. There is little forgiveness for inattention or error on this two-lane road. On the 11 miles of road above the tree line, there are no shoulders, few guardrails, and numerous places where your car could go tumbling down the tundra. With no bike lane, be especially careful when passing road cyclists. Observe posted speed limits on Trail Ridge Road and be aware that rangers patrol the area regularly.

Weather Conditions

A storm can occur at any time, making driving more treacherous. Snow is possible at any time of year, and can create slippery conditions. Dense fog can also force whiteout situations on Trail Ridge Road. If you are headed to Trail Ridge Road late in the day, keep in mind that the park does not plow the road from 4pm to 7am.

Trail Ridge Road is **closed** from the Colorado River Trailhead on the west side to Many Parks Curve on the east side **mid- to late October-Memorial Day** (closures are weather dependent). Trail Ridge Road from Deer Ridge Junction to Many Parks Curve is open year-round, but tends to stay icy even though it is plowed. Snow tires or chains offer a greater level of safety for visitors making a winter trip to the area.

Parking

Decent-sized parking lots are found at Hidden Valley, Rainbow Curve, Forest Canyon Overlook, Rock Cut, Gore Range Overlook, the Alpine Visitor Center, Milner Pass, and Lake Irene. In the summer, the parking lot to the Alpine Visitor Center can get hairy at any time of day with visitors circling around looking for a space. You might even find yourself in a temporary standstill at the junction of Old Fall River Road and the parking lot because of a traffic jam. While other parking lots on Trail Ridge Road can get busy, the turnover is fairly quick and you shouldn't find yourself looking for an empty space for too long.

RVs

RVs are permitted on Trail Ridge Road and a small amount of parking spots for RVs are located at the Alpine Visitor Center. An RV dump station is located at Timber Creek Campground on the west side. The closest dump station on the east side is at Moraine Park Campground.

OLD FALL RIVER ROAD

Estes Park is the closest town to Old Fall River Road. From the junction of Highway 34 and Highway 36 in downtown Estes Park, it is 4.9 miles west to the Fall River Entrance Station. Old Fall River Road usually **opens by July 4.** However, it is **not plowed** and can close earlier in the fall than Trail Ridge Road.

Old Fall River Road is narrower than Trail Ridge Road and is **one-way** with a **15-mph** speed limit. Vehicles (no bicycles permitted) have a length restriction of 25 feet; trailers are not allowed. There are several sections with

Where Can I Find...?

- **Cell Service:** Cell phone service is unreliable along Trail Ridge Road and Old Fall River Road. Consider this a good reason to unplug for a few hours.
- **Firewood and Ice:** On summer evenings, firewood, kindling, and ice are available at the Aspenglen Campground; firewood can be purchased at Timber Creek Campground.
- **Gas:** Plan on fueling up in Grand Lake or Estes Park, where there are numerous service stations. There are no gas stations located in the park.
- **Internet Service:** Free public Wi-Fi is at the Beaver Meadows Visitor Center, Kawuneeche Visitor Center, and the Fall River Visitor Center.
- **Restrooms:** Vault toilets and restrooms are interspersed along Trail Ridge Road at Hidden Valley, Rainbow Curve, Rock Cut, the Alpine Visitor Center, Milner Pass, Lake Irene, and the Colorado River Trailhead. There are no restrooms on Old Fall River Road. The closest toilets are located at the Endovalley Picnic Area, the Alluvial Fan, and the Fall River Visitor Center.

no guardrails where the road drops off considerably. Do not attempt to pass cars on Old Fall River Road, and do not stop in the middle of the road to take photos; doing so creates a hazardous situation.

At their discretion, the park will **temporarily close access** to Old Fall River Road if it becomes too clogged with cars. As visitation has increased, park officials use temporary road closures as a strategy to alleviate congestion in certain high-traffic spots. Arrive outside of **peak visitation hours** (10am-3pm) to avoid getting turned away.

There are two small **parking areas** (larger pullouts) on Old Fall River Road at **Chasm Falls** and **Chapin Creek Trailhead.** Small pullouts suitable for 1-2 cars are at other spots along the road if you need a break from driving.

EMERGENCIES

Visitors to Rocky often experience health-related emergencies on Trail Ridge Road and at the Alpine Visitor Center related to **altitude sickness** or preexisting medical conditions exacerbated by the high elevation. Headaches, lightheadedness, nausea, and fatigue are often altitude-related symptoms that are quickly resolved by returning to lower elevation. If you need medical help, your best option for obtaining emergency services is to notify a ranger at the visitor center. If you are not close to the Alpine Visitor Center, enlist someone to seek help and attempt to call 911 or the park **dispatch center** (970/586-1203). While cell phone service is generally weak to nonexistent on Trail Ridge Road, you might be able to get through. **Emergency phones** are located at the Timber Creek Campground on the west side, the Aspenglen Campground on the east side, and the Lawn Lake Trailhead on Fall River Road.

For vehicle emergencies, pull over, turn on your hazard lights, and set up an emergency hazard triangle. Attempt to call an Estes Park towing company, such as **Bob's Towing and Repair** (800 Dunraven St., Estes Park, 970/586-3122, 8am-5pm Mon.-Sat.) or **Up Top Towing** (875 Moraine Ave., Estes Park, 970/586-4248, open 24/7) for help. Bob's will travel anywhere along Trail Ridge Road to provide people with vehicle assistance. Park police also patrol both roads regularly in the summer.

Kawuneeche Valley

Glacier-carved Kawuneeche Valley is known for vast meadows that hug the banks of the Colorado River.

Eighty percent of Rocky Mountain National Park visitors enter the park from the east—and many of those 80 percent never make their way over to the quieter west side known as the Kawuneeche (pronounced kah-wuh-nee-CHEE) Valley. Yet, many delights found on the east side of the park are also here: fields teeming with wildflowers, streams playing peek-a-boo through the trees, glassy lakes, gushing waterfalls, and fascinating historical sites.

The west side also lays claim to a small section of the Continental Divide National Scenic Trail (CDT), as well as numerous other hiking and horse trails. Wildlife-watchers should come and stay a while, since this is the best place to set eyes on one of the 30-50 moose that reside in the park year-round. The fall elk rut also takes place here, and you can usually listen and watch without a huge crowd of people clamoring for the same photo. Winter brings more snowfall to the west side than to the east, and pleasurable snowshoeing is a given for a good three months or longer.

PLANNING YOUR TIME

Kawuneeche Valley on the west side of the park is accessible to visitors **year-round.** If you have just **one day** to explore the west side, Adams Falls along the East Inlet Trail, the Coyote Valley Trail, and the Holzwarth Historic Site are must-sees. In the summer, sightseeing along the highest portion of **Trail Ridge Road** is a great way to break up a series of hiking days. The stark yet fascinating alpine tundra is within easy reach of the Kawuneeche Valley and contrasts sharply with the west side's lush meadows. Consider spending several days exploring the Kawuneeche Valley, then heading over Trail Ridge Road to the east side of the park for several days of sightseeing. Drive west back over Trail Ridge Road to wrap up your trip. The more ambitious could thru-hike/backpack from the west side to the east via Flattop Mountain; you will need to shuttle a car to Estes Park or arrange to be picked up for this option.

In mid- to late October, **Trail Ridge Road** (Hwy. 34) **closes** immediately after the Colorado River Trailhead on the north end of

Previous: hiking in the Kawuneeche Valley; fly fishing on a tributary of the Colorado River. **Above:** Cascade Falls.

Look for ★ to find recommended sights, activities, dining, and lodging.

Highlights

★ **Moose-Watching:** Keep a lookout for moose near lakes, willows, aspen trees, and even on Highway 34 (page 145).

★ **Holzwarth Historic Site:** Visit this well-preserved 1920s guest lodge in the summer, when tours inside of the buildings are offered (page 146).

★ **Colorado River:** Admire the serpentine form of this life-giving river (page 147).

★ **Lulu City:** Visit the site of an old mining town, where prospectors hoped to find silver and gold (page 148).

★ **Coyote Valley Trail:** Investigate a riparian ecosystem found along the Colorado River (page 148).

★ **Granite Falls:** Look for wildlife in Big Meadows, then relax next to a gorgeous waterfall (page 149).

★ **Shadow Mountain Lookout Tower:** Gaze down upon Grand Lake, Shadow Mountain Reservoir, and Lake Granby at the site of a historic fire lookout tower (page 154).

★ **Continental Divide National Scenic Trail:** Spend a few nights backpacking along Rocky's portion of the CDT (page 156).

★ **Fishing:** Drop a line along the Colorado River, or hike with your gear along one of the valley's trails to a brook or stream (page 158).

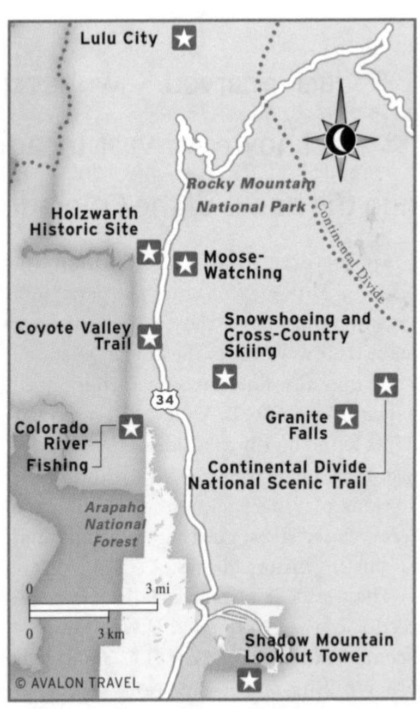

★ **Snowshoeing and Cross-Country Skiing:** Bundle up and stomp or slide through the soft stuff (page 159).

Kawuneeche Valley

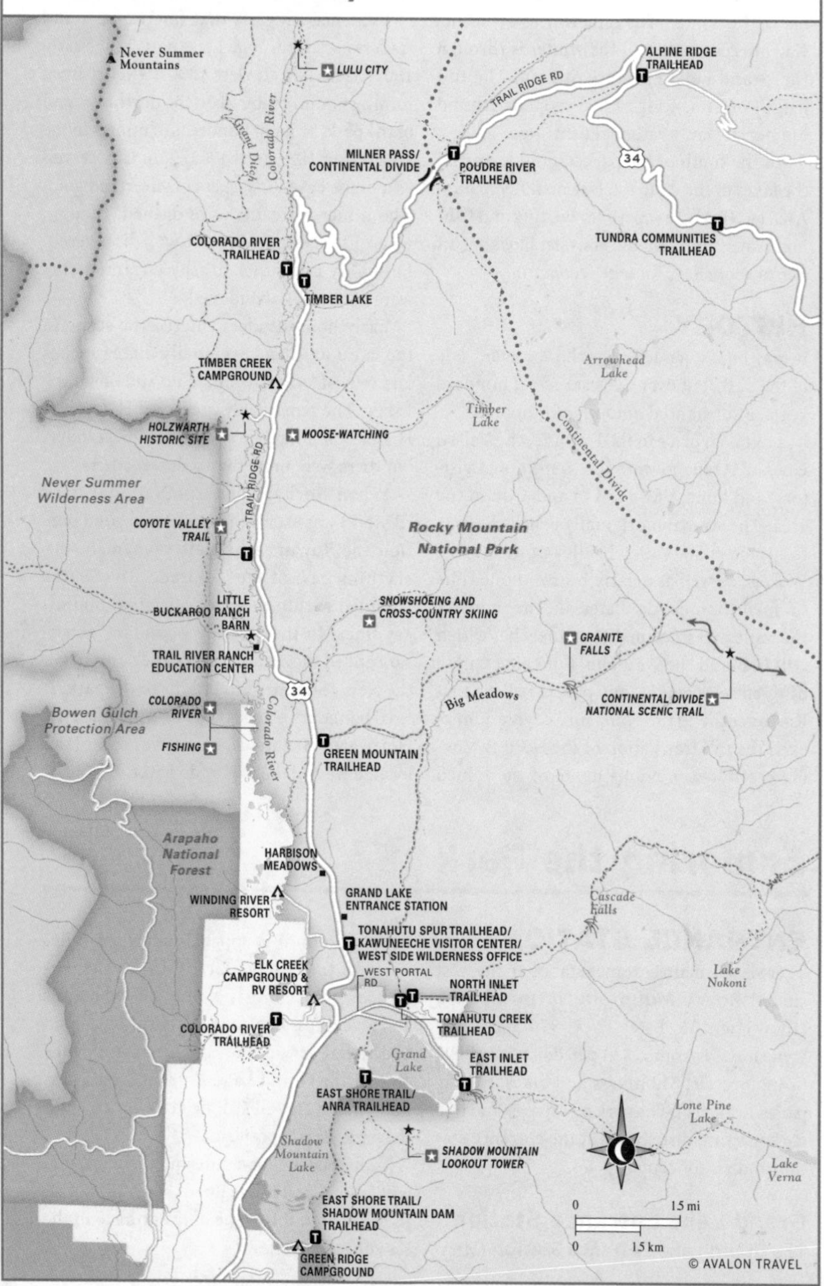

the Kawuneeche Valley, making vehicle travel from the east side to the west side impossible in the winter. The only way to get to the Kawuneeche Valley in the winter is through the Grand Lake Entrance Station. The full length of Trail Ridge Road reopens around Memorial Day, weather permitting.

To the south of the park, Grand Lake and the lakes of the Arapaho National Recreation Area (ANRA) are superb for boating and fishing. Water-lovers should consider blocking off one or more days for lake recreation.

HISTORY

It may be known today as the "quieter" side of the park, but over the last several hundred years, a substantial amount of human activity has taken place in the Kawuneeche Valley. Ute and Arapaho were the first-known visitors, and hunted for food in and around the area. The Arapaho originally called the area the Haquihana Valley (Valley of the Wolf). Wolves, as well as grizzly bears, at one time roamed these lands. Later on, the name of the valley was deemed Kawuneeche, which still honored the Arapaho, but came with a different meaning. Many people believe that Kawuneeche is the word for "coyote"; however, the full translation of the word is "coyote creek"—a previous name of the famed Colorado River, which winds its way through the valley.

Evidence suggests that fur trappers and traders passed through these parts in the early 1800s. Then, in the late 1800s, a short-lived mining boom, centered on the northwest end of the park, brought hundreds of miners to the area. From 1879 until 1883, Lulu City served as a home base for seekers of silver and gold. The miners' dreams were dashed, though, when little valuable metal was discovered. Lulu City and other nearby encampments were eventually abandoned.

Early homesteaders entered the scene in the late 1800s, and eventually dude ranches and tourist lodges sprouted up and down the valley. The remarkably preserved Holzwarth Historic Site was the site of one guest lodge, but there were more than a dozen others.

When Rocky Mountain National Park (RMNP) was established in 1915, a good portion the Kawuneeche Valley—namely, everything east of the Colorado River—was included within the park's original boundary lines. In the 1930s, a boundary extension added the eastern slopes and summits of the Never Summer Mountains to the park. A final boundary extension in 1974 included the Holzwarth Historic Site as well as other land located west of the Colorado River.

Exploring the Park

ENTRANCE STATIONS

There is one main entrance station to the west side of **Rocky Mountain National Park** (1000 Hwy. 36, Estes Park, 970/586-1206, www.nps.gov/romo, $20 per day per vehicle or motorcycle, $10 hikers and bikes, weekly passes available). The park newspaper and free park map are distributed at the entrance station and visitor center.

Grand Lake Entrance Station

The **Grand Lake Entrance Station** (Hwy. 34, year-round) is approximately 1.8 miles north of the town of Grand Lake. This entrance station consists of only staffed booths and an express lane for park pass holders; no additional services or amenities are available. If the Grand Lake Entrance Station is unstaffed, you will still need to pay to enter the park via a deposit slot.

Immediately upon entering the park, you will follow Trail Ridge Road (Hwy. 34) north. In the winter, this is the only entrance to the Kawuneeche Valley.

Fall River and Beaver Meadows Entrance Stations

From Memorial Day to mid- or late October (weather permitting) visitors can enter the park on the east side via the **Fall River Entrance Station** (Hwy. 34) and drive over Trail Ridge Road to the Kawuneeche Valley, a distance of 48 miles. In the summer, east-side visitors can drive Old Fall River Road (east-to-west one-way, opens July 4) west to Trail Ridge Road and then continue on to the Kawuneeche Valley.

During the summer, visitors can also enter the park through the east side **Beaver Meadows Entrance Station** (Hwy. 36). From the entrance station, continue 3 miles northwest on Highway 36 to Trail Ridge Road, then proceed west to the Kawuneeche Valley.

West Side Trailheads

Five trailheads are found south of the Kawuneeche Valley entrance station. These trailheads are fee-free areas of the park, though an **Arapaho National Recreation Area** (ANRA, $5) day-use fee is required to park at the East Shore Trailhead. A pass can be purchased at the Hilltop Boat Launch, located on Jericho Road at the north end of the reservoir (south of the connecting channel between Grand Lake and Shadow Mountain Reservoir).

TONAHUTU CREEK AND NORTH INLET TRAILHEADS

Starting at the intersection of Highway 34 and County Road 278 in Grand Lake, take County Road 278/West Portal Road for 0.3 mile east to the junction of West Portal Road and Grand Avenue. Stay left on West Portal Road, and drive another 0.8 mile east to the next junction. At the trailhead sign, turn left (north) on County Road 663 and drive 0.2 mile. You will arrive at the **Tonahutu Creek Trailhead** first; there is a small parking lot at this spot. The **North Inlet Trailhead** is 0.1 mile to the east of the Tonahutu Creek Trailhead and features an additional parking lot.

EAST INLET TRAILHEAD

From the junction of Highway 34 and County Road 278, take County Road 278 for 0.3 mile east to the junction of West Portal Road and Grand Avenue. Stay left on West Portal Road and drive 2.1 miles to the **East Inlet Trailhead** and parking lot.

EAST SHORE TRAIL: ANRA TRAILHEAD

At the junction of Highway 34 and County Road 278, take County Road 278 east for 0.2 mile to Center Drive. Turn right (south) on Center Drive, and drive 0.2 mile to Marina Drive. Turn left (east) and drive for 0.1 mil to Shadow Mountain Drive. Drive south on Shadow Mountain Drive for just over 0.2 mile until reaching Jericho Road. Turn right (south) on Jericho Road and drive over a wooden bridge that crosses the channel of water between Grand Lake and Shadow Mountain Dam. It is a 0.4-mile drive on Jericho Road to Shoreline Way. Head right (south) on Shoreline Way and drive 0.1 mile to the **East Shore Trailhead** and parking lot.

The trailhead is technically an **Arapaho National Recreation Area** (ANRA) trailhead, but information about Rocky is also provided, since the trail crosses over ANRA and RMNP land. An ANRA day-use fee ($5) or annual pass is required to park in the lot.

EAST SHORE TRAIL: SHADOW MOUNTAIN DAM TRAILHEAD

From the junction of Highway 34 and County Road 278, take Highway 34 south for 2.75 miles and turn left (east) on County Road 66. Drive for 2 miles to the Green Ridge Campground. Continue through the campground to the lakeshore and park your car. This trailhead provides access to the **East Shore Trail.** An ANRA day-use fee ($5) is required.

VISITOR CENTER

Kawuneeche Visitor Center

One information hub for the park is located

on the west side: the **Kawuneeche Visitor Center** (16018 Hwy. 34, 970/627-3471, 8am-6pm daily summer, 8am-4:30pm daily winter), 0.4 mile south of the Grand Lake Entrance Station. The center features a large topographical relief map, educational displays about the Colorado River, a Rocky Mountain Conservancy Nature Store, and an information desk. A short film about the park is screened in the auditorium at visitors' request, and ranger-led programs often meet at this location. The **West Side Wilderness Office** (970/586-1242) is located inside the visitor center and is the place to obtain information about and permits for wilderness camping.

DRIVING TOURS

KAWUNEECHE VISITOR CENTER TO COLORADO RIVER TRAILHEAD

The most interesting driving tour begins by traveling the length of Highway 34 from the Kawuneeche Visitor Center to the Colorado River Trailhead (10 mi). If time allows, step out at the **Coyote Valley Trail** (5.8 mi) and the **Holzwarth Historic Site** (7.8 mi) for a short stroll. In summer, continue east on Highway 34 to cross Trail Ridge Road from west to east.

In the winter, driving the 10 miles of Highway 34 from the Kawuneeche Visitor Center to Colorado River Trailhead is a pleasant journey, taking a half hour to travel one-way. The snowy expanse of **Harbison Meadows** twinkles like a field of diamonds on a sunny day, and you can spot many meandering animal trails stamped out in the snow on both sides of the road. Moose sightings are less frequent in the winter but are still a real possibility. (A driving tour of the Kawuneeche Valley in winter has its limitations, though; have snowshoes in your car if you want to explore for even 15 minutes outside.) Consider a short outing on the **Tonahutu Spur Trail,** which starts at the Kawuneeche Visitor Center, or a brisk snowshoe on the **Colorado River Trail.**

the East Shore Trailhead by Shadow Mountain Dam

TRAIL RIDGE ROAD (SUMMER ONLY)

A stop at **Farview Curve** (14 mi) is a must, as there is an arresting view of the Kawuneeche Valley's vast green meadows. From this location, reasonable stops and/or turnaround points for those short on time include the **Milner Pass/Continental Divide** (16 mi), **Medicine Bow Curve** (20 mi), and the **Alpine Visitor Center** (20.5 mi). Those following the entirety of Trail Ridge Road to the east side should make sure to stop at **Rock Cut** (24.7 mi), **Forest Canyon Overlook** (26.6 mi), **Rainbow Curve** (29.4 mi), and **Many Parks Curve** (33.4 mi). You'll view three ecosystems within the course of your drive: montane, subalpine, and tundra.

Sights

★ MOOSE-WATCHING

Moose are out and about on the west side, and many people come to the Kawuneeche Valley specifically to spot one. Positioning yourself near (but not *too* near) a moose's food source increases the likelihood of seeing one of these hulking creatures. Willows, which are abundant on the valley floor, are particularly delicious fare for moose. They also munch on grass, aquatic plants, aspen bark and leaves, and mosses. Some hot spots for seeing moose are near the **Kawuneeche Valley entrance sign,** around the **Holzwarth Historic Site,** and where the Continental Divide National Scenic Trail crosses Highway 34 (just north of the **Onahu Trailhead**). The **Beaver Ponds Picnic Area** is another good place for observation. Any time of day is a good time to spot a moose, and don't be surprised if you stumble upon one taking a mid-afternoon "bath." The mammals feel right at home wading and even full-on swimming in water.

LITTLE BUCKAROO RANCH BARN

Little Buckaroo Ranch Barn is a not-so-hidden-gem that is part of the park's Trail River Ranch property. This gorgeous barn earned its spot on the National Register of Historic Places because of its unique architecture. (Coors Brewing Company featured the structure in several television commercials.) Officially known as **Little Buckaroo Ranch Barn,** the building is also affectionately called "Betty's Barn" by those who knew its last private owner, Betty Dick.

The barn was originally built in 1942 to house the horses of Frank and Mary Godchaux, a couple who owned this slice of property 1941-1957 and spent summers here. The Godchaux were from Louisiana and were fond of Cajun-style barns, a style frequently constructed in southern Louisiana in the early 20th century. Features include a monitor roof and rustic log slab siding. A monitor roof is a raised structure (with its own smaller roof) found on top of the ridge of a traditional double-pitched roof. Little

Moose are commonly seen on the west side of the park.

Safety, Not "Selfie," First

I once spoke with a wildlife biologist who claimed to have a low-to-moderate level of trepidation around bears, but a rather intense fear of moose. This is why: Moose are large (weighing up to 1,000 pounds), are fast runners (reaching speeds of up to 35 mph), and they have a great ability to harm. When people approach moose, the animals typically don't turn and run, giving an impression that they are rather laidback and mellow. But when aggravated—watch out. A moose can literally stomp a person to death. While a moose's sometimes stoic manner makes them particularly watchable—and relatively easy to photograph—visitors should pay these creatures an enormous amount of respect.

- **Be judicious about giving a moose space;** always keep a distance of at least 25 yards. Pull over only into designated pullouts or parking lots along Highway 34 to view moose. Be aware that a gridlock situation on the road can create safety issues for drivers and a situation where moose feel cornered. If you see that parked cars are starting to amass along the side of the road, consider driving around and forgoing your turn to see and/or photograph a moose in the interests of maintaining safety and keeping traffic moving.
- **Canines** may be "man's best friend," but they are far from being BFFs with moose. If you are traveling through the Kawuneeche Valley with a dog in your car, make sure the pooch is secured before exiting your vehicle. I have seen dogs escape from cars in the park when the vehicle's driver hurriedly opened the door in an attempt to view wildlife; then a frantic situation ensued. Dogs are otherwise not allowed on trails anywhere in Rocky.
- Pay attention to the **body language** of a moose. If you notice that their ears are pulled back, they are rolling their eyes, or in any other way seem aggressive, remove yourself from the situation.
- **Walk slowly** near a moose, and do not walk directly toward them.
- **Use binoculars,** a spotting scope, or telephoto lenses to view moose.

Buckaroo is not considered a 'true' Cajun barn because the Godchaux made a few modifications to the design. Regardless, it is an uncommon design for a Colorado barn. Today, this handsome structure stands vacant in a grassy field and is simply an object of admiration for those who pass by it on the **Bowen Gulch Trail.** This is a sensitive historic building, so do not touch the exterior or make any attempt to enter. The park prefers visitors to observe the barn from the trail.

From the Grand Lake Entrance, travel 4 miles north on Highway 34/Trail Ridge Road. Turn left (west) on an unmarked dirt road. After 0.3 mile, arrive at a small dirt parking area. Park, walk over a bridge, and you will be on the Bowen Gulch Trail. After a short 0.1 mile walk west from the parking lot, you will see the barn. In the winter, the unmarked dirt road is unplowed.

★ HOLZWARTH HISTORIC SITE

Holzwarth Trout Lodge, today known as the **Holzwarth Historic Site,** was one of the first tourist operations in the Kawuneeche Valley. Homesteaders Sophie and John Holzwarth expended considerable effort to maintain their vacation lodge from 1920 to 1929. There were dude ranch activities to host, meals to cook, and guest accommodations to keep in order.

Though the Holzwarth Historic Site no longer functions as real dude ranch, there is still a major operation going on at this location in the summer. Approximately 30 volunteers facilitate a "step back in time" experience for visitors by offering drop-in **tours** (8:30am-4:30pm daily mid-June-Labor Day, free) of the buildings. The property includes multiple sleeping cabins, a taxidermy shop, a main house where meals were served, an

What Is Homesteading?

As a kid, I recall learning to sing "Home on the Range" and feeling uplifted by the tune, especially the lines "Where seldom is heard a discouraging word; and the skies are not cloudy all day." But it wasn't until much later that I fully understood what I was crooning about: the hope and promise felt by early western settlers. If you attend history programs at Rocky, chances are good that you will hear about homesteading and homesteaders. It helps to have a bit of background, and the basics are this: The **Homestead Act of 1862,** signed into law by President Abraham Lincoln, was created to encourage Western settlement and land cultivation. Individuals age 21 or over who were considered the head of the household could acquire a 160-acre parcel of land and officially own it in five years' time. There were stipulations involved, of course: Homesteaders were required to build a home, live on the land, and farm the land. The application to homestead cost a mere $18, which seemed like one heck of a deal until you considered the many costs associated with growing crops and raising livestock. Homesteaders were also challenged by weather and limited access to supplies; the act proved a boon for some, but for others it was a bust. More than 270 million acres of land were ultimately distributed. The Homestead Act remained in effect until 1976.

ice house, and a wood shed. You'll find a mix of original items from the ranch (including taxidermy animals), as well as other artifacts from the early 1920s. Kids in particular love wringing out wet socks using an old-fashioned washbasin that is often set up outside.

An **Old Ranch Campfire** (free) takes place on Fridays; arrive at 7pm for singing and a crackling campfire. Pack a cozy sweater and your own marshmallows to roast.

Holzwarth Historic Site's parking area is located on Highway 34, approximately 7.5 miles north of the Grand Lake Entrance Station. Walk a flat and easy 0.5 mile to the buildings. In the fall, winter, and spring, the buildings are closed, but it is still fun to look around outside.

★ COLORADO RIVER

The **Colorado River** starts on the upper west side of Rocky and winds its way from north to south through the Kawuneeche Valley. The river and its tributaries are found in six other states besides Colorado—Wyoming, Utah, New Mexico, Arizona, Nevada, and California—as well as the country of Mexico. In its entirety, the river is 1,450 miles long and provides water for drinking, hydroelectric power, agricultural use, and recreation.

People have battled over many aspects of the Colorado River for decades, including who should get its water, as well as where, when, why, and how. People have even butted heads over the name of the river. It was named The Grand River until 1921, when one plucky Colorado politician petitioned Congress for a name change that would more specifically honor the location of the river's headwaters. U.S. Representative Edward T. Taylor succeeded in his effort and it thereafter was known as the Colorado, and often the "mighty" Colorado. But these days, the river isn't running so mightily. Thanks to long periods of drought and to water diversion projects along the river, the Colorado no longer flows all the way to its natural end (the Sea of Cortez), a fact that is deeply concerning.

In the Kawuneeche Valley, the Colorado River is located west of Highway 34/Trail Ridge Road. While you can easily view the river from your car window and various pullouts along the road, it's worth it to take a walk on the **Coyote Valley Trail** or the trail to the **Holzwarth Historic Site** to get up close. If your plans on the west side include staying one or several nights at the **Timber Creek Campground,** the Colorado River is located just west of the tent/RV sites. Another great place to view the river is along the **Colorado River Trail** to **Lulu City.**

Recreation

HIKING

★ Lulu City

Distance: 7.4 miles round-trip
Duration: 2 hours
Elevation gain: 350 feet
Effort: moderate
Trailhead: Colorado River (see map p. 149)
Directions: From the Grand Lake Entrance Station, drive 9.6 miles north on Highway 34.

What you'll notice on the way to Lulu City are the big things: the Colorado River; the remains of a prospector's home (Shipler's Cabins); and the large, now-deserted meadow that was once home to 200 miners. Just as interesting, though, are some of the smaller details along the path. Keep a look out for a remarkably green understory along parts of the trail and delicate wisps of spider webs strung between tree branches. On a clear day, sunlight streams through the trees, making pretty patterns appear on the ground. Beauty is found every step of the way on this trek.

From the **Colorado River Trailhead,** walk north on the trail and almost immediately, climb up a short set of natural steps. The trail levels out then travels through forest before arriving at an attractive, tree-dotted **meadow.** At 0.5 mile, find a junction for the **Red Mountain Trail;** stay straight for Lulu City. After leaving the meadow, you will start to gain some nice views of the Colorado River on your left. On the approach to **Shipler's Cabins,** look on the right side of the trail for tailings from Joseph Shipler's silver mine. The tailings are strewn across a hillside and you will also walk through a short section of trail where broken-up rock lines both sides of the path. At approximately 2.3 miles from the trailhead, a pretty meadow and Shipler's ramshackle residence come into view. Just after leaving the meadow, a privy is off the trail if you need to make a pit stop. Otherwise, continue walking through the forest until arriving at a trail junction for **Little Yellowstone.** Stay straight for Lulu City—it is just 0.2 mile farther. Once at Lulu City, you will find a small wooden marker that says "**Lulu City Site.**" Just beyond is the large meadow where various stores, cabins, a hotel, a bar, and a post office used to exist. While the buildings are long gone, stellar views remain. This is a superb place to sit, unpack a picnic, relax, and observe the flow of the Colorado River. Return the way you came, or continue farther north to Little Yellowstone or La Poudre Pass.

★ Coyote Valley Trail

Distance: 1 mile round-trip
Duration: 1 hour
Elevation gain: 10 feet
Effort: easy
Trailhead: Coyote Valley
Directions: From the Grand Lake Entrance Station, drive 5.4 miles north on Highway 34.

This gentle, **wheelchair-accessible,** and

the Coyote Valley Trail

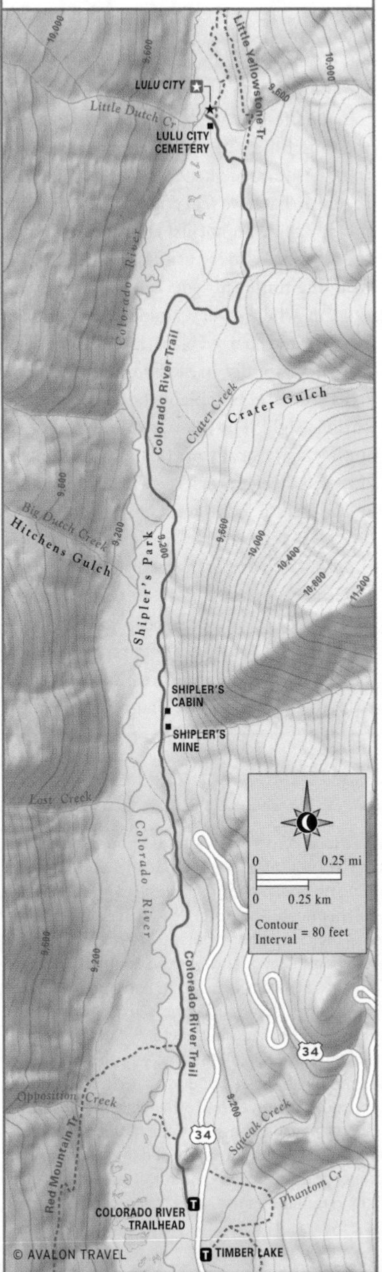

family-friendly trail highlights some of the best scenery the Kawuneeche Valley has to offer: large meadows, the Colorado River, and views of the Never Summer Mountains. Of particular interest is the abundance of life along the edge of the Colorado River, an area known as riparian habitat.

From the parking lot, head west on a wide, packed-gravel path that in just a few paces crosses over the river via a **footbridge.** Take a right (north) after the bridge. Now you are paralleling the river on the right side of the trail; a sprawling mountain meadow is on your left. Stop and listen. The gurgling sound of the water has a soothing and meditative effect, inviting hikers to slow down the pace and notice numerous interpretive signs and wildlife activity on both sides of the trail. Keep a lookout for birds, moose, elk, coyote, and small mammals as you go, and stop to sit on a bench if you wish. There is a **short loop** at the end of the trail that rejoins the main path; return the way you came and consider sticking around for a picnic. Numerous tables are located at the beginning of the trail, just west of the footbridge. Five parking spots at the Coyote Valley Trail are designated for people with disabilities, and bathrooms are wheelchair accessible.

★ Granite Falls

Distance: 10.4 miles round-trip
Duration: 5.5 hours
Elevation gain: 1,406 feet
Effort: moderate
Trailhead: Green Mountain (see map p. 152)
Directions: From the Grand Lake Entrance Station, drive 2.5 miles north on Highway 34.

On this lovely hike, nature proves to be more of a balm than a stimulus, with plenty of opportunities for relaxation and contemplation. Though a longer trek, the elevation gain is spread out over 5.2 miles, meaning you will never huff and puff with overexertion.

In the first 1.8-mile stretch along the **Green Mountain Trail,** ascend gently through forest, cross over several small wooden **footbridges,** and discover some delightful meadow areas on the right (south) side of the trail. Start watching for wildlife early; you could very well stumble upon a moose. Immediately after you see a sign for the **Green Mountain wilderness campsite** (at 1.8 mi), you will be at a trail junction; head left (north) on the **Tonahutu Creek Trail,** referenced as the "Upper Tonahutu" on the trail sign.

Once on the Tonahutu Creek Trail, you will first skirt the west side of **Big Meadows,** the largest montane meadow in Rocky. Along the edge of the meadow are plenty of great spots to stop and enjoy the view. Listen to the grass rustling in the breeze; keep an ear out for woodpeckers and other birds; and note that across the meadow there is a large area of trees scoured by the **Tonahutu Fire,** a blaze started by lightning in 2014. As you hike, you will encounter the remains of an **old log cabin** on the left side of the trail. A second crumbled-down cabin appears shortly after on the right side. Both at one time belonged to a miner named Sam Stone. The trail is nearly flat as it skirts Big Meadows for 0.7 mile to the next trail junction.

You will come to a sign with several choices: Onahu Creek Trailhead, or Flattop Mountain and Bear Lake. Granite Falls is not listed as an option; you will need to follow the arrow for **Flattop Mountain/Bear Lake** to stay on the Tonahutu Creek Trail. Next, follow the trail east and skirt the north side of the meadow. You are now heading directly into the fire-damaged area, and there is a sign warning hikers of potential hazards on the trail. Be aware of burned and creaking/swaying trees that have real potential for tumbling down. At one point (just after the turnoff for the **Sunrise wilderness campsite,** 3.5 miles from the trailhead) you will walk through a section where every single tree has been stripped and charred black, and the landscape feels otherworldly. In the summer, the charred trees are offset by a blanket of wildflowers, a curious sight. For the last 15 minutes or so, until you arrive at your final destination, the trail gets steeper; rock steps have been added to the trail to aid hikers. At last you will arrive at **Granite Falls,** an absolute beauty of a waterfall and one of my favorites in the park.

Head back the way you came, or plan ahead and include this destination on a longer backpacking trip. You might opt to continue on to Flattop Mountain and thru-hike to the east side, or do a loop hike that returns via the

The Hotel de Hardscrabble

Robert "Squeaky Bob" Wheeler ran the first lodge located between Estes Park and Grand Lake, the **Hotel de Hardscrabble.** Though the park had not yet opened in the early 1900s, Wheeler made a keen observation: people who were riding on horseback from Estes Park to Grand Lake had nowhere to stay overnight. He sought to fill that need. The Hotel de Hardscrabble opened along the Colorado River in 1907. As travelers made their way along a horse trail above the Kawuneeche Valley, they could spot Wheeler's property in the distance and were no doubt delighted to see tent-cabins (accommodations made from log and canvas), a main lodge, and a place to bathe (the Colorado River). Wheeler was particularly well known for his adeptness in the kitchen, and for his voice. Whenever he talked excitedly, his voice squeaked similarly to that of a boy going through puberty. Though over the years several stories have circulated as to why this was so, the most plausible is that Wheeler's throat was scarred by illness at a young age. Wheeler and his hotel enjoyed notoriety for hosting President Theodore Roosevelt and other high-profile guests. Wheeler is also remembered for some eccentric hotel management practices that would never fly in this day and age; instead of routinely washing guests' sheets, he sprinkled them with talcum powder. He was also said to have skimped on toilet paper, providing patrons instead with mail-order catalog pages to wipe their behinds. Nothing remains of the hotel today, but the story of this enterprising, quirky man with a distinct voice lives on.

The Harbison Sisters and Harbison Ranch

Early homesteaders **Annie** and **Kitty Harbison** are remembered at the site of the **Harbison Meadows Picnic Pavilion** with an interpretive sign, though their actual properties were located approximately a quarter mile south of the sign, closer to the western entrance of the park. The two are recalled as women who were fiercely devoted to each other and to the land that they tended. They purchased two adjoining lots, totaling 320 acres, and built individual cabins on each, as well as a cabin for their parents and brother. The sisters operated a dairy ranch that supplied fresh milk to the people of Grand Lake, and toiled hard on their land. In 1915 when the park was established, the sisters refused to sell their land to the National Park Service (NPS), and, for many years, stood firm in their decision. In 1938 they finally relented—just a little—by selling a small portion of their property during a re-route of Trail Ridge Road. At one point, Kitty became engaged to a local gentleman but eventually jilted her husband-to-be; she felt her responsibility to the land and her sister would be compromised if she were to be married. After the Harbisons' parents passed away and their brother married and left the property, this inseparable twosome stayed on their adjoined homesteads. Later on, both sisters contracted pneumonia and died within days of each other, after which point the property became part of the park.

The Harbisons were an important family in the history of the area, though there is nothing left of their property other than timothy grass that they planted for their livestock to eat and the remains of an irrigation ditch. If you sit at the picnic pavilion in the summer and gaze south, look for where the sagebrush ends and grass begins—this is one edge of the sisters' property. A local historian conducts tours on this property in the summer, recreating in vivid detail the story of two sisters bound by love for each other and love for the land on which they worked.

North Inlet Trailhead. The Green Mountain Trail and North Inlet Trail make up one small section of the Continental Divide National Scenic Trail (CDT).

Tonahutu Creek Trail to Big Meadows

Distance: 8.4 miles round-trip
Duration: 3.5-4 hours
Elevation gain: 852 feet
Effort: moderate
Trailhead: Tonahutu Spur Trail, located next to the Kawuneeche Visitor Center (see map p. 152)

Big Meadows is the sprawling treat waiting at the end of this hike. Looking at a map, you will see that the Green Mountain Trail provides a much shorter means to this capacious meadow. But if you can, try both routes, if for no other reasons than to get a greater sense of the Kawuneeche Valley's landscape and to experience a portion of the 13-mile-long Tonahutu Creek Trail (Tonahutu is an Arapaho word that translates to "Big Meadows."). This route (or a smaller portion of it) is also fabulous for a cross-country ski or snowshoe outing in the winter.

To start, park at the south end of the **Kawuneeche Visitor Center** parking lot and jump onto the **Tonahutu Spur Trail**. Head east through a lodgepole pine forest on flat ground for 0.7 mile until you reach a **trail junction.** Turn left (north) at the junction toward Big Meadows. The trail continues through lodgepoles until **Harbison Ditch** at around 0.8 mile, marked by a small wooden sign. Harry Harbison, the half-brother of homesteaders Annie and Kitty Harbison, dug the ditch to supply water for Columbine Lake (located outside the park boundaries), once a commercial fish hatchery run by Mr. Harbison.

Tonahutu Creek appears about 1.1 miles from the trailhead. Continue hiking through forest to the **Paintbrush wilderness campsite,** located on the southern end of Big Meadows, approximately 3.5 miles from your starting point. Another 0.5 mile later you will arrive at the junction of the **Green**

Green Mountain and Tonahutu Trails

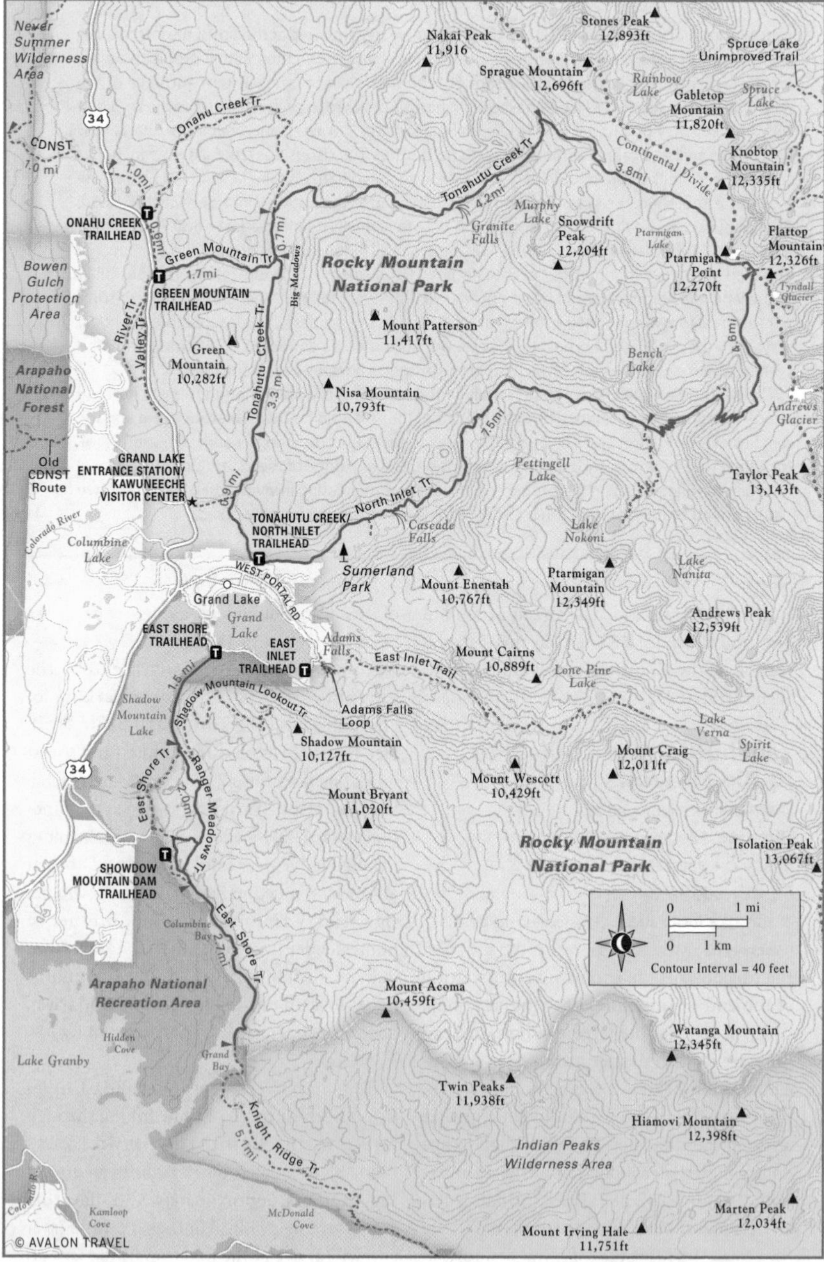

Mountain Trailhead and the **Tonahutu Creek Trailhead.** Continue walking along the edge of the broad expanse of meadow as long as you like, then return the way you came.

Cascade Falls

Distance: 7 miles round-trip
Duration: 3 hours
Elevation gain: 300 feet
Effort: moderate
Trailhead: North Inlet (see map p. 152; park pass not required)

For many people, Cascade Falls is just a quick stop on a larger Continental Divide Trail hike/backpack trip starting or ending at the Green Mountain Trailhead, but this is also a satisfying out-and-back day hike.

The **North Inlet Trail** is flat and wide as it heads east. Five to ten minutes of easy hiking puts you next to the North Inlet Creek, located south of the trail. The creek is placid and mirrorlike in this stretch, and worth stopping to enjoy for a few minutes or longer before continuing on. The sprawling meadow of **Summerland Park** is also here, just shy of the 1-mile mark. Next, you will pass a privately owned house on the north side of the trail, followed by the **Summerland Park group campsite** at 1.2 miles (on your right). Shortly thereafter, you'll cross a small wooden footbridge and walk by a sign for the **Summerland wilderness site.** At this point the trail is flanked by trees on both sides. Travel until you pass yet another wilderness campsite, **Twinberry,** located about 0.5 mile from your destination. Continue northeast on the trail and you will start to hear the rush of water on your right, a sign that you are getting close to the falls. Finally, you will reach a **trail split:** a stock-only path heads up, and another trail heads down to the falls. Walk along the short rocky path to see the falls, tumbling and gushing over an impressive pile of granite. Take a seat on a nearby rock and keep your eyes out for gray birds called water ouzels—also known as American dippers—frolicking in the spray of water. Head back west to your starting point, or continue heading northeast if you planned ahead to hike to Flatttop Mountain and/or loop around to the Green Mountain Trailhead.

Adams Falls

Distance: 0.6 mile round-trip
Duration: 30 minutes
Elevation gain: 80 feet
Effort: easy
Trailhead: East Inlet (see map p. 152; park pass not required)

On the west side of the park, there is no easier waterfall to get to than Adams Falls, making this outing a **favorite among families.** On summer weekends especially, expect to share the trail with many other visitors.

To start, amble east through a forested area at a gentle grade. Very quickly you will arrive at a **sign** directing you toward the falls. Swing right (south) and hike a short distance to a rock-walled **viewing platform.** (The park strongly discourages people from viewing the falls from points outside of the platform; there are big drop-offs to the bottom and injury or

Adams Falls

death is a real possibility.) From the platform, return the way you came or continue east along a short loop trail that connects with the **East Inlet Trail.** At this point, to return to the parking lot, head left (west). You might also consider heading farther right (east) on East Inlet to extend your hiking time. In under 0.5 mile, the landscape opens up to reveal East Meadow—a beautiful grassy expanse of land, cheerfully punctuated with wildflowers in the warm months.

East Shore Trail to Shadow Mountain Dam

Distance: 5.2 miles round-trip
Duration: 2.25 hours
Elevation gain: 100 feet
Effort: easy to moderate
Trailhead: East Shore Trail (see map p. 152), Arapaho National Recreation Area ($5 fee)

Hiking the East Shore Trail in the warm months, you are likely to be treated to a blithe scene: people canoeing, kayaking, or jet skiing. Occasionally, you might hear music floating across the reservoir from someone's watercraft, or catch a snippet of conversation or laughter from a pontoon boat that has temporarily tucked itself into a cove. These are the happy sounds of summer. But even with people so close by, the East Shore Trail still offers plenty of opportunities to get in touch with nature.

Start your hike on a tree-lined trail, part of the Continental Divide National Scenic Trail, in the **Arapaho National Recreation Area.** Good views of **Shadow Mountain Reservoir** appear on the right side of the trail after about 5-10 minutes of hiking. At 0.7 mile, you will have traveled south to the **entry point for Rocky,** though the terrain will not look any different. As you continue, keep on the lookout for wildflowers and wildlife. The trail dips right next to the water at times, then veers away for a few minutes, then heads back toward the water—all along offering wonderful views. However, many of the trees along this stretch were decimated by pine beetles and lie on the forest floor. Those still standing sometimes make loud creaking noises as they sway back and forth.

At 1.5 miles from the trailhead, arrive at a **trail split.** Continue south to **Shadow Mountain Dam** (the other trail leads east to Shadow Mountain Lookout Tower). In less than 50 yards, you will encounter another set of signs; your choices are to stay on the CDT (via the Ranger Meadows Trail) and veer left away from the water, or stay to the right. Though either trail will get you to your destination, **stay right** and continue hiking close to the water. In the last 2 miles of the hike, there are several spots where the trail is muddy and logs have been dragged over the mud for ease of travel. The majority of hikers should not have any problem getting over the logs, but if you have balance issues, hiking poles can be helpful. Stay aware of activity overhead; you are in osprey territory and they are commonly soaring in the sky. You will arrive at the NPS **East Shore Trail** sign, at which point you can turn around, explore the area of the dam, or go fishing.

The Arapaho National Recreation Area requires $5 day-use fee; no NPS fee is necessary. The nearest **fee station** is at the ANRA's Hilltop boat launch, located on Jericho Road at the north end of the reservoir, just south of the connecting channel between Grand Lake and Shadow Mountain Reservoir.

★ Shadow Mountain Lookout Tower

Distance: 9.6 miles round-trip
Duration: 4-5 hours
Elevation gain: 1,533 feet
Effort: strenuous
Trailhead: East Shore Trailhead (see map p. 152), Arapaho National Recreation Area ($5 fee)

At one time, four fire lookout towers in and around Rocky were occupied in an effort to nip natural or human-caused blazes in the bud. Locations included Longs Peak, Twin Sisters, Shadow Mountain, and the North Fork of the Big Thompson River. Today, only the Shadow Mountain Lookout Tower remains. The three-story tower, which was

Where There's Smoke, There's Fire

Quick detection of forest fires saves trees, communities, and lives. Throughout the United States, fire lookout towers were popularly used for early fire detection from the turn of the 20th century through the 1960s. Forest Service employees staffed towers 365 days a year, keeping a watchful eye on the woods for wisps of smoke. Fire towers fell out of favor, though, when aerial detection methods were recognized as a superior, more cost-effective monitoring method. Daily airplane flyovers could detect fire in areas visible from four or five fire towers, and staff could survey the grounds in a fraction of the time needed by employees in the lookout towers. The flyover method is not foolproof though, and if you talk to folks who are passionate about the topic, they will say that there is still plenty of need for fire towers in the present day.

In Rocky, daily flyovers are not the norm; instead, park staff find that smoke reports from the public are highly effective for identifying new fires. With so much development around the park and plenty of folks traveling in the backcountry, there are hundreds of people gazing at the skyline (and sniffing the air) on any given day in months when fire danger is high. In 2013, after decades of not being used, the **Shadow Mountain Lookout Tower** was staffed during a period of extreme fire danger. The tower could be used again in the future, should the right combination of circumstances present themselves, but most of the time it stands vacant.

often occupied by a married couple, was built in 1930 and abandoned at the end of the summer in 1968. In 1978, the lookout was added to the **National Register of Historic Places** due to its rustic architecture. The stone-and-wood building, which is often referred to as a "truncated windmill," is still as attractive as ever today.

From the parking lot, head south on the **East Shore Trail.** Consider this pleasant section of mostly level ground a short warm-up for your legs before the real work begins. As you travel along, enjoy abundant views of **Shadow Mountain Reservoir,** which is just off the west side of the trail. At 1.5 miles, you will reach a trail split; head east on the **Shadow Mountain Trail.** The trail from here on out is a tongue-dragger, heading steadily up Shadow Mountain through the forest. Finally, at 3.3 miles from the last

Shadow Mountain Lookout Tower

trail junction, you will arrive at your destination. Visitors are typically allowed to climb the steep set of stairs to the **wraparound deck** on the tower, though heed signs advising you to stay off the structure; occasionally repairs are being made. Otherwise, there are plenty of large rocks to sit on around the tower for lunch. From the top, enjoy views of Grand Lake, Shadow Mountain Reservoir, and Lake Granby. Return the way you came.

The Arapaho National Recreation area requires $5 day-use fee; no NPS fee is necessary. The nearest **fee station** is at the ANRA's Hilltop boat launch, located on Jericho Road at the north end of the reservoir, just south of the connecting channel between Grand Lake and Shadow Mountain Reservoir.

BACKPACKING

When the itch to hoist a 30-pound pack onto your shoulders and meander into the woods strikes, west-side trails sufficiently scratch that itch. Plenty of wilderness campsites exist throughout the Kawuneeche Valley, with the **East Inlet Trail** proving an especially popular choice for hikers, along with the **Continental Divide National Scenic Trail** (CDT) and thru-hiking to the east side of the park (a car shuttle is needed for this option).

A **permit** is required to camp in the backcountry. For wilderness camping dates May 1-October 31, reservations can be made online (www.pay.gov) or in-person at a wilderness office (not by phone) March 1-October 28. For camping dates November 1-April 30, reservations can be made by phone or in person October 1-April 30. The **West Side Wilderness Office** (970/586-1242) is located in the Kawuneeche Visitor Center.

Denver REI (1416 Platte St., Denver, 800/622-2236, www.rei.com, July-Sept., $949 REI members, $1,049 non-members) offers two backpacking trips in the Kawuneeche Valley; participants meet in Denver and travel by van to the park. Trips run along the East Inlet Trail and North Inlet Trail.

Never Summer Mountain Products (919 Grand Ave., Grand Lake, 970/627-3642, www.neversummermtn.com, 8am-8pm daily mid-June-mid-Sept., 9am-5:30pm daily fall-winter) rents bear canisters.

★ Continental Divide National Scenic Trail

The **Continental Divide National Scenic Trail** (CDT) is mind-bogglingly long—3,100 miles of interconnected trails that stretch from the Canadian border in Montana to Mexico.

In the making since 1962, parts of the trail were initially marked out with blue cans; thus, the route early on was called "The Blue Can Trail." In 1977, the Department of the Interior officially considered a proposal for the Continental Divide National Scenic Trail and in 1978, the CDT formally became part of the National Trails System. Efforts to improve the trail have waxed and waned over the decades, and even today, the CDT is a work in progress. Some parts of the route still consist of dirt roads or pavement. Blue markers or blazes with the official CDT logo help guide hikers in sections where the path is less obvious; but even then, there are points along the route where it is unclear which direction to go, which adds to the adventure.

The trail winds through two other national parks besides Rocky: Yellowstone National Park and Glacier National Park. In RMNP, approximately 30 miles of existing park trails are included in the CDT.

BACKPACKING

Anyone can hike a small or large section of the CDT, or backpack along the route. One popular backpacking trek starts at the **Green Mountain Trailhead.** Take the trail east for 1.7 miles to the **Tonahutu Creek Trail,** and then travel north and west for 8.7 miles to **Flattop Mountain.** Follow the **North Inlet Trail** south, then west, for 12.1 miles to the **North Inlet Trailhead.** To finish out the hike, travel 4.2 miles north on the **Tonahutu Creek Trail,** then 1.7 miles west on the **Green Mountain Trail** back to your starting point.

How to Talk Like a Thru-Hiker

If you plan to hike the entire CDT or just want to chat up people on a section of the trail using the right lingo, get schooled with this newbie's guide to thru-hiker terminology.

- **Flip Flopper:** A hiker who does not trek in a linear fashion along a long-distance trail.
- **MUDs:** Mindless ups and downs. A section of trail that builds up to nothing spectacular, heads down, then up again (and so on).
- **NOBO:** Heading northbound on the trail.
- **PUDs:** Pointless ups and downs. A more mind-numbing version of MUDs; extended in nature.
- **SOBO:** Heading southbound on the trail.
- **Thru-Hiker:** Thru-hikers intend to hike the entire 3,100 mile CDT trail from tip to tail.
- **Trail Angel:** A person who bestows trail magic.
- **Trail Magic:** A sweet surprise bestowed upon a long-distance hiker: often a hot meal or an icy cold beverage.
- **Trail Name:** A nickname that is used frequently and affectionately while on the trail (and often off-trail, too, while still on the hike but having a "zero day"). The best trail names are bestowed while the hike is in progress.
- **Triple Crown:** Three major long-distance hikes are found in North America: the Appalachian Trail, Pacific Crest Trail, and Continental Divide National Scenic Trail. Collectively, they are known as the "Triple Crown." To complete all three hikes is considered the ultimate thru-hiking achievement.
- **Zero Day:** When the legs are tired, the back is tweaked, or a sore throat is coming on, it's a good day to stay put and have a "zero day," on which zero miles are hiked. A zero day can happen in the woods or in a nearby town.

Significant sights along the way include Big Meadows, Granite Falls, Flattop Mountain, and Cascade Falls. Numerous **wilderness campsites** along the route are available for reservation through the park's Wilderness Office (970/586-1242). On the Tonahutu Creek Trail, campsites include Sunset, Sunrise, Lower Granite Falls, Granite Falls, and Tonahutu Meadows. On the North Inlet Trail, reserve a spot at Twinberry, Big Pool, Grouseberry, Porcupine, or July.

THRU-HIKING

CDT "thru-hikers" (people backpacking the entire route) often don't follow a strict path during their journey. There are numerous unofficial (but well-known) alternate routes on which hikers can get sidetracked; such is the case in Rocky. Some options for exploring Rocky as a thru-hiker include (1) taking the **short loop** (hiking the Green Mountain Trail and following the Tonahutu Creek Trail south to its trailhead), continuing south out of the park boundary to your next destination; (2) taking the **long loop** (hiking the Green Mountain Trail to the Tonahutu Creek Trail, following it east to Flattop Junction, then heading southwest on the North Inlet Trail to its trailhead) and staying overnight at a wilderness campsite; or (3) hiking **part of the short loop,** staying overnight in Grand Lake, and exploring **part of the longer route** as a side trip the following day. Option number three is preferable for many thru-hikers because they can't predict exactly what day they will arrive in the park; making reservations in advance for a wilderness campsite can be challenging.

Thru-hikers who bypass the longer route altogether do not get to stand on top of the Continental Divide in Rocky. That opportunity only arises once: at **Flattop Mountain.** Otherwise, the route in RMNP travels near the Continental Divide, not on top of it.

INFORMATION

For those interested in thru-hiking the CDT, the **Continental Divide Trail Coalition** (www.continentaldividetrail.org) is a good source of information, and **Bear Creek Survey** (www.bearcreeksurvey.com) sells numerous map guides for the trail. I particularly love **Phlumf.com;** the person who runs this website, Jonathan Ley, started creating maps for the trail back in 2001 when resources were few. He downloaded USGS maps on a painfully slow dial-up Internet connection and marked them up during his own trek along the CDT. Today, he updates his original maps each year and offers them to interested parties at no charge (though donations are strongly appreciated).

★ FISHING

Fly-fishing aficionados find themselves in good company on the west side. In particular, anglers love the Kawuneeche Valley's streams. Favorite spots to cast a line include the **North Inlet, East Inlet,** and **Tonahutu Creek.** Do not expect to catch any monsters in these waterways, but the fishing is still good fun. Brook trout are the most plentiful, while brown trout and rainbow trout are harder to come by. Colorado River Cutthroats (a subspecies of cutthroat trout that is native to the Colorado River) are found in west-side lakes such as **Lake Nanita** and **Timber Lake. Paradise Creek,** located on the south end of the park, is great for catch-and-release cutthroat trout; however, it is a trek to get to this remote area, and there is no overnight camping in the region. Rocky's stretch of the Colorado River is also a popular and superb waterway to fish. The river predominately contains brook trout, though other varieties of trout are present. Easy access spots for the Colorado include the **Coyote Valley Trail** and the **Holzwarth Historic Site.**

Upper Columbine Creek, in the southwest corner of the park, is closed to fishing to protect native cutthroat trout, and the Lake Nanita outlet is also closed waters. Additional rules and restrictions apply to Rocky's streams and rivers; it is important to review the park's fishing guidelines ahead of a visit.

During the **elk rut** (Sept. 1-Oct. 31) anglers cannot access certain sections of the Colorado River 5pm-7am. The park restricts foot-traffic access to Harbison Meadow and the Holzwarth Historic Site meadow so elk have the space they need to mate.

A Colorado fishing license must be obtained before fishing Rocky's waters. Pick one up at **Rocky Mountain Outfitters** (900 Grand Ave., Grand Lake, 970/798-8021, www.rkymtnoutfitters.com, 7am-6pm Mon.-Fri., 6:30am-6pm Sat.-Sun.) or **Lakeview Conoco** (14626 Hwy. 34, Grand Lake, 970/627-8252, 6am-9pm Tues.-Thurs., 6am-10pm Fri.-Sat.). Alternatively, purchase a fishing license online through the **Colorado Parks and Wildlife** (ww.cpw.state.co.us).

In the summer, the park typically offers a weekly **Ranger's Fly-Fishing School** (3 hours, free). Casting techniques are discussed and practiced, and other topics are covered. Participants do not actually catch fish during these sessions, but will gain some of the know-how needed to do so on their own time. Equipment can be borrowed from the ranger if you do not have your own. Check the park newspaper or consult with the Kawuneeche Visitor Center (970/627-3471) for details.

HORSEBACK RIDING

Guided horseback rides on the west side are offered by **Winding River Resort** (1447 County Road 491, Grand Lake, 970/627-3215, www.windingriveresort.com, Memorial Day-Sept., reservations required). Eight scheduled rides leave its facility daily; one-hour rides are $45 pp and two-hour rides are $65 pp. These

One Woman's Fight to Stay in Rocky

Trail River Ranch (on the west side of Highway 34, near the Bowen Gulch Trail) was originally homesteaded in 1919 and remained a privately owned property within Rocky until 2006. Fred and **Betty Dick,** who were the last people to own the ranch, summered on the property beginning in the 1970s. The couple believed that they had an agreement with the park to spend the rest of their lives in their home, but at one point the Park Service notified the Dicks that they only had a 25-year contract to stay, with an end-date in 2005. Fred Dick passed away in 1992, but Betty still used the cabin up until the contract's expiration date. She wanted to spend her remaining years in the cabin and rallied for her cause. The Grand Lake community, local and regional news entities, and Colorado politicians stepped in to help Dick, a well-respected philanthropist. Ultimately, an act of Congress allowed Dick to stay put at Trail River Ranch. She passed away in 2006, just months after she was granted the legal right to reside in the park. After her passing, the NPS took over the property. A group of interested local citizens called the Friends of Trail Ridge Ranch formed and served as stewards of the property until the Rocky Mountain Conservancy took over management of the ranch in 2015. The buildings, which sit on eight acres of land, are not open to visitors.

loop rides depart directly from the resort and follow the Colorado River. Winding River Resort also offers 14 campsites for visitors who wish to snooze right next to their horse. These popular sites have a base price of $46/night and include water and electricity. The fee for horses is $15 for one and $20 for two.

Equestrians are welcome to bring their own horse to the west side. Review current trail conditions and rules and regulations regarding stock use before entering the park. There are six **wilderness campsites** designed for stock; reserve ahead through the wilderness office (inside the Kawuneeche Visitor Center).

BIKING

Road cycling in the Kawuneeche Valley is limited to **Highway 34.** Some cyclists choose to ride 10 miles out and back from the Grand Lake Entrance Station to the Colorado River Trailhead; others challenge themselves with the more strenuous option of going over Trail Ridge Road (summer only). There is a decent shoulder on the road from the Grand Lake Entrance Station to the Colorado River Trailhead; from that point onward cyclists find themselves riding on the white line, making safety more of an issue. In the spring and the fall, west-side cyclists often enjoy a short car-free spell of Trail Ridge Road, when the road barrier is up for automobiles but bicycles are still allowed. A **permit** ($10/day or $15/week) is required. Be sure to wear a good helmet and reflective clothing, and carry a small repair kit with you.

If the thought of zipping 20 miles downhill on Trail Ridge Road from the Alpine Visitor Center sounds fun, consider hiring **Mountain Transit Adventures** (www.mtagrandlake.com, 970/888-1227, year-round) to shuttle you to the top. The service charges $125/hour for bus transportation (with a capacity of 40 passengers) and $80/hour for transportation via 12-passenger van.

WINTER SPORTS

★ Snowshoeing and Cross-Country Skiing

Trails on the west side are open to both snowshoers and cross-country skiers. When it comes to snowshoeing, my preference is to amble along at an easy pace on terrain with a gentle grade, focusing more on the scenery than the workout (though breaking trail through fresh snow can be a workout even on flat ground!). The Kawuneeche Valley has several options that fit the description of "slow and easy" (for both skiing and snowshoeing). The 2.3-mile **Sun Valley Loop** (starts at Harbison Meadows) and **Coyote Valley Trail** are good for beginners. For an intermediate-level outing, consider taking the **Colorado River Trail** to **Lulu City,** the **Tonahutu Spur Trail** (next to the Kawuneeche Visitor Center) to **Big Meadows,** or the **Green Mountain Trail** to **Big Meadows.** It is fun to explore just short parts of trails, too. I once snowshoed up the Timber Lake Trail for just 20 minutes, became captivated by a feisty Abert's squirrel careering through the woods, and eventually returned to the parking lot.

Never Summer Mountain Products (919 Grand Ave., 970/627-3642, www.neversummermtn.com, 8am-8pm daily mid-June-mid-Sept., 9am-5:30pm daily fall-winter) offers cross-country ski and snowshoe rentals for adults and children.

Regardless of what you strap on your feet, make sure that you are following winter trail etiquette. In the snowy months, numerous signs posted in the Kawuneeche Valley (and in other areas of the park) advise recreationists to "share the trail, not the track." Snowshoers should be conscientious about preserving cross-country ski tracks that are set by others in the snow: whenever possible, hike to the side of those ski tracks (cross-country skiing in lumpy snow isn't a barrel of fun).

Entertainment and Shopping

RANGER PROGRAMS

An appealing line-up of ranger-led **talks, hikes,** and **educational programs** is available throughout the year on the west side. History- and ecology-based talks often take place at the **Kawuneeche Visitor Center;** in the summer, rangers present an entertaining and educational nightly program at the **Timber Creek Campground Amphitheater.** Also on the summer schedule are ranger-led wildflower hikes and heritage walks.

A handful of kid-specific programs are offered. A summertime campfire program at **Holzwarth Historic Site** (7pm Fri.) is especially popular with families. Other evening programs include twilight walks and stargazing. If your goals for a fulfilling west-side visit include some learning, pick up the park newspaper for a ranger-led program schedule, or chat with staff in the visitor center about upcoming programs.

Winter Tours

In the heart of winter, the west side offers free ranger-led snow sports. Choose from a 1.5-hour **cross-country ski tour** (one a week late Dec.-Jan.) and a 2-hour beginner or intermediate **snowshoe tour** (one a week late Dec.-early Mar.). Tours are open to participants age 8 and older; equipment is not provided. All programs require advance reservations; stop by the Kawuneeche Visitor Center (970/627-3471) to reserve your spot.

Rocky Mountain Conservancy Field Institute

The **Rocky Mountain Conservancy Field Institute** (48 Alpine Cir., Estes Park, 970/586-0108, www.rmconservancy.org) runs educational programs on the west side. Topics run the gamut, from hummingbirds ($60) to mushroom hunting ($80). Pre-registration for classes through the Rocky Mountain Conservancy is required. Check the Field Institute's catalog for offerings specific to the Kawuneeche Valley and Grand Lake area.

SHOPPING

The **Kawuneeche Visitor Center** (16018 Hwy. 34, Grand Lake, 970/627-3471, 8am-6pm daily summer, 8am-4:30pm daily winter) carries Rocky Mountain Conservancy goods, including plush toys, books, and clothing. Proceeds from merchandise sales benefit various park initiatives.

Camping

Camping is the only form of overnight accommodation. Grand Lake and the town of Granby (a 20-minute drive south from the Grand Lake Entrance Station) serve as great jumping-off points for the west side, with a variety of accommodations available in both towns. In the summer and fall, it is possible to stay overnight in Estes Park and drive over Trail Ridge Road for a long day trip to the west side of the park.

INSIDE THE PARK

Timber Creek Campground

The west side's only campground is **Timber Creek Campground** (Hwy. 34, www.nps.gov/romo, late May-early Nov., $26), 10 miles north of Grand Lake. All 98 RV and tent sites are first-come, first-served. Shade is sparse, as mountain pine beetles did a number on the trees and most were removed; precious few remain. Campsite amenities include a tent pad, grill, and fire pit; restrooms; an amphitheater for ranger-led programs; a dump station; water; and dishwashing sinks. Firewood is sold here, but not ice. Bear boxes must be shared. A few minutes' walk takes campers down to the shores of the Colorado River, where fishing and relaxing are popular pastimes.

Dispersed Camping

Numerous wilderness campsites are found along trails east of Highway 34. As you explore your options, consider sites on the **Onahu Creek Trail, Tonahutu Creek Trail, North Inlet Trail,** or **East Inlet Trail.**

OUTSIDE THE PARK

If you want to park your RV or pitch a tent outside the park, there are two options. **Elk Creek Campground and RV Resort** (143 County Rd. 48, Grand Lake, 970/627-8502, www.elkcreekcamp.com, May 15-Oct.15) has 13 tent sites ($29), 50 RV sites ($40-45), 14 cabins ($59-64), and 1 tipi ($40) that may be reserved. On-site amenities include a trout pond, game arcade, and a shower room.

Winding River Resort (1447 County Rd. 491, Grand Lake, 970/627-3215, www.windingriverresort.com, Memorial Day-Sept.)

Timber Creek Campground

has 14 tent or RV sites (water/electric) with horse corrals ($46, plus $15-20 for horses), 39 tent-only sites ($35), 43 full-hook up RV sites ($49), 8 cabins ($210-275), and 2 lodge rooms ($110-135). The resort offers a number of unique recreational opportunities. Among them is a small sleigh and carriage museum where you can ogle Santa-worthy transportation that dates back to the 1800s. The facility also hosts "cowboy church" on Sundays next to the Colorado River, a decidedly casual affair with worshipers toting their own lawn chairs.

Campgrounds around the **Arapaho National Recreation Area** (www.fs.usda.gov) are a reasonable option for Kawuneeche Valley visitors; the closest to the park entrance is **Green Ridge Campground** (78 sites, 877/444-6777, www.recreation.gov, mid-May-late Sept., $19 singles, $38 doubles) 4.5 miles away. From the junction of Highway 34 and County Road 66, drive 1.4 miles east.

Food

INSIDE THE PARK

Want grub on the west side? Your options are limited to: (1) driving up Trail Ridge Road (summer only) to **Café in the Clouds** (Trail Ridge Rd. and Old Fall River Rd., www.trailridgegiftstore.com, 10am-4:30pm daily late May-June and Aug.-mid-Oct.; 9am-5:30pm late June-Aug., $6-10); (2) driving into Grand Lake; (3) packing a picnic.

Picnicking

Picnic tables are plentiful in the Kawuneeche Valley; find them at the Beaver Ponds, Bowen/Baker Trailhead, Colorado River Trailhead, Coyote Valley Trailhead, Holzwarth Historic Site, Kawuneeche Visitor Center, and Timber Lake Trailhead. Picnicking is not allowed in the Timber Creek Campground Memorial Day-September.

Harbison Meadows (on the left side of Hwy. 34, north of Grand Lake Entrance Station) has an especially nice pavilion, but this particular spot may be reserved for a wedding. Otherwise, all other picnic spots on the west side are first-come, first-served.

Transportation and Services

DRIVING

Grand Lake is considered the gateway town for the Kawuneeche Valley. From Grand Lake, it is 1.3 miles north on Highway 34 to the Kawuneeche Visitor Center; approximately 0.4 mile beyond is the entrance station. **Highway 34** (also known as Trail Ridge Road) travels the length of the Kawuneeche Valley; trailheads line the road and feature ample parking spaces. Observe posted speed limits while driving park roads; Highway 34 is patrolled and wildlife crossings are common.

For emergency roadside assistance and towing, contact **Pete's Towing and Mobile Repair** (970/887-0066, open 24/7) in Granby; there are no vehicle service stations in Grand Lake.

Winter Travel

In winter, Highway 34 and the trailhead parking lots are regularly plowed and accessible, but the road closes north of the Colorado River Trailhead. The short road leading to the Coyote Valley Trailhead closes in the winter, but visitors can still park on Highway 34 and snowshoe down to the trail.

Snow tires or all-season tires are helpful to have in the winter months. Even if you do

Where Can I Find...?

- **Bank/ATM:** The nearest bank with an ATM is Grand Mountain Bank (902 Grand Ave., Grand Lake, 970/627-9500, www.grandmountainbank.com).
- **Emergencies:** Call the park's dispatch center (970/586-1203) or seek help at the Kawuneeche Visitor Center. The nearest medical facility is Middle Park Medical Center - Granby Campus (1000 Granby Park Dr. South, Granby, 970/887-5800, www.mpmc.org, open 24/7).
- **Firewood:** Firewood can be purchased at the Timber Creek Campground on summer evenings.
- **Gas:** The nearest place to fill up is at the Lakeview Conoco (14626 Hwy. 34, Grand Lake, 970/627-8252). There are no gas stations inside the park.
- **Internet Service:** The Kawuneeche Visitor Center is one of three Wi-Fi hot spots in the park.
- **Restrooms:** Toilets are located at the East Inlet Trailhead, Tonahutu Creek/North Inlet Trailheads, Green Mountain Trailhead, Coyote Valley Trailhead, Bowen/Baker Trailhead, Timber Lake Trailhead, and Colorado River Trailhead. Bathrooms are also located at the Timber Creek Campground and the Kawuneeche Visitor Center.
- **Laundry and Showers**: Your best option to get clean is to secure overnight accommodations in Grand Lake with shower facilities. The nearest place to wash clothes is at East Side Laundromat (601 E. Jasper Ct., Granby, 970/887-3889, 7am-10pm daily).

not need them within the park, they can be a necessity when staying nearby. One winter trip to Rocky, I ended up stranded in a condominium in Granby for two days because of snow and blowing snow on Highway 34. (My car was still outfitted with summer tires; as a result, I missed out on a few days of activity.) If you end up traveling to the west side via Berthoud Pass (U.S. Hwy. 40), the road can be snowy, slick, and wet in the winter. Bottom line: travel with snow tires in the winter.

RVs

RV travel is straightforward on Highway 34 in Kawuneeche Valley. Limited RV parking is located at the Kawuneeche Visitor Center and a dump station is available at the Timber Creek Campground. If you decide to proceed past the Colorado River Trailhead on Highway 34/Trail Ridge Road, know that the road gets windy in parts; however, RVs are still permitted.

Parking lots are located at the Kawuneeche Visitor Center, Harbison Meadows, Green Mountain Trailhead, Onahu Trailhead, Coyote Valley Trailhead, Bowen/Baker Trailhead, Holzwarth Historic Site, Beaver Ponds, Timber Lake Trailhead, and the Colorado River Trailhead.

BUS AND SHUTTLE

Mountain Transit Adventures (www.mtagrandlake.com, 970/888-1227, year-round) is the only charter bus and shuttle service serving the Grand Lake area. With a fleet of five buses and three 12-passenger vans, MTA transports passengers (primarily groups) to destinations around Grand Lake, the Kawuneeche Valley, and beyond. In the summer, shuttles to the trailheads are common, as are trips up Trail Ridge Road to the Alpine Visitor Center to drop off groups of downhill cyclists. Rates are $125/hour for transportation by bus (capacity of 40 passengers) and $80/hour for a shuttle via 12-passenger van. MTA will work with individuals and smaller parties on shuttle pricing on a case-by-case basis. Transportation is available any time of the day and buses are wheelchair accessible.

Lumpy Ridge and the Mummy Range

Whether you experience Lumpy Ridge and its surroundings suspended in the air on a climbing rope or with two feet planted firmly on terra firma, you are likely to fall in love with this unique area.

Located in the northeastern corner of the park, Lumpy Ridge is in a class all its own. This conspicuous land mass first formed when magma hardened into granite some 1.4 billion years ago. Over time, with weathering, a geologic process called "exfoliation" caused minerals to slough off the rock in layers, revealing unique, knobby formations. Lumpy Ridge is of such geologic interest that school groups often come here to study its features.

Not just a scientific curiosity, Lumpy Ridge's lumps and bumps are beloved by rock climbers. Along its walls are hundreds of climbing routes. As soon as park officials lift annual raptor-nesting closures in the area in mid-summer, people come here to get their climbing fix. Hiking and trail running rival rock climbing as other popular pastimes. It's tough to decide which are more beautiful: the views of MacGregor Ranch from Lumpy Ridge, or vice versa.

If solitude is your goal, consider the Long Draw and Corral Creek region in the far northern section of the park ground zero for adventure. The majority of visitors to Rocky do not explore this area: access is more difficult, no amenities are close by, and no roads are within the park boundaries. As a result, you can hike a trail here for hours or days and encounter only a few people—or none at all. Favored activities in this remote region include fishing, backpacking, hiking, and wildlife-watching.

PLANNING YOUR TIME

It helps to look at this section of the park as not just one region, but three: the **Lumpy Ridge/Cow Creek** region (northeast), **Mummy Range** (north central), and **Long Draw Road/Corral Creek** region (northwest). While these designations are rather rough, they can at least help you narrow down the general area that you would like to visit.

Previous: pack llamas on the North Boundary Trail; a teaser on the way to Bridal Veil Falls. **Above:** the Mummy Pass Trail.

Lumpy Ridge and the Mummy Range

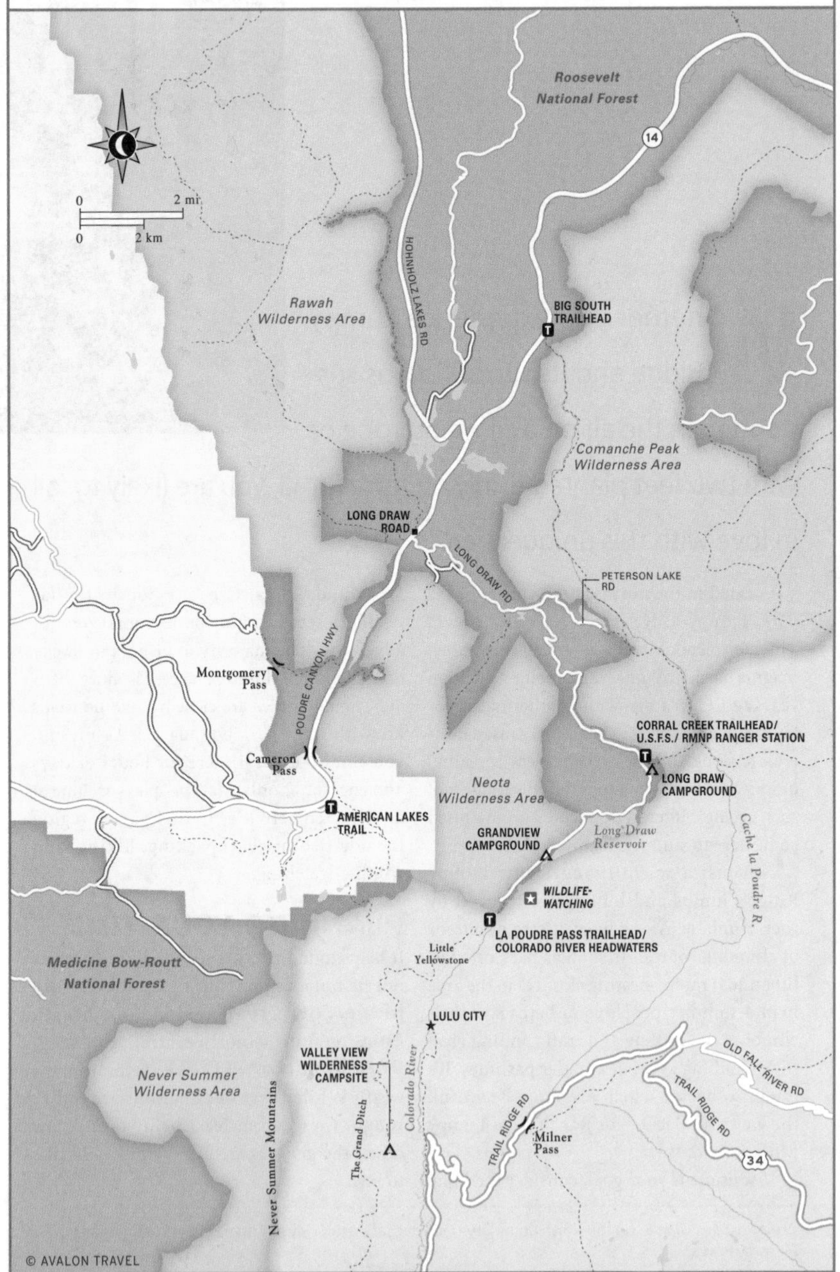

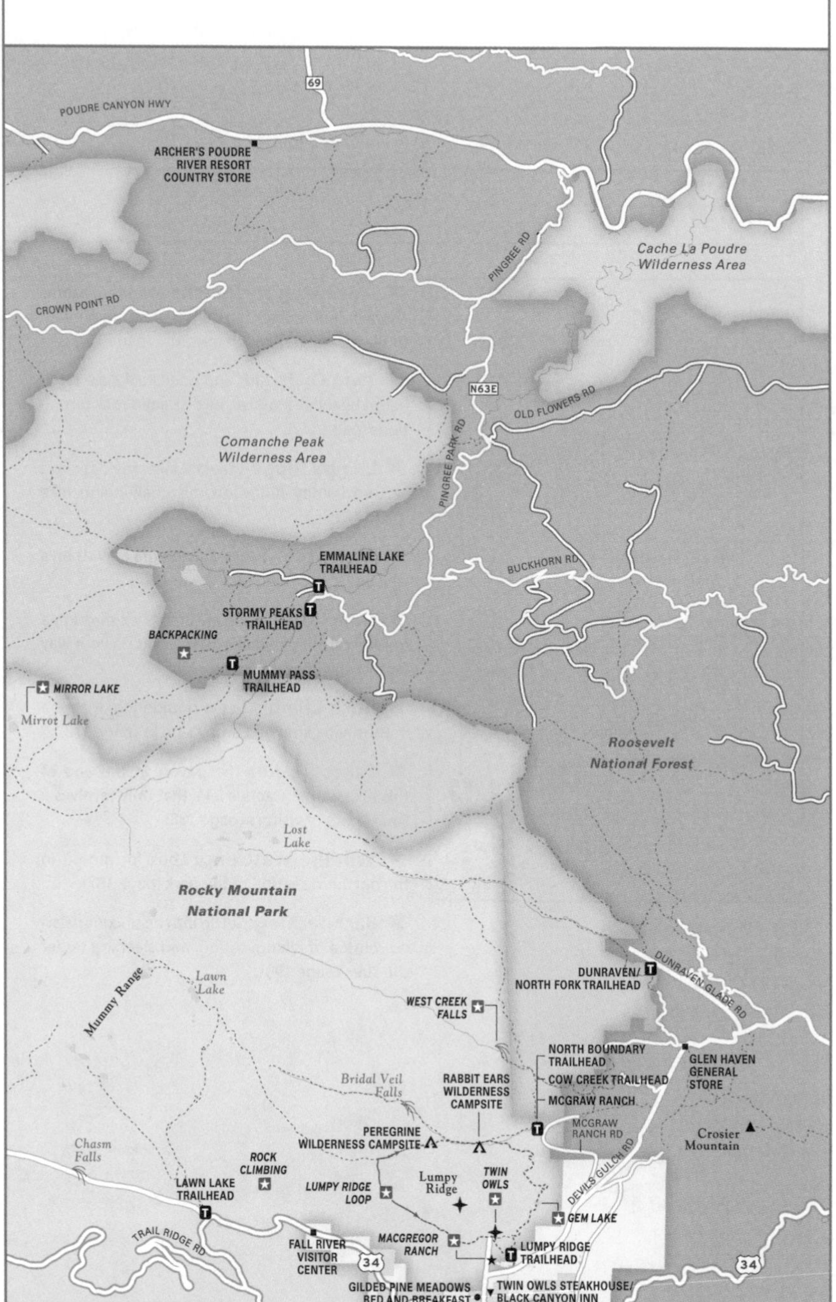
69
POUDRE CANYON HWY
ARCHER'S POUDRE RIVER RESORT COUNTRY STORE
CROWN POINT RD
PINGREE RD
Cache La Poudre Wilderness Area
N63E
OLD FLOWERS RD
PINGREE PARK RD
Comanche Peak Wilderness Area
EMMALINE LAKE TRAILHEAD
BUCKHORN RD
STORMY PEAKS TRAILHEAD
BACKPACKING
MUMMY PASS TRAILHEAD
MIRROR LAKE
Mirror Lake
Roosevelt National Forest
Lost Lake
Rocky Mountain National Park
DUNRAVEN/ NORTH FORK TRAILHEAD
DUNRAVEN GLADE RD
Mummy Range
Lawn Lake
WEST CREEK FALLS
NORTH BOUNDARY TRAILHEAD
GLEN HAVEN GENERAL STORE
COW CREEK TRAILHEAD
Bridal Veil Falls
RABBIT EARS WILDERNESS CAMPSITE
MCGRAW RANCH
MCGRAW RANCH RD
PEREGRINE WILDERNESS CAMPSITE
Crosier Mountain
Chasm Falls
ROCK CLIMBING
DEVILS GULCH RD
Lumpy Ridge
TWIN OWLS
LAWN LAKE TRAILHEAD
LUMPY RIDGE LOOP
GEM LAKE
TRAIL RIDGE RD
FALL RIVER VISITOR CENTER
MACGREGOR RANCH
LUMPY RIDGE TRAILHEAD
34
GILDED PINE MEADOWS BED AND BREAKFAST
TWIN OWLS STEAKHOUSE/ BLACK CANYON INN

Look for ★ to find recommended sights, activities, dining, and lodging.

Highlights

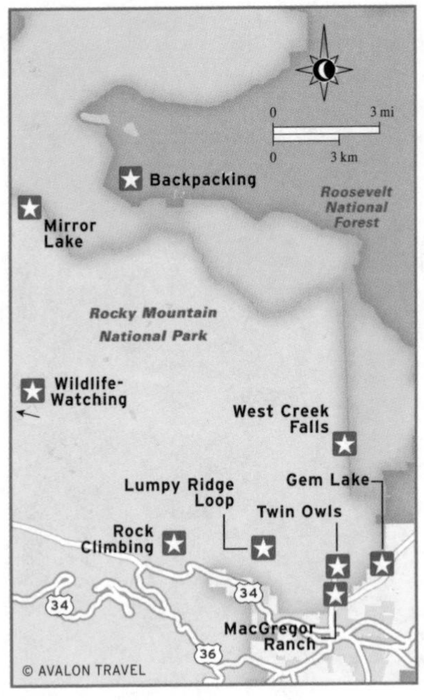

★ **MacGregor Ranch:** Wander rooms chock-full of archaic household items in a beautifully maintained ranch museum (page 170).

★ **Twin Owls:** Kids and adults alike are fascinated by these massive, bird-shaped rock formations (page 172).

★ **Lumpy Ridge Loop:** Make one big circle around Lumpy Ridge on this challenging hike (page 173).

★ **West Creek Falls:** Escape the crowds on a trek out to secluded falls (page 174).

★ **Gem Lake:** In the autumn, kick through a golden carpet of fallen aspen leaves on your way up to a shallow lake (page 176).

★ **Rock Climbing:** Go bouldering or take a multi-pitch climb on Lumpy's rocks (page 178).

★ **Mirror Lake:** The payoff at the end of this hike is an attractive lake that only receives a smattering of visitors (page 183).

★ **Wildlife-Watching:** Look for moose in the northern section of the park (page 187).

★ **Backpacking:** Settle into an uncomplicated routine of hiking, eating, and sleeping under the stars (page 190).

No single entrance station grants access to this region's sights and trails. In some cases, travel into Rocky is via trails that originate outside of the park boundary.

A reasonable plan for most visitors is to spend **2-5 days** exploring one region, either backpacking or camping outside of the park and day hiking.

Lumpy Ridge

Lumpy Ridge can transfix climbers for days and they may find no reason to explore elsewhere during their stay. The typical visitor, though, will be satisfied by making 1-2 day trips to the area during a week-long getaway to the east side. Since there are only three wilderness campsites around Lumpy, most visitors end up staying overnight at established campgrounds on the east side or in Estes Park. If your time is limited, a visit to Gem Lake should be at the top of your list. Also consider hiking west for just a mile or two on the Black Canyon Trail; in doing so, you will be able to get a good look at MacGregor Ranch, the Twin Owls, and many of Lumpy Ridge's other rock features.

ENTRANCES

The following trailheads provide access to the Lumpy Ridge/Cow Creek region. National Park fees are not required at these trailheads; however, if you plan to backpack in, you must purchase a wilderness camping permit in advance from the park's wilderness office (970/586-1242).

Lumpy Ridge and Gem Lake Trailheads

From the intersection of Highway 34 and MacGregor Avenue in Estes Park, take MacGregor Avenue northeast for 1.3 miles to the turnoff for the **Lumpy Ridge Trailhead** and **Gem Lake Trailhead.** Drive another 500 yards north on Lumpy Ridge Road to the parking lot. Vault toilets are available. These trailheads access the **Twin Owls, Lumpy Ridge,** and **Gem Lake Trails.**

Cow Creek Trailhead

From the intersection of Highway 34 and MacGregor Avenue in Estes Park, travel 3.4 miles northeast on MacGregor Avenue/Devils Gulch Road to McGraw Ranch Road. An electronic sign at the start of the road will tell you if the parking lot is full. If it's not, travel 2.1 miles on McGraw Ranch Road to the **Cow Creek Trailhead** parking area. Vault toilets are on the Cow Creek Trail (behind McGraw Ranch). This trailhead accesses the **West Creek Falls** and **Bridal Veil Falls Trails.**

Do not attempt to park anywhere other than a designated spot; parking rules are strictly enforced and cars will be towed. To start hiking, walk toward **McGraw Ranch** (an historic ranch-turned-park-research facility) and follow the small sign next to the green gate that says "Trail."

Dunraven and North Fork Trailheads

Hikers use this **Roosevelt National Forest** trailhead to access Rocky. From the intersection of Highway 34 and MacGregor Avenue in Estes Park, travel northeast on MacGregor Avenue/Devils Gulch Road for 8.8 miles to Dunraven Glade Road. Turn left, then travel 2.1 miles to the trailhead and parking area. Vault toilets are available.

Visitors will hike about 3 miles through the Roosevelt National Forest's Comanche Peak Wilderness, on the **North Fork Trail,** before arriving at the boundary of Rocky. This trailhead also provides access to the **Stormy Peaks Trail.**

Earl of Dunraven

After several visits to Estes Park in the late 1800s, a member of the British royalty, the Earl of Dunraven, became so enamored with the area that he used his power and vast wealth to try to take over the entire community. His goal was to establish his own private hunting grounds. He first went about this land-grab legally, and at one point legitimately owned 8,000 acres of land in the area. However, the earl also resorted to conniving ways to get what he wanted. First, he convinced numerous men to purchase homesteading plots; then, in rapid fashion, purchased the plots from these men and called them his own. The earl never used these alleged homesteading plots in accordance with the **Homestead Act of 1862,** of which one section required settlers to live on and improve their land for a period of five continuous years in order to own it. Though some walked away with money in their pockets and satisfied with this arrangement, the earl's activities riled up many others in the community. At one point the earl controlled—both legally and illegally—15,000 acres of land in Estes Park. In 1877, he built **The English Hotel,** a lodge in Estes Park that was popular with visitors.

For reasons that are not completely clear, the earl eventually left Estes Park in the early 1880s. He sold his land in 1908 and his hotel burned down in 1911. Still, the earl's memory lives on in Rocky and in surrounding areas: a restaurant, trailhead, lake, mountain, and street all bear his last name.

VISITOR CENTERS

Fall River Visitor Center

The **Fall River Visitor Center** (3450 Fall River Rd., 970/586-1206, www.rockymountaingateway.net, 9am-4pm Fri.-Sat. mid-May; 9am-5pm daily late May-mid-Oct.; limited hours Nov.-Dec.) is located 6 miles west of Lumpy Ridge via Highway 34. The visitor center has restrooms, a Rocky Mountain Conservancy Store, and interpretive displays; in the same complex are The Trailhead Restaurant and the Rocky Mountain Gateway Gift Shop.

Beaver Meadows Visitor Center

The **Beaver Meadows Visitor Center** (1000 Hwy. 36, 970/586-1206, www.nps.gov/romo, 8am-4:30pm daily mid-Oct-mid-May, 8am-5pm daily mid-May-mid-June, 8am-6pm daily mid-June-early Sept., 8am-5pm daily early Sept.-mid-Oct.) is located 5 miles southwest of Lumpy Ridge via Highway 36. Inside are park literature and maps, a staffed information desk, a Rocky Mountain Conservancy Store, and a small theater.

Wilderness camping permits for Lumpy Ridge can be obtained at the **East Side Wilderness Office** (located in a building near the Beaver Meadows Visitor Center, 970/586-1242, open daily, hours vary seasonally). The office also serves as a resource for people who are interested in rock climbing on Lumpy Ridge (and in other areas of the park). Some of the staff have extensive knowledge of the park's climbing routes and can give recommendations to visitors. The office also has several rock-climbing books available for perusal.

SIGHTS

★ MacGregor Ranch

Get ready for a respite from modern-day pressures upon arrival at **MacGregor Ranch** (180 MacGregor Ln., 970/586-3749, www.macgregorranch.org, 10am-4pm Tues.-Sat. June-Aug.; $5 adults, children under 18 free), a privately owned ranch, museum, and youth education center. A trip to this remarkably preserved ranch is a great way to develop an understanding of early pioneers. MacGregor Ranch (est. 1873) is the only ranch that is currently operational within Rocky's boundaries. It is still around largely because of one family's fierce pride and tenacity, and because of

MacGregor Ranch

a legal agreement with Rocky called a conservation easement.

Original homesteaders Alexander and Clara MacGregor put plenty of sweat equity into their land, which was used for cattle ranching and (later) as guest accommodations. The MacGregor family controlled the property for three generations; during those years, family members lived on-site and managed its daily operations. The last surviving MacGregor—Muriel (granddaughter of Alexander and Clara)—requested in her will that the ranch be run by a charitable trust and primarily function as an educational center.

Muriel's wishes were granted. However, the trust was initially land-rich but cash-poor. A significant award from the Colorado State Historical Fund allowed the trust to restore many buildings that were in a state of disrepair. Today, 28 structures on the property are listed on the National Register of Historic Places. A conservation easement purchased by Rocky allowed the ranch to keep operating, while also ensuring that high rises and minimalls would never be built on the property. The park secured the 1,221-acre conservation easement in 1983, and it was a win-win for all involved.

Today, horses relax under shade trees, their tails swaying contentedly. Vegetables sprout in a sprawling garden. Local volunteers informally lead visitors around an eight-room house that brims with artifacts from a bygone time. A **self-guided tour** of the ranch's many outbuildings, which include a blacksmith shop and a root cellar, is another pleasant diversion. The views from the ranch are enviable; cast your eyes in any direction on a bluebird day and you will be treated to lush green, bucolic scenery. To the north, Lumpy Ridge and the Twin Owls seem close enough to touch. Just as they did more than a century ago, ranch hands actively tend to the land and cattle. Don't hurry; allot several hours to unwind at the ranch. By the time you leave, your cortisol (stress hormone) levels will most likely be lower.

Every summer, the ranch runs **Heritage Camp** (9am-2pm across four days in July, $250), a popular program for children who have completed third, fourth, and fifth grades. Participants engage in a wide variety of activities, which can include cooking meals from scratch, using a washboard to clean clothes, and gathering eggs from a henhouse. Only three or four sessions are held each summer, and spots must be reserved in advance.

A small gift shop on the property, **Maude's Mercantile** (10am-4pm Tues.-Sat. June-Aug.), sells curios, baby bibs sewn by volunteers, and books about local history.

To get there from Highway 34 and MacGregor Avenue in Estes Park, take MacGregor Avenue north for 0.7 mile to the ranch entrance.

McGraw Ranch

While the vast majority of Rocky's visitors come to the area for recreation and relaxation, some arrive with their sleeves rolled up, ready to work. Visiting scientists and researchers

Lumpy's Raptors

Humans and wildlife coexist every day of the year in the park. Most of the time an exchange of glances between person and beast—or person and bird—is all that transpires. But at times, greater protection than usual is needed for certain animals. From **March 1 to July 31** many sections of Lumpy Ridge are closed so that birds of prey can court and procreate. Lumpy Ridge has the largest concentration of birds of prey in any one area of the park, including **goshawks, peregrine falcons, turkey vultures, red-tailed hawks, prairie falcons,** and **Cooper's hawks.** The ledges, cliffs, and cavities found in the area are prime spots for nesting, and Lumpy Ridge's cliffs are ideal places for these birds to perch and peer down at the ground in order to identify prey—including smaller birds and rodents.

Humans can have a deleterious effect on the nests of birds of prey, but these temporary closures are also in place to protect climbers. In the past, incidents have been documented of raptors hassling people while they were scaling the rocks. Closure signs are visible at the trails leading to Lumpy's rock features; to be clear, not only is the rock off-limits, the trails approaching each of the climbing areas are, too.

You might expect Lumpy Ridge to be a great area for bird-watching, but that is not always the case. In order to lower people's expectations, one naturalist who has led bird-watching hikes here eventually changed the name of his program from "Raptors of the Ridge" to "Bird-Watching on Lumpy Ridge." Birds of prey just aren't that easy to spot on Lumpy Ridge; if they are sitting on their nests or tending to their young, you will not see them at all. So go ahead and bring along some binoculars while you hike in the area, but know that seeing a raptor is by no means guaranteed.

conducting studies in the park have a handful of lodging options to choose from—and McGraw Ranch is one of them. Built in the late 1800s, McGraw Ranch has been a cattle ranch and a guest ranch. After purchasing the buildings and land, the National Park Service initially planned to remove the structures and return the land to its natural state. Local citizens helped to chart a different course: re-purposing the ranch into a research and learning center. Restoration of the facility was completed in 2003 and cost $2 million (accomplished jointly with the National Trust for Historic Preservation).

Today, researchers spend weeks or months at **McGraw Ranch** (McGraw Ranch Rd.), dipping in and out of the park to study everything from slime molds to cheatgrass. In addition to cabins, the ranch also has a kitchen, field lab, and researcher work space. McGraw Ranch is **not open to the public,** but visitors can view the outside of the buildings as they hike along the first part of the **Cow Creek Trail.** Historians particularly note the Rocky Mountain Rustic—or stick-style—architecture of an old outhouse located on the property.

To get to McGraw Ranch from the intersection of Highway 34 and MacGregor Avenue in Estes Park, travel 3.4 miles north on MacGregor Avenue to McGraw Ranch Road. If the parking lot is full, an electronic signboard at the start of the road will be lit up. Turn left at McGraw Ranch Road and travel 2.1 miles to the parking area.

RECREATION

Hiking

★ TWIN OWLS

Distance: 1.2 miles round-trip

Duration: 40 minutes

Elevation gain: negligible

Effort: easy

Trailhead: Lumpy Ridge (see map p. 173)

The first time you peer up at Longs Peak and try to find the shape of a beaver in the mountain's ridge line, you might do as I did—squint a little, cock your head one way, then the other, and then finally make out the shape

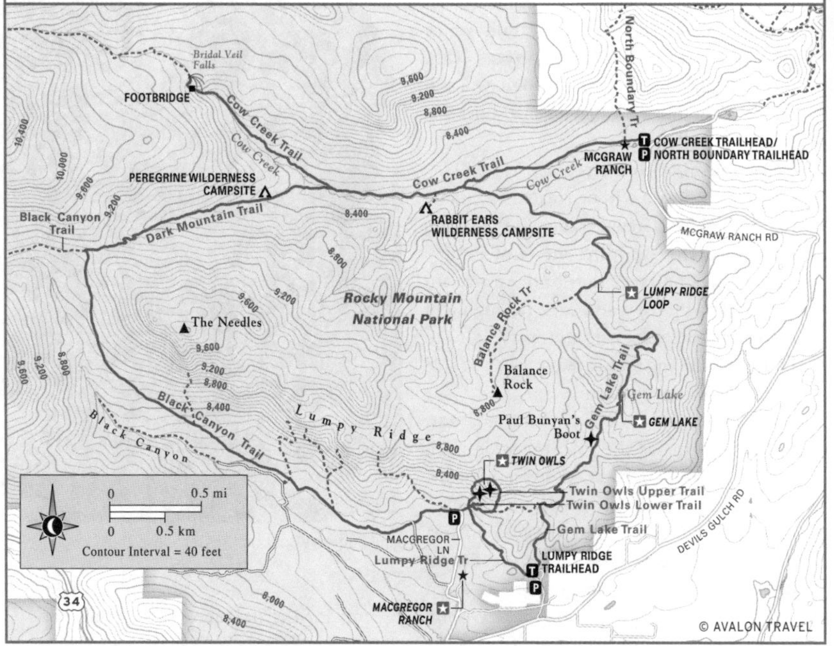

of the beaver's back and tail. With the Twin Owls, you do not need a keen imagination to see the heads, bodies, and wings of two birds perched proudly atop Lumpy Ridge. Many people simply admire the owls from various locations in Estes Park and while driving north on Devils Gulch Road.

The Twin Owls are accessed from the Lumpy Ridge Trailhead. From the parking lot, look for a sign pointing to the **Twin Owls/ Black Canyon Trail.** Follow the trail for 0.6 mile to reach the short spur trail leading to the Owls. The trail forks, providing climber access to the **lower Twin Owls** (left) and **upper Twin Owls** (right). The views of the Owls from the trail are the real prize on this short hike.

The Twin Owls see heavy **rock climbing** traffic in the summer, with several dozen climbing routes with varying degrees of technical difficulty on this rock formation. If you aspire to scale the Owls, know that they are closed to climbers March 1-July 31 for raptor breeding and nesting season.

★ LUMPY RIDGE LOOP

Distance: 10.7 miles round-trip
Duration: 5 hours
Elevation gain: 2,584 feet
Effort: very strenuous
Trailhead: Lumpy Ridge (see map p. 173)

This incredibly scenic, versatile loop, commonly referred to as the Lumpy Ridge Loop, can be enjoyed as a hike, a backpacking trip, or a challenging trail run. While these directions take hikers clockwise around the loop, the circuit can be traveled in either direction.

Starting from the Lumpy Ridge parking lot, follow the small sign at the trailhead pointing toward the **Twin Owls/Black Canyon Trail.** During this first stretch, you will experience great views of the Twin Owls. In the springtime, look for pasque flowers on the sides of the trail, one of the earliest-appearing wildflowers in Rocky. At around 0.6 mile, you will arrive at an emergency telephone and a **trail junction.** Follow the sign pointing west to Lawn Lake and climber access trails, which take hikers along the **Black Canyon Trail.** Immediately after you pass the sign, you will see a park building located down a short dirt road to your right.

As you hike this stretch of the Black Canyon Trail, you will be treated to fantastic views of MacGregor Ranch to the south, and to equally stunning views of Lumpy Ridge's rock outcroppings to the north. In my opinion, this easy section is the highlight of the whole hike. Numerous trails leading to Lumpy's climbing areas are on the right side of the Black Canyon Trail.

At 2 miles, you will encounter a **green gate.** Once inside the gate, the wide-open terrain changes to forest, and you will start to climb in elevation. At approximately 3 miles from the trailhead, cross over an area of land damaged by the **Colorado Flood of 2013.** Trees are uprooted in this area and you can see rocks and debris that have slid down the mountain. Continue to steadily climb up the trail through forest until you reach a **trail junction.** Head east here, following the arrows for the **Peregrine** and **Cow Creek wilderness campsites,** and the Cow Creek Trailhead. You are now on the **Dark Mountain Trail,** descending east toward Cow Creek. At 1.5 miles into this stretch, you will come across the **Peregrine Wilderness Site,** a great place to sleep if you wish to split up your journey into two days. In approximately 0.2 mile (about 5.6 miles from the trailhead), you will come to a trail junction; continue east toward the **Cow Creek Trailhead.** Another wilderness camping spot is just ahead—**Rabbit Ears**—along with a trail junction for Gem Lake and the Lumpy Ridge Trailhead. Head right (south) on the **Gem Lake Trail.** You are now 6.4 miles into your hike. As you walk uphill, you will encounter another area of trail damage caused by flooding.

Around 8 miles into the loop, look for a turnoff for the Balanced Rock Trail; continue on the Gem Lake Trail through the forest. During this uphill stretch to Gem Lake, you might find that your legs are getting tired. A place to rest is just ahead: attractive **Gem Lake.** Once you are at the lake, the hard work is over—from here to the parking lot (1.7 miles), the trek is downhill. Be sure to stop at the pile of rocks named **Paul Bunyan's Boot,** located 0.3 mile from Gem Lake; then hike back to where you started.

Paul Bunyan's Boot on the Gem Lake Trail

★ WEST CREEK FALLS

Distance: 4.8 miles round-trip
Duration: 2.5 hours
Elevation gain: 1,434 feet
Effort: moderate
Trailhead: Cow Creek (see map p. 175)

This waterfall hike is very lightly traveled; you might see only one or two people on the trail, or none at all. However, the elevation profile may be a deterrent for some—this trail goes up, then down, then up again. Thus, some cardio is involved on the return trip to your car.

West Creek Falls

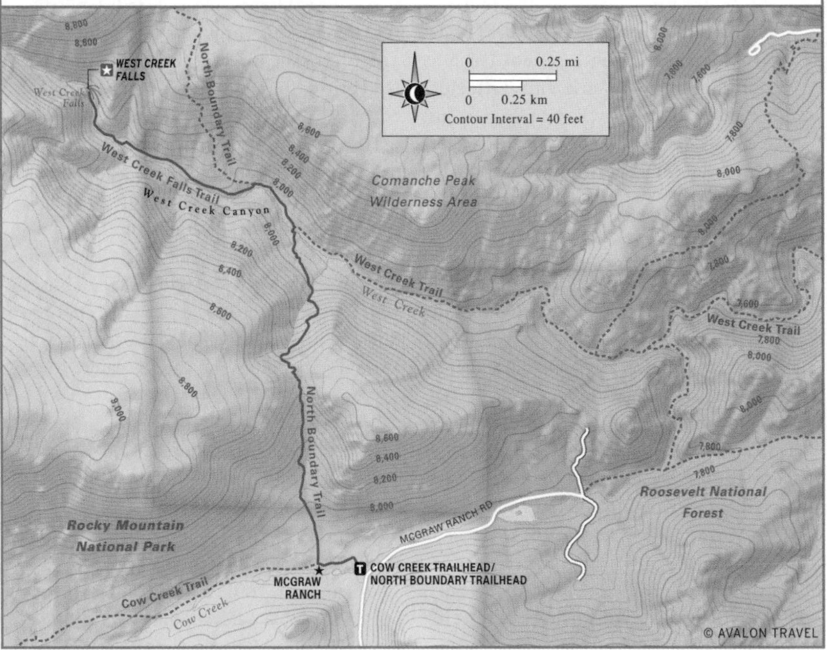

Don't let that fact stop you from enjoying this wonderfully secluded spot, best visited in the **spring,** when the falls gush with gusto.

Arrive early at the Cow Creek Trailhead, because the parking lot fills up quickly on summer mornings and there is no overflow parking on the roadside. Follow the trail sign next to **McGraw Ranch;** for 0.1 mile, walk west on the dirt road, behind the buildings of the research facility, to the **North Boundary Trailhead.** Then, start a steady climb north on the North Boundary Trail, keeping your eyes peeled for wildflowers—western wallflowers, penstemon, larkspur, mountain iris, paintbrush, or, one of my favorites, tall chiming bells. In late spring, you might even stumble upon fairy slipper orchids, which are not commonly seen in the park. After climbing steadily uphill for 0.8 mile, you will reach the top of a ridge and drop down through the forest into West Creek Canyon. At 1.5 miles, a log **footbridge** crosses over West Creek. Cross the bridge and gradually ascend once again, following a sign for the North Boundary Trail. At 1.7 miles, the trail briefly splits, then becomes one again. A sign for the **West Creek Falls** spur trail appears at 1.8 miles. Head west for 0.7 mile to your destination; West Creek will be on your left. The trail is rather awkward in spots due to damage from the Colorado Flood of 2013, but this is nothing to be concerned about. Finally, the waterfall appears. Watch your footing walking over the rocks, as it can be slippery close to the falls. Eat a snack or lunch, then return to the parking lot the way you came.

BRIDAL VEIL FALLS

Distance: 6.1 miles round-trip
Duration: 3 hours
Elevation gain: 1,060 feet

Effort: moderate

Trailhead: Cow Creek (see map p. 173)

If the name of this hike sounds familiar, it might be because a number of other "Bridal Veil Falls" are at other locations (such as Yosemite National Park and Telluride, Colorado) in the country. For obvious reasons, "bridal veil" is a popular descriptor for a glittering cascade of white, frothy water.

To get on the Cow Creek Trail, walk toward **McGraw Ranch** from the Cow Creek parking area. A small sign says "trail" and will lead you along the side of a closed gate; shortly thereafter, another sign points left toward the trail. At this point, you are walking behind the buildings of the ranch. (A vault toilet is here if you need it.) Continue walking along the flat, wide dirt road, passing the North Boundary Trail marker on your right. Advance through a grassy meadow dotted with trees until the path narrows from double track into single track. At the trail split for **Gem Lake**—approximately 1.2 miles from the trailhead—continue straight (west) toward the falls. The **Rabbit Ears wilderness campsite** is located near this trail junction. Continue walking 0.8 mile through trees to the next trail junction with the **Black Canyon Trail.** Stay to the right (northwest) to continue to the falls, which are 1.2 miles away. (If you stay to the left at the fork, you will arrive at the Peregrine wilderness campsite in 0.2 mile.)

After passing through another meadow area, cross Cow Creek on a wooden **footbridge.** From here, the trail gets markedly more uneven, with protruding tree roots on the path and continues steadily uphill. Shortly before arriving at the main attraction, look just off the trail for a miniature waterfall spilling into a small pool. Continue on the uneven path, cross a big slab of rock, and then hike up a set of **rock steps** to the falls. Finish your journey at the base of the falls, or, for a different perspective, climb above the falls via a social trail. Return the way you came.

★ GEM LAKE

Distance: 3.2 miles round-trip

Duration: 1.75 hours

Elevation gain: 1,000 feet

Effort: moderate

Trailhead: Lumpy Ridge/Gem Lake (see map p. 173)

The Gem Lake Trail starts out at 7,852 feet, one of the lowest-elevation areas in Rocky. From the Lumpy Ridge parking lot, follow the small trail sign pointing right toward **Gem Lake.** After a few minutes of hiking, you will arrive at the official **Gem Lake Trailhead**

Gem Lake

sign. A welcoming cluster of aspen trees just beyond invites hikers along this pretty path. In the summer, keep an eye out for wildflowers and the occasional wild berry bush along the first stretch of mostly shady trail. At 0.5 mile, you will reach the junction of the **Black Canyon Trail** and the Twin Owls View Trail; follow the arrow pointing east to Gem Lake. Now ascending steadily, you will see a continuing trend of boulders, rock formations, and more boulders along the trail. At approximately 0.2 mile from the Black Canyon Trail junction, a commanding view of Estes Park and Lake Estes opens up on the right (east) side of the trail. This is a great spot to stop for a swig of water.

As you continue, more aspens dot the landscape. Rocks become larger and more impressive, and the trail gets steeper in parts; rock steps aid hikers in some spots. Take one more break from the uphill slog at approximately 0.3 mile from your final destination. A sign does not identify **Paul Bunyan's Boot,** but you will know it when you see it: a set of rocks that looks strikingly similar to a boot with a hole in the sole. Get a boost from a friend and sit on top of the boot for a memorable photo.

Just before you arrive at Gem Lake, you will find a privy a few paces off of the trail; then **Gem Lake** itself appears. This shallow lake is partially bordered by a granite wall and features a small sand beach. The water is bracing, but restorative for aching feet. Aggressive rodents vie for crumbs at this spot, and lunching visitors often cave in to their demands—don't play their game. After cooling off your feet and soaking in the beauty of this special place, head back down the trail to the parking lot.

Backpacking

LUMPY RIDGE LOOP

Several good backpacking itineraries exist in the Lumpy Ridge area. One option is to hike the 10.7-mile **Lumpy Ridge Loop,** traveling either clockwise or counterclockwise from the Lumpy Ridge Trailhead, and spend a night at either the **Peregrine** or **Rabbit Ears wilderness campsites,** both of which are located off the Cow Creek Trail. These sites are handy for backpacking the entire Lumpy Ridge Loop, or they can be used for an overnight on the way to (or from) Bridal Veil Falls.

Permits for these wilderness sites must be acquired in advance of a trip. Reservations can be made online (www.nps.gov/romo) March 1-October 28 for camping dates May 1-October 31. The **East Side Wilderness Office** (970/586-1242, hours vary seasonally), located in a building just next to the Beaver Meadows Visitor Center, is the closest office to Lumpy Ridge.

McGregor Mountain is a group campsite located off the Black Canyon Trail; this spot is most appropriate for backpackers heading west of Lumpy Ridge to the Mummy Range.

NORTH BOUNDARY TRAIL TO LOST LAKE

The **North Boundary Trail** (accessed from the Cow Creek Trail behind McGraw Ranch) is a remote path that travels through both Rocky Mountain National Park (RMNP) and the Comanche Peak Wilderness for 6.6 miles (one-way). At its endpoint in the north, the trail connects with the **Lost Lake Trail.** There are numerous backcountry campsites located near this trail junction. To get to **Lost Lake,** hike an additional 3.9 miles west on the Lost Lake Trail.

NORTH FORK TRAIL TO LOST LAKE

This popular 19.4-mile (round-trip) trek starts outside the park at the North Fork/Dunraven Trail and includes trail time in the Comanche Peak Wilderness. A number of wilderness campsites are located along the trail, including **Happily Lost** and **Lost Lake.** The Lost Falls Wilderness Site, which is noted on older versions of park maps (such as National Geographic's *Trails Illustrated* map), was destroyed in the Colorado Flood of 2013.

LAWN LAKE

From the Lumpy Ridge Trailhead, backpacking to **Lawn Lake** is a 9.6-mile one-way trek west on the Black Canyon Trail. After spending some time at the lake (and perhaps traveling 1.5 miles west to check out Crystal Lake and Little Crystal Lake), you can finish your adventure by hiking 6.3 miles south on the Lawn Lake Trail to arrive at the **Lawn Lake Trailhead.** A car shuttle is needed for this option.

Wilderness campsites are located along the Black Canyon Trail leading up to Lawn Lake, though visitor's options might be limited. **Tileston Meadows, Lower Tileston Meadows,** and **Bighorn Group** campsites were closed for a period due to pine beetle damage. Check with the wilderness office (970/586-1242) for the current status. Wilderness campsites are also located along the Lawn Lake Trail.

STORMY PEAKS TRAIL TO NORTH FORK TRAIL

The **Stormy Peaks Trail** starts outside of the park boundary, eventually traveling south into Rocky and connecting with the North Fork Trail to Lost Lake. From there, you can hike east to the Dunraven/North Fork Trailhead. **Stormy Peaks South, Happily Lost,** and **Halfway** are possible wilderness campsites. A car shuttle is needed for this trek.

For specific information about Stormy Peaks and other trailheads located on National Forest land, contact the **Arapaho and Roosevelt National Forests** (www.fs.usda.gov) or the U.S. Forest Service Canyon Lakes Ranger District (970/295-6700). This backpacking trip is 13.9 miles (one-way), with 7.5 miles of hiking in the National Forest.

★ Rock Climbing

Lumpy Ridge has a compelling story as the park's most popular rock-climbing destination. The area started to gain attention in the 1950s; since then, thousands of people have tested their climbing chops on Lumpy Ridge's grand granite cracks and faces, and have lived to tell about it.

As rock-climbing equipment and techniques have become more sophisticated, climbers have tackled more difficult routes over the years. First ascents are still being achieved on Lumpy Ridge, and its history is still unfolding.

The first thing to know about rock climbing on Lumpy Ridge is that only traditional or "trad" climbing is allowed. This means that climbers must place and remove their own protection as they climb; there are no bolts in the rock, and visitors cannot permanently attach bolts or other equipment. The second thing to know is that while granite is often smooth and almost marblelike in appearance, Lumpy Ridge's granite is coarse to the touch. Its lumps and bumps can actually scrape you.

The third bit of important information is that this outstanding climbing location hasn't been loved too much. Lumpy Ridge offers much in the way of variety, challenge, and superb views, but it isn't swarming with people. If you are a climber looking for a new challenge and a less-crowded scene, this is a great place to do it.

Many climbers also enjoy bouldering at

Bouldering is a popular activity around Lumpy Ridge.

Lumpy Ridge. Bouldering is climbing fairly low to the ground without ropes and a harness; a thick mat called a crash pad is used as protection in case of a fall.

ROUTES

Easier climbs on Lumpy Ridge include **Batman and Robin** and **Magical Chrome-Plated Semiautomatic Enema Syringe** or "Chrome-Plated" for short. More advanced climbers will be challenged by **Pear Buttress** on **The Book** formation. **The 37th Cog in Melvin's Wheel** is another great climb with a moderate amount of difficulty. If you are an expert climber, consider adding to your short list **Fat City** or **Crack of Fear** on the Twin Owls.

To access Lumpy Ridge's climbing features, park at the Lumpy Ridge Trailhead. Hike approximately 0.6 mile north to the Black Canyon Trail. Various spur trails located along the Black Canyon Trail take climbers directly to the rock. These spur trails are not indicated on the park's free handout map; however, wooden signs direct climbers to some of the most popular areas, including the **Twin Owls, Batman, Checkerboard, The Book, The Pear,** and **Sundance.**

At the junction of the Black Canyon Trail and climber access trails for Batman and Checkerboard, disposable travel toilet kits—known informally in the climbing community as "**wag bags,**" are located in a dispenser. In an effort to discourage climbers from leaving human waste at popular climbing spots along Lumpy Ridge, the park offers these kits at no charge. Each kit contains a bag for solid waste, toilet paper, and an antibacterial wipe. Once used, bags should be packed out and deposited in a trashcan, not in a vault toilet.

GUIDES

The **Colorado Mountain School** (341 Moraine Ave., 800/836-4008, www.coloradomountainschool.com) offers guided rock climbing in the Lumpy Ridge area. Every other Friday in the summer, a discounted group climb takes place: the **Lumpy Ridge Classic Climb** (8am-4pm, $195). This full-day outing takes place at a variety of locations along Lumpy Ridge and is open to climbers with prior experience on multi-pitch routes. The Colorado Mountain School also offers private, guided climbing. Prices vary depending on the size of the party; a half-day, private guide for two people costs $145 pp; a full day runs $225 pp.

Kent Mountain Adventure Center (970/586-5990, www.kmaconline.com) also offers private, guided climbing. Three to four hours of climbing for two people costs $135 per person; a full day for two is $245 per person.

INFORMATION

One of the best ways to gather information about specific climbs is to visit the **Mountain Project** (www.mountainproject.com). Entire guidebooks are dedicated to the topic of RMNP climbing. Bernard Gillett's *Rocky Mountain National Park: The Climber's Guide, Estes Park Valley* contains comprehensive information about Lumpy Ridge. If you can get your hands on an old copy of Scott Kimball's *Lumpy Ridge—Estes Park Rock Climbs* (published in 1986 by Chockstone Press), you will find that it is an illuminating read. Bouldering enthusiasts consult Jamie Emerson's *Bouldering Rocky Mountain National Park & Mount Evans.*

FOOD AND ACCOMMODATIONS

There are no established campgrounds in the Lumpy Ridge region, only backpacking wilderness campsites (permit required). Two lodging options in Estes Park provide the closest park access.

Black Canyon Inn's (800 MacGregor Ave., Estes Park, 970/586-8113, www.blackcanyoninn.com, $195 and up) convenience to the Lumpy Ridge Trailhead is one of its main selling points; the other is its close proximity to the on-site Twin Owls Steakhouse. One-, two-, and three-bedroom condos are available for rent. Each unit is privately owned and furnished according to the owners' individual tastes. In the summer season, there is

Connect to the Climbing Community

Climbers speak a language all their own. If you are part of the tribe but not yet connected to the Estes Park/RMNP climbing community, that problem is easily remedied. One of the best things you can do is head to **Ed's Cantina and Grill** (390 E. Elkhorn Ave., Estes Park, 970/586-2919, www.edscantina.com, 11am-9pm Mon.-Thurs., 11am-9:30pm Fri.-Sat.). An avid climber owns the restaurant; many employees are climbers as well. Pieces of climbing equipment are incorporated into the bar top (where many celebratory margaritas have been consumed), and autographed pictures of famous climbers adorn one of the restaurant's walls. Start talking with folks, and soon you will be connected.

Another strategy is to call up or visit a local guide service in town. **Colorado Mountain School** (341 Moraine Ave., 800/836-4008, www.coloradomountainschool.com) offers itself as a resource to the climbing community and will happily share information about routes and other topics, regardless of whether you are interested in signing up for a course or hiring a private guide.

RMNP climbing rangers are out and about on Lumpy Ridge during the summer; if you run into one, feel free to ask him or her questions regarding the area.

Going directly to a climbing area (**Lumpy Ridge, Longs Peak, or Lake Haiyaha**) or the **Epic Climbing Gym** at the **Estes Park Mountain Shop** (2050 Big Thompson Ave., 970/586-6548, www.estesparkmountainshop.com, 8am-9pm daily) is a guaranteed way to meet like-minded folks in a jiffy.

Online, **Mountain Project** (www.mountainproject.com) has a public forum, maps—or "topos"—of local routes, and a climbing partner finder tool.

a four-night minimum; during the rest of the year, there is a three-night minimum stay. If you have a shorter visit in mind, reservationists can sometimes squeeze visitors into a gap between existing reservations. A heated pool on-site is open in the warm months.

The **Gilded Pine Meadows Bed and Breakfast** (861 Big Horn Dr., Estes Park, 970/586-2124, www.gildedpinemeadows.com, June-Sept., $120-157) is approximately 1 mile from the Lumpy Ridge Trailhead. The house was built around the turn of the 20th century, and memorabilia from its original owners, James and Fannie Boyd, are found inside. James Boyd was a town trustee for Estes Park in the 1920s; he also built the original headquarters building for RMNP (now located at the Estes Park Museum). Visitors have their choice of a guest room, suite, or cottage. The inn's proprietors cook up a hot breakfast for visitors; Mexican quiche and German pancakes are often on the menu. An outdoor hot tub is available for post-hike soaking.

"Rustic elegance" is a fitting description for the decor at ★ **Twin Owls Steakhouse** (800 MacGregor Ave., Estes Park, 970/586-9344, www.twinowls.net, 5pm-9pm daily May-Oct., 5pm-9pm Fri.-Sun. Nov.-Apr., $30). The log building features beautiful oak floors, open ceiling beams, and a gorgeous stone fireplace. From the main dining room, a staircase leads up to an intimate balcony area that is great for people-watching (or popping the question). Entrées include buffalo filet and prime rib. For a uniquely regional dining experience, consider ordering the elk medallions as your main course. Though the Twin Owls is less than 1 mile from the Lumpy Ridge Trailhead, you'll want to get cleaned up after a hike or a climb before arriving at dinner; this is more of a fine-dining experience.

About 3 miles south of the Dunraven/North Fork Trailhead is the tiny community of Glen Haven. In 2013, Glen Haven was hard hit by flooding and the survival of the **Glen Haven General Store** (7499 County Rd. 43, Glen Haven, 970/586-2560, www.glenhavengeneralstore.com, 9am-6pm daily May-Oct.) was uncertain. However, the community dug in and helped this iconic establishment—originally built in 1919—open its doors again, to the relief of cinnamon-roll lovers everywhere. The store's generously sized, rich rolls are thickly spread with sweet icing and are available all day long. Other food items include ice cream, sandwiches, candy, and drinks; quilts, craft items, and log furniture are also for sale. Mostly, people just clamor for those rolls. The store sells ice, but not firewood.

TRANSPORTATION AND SERVICES

Driving

Estes Park is the gateway town for Lumpy Ridge. To reach the **Lumpy Ridge Trailhead** from the intersection of Highway 34 and MacGregor Avenue in Estes Park, take MacGregor Avenue northeast for 1.3 miles. At the turnoff for the Lumpy Ridge and Gem Lake Trailheads, turn left. Drive another 500 yards north on Lumpy Ridge Road to the parking lot. To reach the **Cow Creek Trailhead,** you'll take MacGregor Avenue north for 3.4 miles, then turn left (north) on McGraw Ranch Road. The parking area is 2.1 miles ahead.

In the winter, roads to these trailheads are plowed. Chains are not required for vehicles traveling to this area in the winter. Snow tires or all-season tires are handy to have, however, in the snowy months.

For emergency roadside service, contact **Bob's Towing and Repair** (800 Dunraven St., Estes Park, 970/586-3122) or **Up Top Towing** (875 Moraine Ave., Estes Park, 970/586-4248).

Parking

Visitors may only park in official parking spots at Lumpy Ridge and Cow Creek Trailheads. There are no RV parking spots. Several spaces for horse trailers are available at the Lumpy Ridge Trailhead.

Emergencies

In an emergency, call 911 or the park's **dispatch center** (970/586-1203). Cell phone service is intermittent in the Lumpy Ridge area, but there is an emergency phone on the Cow Creek Trail, attached to one of the McGraw Ranch cabins. (Walk on the path behind the buildings and look for a brown sign that says Emergency Phone with an arrow.) An informational sign in front of the property also indicates the phone's location.

Another emergency phone is located at Lumpy Ridge next to the sign for the climber access trails for the Twin Owls. From the Lumpy Ridge/Twin Owls parking lot, hike 0.6 mile northwest to the Twin Owls/Black Canyon Trail.

Mummy Range

A set of impressive peaks juts up along the Mummy Range located in the north-central region of the park. The range includes Mount Chapin, Mount Chiquita, Ypsilon Mountain, Desolation Peaks, Fairchild Mountain, Hagues Peak, Rowe Peak, Rowe Mountain, Mummy Mountain, and Dunraven Mountain. If you have loads of stamina, good route-finding abilities, and mountaineering skills—and are the ambitious type—you might want to scale one or all of these peaks. The park does not maintain trails to the top of each mountain, but well-traveled routes have been established. (Lisa Foster's *Rocky Mountain National Park: The Complete Hiking Guide* has good maps to get you started with planning.)

Otherwise, access to Ypsilon Lake, Lawn Lake, Crystal Lake, and Little Crystal Lake is possible from the **Lawn Lake Trailhead** off Endovalley Road. A backpacking trip to Lawn

Lawn Lake

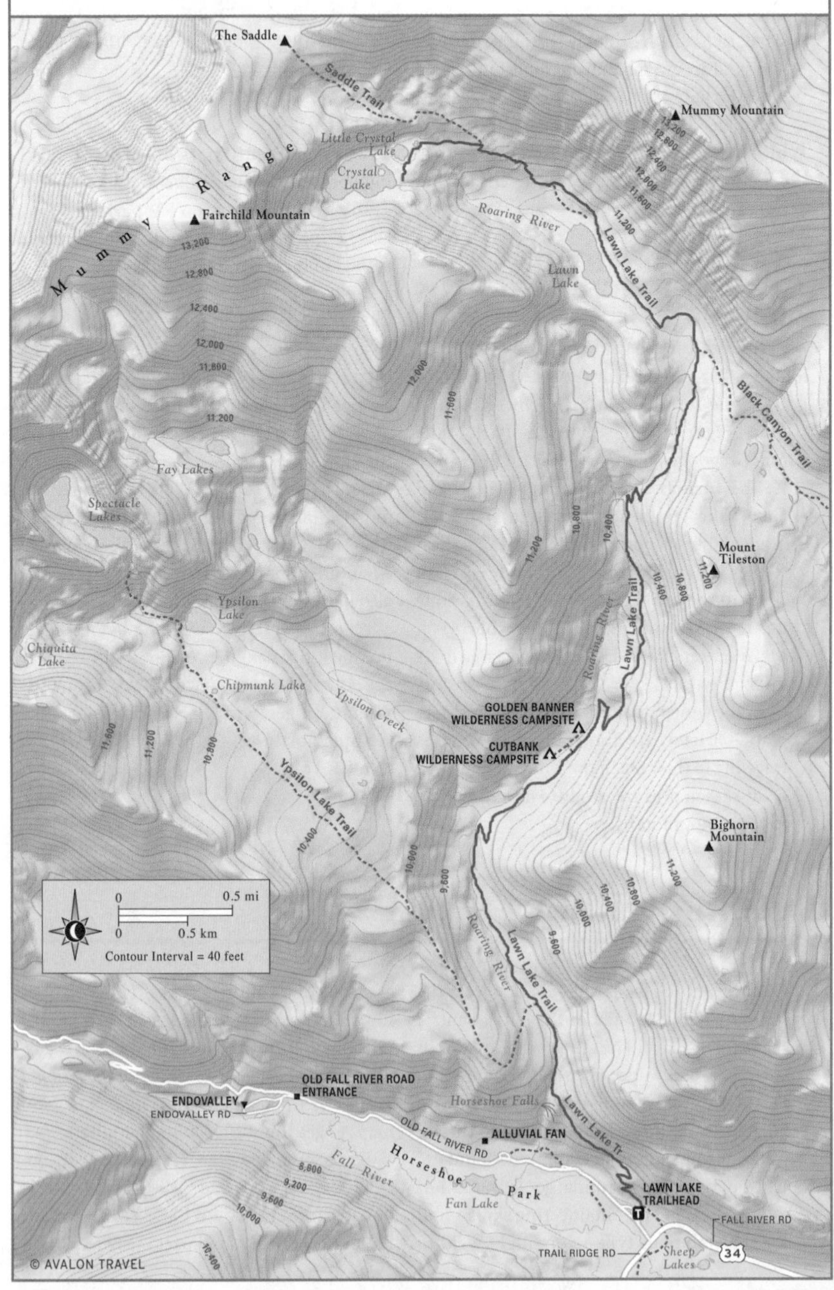
The Saddle
Saddle Trail
Mummy Mountain
Little Crystal Lake
Crystal Lake
Mummy Range
Fairchild Mountain
Roaring River
Lawn Lake
Lawn Lake Trail
Black Canyon Trail
Fay Lakes
Spectacle Lakes
Mount Tileston
Ypsilon Lake
Chiquita Lake
Chipmunk Lake
Ypsilon Creek
GOLDEN BANNER WILDERNESS CAMPSITE
CUTBANK WILDERNESS CAMPSITE
Ypsilon Lake Trail
Bighorn Mountain
0 0.5 mi
0 0.5 km
Contour Interval = 40 feet
OLD FALL RIVER ROAD ENTRANCE
ENDOVALLEY
ENDOVALLEY RD
Horseshoe Falls
Lawn Lake Tr
OLD FALL RIVER RD
ALLUVIAL FAN
Horseshoe Park
Fall River
Fan Lake
LAWN LAKE TRAILHEAD
FALL RIVER RD
TRAIL RIDGE RD
Sheep Lakes
34
© AVALON TRAVEL

Lake or Crystal Lake can originate from either the Cow Creek Trailhead or Lumpy Ridge Trailhead.

Traveling into the Mummy Range, you might be treated to a bighorn sheep sighting. There are no guarantees, but if you hike to **Ypsilon Lake** or **Lawn Lake,** you could spot some curly or straight-horned creatures. Sheep from the Mummy herd spend extensive time in this area. In the spring and early summer, mammals from the herd can often be found along Trail Ridge Road or at Sheep Lakes.

Wildland Trekking (800/715-4453, www.wildlandktrekking.com, $1,240 pp includes a guide, meals, and most gear) offers a five-day backpacking trip in the Mummy Range. The Mummy Range Trek starts at Chapin Pass Trailhead and takes backpackers to various destinations in the northern region of the park, including Mirror Lake, Mummy Pass, and Sugarloaf Mountain.

RECREATION

Hiking and Backpacking

LAWN LAKE

Distance: 12.4 miles round-trip
Duration: 7 hours
Elevation gain: 2,249 feet
Effort: very strenuous
Trailhead: Lawn Lake (see map p. 182)
Directions: From the Fall River Entrance Station, travel 2.2 miles west on Highway 34 to Endovalley Road and turn right. The Lawn Lake Trailhead is 0.1 mile west on Endovalley Road, on the right-hand side.

The hike to Lawn Lake is a long one, which is why many visitors choose to split up the journey into two days. Two wilderness campsites (**Cutbank** and **Golden Banner**) are located along the trail, and two more can be found next to the lake (one of them is a wilderness stock campsite). Otherwise, if you are cranking out this hike all in one day, get an early start. Be sure to wear sturdy hiking boots, since some spots along the trail are rather rocky.

From the trailhead sign, start hiking north along the **Lawn Lake Trail.** At approximately 1 mile, you will see extensive damage from the Lawn Lake Flood of 1982, a devastating event caused by the failure of a dam that once existed at the lake. People often linger here for a short time, surveying the scene. At 1.4 miles, find a **junction** for the Ypsilon Lake Trail. Head straight to continue on to Lawn Lake. For the next 4 miles, the trail climbs steadily uphill through forest until it meets up with the **Black Canyon Trail,** which is another route to get to Lawn Lake.

From the junction, hike an additional 0.7 mile to **Lawn Lake.** The subalpine scenery at the lake (which is one of the largest in the park) is wonderful; small stands of trees are located in clusters around the lake. From the lake's banks, find excellent views of Mummy Mountain, Hagues Peak, and Fairchild Mountain. If your step is still sprightly, consider traveling approximately 1.5 miles farther north to explore **Little Crystal Lake** and **Crystal Lake;** then return the way you came.

If you brought along a **fishing** pole, expect to find greenback cutthroats in Lawn Lake and Crystal Lake.

★ MIRROR LAKE

Distance: 11.6 miles round-trip
Duration: 6 hours
Elevation gain: 1,000 feet
Effort: very strenuous
Trailhead: Corral Creek (see map p. 184)

This is a hike that keeps on giving. The scenic Cache la Poudre, a beautiful lake, the possibility of spotting moose, great birdwatching, attractive meadows, and a bounty of wild blooms are among its rewards. Other small treasures along the trail include puffball mushrooms, which look like large golf balls peeking out of the grass. Mirror Lake is often a backpacking destination rather than a day hike, but it works well as both. Being acclimated to higher elevations before setting out is helpful, since the trailhead sits above 10,000 feet.

The first section of terrain lies in the

Mirror Lake

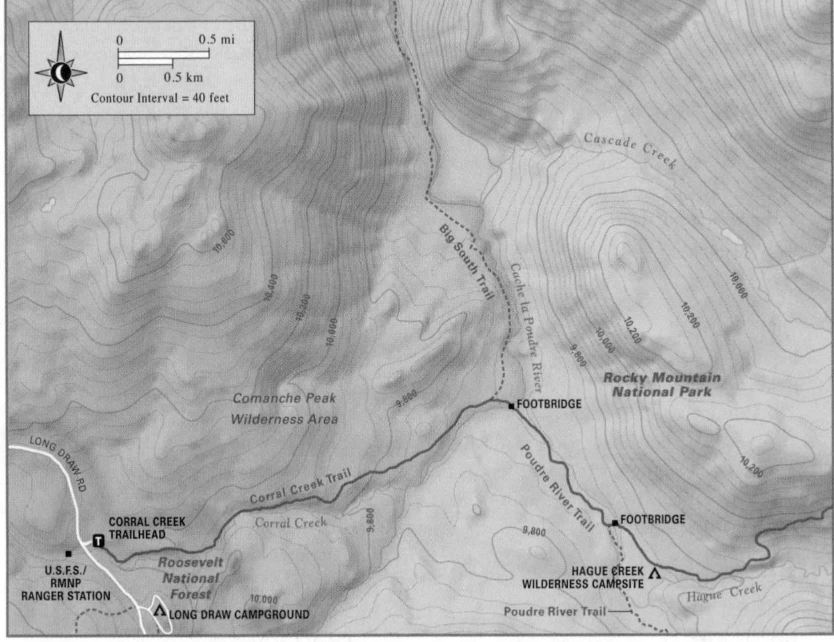

Roosevelt National Forest. Travel along an easy downhill stretch of path with great views of Corral Creek on the south side of the trail. At approximately 1 mile, there is a trail split for the Big South Trail and RMNP. Head southeast on the **Poudre River Trail,** cross over a **footbridge,** and enter the park. The trail now parallels the **Cache la Poudre River.** You will be tempted to linger here for a while; this is one of the most scenic stretches of the entire hike.

At the next junction (1.8 miles from the trailhead), head east on the **Mummy Pass Trail** to Mirror Lake. Cross over a **footbridge** and pass by a sign for **Hague Creek wilderness campite** and group site; you will also see a separate sign for a privy. If it's the height of summer, you might find a lovely patch of wildflowers tucked in along the trail within five minutes of walking past these signs. This is a good place for a water break.

Continue past a sign for the **Desolation wilderness campsite** (2.3 miles from the trailhead) and peek at the pretty meadow just beyond. This is a gorgeous spot, and you might see moose. Continue hiking east along the Mummy Pass Trail through a forested area at a **junction for Mirror Lake** and Mummy Pass (2.4 miles from the previous trail). Head north to Mirror Lake, and hike approximately 0.6 mile to a junction with the Comanche Peak Trail. Stay left on the **Mirror Lake Trail.** The final mile to the lake is enchanting, with many different wildflowers, a small waterfall along Cascade Creek, and views of the surrounding mountains. Keep an eye out for Parry's primrose on this stretch, a particularly beautiful flower found in wetlands. You will arrive at the turnoff for Mirror Lake's three **wilderness campsites.** Then, finally, the lake appears. Eat lunch, bask in the sunshine, and rest up before heading back the way you came.

Long Draw and Corral Creek

There is something to be said for having modern conveniences close-by while visiting Rocky, and that's why so many visitors opt to stay in Grand Lake or Estes Park while exploring the park. This northern corner offers much in the way of scenery and experiences, but little in the way of amenities. A trip here means you will be far away from gas stations, cell phone reception, hotels and—if you should find yourself in trouble—emergency services.

Long Draw Road and the Cow Creek Trailhead offer access to lakes, streams, rivers, hiking, and backpacking trails, and wilderness campsites. You can stand on top of the Continental Divide and see the headwaters of the Colorado River. There are no traffic jams on the trails. The north is—simply put—fabulous.

There is only a short window of time each year to access this area by car: from **July** until the first major snowfall. Long Draw Road, the area's only road, is otherwise unplowed and closed to regular vehicles (but open to snowmobilers, cross-country skiers, and snowshoers).

ENTRANCES

Long Draw Road is located just outside of the park's northwestern boundary. There is no vehicle access to Long Draw Reservoir/Corral Creek from within the park.

From the intersection of Highway 34 and E. Elkhorn Avenue in downtown Estes Park, drive 30 miles east on Big Thompson Ave./ Highway 34 toward Loveland.

From the intersection of Highway 34 and Highway 287, drive 22 miles north on Highway 287 to Highway 14. Continue 54 miles west on Highway 14 to Long Draw Road. Then drive southeast on Long Draw Road for 8 miles to the **Corral Creek Trailhead** and the **U.S. Forest Service/RMNP Ranger Station.** No fees are required.

To reach the **La Poudre Pass Trailhead,** drive 13.5 miles southeast on Long Draw Road until it ends in a turn-around. There are vault toilets, but no services.

Vault toilets are located on Long Draw Road near the northeast corner of Long Draw Reservoir and at La Poudre Pass. There are no toilets at the Corral Creek Trailhead, so plan accordingly.

VISITOR CENTER

At the **U.S. Forest Service/Rocky Mountain National Park Ranger Station** (Long Draw Rd., 8am-5pm Fri.-Mon. July-Sept.) you can find information about both the Roosevelt National Forest and Rocky Mountain National Park. Stop by for information about trails, camping, roads, and sights. **Wilderness camping permits** can be purchased inside.

The station is usually staffed by one National Park Service (NPS) ranger who is equipped with a radio; in case of emergency, this is the only place in this region to request help.

On some maps, **La Poudre Pass Ranger Station** (Grand Ditch Rd., south of Long Draw Reservoir) is listed as a patrol cabin. Rocky employees working in the area use this log cabin; however, it is not an information station for visitors.

SIGHTS

Long Draw Reservoir

Long Draw Reservoir is the main focal point along Long Draw Road. The dam was built along La Poudre Pass Creek in the late 1920s; the reservoir serves now as a water storage area for the Grand Ditch water diversion project.

This body of water entices recreationists with its remoteness and attractive surroundings. From the beginning of Long Draw Road, drive approximately 9 miles south to gain your first glimpse of the reservoir (there is parking here). Non-motorized **boating** is allowed on the lake; one boat ramp is available 9.3 miles from the beginning of the road. Two additional parking areas (at 10.4 mi and 10.5 mi) are convenient for **fishing** access; cutthroats are found in the lake. **Grandview Campground** is located along the reservoir's western edge.

Grand Ditch

A privately owned ditch with origins in the northwestern corner of Rocky has, over time, been met with mixed opinions. The **Grand Ditch** is a 14-mile long canal that captures snowmelt on the western side of the Continental Divide for agricultural use in the eastern part of the state. Workers using rudimentary tools and dynamite began work on the Grand Ditch in 1890. Digging out just 2 miles of the canal took two years' time, and the slow-moving project was not fully completed until 1936. The Grand Ditch still operates today because its owners have water rights that pre-date Rocky's designation as an official national park in 1915.

Some groups consider the Grand Ditch a remarkable engineering feat; others consider it an unsightly scar upon the earth. By diverting significant runoff from the Never Summer Mountains each year, the ditch adversely affects the Kawuneeche Valley's delicate ecosystems. It has reduced water flow to the valley's wetlands and has allowed exotic plant species to prosper in the region. The Grand Ditch has also caused substantial injury to the environment: during a major breach in May 2003, water rose up and over the passageway, setting off a massive landslide that—among other things—extensively damaged riparian habitat around **Lulu Creek** and the **Colorado River.** In an out-of-court settlement, Water

Storage and Supply Company (owners of the ditch) paid Rocky $9 million to cover the cost of the damage. Restoration of this area of the park is still ongoing.

Liked or disliked, the Grand Ditch features significantly in the area's history, and is listed on the National Register of Historic Places.

★ Wildlife-Watching

Big, brown, beautiful moose are active in the northwestern corner of the park. Moose prefer eating willows, grasses, and shrubs, and have a preference for marshy areas. I have personally viewed moose along **La Poudre Pass Creek**—just south of Long Draw Reservoir—and in the large meadow just beyond the junction of the **Mirror Lake Trail** and the **Mummy Pass Trail.** There are certainly scores of other locations at which you might sneak a peek. Always stay a distance of at least 25 yards away when viewing moose, as the animal's behavior can be unpredictable and dangerous to humans.

RECREATION

Hiking

COLORADO RIVER HEADWATERS AND THE GRAND DITCH

Distance: 1-14.3 miles one-way
Duration: 30 min. to multiple days
Elevation gain: negligible
Effort: easy to strenuous
Trailhead: La Poudre Pass (see map p. 188)

Thousands of Colorado residents and farmers who live on the east side of the Continental Divide depend on water collected from the west side of the park. This water is diverted through two separate, large-scale efforts: The Colorado-Big Thompson Project (a federal water diversion project) and The Grand Ditch (a canal owned and managed by a private company in Fort Collins). Water from the Colorado River travels underneath Rocky in a tunnel to the east side and is then stored in reservoirs before being distributed to farms and municipalities. Water from the Grand Ditch is used for irrigation by farmers and ranchers; it flows into the Long Draw Reservoir, then travels along the Cache la Poudre River to a location north of Fort Collins.

This outing gives visitors a look at two spots of significance to west-side water diversion. The journey can be done as a quick day hike or a multiday backpacking trip. For the latter, arrange for a car shuttle in the Kawuneeche Valley if you are hiking one-way.

Getting to the Colorado River headwaters is easy. From the **La Poudre Pass Trailhead,**

a moose grazing next to La Poudre Pass Creek

La Poudre Pass

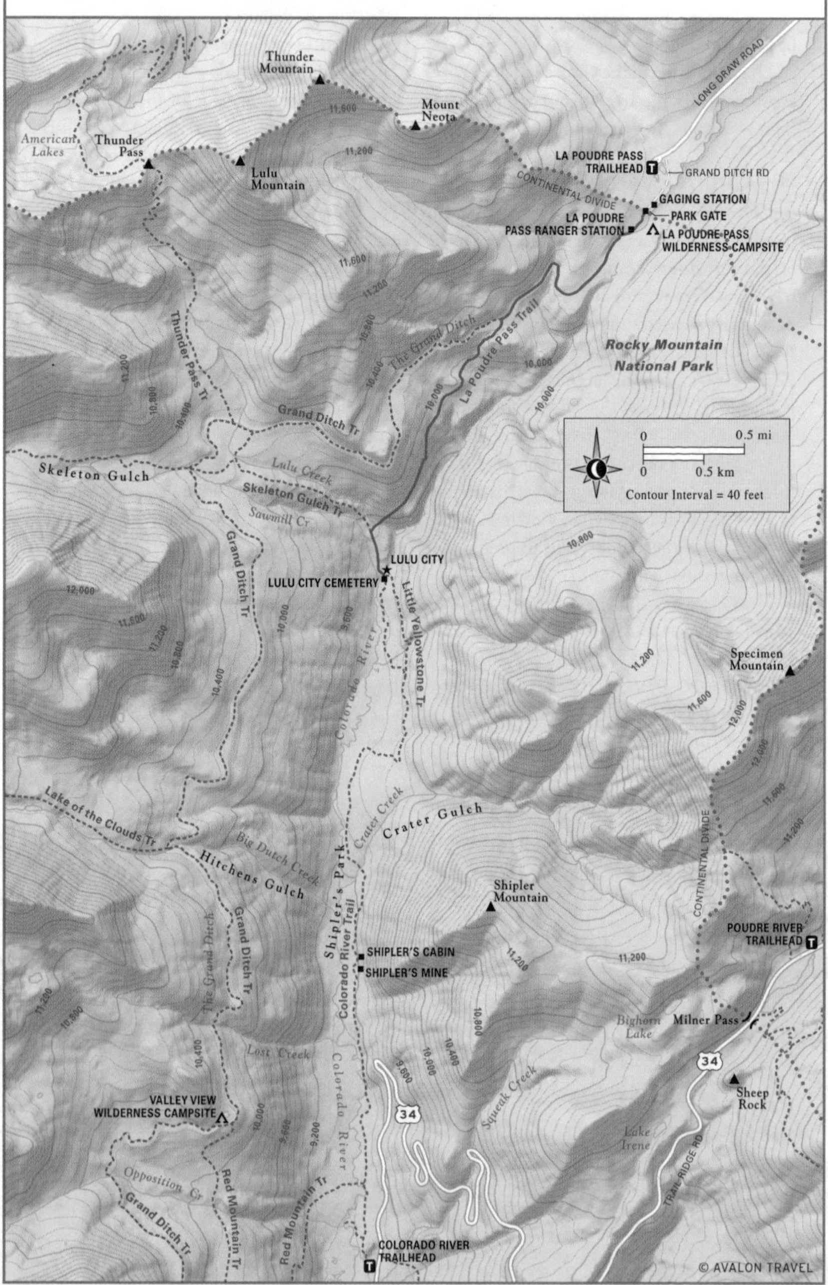

walk a few minutes south through an open field for less than 0.1 mile to **Grand Ditch Road.** Walk another two minutes south on Grand Ditch Road, keeping a lookout on your left for a **gaging station**—a small white building with an antenna on top. The station is used to measure the water flow in the Grand Ditch. Venture east off the road and cross over a short, narrow **bridge** that is just next to the station. After roughly 200 feet of walking on mostly level ground, you will arrive at a sign for the **headwaters.** Don't expect to be knock-your-socks-off wowed by what you see—it's just wet, marshy ground. Slowly but surely, though, that wet, marshy ground turns into a tiny trickle, then a small stream, and then a full-fledged river—and a remarkable one at that.

Backtrack to the road and walk less than 0.1 mile south to a **gate.** After walking around the gate, you will enter RMNP. Shortly thereafter is the **La Poudre Pass Ranger Station** on your right; cross over a small **bridge** and walk directly next to the Grand Ditch. Grand Ditch Road (a dirt road) travels next to the 20-foot wide, 6-foot deep ditch for 14 miles and offers some nice scenery, including spectacular views of the Kawuneeche Valley. Wildflowers bloom alongside the road in the summer. A less-wonderful sight is about 2 miles south of La Poudre Pass; here you can see where the ditch was breached in 2003 and a major landslide took place. The trail along the Grand Ditch ends about 3 miles west of the of the Bowen/Baker Trailhead.

Several hiking trails connect to the Ditch Road, affording access to additional sights like **Skeleton Gulch** and **Lake of the Clouds.** If backpacking along the Grand Ditch, **Valley View** wilderness campsite is a good overnight stopping point.

The Grand Ditch Road was a source of curiosity for me for a long time; in my conversations with park rangers, I had heard about it repeatedly, and I had seen from Trail Ridge Road the road "scar" that runs across the Never Summer Mountains. I needed to see the ditch and the road close-up, with my own eyes. However, if you are eager to hit some trails (not a flat road) and want to experience wilderness when you visit the park, this sight/hike belongs lower down on your to-do list. And, if you are planning a backpacking trip to Skeleton Gulch or Lake of the Clouds (west of the ditch), know that road walking will make up a considerable portion of your journey.

LITTLE YELLOWSTONE

Distance: 3.2 miles round-trip
Duration: 1.25 hours
Elevation gain: - 75 feet
Effort: easy to moderate
Trailhead: La Poudre Pass (see map p. 188)

It is possible to arrive at Little Yellowstone from two different directions: the longer route starts at the Colorado River Trailhead in the Kawuneeche Valley and heads north. The shorter route starts from the La Poudre Pass Trailhead and heads south.

For this option, park at the La Poudre Pass Trailhead and walk on a flat, narrow path through a grassy field for less than 0.1 mile to **Grand Ditch Road.** Turn right (south) on the road and walk for several minutes to a **gate.** Walk around the gate on the right side to enter the park. After a few minutes of walking, pass the **La Poudre Pass Ranger Station,** where a short trail leads up to the **La Poudre Pass wilderness campsite.** Cross over a small **bridge,** and continue south along Grand Ditch Road. The Grand Ditch's waters will course steadily along on the right. To the east, you will soon see views of Specimen Mountain. Walk 1.3 miles on the road until you see a sign on the left (east) side of the road for **Little Yellowstone.** The Little Yellowstone trail heads downhill through a forest; at approximately 0.4 mile, you will arrive at a good viewpoint for a landscape that resembles (on a much smaller scale) the Grand Canyon of the Yellowstone in Yellowstone National Park. The eroded rock here is a result of an eruption that occurred in the Never Summer Mountains many millions of years ago. The rock, distinguished by its white, pale pink, and gray tones, is unlike that found in other areas of the park.

You can continue past this viewpoint to other destinations, including Lulu City to the south, and Skeleton Gulch to the southwest. At the very least, continue a few more minutes along the trail to a small but picturesque (unnamed) **waterfall.** Return the way you came.

★ Backpacking

Multiple destinations in this northwestern region can feel just beyond the reach of a comfortable day hike. That's why backpacking is the preferred activity. Possible itineraries include **Mirror Lake, Mummy Pass,** and **Chapin Creek,** as well as **Skeleton Gulch** and **Lake of the Clouds** (hikers must travel on an unmaintained trail to this location).

On the Mummy Pass Trail, the **Hague Creek** and **Desolation** wilderness sites are great for solitude-seekers. Some hikers prefer to travel to Mummy Pass from outside the park boundary; the **Emmaline Lake Trail,** located on National Forest land north of the park, provides access.

Mirror Lake has **three wilderness campsites** to choose from. Skeleton Gulch has one campsite (**Skeleton Gulch**), and near Lake of the Clouds, **Dutch Town** is a fine place to spend the night.

PERMITS

To occupy a wilderness campsite, you must obtain a permit. March 1-October 28, **online reservations** (www.nps.gov/romo) can be secured for wilderness camping dates May 1-October 31, or visit a wilderness office. Permits can be picked up at either the **East Side Wilderness Office** (next to the Beaver Meadows Visitor Center) or the **West Side Wilderness Office** (inside the Kawuneeche Visitor Center); neither are very convenient if you are traveling in this region of the park.

Other permit locations include the **U.S. Forest Service/RMNP Ranger Station** (Long Draw Rd., no phone, 8am-5pm Fri.-Mon. July 1-Sept.) and the **Colorado State University Mountain Campus** (Pingree Park Rd., 970/881-2150, www.mountaincampus.colostate.edu, 7am-7pm daily mid-May-mid-Oct.), north of the park's northern boundary; directions to this remote campus are available online. Inquire about RMNP wilderness permits at the main office in the dining hall building.

For more information, contact the park's wilderness office (970/586-1242).

Mirror Lake has three wilderness campsites for backpackers.

Research Natural Areas

On some maps of Rocky, you will see three large, shaded areas that are defined as "research natural areas." Two of these areas are located in the north end of the park: **Specimen Mountain** and **West Creek.** An additional natural area, **Paradise Park,** is located at the southern end of the park. Rocky became a designated United Nations Educational, Scientific, and Cultural Organization (UNESCO) international biosphere reserve in 1976. As a result of this designation, these three regions of the park were set aside for scientific research purposes. They are free of hiking and horse trails, roads, and human development.

ROOSEVELT NATIONAL FOREST

Big South Trail and **Mummy Pass Trail** lead into Rocky's northern region. For information about these trails, contact the **Arapaho and Roosevelt National Forests** (www.fs.usda.gov) or U.S. Forest Service Canyon Lakes Ranger District (970/295-6700).

STATE FOREST STATE PARK

The **American Lakes Trail** in the **State Forest State Park** (970/723-8366, www.cpw.state.co.us) connects to Rocky's Thunder Pass Trail in the Never Summer Mountains (and the Thunder Pass Trail connects with Grand Ditch Road). From the tiny community of Gould (on the west side of the park), travel east on Highway 14 for 6.9 miles. Turn right at the park's Crags Entrance (County Road 62) and follow the dirt road for approximately 1.4 miles to the American Lakes Trailhead. Visitors need to purchase a Colorado State Parks Pass ($7/day) for their vehicle; a fee station is located at the Crags Entrance.

Fishing

In this region, you'll find plenty of great spots to fish. At **Hague Creek,** expect to catch cutthroat and brook trout. At **Mirror Lake,** fish for both brook trout and brown trout. Along the **Cache la Poudre River,** cast for brook trout and cutthroat trout. Anglers should review Rocky's fishing rules and regulations on the park website (www.nps.gov/romo) before embarking on an outing.

Just outside the park boundary you can fish **Long Draw Reservoir** for cutthroat trout. Bait fishing is not allowed at the reservoir, and the bag-and-possession limit for trout is two. In **La Poudre Pass Creek,** above the reservoir, you can also find cutthroat trout.

To fish inside or outside of the park boundary, individuals age 16 and over must carry a current Colorado fishing license; obtain yours through the Colorado Parks & Wildlife (www.cpw.state.co.us).

Boating

Nonmotorized boats are allowed within Rocky, and some people make the extra effort of carrying their boat and gear along trails to get to desirable waters. On the northwestern side of the park, kayaking enthusiasts get on the **Cache la Poudre River** by parking at the Corral Creek Trailhead, then portaging their kayaks east along the Corral Creek Trail to the confluence of La Poudre Pass Creek and the Poudre River. Once on the water, kayakers paddle north to Highway 14.

Winter Sports

In the snowy months, Long Draw Road becomes the **Long Draw Winter Recreation Area.** Snowmobiling, snowshoeing, and cross-country skiing are permitted on the road. (Snowmobiling is not allowed.) In the greater Cameron Pass area, a number of trails can be used by winter sports enthusiasts. For winter recreation maps and more information, contact the U.S. Forest Service's Canyon Lakes Ranger District office (970/295-6700, www.fs.usda.gov).

CAMPING

Along the entire stretch of **Long Draw Road,** between Highway 14 and La Poudre Pass, are 29 **designated camping sites** (first-come, first-served, free), each marked with a brown signpost that specifies the site number. Designated sites have no services or amenities, and reservations are not required. Some spots are suitable for tents-only, while others are large enough to accommodate RVs.

Grandview Campground

Of the two U.S. Forest Service campgrounds in the area, **Grandview** (Long Draw Rd., 970/295-6700, www.fs.usda.gov, July-mid Nov., $16 single sites, $32 double sites, cash or check only, mid-Oct.-mid-Nov., free) is by leaps and bounds more scenic. Depending on which site you get, you may enjoy views of La Poudre Pass Creek, Long Draw Reservoir, and/or the peaks of Rocky and the Neota Wilderness. Nine tent-only campsites are available and they are first-come, first-served. Each site has a fire pit with grate and a picnic table. Potable water and vault toilets are also available.

From the junction of Highway 14 and Long Draw Road, drive 12 miles south on Long Draw Road to the campground.

Long Draw Campground

Long Draw Campground (Long Draw Rd., 970/295-6700, www.fs.usda.gov, July-mid Nov., $16 single sites, $32 double sites; cash or check only; mid-Oct.-mid-Nov., free) is a 25-site campground just a short drive from the Corral Creek Trailhead. Sites are shaded, and deer are frequent visitors. Each tent site has a picnic table and fire pit with a grate; all sites are first-come, first-served. Smaller RVs must fit in established parking spots, which range 25-55 feet in length. Amenities (summer only) include vault toilets and water. Firewood ($5) is available from the campground host; otherwise, dead and downed wood can be gathered.

From the junction of Highway 14 and Long Draw Road, drive 10 miles south on Long Draw Road to the campground.

TRANSPORTATION AND SERVICES

Driving

From the beginning of **July,** 13.5-mile **Long Draw Road** opens to car, truck, and RV traffic. The road is dirt and gravel, and has a 20-mph speed limit. After the first significant snowfall, the road closes for the winter. Winter enthusiasts are able to use snowmobiles and skis to get around. Road status updates are posted by the Arapaho and Roosevelt

a prime spot at the Grandview Campground

National Forests (www.fs.usda.gov) and on the Canyon Lakes Ranger District Twitter page (twitter.com/usfsclrd).

PARKING

Parking lots are located at the Corral Creek Trailhead and La Poudre Pass.

Services

WALDEN

If you arrive at Long Draw Road from the west, stock up on firewood, ice, and grocery items at the **North Park Super's** (33482 North Hwy. 125, 970/723-8211, 8pm-9pm Mon.-Sat., 9am-6pm Sun.) in the town of Walden. There are also several small mom-and-pop stores located on Highway 14 in Walden and Gould.

From North Park Super's, travel 1.4 miles south on Highway 125 to 6th Street. Drive east four blocks, then head south on Highway 14 for 34 miles to the turnoff for Long Draw Road. Travel southeast of Long Draw Road for 8 miles to the Corral Creek Trailhead. The full (one-way) trip is approximately 43 miles.

BELLVUE

If you enter the park from the east (or from a Roosevelt National Forest trailhead outside of the park), stock up on supplies at **Archer's Poudre River Resort Country Store** (33021 Poudre Canyon Hwy., Bellvue, 970/881-2139, 7am-7pm daily year-round). The store carries ice, camping gear, and groceries.

From the Country Store, it is a 28-mile drive to the Corral Creek Trailhead. Drive 20 miles west, then south, on Highway 14 to Long Draw Road; then drive southeast on Long Draw Road for 8 miles to the Corral Creek Trailhead.

EMERGENCIES

In an emergency, your closest resource is the **U.S. Forest Service/RMNP Ranger Station** (Long Draw Rd., 8am-5pm Fri.-Mon. in summer), across from the Corral Creek Trailhead. There is no cell phone service. Carrying a SPOT messenger device or satellite communicator provides some assurance that you can reach first responders in case of a true emergency.

Gateways

The small towns of Estes Park and Grand Lakes bracket the park's east and west sides, offering services, accommodations, and an appeal all their own.

An unusual mix of attractions greets visitors to Estes Park, a town of roughly 6,000 full-time residents located down the road from the park's headquarters. The historic and regal Stanley Hotel, perched on a hill, is a truly breathtaking sight and seemingly stands watch over the town below. The downtown shopping strip is touristy, filled with numerous T-shirt and old-fashioned candy shops. Still, you can discover true gems here during downtime from the park, including a fabulous independent bookstore and a great place to score a one-of-a-kind skein of yarn. Residents of Estes Park are fiercely proud of their town's rich history, and are happy to share with visitors their best-loved hikes in the park or favorite spots for grabbing a nosh. Ample options are available for lodging, dining, groceries, gas, and other trip essentials.

On the west side of the park, the town of Grand Lake (population 450) is small and sweet, hugging up against the shores of its namesake body of water—the largest natural lake in Colorado. Features include a delightful beachfront for sunning and a quaint boardwalk peppered with shops and restaurants. This is the ideal entry point for visitors who intend to explore the park's Kawuneeche Valley, and a natural fit for water sports enthusiasts wanting to plunge their toe, boat, or stand-up paddleboard into one or all of the Arapaho National Recreation Area's five reservoirs. Grand Lake's brick-and-mortar businesses are well stocked with vacation essentials, from firewood to fly rods. As in Estes Park, many visitors to this area are multigenerational families for whom visiting the lake is a time-honored tradition.

Previous: golf course in Estes Park; sheets of ice on Grand Lake in April. **Above:** sculpture of Joel Estes, founder of Estes Park.

Look for ★ to find recommended sights, activities, dining, and lodging.

Highlights

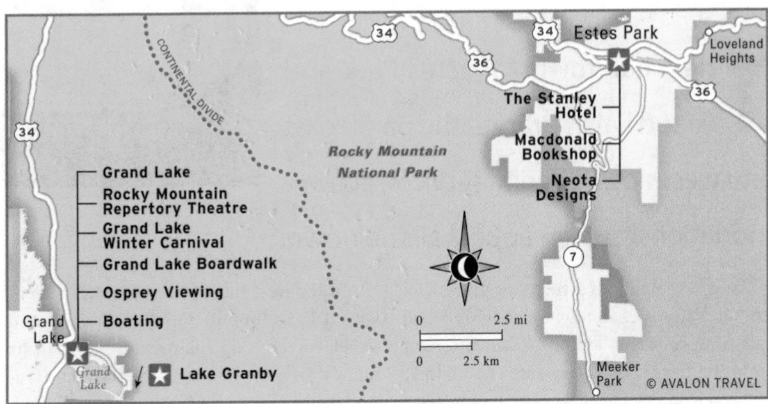

★ **The Stanley Hotel:** Request the "Ghost Adventure Package" for your overnight stay at this historic hotel, and you'll be guaranteed accommodations on the "haunted" fourth floor (page 198).

★ **Macdonald Bookshop:** Pick up a book about local history or check out an author event at Estes Park's independent bookstore (page 209).

★ **Neota Designs:** Be the envy of your friends at the next knitting party with a hand-painted skein of yarn (page 209).

★ **Grand Lake:** Come prepared to enjoy Colorado's largest natural lake with a boat, fishing rod, or a swimsuit (page 220).

★ **Rocky Mountain Repertory Theatre:** See live performances that rival Broadway at this Grand Lake theater (page 229).

★ **Grand Lake Winter Carnival:** Say *sayonara* to the winter doldrums at Grand Lake's frosty annual celebration (page 230).

★ **Grand Lake Boardwalk:** Stroll this charming walkway lining Grand Lake's main street. (page 231).

★ **Lake Granby:** Tour Grand County's largest lake in a motorboat or enjoy the views from the shore (page 238).

★ **Osprey Viewing:** Check out osprey nests on this self-guided driving, boating, or biking tour (page 240).

★ **Boating:** Take your pick of rentable watercraft at multiple marinas in the Arapaho National Recreation Area (page 241).

Estes Park

In 1859, gold miner Joel Estes laid claim to the land now known as Estes Park, but his feet were certainly not the first to tread this corner of the earth. Historians have traced human activity in the area to at least 12,000 years ago. Artifacts found in and around the region tell a story of Paleo Indians, Ute Indians, and Arapaho Indians spending as much as entire summers here, hunting and trapping animals. The landscape of Estes Park was first described on paper in 1846, in Rufus B. Sage's book, *Rocky Mountain Life: or, Startling Scenes and Perilous Adventures in the Far West, During an Expedition of Three Years.* Sage, a hunter, dubbed the area a "charming retreat for someone of the world-hating literati." He waxed poetic in his tome about mountain ridges, rocks, and rivers in the area. Based on Sage's descriptions, historians speculate that he camped somewhere near Marys Lake during his visit.

Kentuckian Joel Estes, the area's first true settler, originally sought riches in Colorado during the 1859 gold rush. After arriving in Denver with his family, Estes spent several months determining his next move, finally opting to establish a cattle ranch in Fort Lupton rather than mine for gold. He stumbled on the area now known as Estes Park by accident while on an expedition with his eldest son. In 1860, he built two cabins and a stock corral on the land, and eventually moved his herd of cattle from Fort Lupton. After enduring various hardships on the

Greater Estes Park

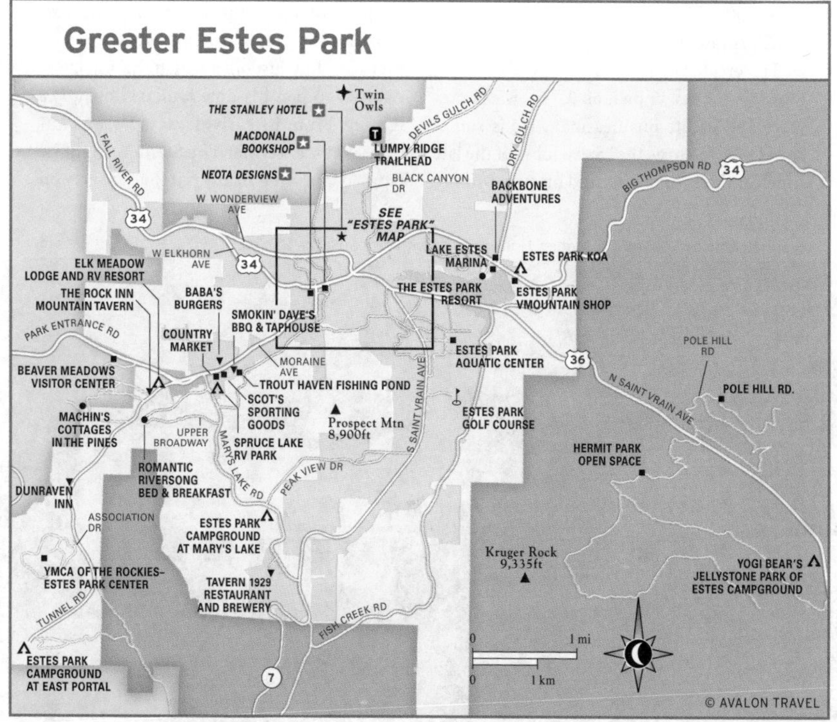

ranch, particularly in the winter months, Estes and his family called it quits in 1866. Two years prior to leaving, though, they were visited by the editor of the then *Rocky Mountain News,* William N. Byers, who was making a bid for the summit of Longs Peak. Byers named the valley Estes Park in a newspaper account of his adventures, and thus it was known from that time forward. When the Estes family moved away, a man named Griff Evans took over the land and turned the Estes property in the area's first guest ranch.

SIGHTS

★ The Stanley Hotel

There is no missing **The Stanley Hotel** (333 Wonderview Ave., 970/577-4000 or 800/976-1377, www.stanleyhotel.com) when you drive into Estes Park. With a brilliant white exterior, red roof, dome-topped cupola, and grand veranda, the multi-story, Georgian-style hotel is eye-catching and wholly impressive. Multiple other cottages and buildings are found on the hotel's sprawling, 35-acre grounds.

The creator of The Stanley, Freelan Oscar Stanley—better known as F. O.—was a creative and astute businessman. He is sometimes referred to as the "Steve Jobs" of the late nineteenth century. F. O. and his twin brother Francis Edgar (F. E.) invented the Stanley Steamer steam car, developed their own highly-coveted line of violins, and created a piece of photographic equipment—purchased by the Eastman Kodak Company—that earned these sharp-as-tacks brothers their fortunes. Surpassing all of the brothers' inventions is F. O.'s biggest legacy: his namesake lodge. If he were still alive today, F. O. would surely be pleased with the way that his hotel has thrived.

After he received a diagnosis of tuberculosis in 1903, F. O. traveled from the East Coast to Estes Park to experience the reportedly curative properties of "rarified" (high altitude) air. He bounced back from ill health in a startlingly short amount of time, and subsequently became active in the Estes Park community. The Stanley, which opened for business in 1909, first served as luxurious accommodations for F. O. and his wife Flora's high-society East Coast friends. The hotel thrived for many decades, but started showing signs of age in the 1970s. Enter horror-book author Stephen King, who, in 1974, after spending just one night at the hotel, was inspired to pen his now famous book, *The Shining.* From its early days, there was anecdotal evidence that The Stanley might be haunted, but King firmly put the property on

Stephen King catapulted The Stanley Hotel to fame with his book, *The Shining.*

the map as a paranormal hot spot. Today, people from all over the world stay at The Stanley in hopes of hearing, seeing, smelling, or feeling something unusual in the halls and rooms of the hotel. There is a resident psychic in the building, and paranormal investigation tours, night ghost tours, and elaborate Halloween celebrations (all activities open to the public, not just overnight guests) routinely sell out. Whether the grounds are haunted is up to you to decide. Just don't be surprised if you hear kids running and laughing in the hotel halls when no children are around, or if you smell a whiff of Flora Stanley's rose-scented perfume in the Music Room.

Well-heeled types still flock here, often to stay at **The Lodge at The Stanley** ($369-499 for rooms and suites), which offers boutique accommodations next to the main hotel, and to sip one of the 1,000 expressions of whiskey at the **Cascades Restaurant** (970/577-4001, whiskey bar open 11am-11pm).

In the summer, outdoor retailer Recreational Equipment, Inc. (REI) occupies a large tent on the front lawn of the hotel. A variety of outdoor courses and activities take place in the tent—dubbed **REI Basecamp at The Stanley Hotel**—from free classes on knot tying and first aid, to evening shindigs with live music and s'mores. Activities are open to hotel guests and the general public. People can also register for a variety of guided hikes through REI Basecamp's **Iconic Hikes of Rocky Mountain National Park program** (970/577-4000, www.stanleyhotel.com, $65 REI members, $75 non-members). Stop by the tent or check online for reservation and registration details.

Advance reservations for any activity, meal, or overnight stay at The Stanley are highly recommended. Those without reservations can still stroll the hotel grounds for free—don't miss *The Shining*-inspired hedgemaze out front—and wander about the lobby, where an old Stanley steam car is parked.

Estes Park Museum

A trip to the **Estes Park Museum** (200 4th St., 970/586-6256, www.estes.org/museum, 10am-5pm Mon.-Sat., 1pm-5pm Sun. May-Oct., 10am-5pm Fri.-Sat., 1pm-5pm Sun, Nov.-Apr., free) is a must-do for anyone wanting to learn about the region's history. The donation-based museum is home to more than 26,000 artifacts, from ski equipment to furniture, and includes displays that arouse curiosity in kids and adults alike. In one exhibit, patrons are invited to sit around a glowing "campfire" and listen to stories told by Estes Park pioneers. Just out the back door of the main building is a historic cabin from 1908 that was relocated from downtown. The original National Park Service headquarters building for Rocky was also moved onto the property and now houses a rotating exhibit. Perhaps the most impressive aspect of the museum is its publishing arm—the Estes Park Museum Friends & Foundation, Inc. Press—that produces numerous books that are sold in the bookstore. Well-stocked with other book titles of regional interest, the store is a treasure trove for any local history junkie. To delve deeper into the museum's collection, ask the Curator of Collections about items available for researchers and students, including maps, negatives, and oral history recordings.

Estes Park Aerial Tramway

A sign that summer has arrived in Estes Park is the sight of the **Estes Park Aerial Tramway**'s (420 E. Riverside Dr., 970/586-3675, www.estestram.com, 9am-6pm daily late May-early Sept., adults $12, seniors $11, children 5 and older $8, children under 5 free) gleaming red cabins traveling up and down Prospect Mountain during daylight hours. The tram, which has operated since 1955, whisks passengers to an observation platform, a snack/drink counter called the **Beam Me Up Café** (open until 2 pm), and a gift shop, in a matter of minutes. Views of the valley below are impressive. Modeled after tramways in Europe, the Estes Park tram features a "free span," meaning that there are no towers between the top and bottom stations for support. Expect to wait in line at the height of summer. Though feeding wildlife (anywhere) is

Estes Park

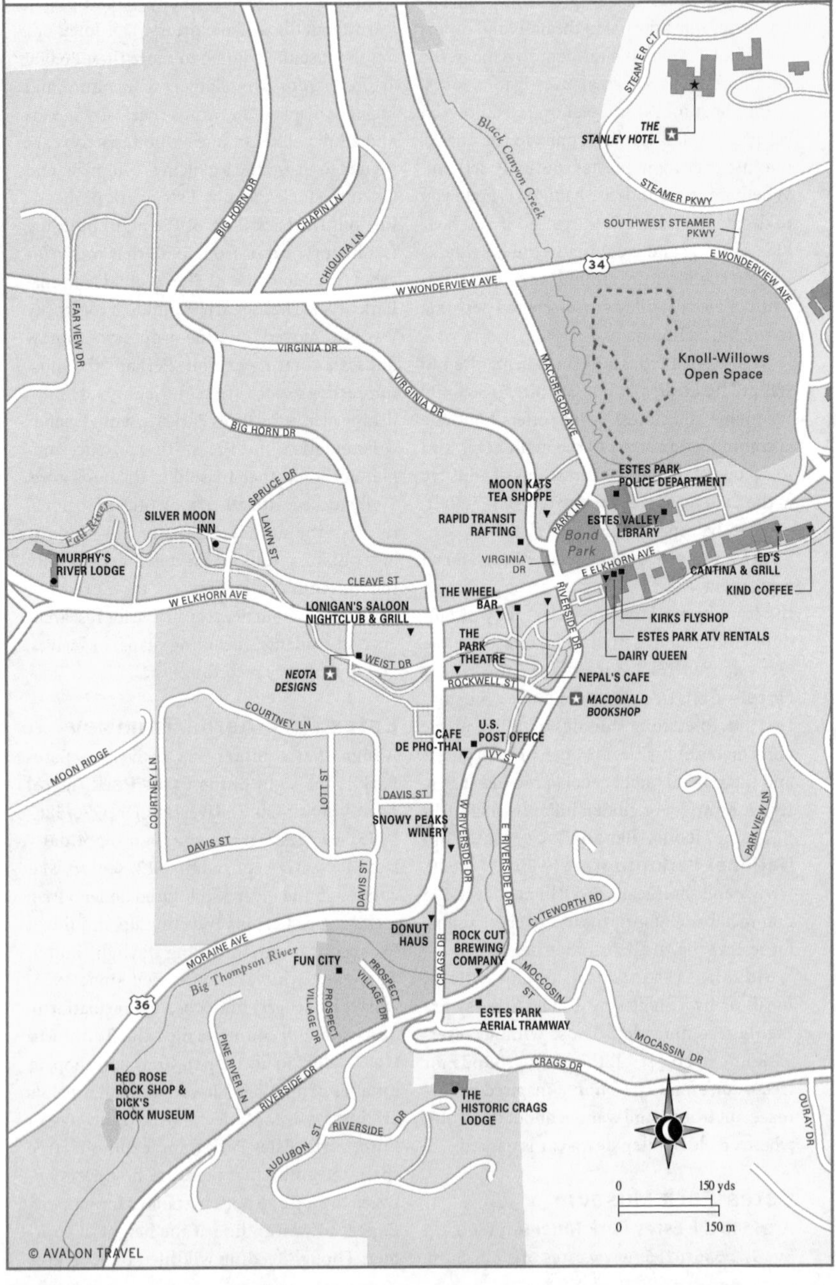

STEAMER CT
THE STANLEY HOTEL
Black Canyon Creek
STEAMER PKWY
SOUTHWEST STEAMER PKWY
34
E WONDERVIEW AVE
W WONDERVIEW AVE
BIG HORN DR
CHAPIN LN
CHIQUITA LN
FAR VIEW DR
VIRGINIA DR
MACGREGOR AVE
Knoll-Willows Open Space
BIG HORN DR
SPRUCE DR
LAWN ST
ESTES PARK POLICE DEPARTMENT
MOON KATS TEA SHOPPE
PARK LN
ESTES VALLEY LIBRARY
Bond Park
RAPID TRANSIT RAFTING
SILVER MOON INN
Fall River
MURPHY'S RIVER LODGE
VIRGINIA DR
E ELKHORN AVE
ED'S CANTINA & GRILL
KIND COFFEE
CLEAVE ST
W ELKHORN AVE
THE WHEEL BAR
RIVERSIDE DR
LONIGAN'S SALOON NIGHTCLUB & GRILL
KIRKS FLYSHOP
ESTES PARK ATV RENTALS
DAIRY QUEEN
THE PARK THEATRE
WEIST DR
NEOTA DESIGNS
NEPAL'S CAFE
ROCKWELL ST
MACDONALD BOOKSHOP
COURTNEY LN
CAFE DE PHO-THAI
U.S. POST OFFICE
IVY ST
MOON RIDGE
COURTNEY LN
LOTT ST
DAVIS ST
SNOWY PEAKS WINERY
W RIVERSIDE DR
E RIVERSIDE DR
PARK VIEW LN
DAVIS ST
DAVIS ST
CYTEWORTH RD
DONUT HAUS
ROCK CUT BREWING COMPANY
CRAGS DR
MORAINE AVE
FUN CITY
PROSPECT
VILLAGE DR
MOCCOSIN ST
Big Thompson River
36
VILLAGE DR
PROSPECT
ESTES PARK AERIAL TRAMWAY
MOCASSIN DR
CRAGS DR
PINE RIVER LN
RED ROSE ROCK SHOP & DICK'S ROCK MUSEUM
RIVERSIDE DR
THE HISTORIC CRAGS LODGE
OURAY DR
AUDUBON ST
RIVERSIDE DR
0 150 yds
0 150 m

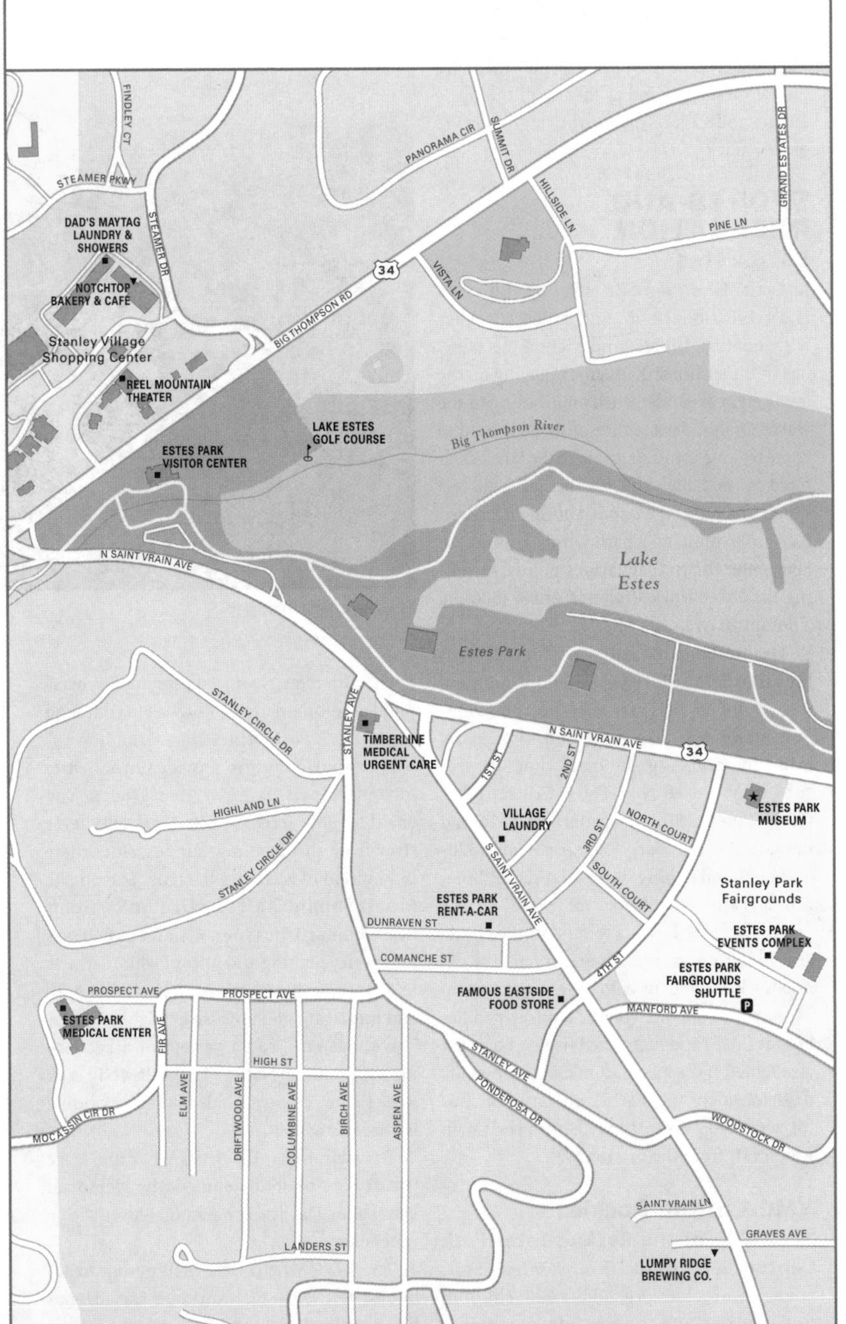
FINDLEY CT
STEAMER PKWY
STEAMER DR
PANORAMA CIR
SUMMIT DR
GRAND ESTATES DR
HILLSIDE LN
PINE LN
VISTA LN
34
BIG THOMPSON RD
DAD'S MAYTAG LAUNDRY & SHOWERS
NOTCHTOP BAKERY & CAFÉ
Stanley Village Shopping Center
REEL MOUNTAIN THEATER
LAKE ESTES GOLF COURSE
Big Thompson River
ESTES PARK VISITOR CENTER
N SAINT VRAIN AVE
Lake Estes
Estes Park
STANLEY CIRCLE DR
STANLEY AVE
TIMBERLINE MEDICAL URGENT CARE
1ST ST
2ND ST
N SAINT VRAIN AVE
34
ESTES PARK MUSEUM
HIGHLAND LN
VILLAGE LAUNDRY
NORTH COURT
3RD ST
S SAINT VRAIN AVE
SOUTH COURT
Stanley Park Fairgrounds
STANLEY CIRCLE DR
ESTES PARK RENT-A-CAR
DUNRAVEN ST
ESTES PARK EVENTS COMPLEX
COMANCHE ST
4TH ST
ESTES PARK FAIRGROUNDS SHUTTLE
PROSPECT AVE
PROSPECT AVE
FAMOUS EASTSIDE FOOD STORE
MANFORD AVE
ESTES PARK MEDICAL CENTER
FIR AVE
HIGH ST
STANLEY AVE
PONDEROSA DR
WOODSTOCK DR
MOCASSIN CIR DR
ELM AVE
DRIFTWOOD AVE
COLUMBINE AVE
BIRCH AVE
ASPEN AVE
SAINT VRAIN LN
GRAVES AVE
LANDERS ST
LUMPY RIDGE BREWING CO.

generally discouraged, the tramway sells peanuts by the scoop or by the bag in its Beam Me Up Café. Many emptied peanut shells are visible on the ground at the top of the tram, and the rodents are—not surprisingly—on the greedy side.

Estes Park Aerial Tramway

SPORTS AND RECREATION

Lake Estes

Just east of downtown Estes Park, **Lake Estes** is a recreational hub, and especially busy with boaters, bikers, and picnicking families in the summer. Kids enjoy playing on the lake's strip of sandy beach and wading in the water. On hot days, a slice of shade is hard to come by unless you snag one of the lake's sheltered picnic tables; consider bringing along a beach umbrella for extended outings. A paved 3.75-mile, multi-use path winds around the lake; enter the trail at various points, including the **Estes Park Visitor Center** (500 Big Thompson Ave.).

The most popular entry spot for the lake is the **Lake Estes Marina** (1770 Big Thompson Ave., 970/586-2011, www.evrpd.com, 9am-5pm daily Apr-mid-June; 8am-6pm daily mid-June-mid-Aug.; hours in shoulder seasons vary; closed Nov.-Feb.). Cruiser bikes ($7/half hour, $9/hour), pedal carts ($14/half hour, $23/hour), boats ($12-32/half hour, $20-60/hour), and fishing rods and reels ($2/hour, $10/day) are available for rent.

Most rental boats are first-come, first-served; pontoons must be reserved. Try canoeing, kayaking, or enjoy a leisurely tour in a foot-pedal-operated boat. Stand-up paddleboards (SUP) and motorized fishing boats are also rented at the marina. On especially windy days, for safety, the marina will only rent motorized boats. Visitors may launch their own watercraft from the marina ($5).

YMCA of the Rockies

The **YMCA of the Rockies-Estes Park Center** (2515 Tunnel Rd., 970/586-3341, www.ymcarockies.org, adults $20, children under age 13 $10) is a small town within a town, with more than 1,000 employees, overnight accommodations, its own zip code, and its own U.S. Post Office. One of the "town's" primary purposes is to provide fun activities for individuals, families, and groups. You could feasibly arrive in Estes Park and never stray from this bustling campus, since there is a myriad of activities to enjoy. The on-site **Mootz Family Craft and Design Center** is heaven for artistic types, with scads of beads for jewelry making and piles of white T-shirts to tie-dye. Roller-skating, archery, disc golf, and miniature golf are also available. YMCA "hike masters" lead a variety of hikes into Rocky Mountain National Park (RMNP) each week in the summer; guided horseback riding is available as well.

For swimmers, the YMCA has one large **indoor pool** (6am-8pm daily Memorial Day-Labor Day; seasonal hours vary) with a waterslide.

The YMCA's **zip line** ($20 pp, up to 1.5 hours) is the perfect antidote for adrenaline junkies. Strapped into a safety harness, participants take a leap of faith off a 30-foot-high wooden platform and whiz for 800 feet along a cable at speeds up to 30 mph. Participants must be 12 years or older and weigh 80-220 pounds. A YMCA day pass is required. Reservations are recommended.

Many on-site activities are included in the price of an overnight stay at the YMCA, though additional fees may apply. A day pass includes the use of a variety of other recreational facilities, so make the most of your money by planning a half- or full-day on the grounds.

Hiking

People don't tend to flock to Estes Park for the hiking; they come for the hiker's paradise that sits right next door in the national park. However, visitors who want to stroll or hike without actually entering the park boundaries still have options. The delightful and flat **Downtown Riverwalk** (1 mi) starts at the **Estes Park Visitor Center** (500 Big Thompson Ave.) and runs through the heart of downtown, ending at the Performance Park amphitheater. The sidewalk runs alongside Fall River and features many benches and picnic tables. Surprises along the way include a small musical garden and several free book-exchange boxes. Walking on the path is not only a good way to ease into the elevation on day one of your trip, it also offers a more pleasant way to access downtown shops and restaurants than the often-hectic Elkhorn Avenue. You can extend your walk well beyond 1 mile to include other streets in the downtown.

A ride on the **Estes Park Aerial Tramway** (420 East Riverside Dr., 970/586-3675, www.estestram.com, 9am-6pm daily late May-early Sept., adults $12, seniors $11, children 5 and older $8, children under 5 ride free) takes passengers near the summit of 8,900-foot **Prospect Mountain** where several social trails can be explored on foot. The trails are unmarked, so be aware of what direction you are going. Walking up a dirt road near the upper terminal takes visitors to the peak of the mountain.

Knoll-Willows Open Space (335 E. Elkhorn Ave., behind the Estes Valley Public Library, free), or simply "The Knoll," encompasses 20 acres and is accessible from downtown. Find historical structures, several short hiking trails, and wetlands that teem with wildlife along Black Canyon Creek.

the Downtown Riverwalk

THE WALTER TISHMA WAY

Those who enjoy hiking but can't do without a cozy bed at night might be enticed by a multiday inn-to-inn trek along the Walter Tishma Way with **Footpaths of the World** (970/586-2995, www.footpathsoftheworld.com, info@footpathsoftheworld.com, May-Sept., 5 nights/4 days $1,240 pp, $940 pp for double occupancy). Guides David and Phebe Novic bring to Estes Park this unique form of adventure travel that is widely popular in Europe. The couple offers guided and self-guided tours for up to six days that use Rocky's hiking trails on the east side of the park. At the end of each day, hikers sleep deeply at well-regarded lodges and B&Bs in Estes Park and in nearby Allenspark. Luggage is shuttled from inn to inn, and breakfast and sack lunches are included in the package price.

Biking

ROAD BIKING

The **Devils Gulch to Dry Gulch** (9 mi one-way) loop is a favorite ride of locals. The ride consists of moderately challenging, rolling terrain—mostly through an attractive rural area. The mountain scenery is fantastic; along the way, you'll have great views of Lumpy Ridge and Longs Peak.

To begin, park at the junction of Highway 34 and MacGregor Avenue. Parking spots are located south of Highway 34 (E. Wonderview Ave.) along the sides of MacGregor Avenue, across from the Knoll-Willows Open Space. Ride your bike north on MacGregor Avenue. After 0.7 mile, at the fork in the road, stay right to continue on Devils Gulch Road. Continue for 3 miles until you see another fork in the road. Stay right to get on H-G Road. After 0.4 mile, take another right turn on Dry Gulch Road (heading south). In 2.8 miles, turn right (west) on Highway 34, and travel back to your starting point.

MOUNTAIN BIKING

Estes Park doesn't have the same kind of buffed-out, mountain bike trail system as you will find in other Colorado mountain towns—like Salida or Crested Butte—but there are still decent places to shred nearby. One of the most popular spots is **Crosier Mountain,** with three access trails located on County Road 43 between the towns of Glen Haven (8 mi northeast) and Drake (13 mi northeast). Mountain bikers also enjoy **Hermit Park Open Space** (2 mi southeast of Hwy. 36, Mar.-mid-Dec., $6/vehicle). There are 2.8 miles of trails, plus access to 12 additional miles of trails on U.S. Forest Service land. **Pole Hill** is another good spot for mountain biking. From the intersection of Highway 34 and Highway 36 in Estes Park, take Highway 36 east for 3.7 miles; turn left on Pole Hill Road and travel 0.8 mile to the brown U.S. Forest Service road marker (labeled 122). Parking is limited. From here, numerous loop-ride options present themselves as you travel east. Be prepared to share the road with four-wheel drive vehicles.

BIKE RENTALS

The **Estes Park Mountain Shop** (2050 Big Thompson Ave., 970/586-6548, www.estesparkmountainshop.com, 8am–9pm daily year-round) offers several types of road bikes ($55/day) and mountain bike rentals ($39-60/day).

Boating

Rapid Transit Rafting (161 Virginia Dr., www.rapidtransitrafting.com, 970/577-7238 or 800/367-8523, $70-115 pp) is the only rafting outfitter based in Estes Park that includes same-day transportation to and from river launch points outside of the town.

Most whitewater kayakers head out of town to paddle the Cache la Poudre River. But if you just want a short outing to get your boat wet, launch your kayak during spring runoff on the Big Thompson River behind the **Dairy Queen** (218 E. Elkhorn Ave.), and get take-out at **Kind Coffee** (470 E. Elkhorn Ave.). Locals refer to this stretch of river as the "Dairy Queen Hole"; it is considered a Class II (novice) run when water levels are high.

Bait fishing is popular at Marys Lake.

Fishing

Fishing opportunities abound in Estes Park; all you need is a license (if you are 16 years or older) and gear to enjoy this classic pastime. The **Big Thompson River**—which runs right through town—is highly popular with anglers, who also relish fishing the **Fall River. Marys Lake** and **Lake Estes** are stocked in the summer and bait fishing is allowed in both spots. Fishing doesn't get any simpler or easier than at the privately owned **Trout Haven Fishing Pond** (800 Moraine Ave., 970/577-0202 or 800/794-7857, www.trouthavenfishing.com, 9am-4pm Mon.-Thurs., 11am-5pm Fri.-Sun., year-round); fish are $1 per inch. You don't have to have a license or even your own gear—just an eagerness to cast a line. This is a great setting for introducing kids to the sport.

For fishing gear, rentals, and licenses, try **Lake Estes Marina** (1770 Big Thompson Ave, 970/586-2011, www.evrpd.com, 9am-5pm daily Apr.-mid-June; 8am-6pm daily mid-June-mid-Aug.; shoulder season hours vary; closed Nov.-Feb.), **Kirks Fly Shop** (230 E. Elkhorn Ave., 970/577-0790, www.kirksflyshop.com, 7am-8pm daily summer, 8am-5pm daily winter), **Scot's Sporting Goods** (870 Moraine Ave., 970/586-2877, www.scotssportinggoods.com, 9am-5pm daily May; 8am-8pm daily June-Aug.; 9am-5pm daily Sept.-mid-Oct.), or **Estes Park Mountain Shop** (2050 Big Thompson Ave., 970/586-6548, www.estesparkmountainshop.com, 8am-9pm daily year-round). The latter three businesses also offer guided fly-fishing trips.

Licenses can also be purchased by phone or online from **Colorado Parks & Wildlife** (800/244-5613, www.cpw.state.co.us).

Rock Climbing

The highly visible rock outcroppings on the east side of **Marys Lake** are great for beginner-level top-rope climbs. Inside the Estes Park Mountain Shop, find the **Epic Climbing Gym** (2050 Big Thompson Ave., 970/586-6548, www.estesparkmountainshop.com, 8am-9pm daily year-round, 3 climbs/$15 for beginners). For rock-climbing instruction, contact the **Colorado Mountain School** (341 Moraine Ave., Estes Park, 800/836-4008 ext. 3, www.coloradomountainschool.com).

OUTFITTERS

The priciest overnight accommodations in Estes Park don't come with luxurious sheets or even indoor plumbing. In fact, you might not get any shut-eye at all while suspended high above the ground on a portaledge (a special type of tent utilized by rock climbers), but you will never forget the experience. **Kent Mountain Adventure Center's** (970/586-5990, www.kmaconline.com, May-Sept., $1,200 pp, $800 pp for two people) Cliff Camping package includes guided climbing, a cozy portaledge on which to sleep, and all the gear and food (snacks, dinner, and breakfast) needed for your overnight stay. A professional photographer can also be enlisted to document this once-in-a-lifetime adventure.

Swimming

The indoor **Estes Park Aquatic Center** (660 Community Dr., 970/586-2340, www.evrpd.com, 6am-7pm Mon.-Fri and 11am-3pm Sat. June-Aug. 15, limited hours Labor Day-Memorial Day, adults $6.75, youth 3-17 years $6.25, children under 2 free) has one 25-yard pool, a waterslide, a diving well, and a baby pool. Another option for cooling off is **Fun City** (455 Prospect Village Dr., 970/586-2828, www.funcityofestes.com, 10am-8pm daily summer) which has a bumper boat attraction ($2 for passengers, $6 to drive). This pricey ride is over within a matter of minutes, so to actually get soaking wet you might need to go twice.

ATV Riding

Many ATV lovers were saddened when damage from the Colorado Flood of 2013 closed a number of trails in the Roosevelt National Forest. Today, all of the trails are back up and running and can be enjoyed on 1-6-person ATVs. Popular areas include **Pole Hill Road,** southeast of Estes Park, and **Bunce School Road,** south of Allenspark. The ATV season runs from May until late fall. For information, maps, and rentals, **Estes Park ATV Rentals** (222 E. Elkhorn Ave., 970/577-7400, www.estesparkatvrentals.com) is a great resource, as is **Backbone Adventure Rentals** (1851 North Lake Ave., 970/235-5045, www.backbonecycles.com).

Hunting

Hunting is illegal in Rocky Mountain National Park, but is allowed on private lands and in the Roosevelt National Forest just east of Estes Park. Hunting season runs **end of August-mid-January** and primarily centers on deer and elk. A hunting license is required and may be obtained from **Colorado Parks & Wildlife** (800/244-5613, www.cpw.state.co.us, $34-254 for CO residents, $379-2,084 for non-residents). Big game such as moose, bear, and bighorn sheep can be hunted, but only a handful of tags are available each year to Colorado residents through a limited license draw. The deadline for the lottery system is the first Tuesday in April of each year. **Estes Park Outfitters** (970/215-7064, www.estesparkoutfitters.com) is the only big-game hunting outfitter in the area and offers five-day guided hunts ($2,850-5,850) complete with accommodations and meals. Longtime local and business owner Tim Resch lives and breathes hunting; he knows his stuff.

Golf

At Estes Park's two public golf courses, the most common cause of golfer distraction is an unusual and delightful one: herds of elk tromping across the greens. The 9-hole par-31 **Lake Estes Golf Course** (690 Big Thompson Ave., 970/586-8176, www.evrpd.com, 7am-6:30pm daily, $13-18) closes temporarily mid-Sept.-Nov. 1 for elk rutting season. Otherwise, the course is open the rest of the year. Winter golf (Nov.1-mid-Apr.) is a bargain at $8 for all-day play. Elk are also frequent visitors to the 18-hole, par-72 **Estes Park Golf Course** (1480 Golf Course Rd., 970/586-8146, www.evrpd.com, mid-Apr.-Oct. 31, 7am-7pm daily, $35-51). Expect fantastic mountain views from each course. At the Estes Park Golf Course, the **Hangar Restaurant** (970/586-8146 ext. 3, 8am-2pm daily Apr.-Oct. 31) offers breakfast and lunch. Both golf courses have pro shops.

Geocaching

You can use a park map or recommendations from friends or rangers to guide your adventures in and around Rocky. Or, you can go on a geocaching tour. Get started by loading the official geocaching app (www.geocaching.com) on your phone and pulling up the **Across the Divide GeoTour.** The tour consists of numerous Global Positioning System (GPS) coordinates for locations in Grand Lake, Estes Park, and RMNP. From this point, you can navigate (using your phone loaded with the geocaching app or another GPS device) to each set of coordinates, where various "caches" are located. In the park, caches might include a sign or a pretty view; in locations outside the park, you might be challenged to find a concealed physical cache in a small container. Souvenir geocoins are distributed to participants after staff at the **Grand Lake Visitor Center** (West Portal Rd. and Hwy. 34, 970/627-3402, Grand Lake, www.grandlakechamber.com, 10am-4pm daily Memorial Day-Labor Day, 10am-2pm daily Sept.-May) or at the **Estes Park Visitor Center** (500 Big Thompson Ave., 970/577-9900) verify your found caches. The game is free and family-friendly; pay a visit to either gateway town's visitor center to get the full scoop.

ENTERTAINMENT AND SHOPPING

Watering Holes

Libations are easy to come by in Estes, with no shortage of restaurant bars to belly up for happy hour or an after-dinner cocktail. Within town limits, try these breweries for hoppy beverage quaffing: **Lumpy Ridge Brewing Co.** (531 S. Saint Vrain Ave., 812/201-3836, www.lumpyridgebrewing.com, 3pm-7pm daily), **Rock Cut Brewing Co.** (390 W. Riverside Dr., 970/586-7300, www.rockcutbrewing.com, 11am-10pm daily), and **Tavern 1929 Restaurant and Brewery** (2625 Marys Lake Rd., 970/586-5958, www.maryslakelodge.com, 2pm-9pm Wed.-Sun.) Vino-lovers enjoy **Snowy Peaks Winery** (292 Moraine Ave., 970/586-2099, 11am-5pm Mon.-Thurs., 11am-6pm Fri.-Sun.).

The Wheel Bar (132 E. Elkhorn Ave., 970/586-9381, www.thewheelbar.com, 10am-2am daily) and **Lonigan's Saloon, Nightclub and Grill** (110 W. Elkhorn Ave., 970/586-4346, www.lonigans.com, 11am-2am daily) both have a dive-bar feel (e.g., gaudy, upholstered swivel chairs, and Slim Jims and lighters for sale at The Wheel Bar; a hot-pocket fridge and microwave for late-night munchies at Lonigan's) and are favorite hangouts for locals and tourists alike. The Wheel Bar staff mixes a mean Bloody Mary, while Lonigan's is known for its entertaining open mike and karaoke nights. Lonigan's also serves a full restaurant menu, including an especially delish Irish Burger.

Theater and Cinema

You can't miss the 80-foot high tower of **The Park Theatre** (130 Moraine Ave., 970/586-8904, www.historicparktheatre.com, May-Oct., show times vary, adults $9, children under 12 years $6, seniors 65 and older $7.50) as you drive through town—especially at night when its decorative green neon lights are glowing. This historic landmark is notable for being the oldest running movie theater in the country. Constructed in 1913, the building looks much the same as it did more than a century ago. The theater's walls are covered in rugs for sound absorption and a projector from 1917 sits on display in the lobby. The carpet on the floor of the theater is original, as are the wooden seats (the seat pads, thankfully, have been updated for comfort). Along with showing first-run films, the theater screens a wide variety of other fare, including Denver Broncos games during football season, the *Rocky Horror Picture Show* around Halloween, and horror flicks during the Stanley Film Festival. Because the theater is smack in the middle of downtown with no dedicated parking, allow extra time to find a spot at one of the nearby public lots.

The **Park Theatre Café** (11am-6:30pm daily, $4-10) is connected to the theater and offers sandwiches, quiche, and chili; there is a concession stand inside the main building. Patrons can order food from the café and eat off trays while they watch a film.

A second option for moviegoers is the **Reel Mountain Theater** (543 Big Thompson Ave., Stanley Village, 970/586-4227 for show times, 970/577-1686 for box office, www.reelmountain.com, daily year-round, show times vary). This small family-owned movie theater has three screening rooms and shows first-run films. A variety of candy, drinks, and food items are available for purchase. The popcorn is prepared in coconut oil and expertly seasoned and is finger-licking delicious.

Festivals and Events

ROOFTOP RODEO

Attending the rodeo is tradition for thousands of Coloradans each year, and several dozen events are held around the state. Estes Park's **Rooftop Rodeo** (1209 Manford Ave., Stanley Park Fairgrounds, 970/586-6104, www.rooftoprodeo.com, $15-30, early July), which takes place at 7,500 feet in elevation, is promoted as a "Rodeo with Altitude!" For many people, a night at the rodeo arouses all kinds of patriotic feelings, but you certainly don't have to be a flag-waver to enjoy one of the most classic forms of entertainment in the West. This fast-paced event includes barrel-racing and team-roping competitions, dopey-looking rodeo clowns, and humans being bucked around like puppets on the backs of ornery bulls. The rodeo is family-friendly, and kids especially love donning suspenders and face paint for "Dress Like a Rodeo Clown" night. **Behind the Chutes Tours** (adults $10, children 11 and under $5), which give attendees a behind-the-scenes look at rodeo logistics, are very popular. You can buy admission tickets and tour tickets in advance. Food and beverages are available for purchase.

STANLEY FILM FESTIVAL

Over the course of four days each spring, the historic Stanley Hotel is transformed from mildly creepy to pee-your-pants scary during the **Stanley Film Festival** (333 Wonderview Ave., 970/577-4000, www.stanleyfilmfest.com, Apr., individual tickets $11, festival passes $95-295), a celebration of the horror genre that has gained worldwide recognition since its debut in 2013. The hotel is awash in blood-red light each night, and all manner of ogres and villains troll the hotel grounds. The long weekend is jam-packed with feature- and short-film screenings, panel discussions, and a student competition and awards ceremony. You can attend events with several types of festival passes or with tickets purchased à la carte. Some of the best parts of the event are totally free. On one visit, I witnessed a woman experience an insane asylum through virtual reality goggles; shortly afterward, I was treated to the discordant and barbaric sounds of Denver's Itchy-O Marching Band. Yes, this is weird stuff, and kids should be left behind. Lodging must be reserved separately and in advance.

LONGS PEAK SCOTTISH-IRISH HIGHLAND FESTIVAL

Throngs of men, women, children, and dogs of Scottish and Irish background descend on Estes Park the first weekend after Labor Day for the **Longs Peak Scottish-Irish Highland Festival** (800/903-7837, www.scotfest.com, adults $25, children age 5-15 $10, children under 5 free), one of the largest gatherings of its kind in the United States. A staggering number of events are held over the course of this four-day celebration at the **Estes Park Events Complex** (1125 Rooftop Way, Estes Park): dancing, bagpipe playing, and a jousting competition among them. It's normal to see jaunty men walking around town in colorful kilts and high knee socks during the festival, which never fails to coax smiles from passersby. Scottish athletic events are a huge hit, and largely involve flinging objects into the air: There's the caber toss, sheaf toss, weight throw, and hammer throw. There's no shortage of booze—namely whiskey and beer—at many events. The hour-long, kick-off parade on Elkhorn Avenue is free of charge and a must-see. Concerts command an additional fee.

ELK FEST

Elk mating season in Estes Park and Rocky reaches a fever pitch in October, which is why many locals refer to the month as "Elktober." In particular, the first weekend of Elktober is set aside for a special elk celebration: **Elk Fest** (www.visitestespark.com, free; 5K race admission: adults $25, youth 14 and under $23). This event primarily takes place in Bond Park in the center of town (on E. Elkhorn Ave. at Virginia Dr.) and includes a 5K Rut Run, bus tours, storytelling, music, food, and children's activities. If you can attend just one event,

Macdonald Bookshop has a fabulous selection.

plan to view or participate in the wildly entertaining elk bugling contest, open to kids and adults.

Shopping

Rock enthusiasts and even those with mild geologic curiosity will love ducking into the **Red Rose Rock Shop and Dick's Rock Museum** (490 Moraine Ave., 970/586-4180, www.redroserockshopestes.com, 8am-8pm daily summer, 10am-5pm Mon.-Thurs. and 9am-6pm Fri.-Sun. winter) to comb their fingers through baskets and bins of earthly gems. The majority of merchandise in the store comes from outside of Colorado, with only one set of shelves dedicated to regionally sourced rocks and minerals. Nonetheless, this is a fine place to pick up gifts for friends, and worth wandering through to admire the owner's personal collection of stones (Dick's Rock Museum). The best part of the shop is the fluorescent specimen room, in which rocks are illuminated with black lights.

★ MACDONALD BOOKSHOP

Indie bookstore **Macdonald Bookshop** (152 E. Elkhorn Ave., 970/586-3450, www.macdonaldbookshop.com, 8am-9pm daily summer, 8am-6pm daily winter) has survived numerous challenging times—including a damaging flood—since its beginnings in 1928. This is one of those instantly loveable, small bookshops with friendly staff members who are voracious readers, plus nooks in which you can easily get lost for an hour or more. Amidst a well-curated selection of current titles exists a large number of books about Western history, plus tomes by local authors and a fantastic classics and poetry section. Original owners Ed and Jessica Macdonald used to live in this old Forest Service cabin, selling books out of their front room; the store is still family-run.

★ NEOTA DESIGNS

Deb Coombs, proprietor of **Neota Designs** (156 Wiest Dr., 970/586-8800, www.neotadesigns.com, 2pm-5pm Mon.-Thurs., 10am-5pm Fri.-Sat., noon-5pm Sun. Jan.-mid-May; 1pm-5pm Mon.-Thurs., 10am-5pm Fri.-Sat., noon-5pm Sun. mid-May-Dec.) started hand-painting yarn for her own projects in the early 1990s and eventually turned her home hobby into a business. Self-taught in her craft, Coombs has held her secret technique close to the vest all of these years. Whatever the process is to make her beautiful skeins of yarn—with nature-inspired names like Jeweled Nights and Golden Meadow—it is a messy one, and done right on-site in a cramped kitchen and bathroom (the loo has been taken over by a steam pot and deemed off-limits to customers). In addition to yarn, hand-woven shawls, scarves, and other accessories are available for purchase.

OUTDOOR GEAR

A lot more than shopping occurs at the independently owned **Estes Park Mountain Shop** (2050 Big Thompson Ave., 970/586-6548, www.estesparkmountainshop.com, 8am-9pm daily year-round). Besides 5,000 square feet of retail space filled with outdoor clothing and gear, the store features summer and winter gear rentals; an indoor climbing gym; and guided hikes, fly-fishing trips, and other outings. Employees are friendly and extremely knowledgeable about the area. Also, the shop is involved in numerous charitable events and efforts in the Estes Park community. Adventure films are screened periodically in the climbing gym.

Kirks Flyshop (230 E. Elkhorn Ave., 970/577-0790, www.kirksflyshop.com, 7am-8pm daily summer, 8am-5pm daily winter) is only a fraction of the size of Estes Park Mountain Shop, but the goods it sells are high quality. Find outdoor books, maps, and gear at Kirks, and a superb selection of fly-fishing gear, clothing, and hand-tied flies. The shop also offers expertly guided mountain outings, including llama pack adventures and overnight float-and-fish trips. Winter and summer gear can be rented through the store.

hand-painted yarn at Neota Designs

FOOD

Breakfast and Lunch

Upbeat 1920s-era jazz tunes and the tinkling of teacups are the norm at **Moon Kats Tea Shoppe** (205 Park Ln., 303/437-9514, www.moonkats.com, 11am-5pm Tues.-Sat., 10am-5pm Sun., $4-11), a favorite of brunch-goers. Cat lovers will find kindred spirits in hands-on owner/chefs Rob and Staci Leavitt, who genuinely gush over their two feline companions, Hansel and Gretel, any chance they get. The shop is located at the site of an old inn called The Prospector, and features original wood flooring from the early 20th century. The tea menu is extensive and features several proprietary blends. Tasty and reasonably priced salads, sandwiches, and baked goods round out the menu at this sunny and spacious café.

Folks who opt for gluten-free will be thrilled to learn that nearly everything on **Notchtop Bakery & Cafe**'s (459 E. Wonderview Ave., 970/586-0272, www.thenotchtop.com, 7am-3pm daily, $6-13) extensive menu can be made with alternative flours and breads. The restaurant has found a great niche catering to gluten-free customers, and also offers a variety of vegan and vegetarian items. Try the Dragon's Egg Rock Benedict, a delightfully spicy dish featuring chipotle hollandaise sauce and green chili pancakes. Notchtop's portions are generous and prices are reasonable.

Wait until after 10am to get your doughnut fix at **Donut Haus** (342 Moraine Ave., 970/586-2988, www.donuthaus-estespark.com, 6am-noon daily, Memorial Day-Labor Day, 6am-noon Tues.-Sun. in the winter, $1-2.50) and you might find yourself out of luck. Workers at the bakery produce several thousand fresh donuts each day, which are often sold out by mid-morning in the summer. Along with donuts and their holes, the bakery sells breads and rolls, breakfast burritos, muffins, and other baked goods. Daily specials like the devil's food cake donut and blueberry cake donut disappear especially fast. Parking is limited.

Locals regularly congregate at **Kind Coffee** (470 E. Elkhorn Ave., 970/586-5206, www.kindcoffee.com, 6:30am-8pm daily Memorial Day-Labor Day, 6:30am–6pm daily the rest of the year) and visitors quickly fall in love with this café located on the town's Riverwalk. In addition to coffee and tea, the café sells breakfast burritos, baked goods, bagels and cream cheese, and bottled drinks. Wi-Fi is free; two relatively quiet rooms off of the main café are available for settling in and getting work done. The outside patio, situated next to the Big Thompson River, is great for sprawling in the sun and socializing. Best of all, Kind Coffee sells and pours its own organic, fair trade java. With names like Estes Perk, Longs Peak, and Bear Lake Breakfast, a one-pound bag of beans is the perfect consumable souvenir to pack in your suitcase.

Barbeque

Pig, chicken, and cow tchotchkes are found throughout ★ **Smokin' Dave's BBQ & Taphouse** (820 Moraine Ave., 907/577-7427, www.smokindavesq.com, 11am-8pm daily, $9-25), a cheerful and bustling restaurant that is a standing favorite among locals and visitors. With your belt loosened and arm sleeves rolled way up, dig into heaping plates of tender, melt-in-your-mouth smoked meats doused in your choice of homemade sauces. Comfort food sides like spiced apples and Southern green beans taste as though they were lovingly prepared in a favorite grandmother's kitchen.

Burgers

When you are in need of eats that are quick and affordable but you don't want to submit to the golden arches (yes, there's one on Big Thompson Ave.), **Baba's Burgers** (861 Moraine Ave., 970/586-1171, www.babasburgers.com, 11am-9pm Mon.-Fri., 11am-10pm Sat.-Sun., $2-8) is a great, locally owned and operated "fast food" option. In addition to classic beef patties, the restaurant offers elk and buffalo burgers, chicken sandwiches, hotdogs, gyros, and various fried veggies. Sit inside or out, or order a sack of freshly made sandwiches at the drive-through window. This no-frills dining out experience is great for travelers on a budget and families.

Italian

Some restaurants in Estes Park reduce their hours during the slower seasons, but the **Dunraven Inn** (2470 Tunnel Rd., 970/586-6409, www.dunraveninn.com, 4pm-9pm daily, $15-29) isn't one of them. A loyal following of local clientele enables the restaurant to stay open daily year-round. The main dining room is elegant while the bar area is funky, with signed dollar bills plastered over every inch of wall space. As the story goes, the original owner of the restaurant hung up one of the first dollars received when the restaurant opened—which was signed "good luck"—and things took off from there. The Dunraven's menu is heavily focused on Italian dishes, with a selection of seafood and steak selections rounding out the options. The drink menu is extensive, featuring fine wines, specialty cocktails, and a unique selection of beers. Staff members accommodate special dietary needs.

Mexican

Ed's Cantina & Grill (390 E. Elkhorn Ave., Estes Park, 970/586-2919, www.edscantina.com, 11am-9pm Mon.-Thurs., 11am-9:30pm Fri.-Sat., $6-18) is a favorite of tourists and locals, and also finds a special niche with the rock-climbing community. The restaurant owner is a climber, and a number of Ed's employees have an affinity for the sport as well. On one of the restaurant's walls you'll find large autographed photos of well-respected climbers who have patronized the restaurant. The extensive menu features a mix of Mexican and American fare. You can't go wrong by ordering anything off the list of specialties, which includes Rocky Mountain trout and bison enchiladas. The kale-blueberry salad is superb. Family-friendly.

Nepalese

★ **Nepal's Café** (184 E. Elkhorn Ave., 970/577-7035, 11am-9pm daily, $11-16) is a lovely treat any time, but especially when damp and chilly Rocky Mountain weather moves in. In this warm and comforting space, no more than a dozen tables are crammed within inches of each other in the main dining room, and the hum of conversation and clattering of dishes from the kitchen can be heard from any table. The food is delicious and includes curries, kormas, noodle dishes, momos, and flatbreads with various levels of spiciness. For a sweet treat, accompany your meal with a glass of mango saffron lemonade.

Steakhouse

★ **The Rock Inn Mountain Tavern** (1675 Hwy. 66, 970/586-4116, www.rockinnestes.com, open daily at 4pm, closing times vary with the weather and season; Sundays 10am-2pm, $10-33) feels every bit an authentic old-style tavern with its rich wood-and-rock interior, hearty fare, and bar stools that don't sit unoccupied for long. This is a great place to unwind after a day of outdoor adventure and has a less touristy vibe than many other restaurants in town. The steaks are delicious—juicy and thickly cut—and a pot of locally blended tea is a sublime way to top off a meal. Most evenings in the summer, a musical act entertains diners, and on Friday nights, booty-shaking takes place until late. The Rock serves dinner and Sunday brunch, and does not take reservations.

Thai and Vietnamese

Cafe de Pho-Thai (225 W. Riverside Dr., 970/577-0682, www.cafedephothai.com, 11am-9pm daily spring/summer, 11:30am-8pm daily fall/winter, $8-14) is a hidden gem, tucked into an inconspicuous space next to the town's post office. There is nothing fancy about the restaurant's décor; the main attraction here is the food, which includes delicious soups, noodles, curries, stir-fries, and salads. The Vietnamese fresh spring rolls are excellent. Service is prompt and friendly. Make reservations for this spot, as only a dozen or so tables are available.

Nepal's Cafe is a local favorite.

Groceries

Shopping at the one major grocery chain store in Estes Park can be stressful in the summer. The aisles are clogged with carts and most people are in a rush. Locally owned **Country Market** (900 Moraine Ave., 970/586-2702, www.nationalparkvillage.com, 7am-8pm daily) is just as busy, and a lot smaller, but offers a more pleasant shopping experience. The store has a fine selection of canned and boxed foods, produce, dairy items, baked goods, a deli, and ice cream/coffee counter. Ice can sell out early afternoon in the high season, so plan accordingly. A small selection of snacks, drinks, picnic items, ice, and firewood is available at the **Famous Eastside Food Store** (381 S. St. Vrain Ave., 970/577-7114, 8am-10pm daily spring and fall-winter, 6am-11pm daily Memorial Day-Labor Day). In the summer, produce, breads, cheeses, and flowers are for sale at the **Estes Valley Farmers Market** (Bond Park, on E. Elkhorn Ave. at Virginia Dr., 303/775-9058, 8am-1pm Thurs. June-Oct.). Factor in a separate trip to

Estes Valley Farmers Market

a local liquor store for purchasing booze, since Colorado laws prohibit grocery and convenience stores from selling full-strength alcohol. Three-two beer (3.2 percent) is as strong as you can get in a supermarket.

ACCOMMODATIONS

Know this: all bets are off if you show up in Estes Park in need of lodging on a weekend or holiday after Memorial Day and before Labor Day. It's not impossible to find a place to stay, but it can be difficult to find that perfect situation. If you wait until the last minute, expect that prime units will be long gone (e.g., don't expect to snag a river-view room in a lodge along the Fall River). Lodges and inns often require a two- or even three-night minimum stay during this peak season. Sometimes, you can land a room for a single night if there is a gap between existing reservations, but do not count on it. For the best selection, start your research months—not weeks—before you arrive.

In the winter and shoulder seasons, finding a place to stay is considerably less difficult and prices are lower. Many hotels and lodges have promotions during slower times. While you can find good rates by using one of the popular travel booking websites, it's also a good idea to check the official Estes Park website (www.visitestespark.com) for current lodging specials.

Hundreds of private home rental listings for Estes Park are located online (www.vrbo.com or www.airbnb.com). Always pay close attention to the fine details of rental property listings before fully committing. Some homeowners tack on hefty cleaning fees to the final rental price, some don't; some require guests to provide their own towels and sheets, while others have the linen closet stocked and ready. Price-wise, a home rental can sometimes be more affordable than a hotel. As long as there are no surprises, these unique stays can make for a memorable visit to Estes Park.

$100-200

Throughout the **YMCA of the Rockies-Estes Park Center**'s (2515 Tunnel Rd., 970/586-3341, www.ymcarockies.org) 860-acre grounds are a variety of accommodations, including simply appointed hotel-style lodge rooms, vacation homes, and standalone cabins ($149 and up). Family reunion cabins—which sleep up to 80 people—book up several years in advance ($1,950-3,900). Overnight guests may choose to immerse themselves in the myriad of family-oriented activities offered on-site as much or as little as they please, and have the option of purchasing a meal voucher for the dining hall. The YMCA's lodging options are more suitable for the social butterfly than the recluse, since more than 1,000 conference groups stay here each year; in the summer, the grounds are bustling with people.

Murphy's River Lodge (481 W. Elkhorn Ave., 970/480-5081, www.murphysriverlodge.com, $169 and up) offers a variety of rooms, but the best are the River Rooms and River Front Condos (snag an upper level unit if you can). The rushing, hypnotic sounds of the

Fall River set the stage for a relaxing vacation and deep sleep after a full day of activity. While some of the lodge's furniture is on the older side, rooms are otherwise spotless and cheerful. No need to get in your car for a meal downtown—the main drag is a 10-minute walk from the hotel. Features an indoor heated pool and an adults-only hot tub.

Machin's Cottages in the Pines (2450 Eagle Cliff Rd., 970/586-4276, www.machinscottages.com, late May-early Oct., from $126) is technically located within the national park boundary, and a 1.2-mile hiking trail that starts on the property takes people to Bear Lake Road near the Moraine Park Discovery Center. Vehicle access to Rocky is not possible from this location, however; guests otherwise need to use established park entrances for accessing sights and trails. Cottages can be booked a year in advance, and it is wise to call early for reservations. For many guests, a stay at Machin's has been a family tradition for years or even a decade or longer. Cottages (one-, two- and three-bedroom) are simply furnished, and each has a deck or porch and wood-burning fireplace. On-site amenities include a playground, shuffleboard, and a small gift shop. The main draw at Machin's is peace and quiet.

If you ask around town for family-friendly accommodations and activities in Estes Park, you will quickly be weighted with recommendations. A harder task is finding spots reserved for just adults. **StoneBrook on Fall River** (1710 Fall River Rd., 970/586-4629, www.stonebrookresort.com, $175-235) offers just that—a special retreat for grown-ups. What you won't find here: a playground, mini-golf, or a game room. What you will find are in-room whirlpool tubs, an outdoor hot tub, gas fireplaces, and king beds. Featuring both cottages and suites, this lodging option is well-suited for a romantic getaway, or simply for those seeking some quiet time. Several hammocks on the back of the property, strung between trees next to the Fall River, are great places to take a siesta.

the Meadow Bright room at the Romantic RiverSong Bed & Breakfast

$200-250

In the lobby of the **Silver Moon Inn** (175 Spruce Dr., 970/586-6006, www.silvermooninn.com, $205-210 summer), guests are invited to help themselves to a bag of popcorn from the retro-style popper whenever they please. It is little surprises like this that make a stay at the hotel enjoyable. In addition, hotel staff members host spontaneous marshmallow roasts several times a week during the summer. The most popular gathering spot before retiring for the evening is in front of the hotel along the banks of the Fall River. Guests linger around campground-style fire rings long after the sun goes down. Rooms are cozy and well-appointed.

Upon arriving at the ★ **Romantic RiverSong Bed & Breakfast** (1766 Lower Broadview Rd., 970/586-4666, www.romanticriversong.com, $213-375) you'll crush hard on the property's 27 acres of manicured lawns, hiking trails, and riverside seating; then you'll fall head-over-heels in love after viewing your quarters: generously sized, luxurious, and full of whimsical details. Indeed, the stage is set perfectly here for romance, and not in a trite, hearts-and-flowers kind of way. Every room has its own theme and unique touches. The bed frame in the Wood Nymph room is fashioned out of willow branches and encircled by a glimmering string of lights; the Meadow Bright room boasts a massive rock fireplace next to a two-person, jetted tub. Breakfast is served in a dining room bathed in sunlight and features such favorites as giddy-up grits and stuffed French toast. Your choices for lazy afternoon activities include lawn chess and a streamside massage.

Over $250

Options—you have lots of them at **The Stanley Hotel** (333 Wonderview Ave., 970/577-4000 or 800/976-1377, www.stanleyhotel.com, from $259). The hotel today is not just a hotel; it is a collection of properties, including a boutique hotel next door to the main hotel, nearby condominiums, and a lodge that is a 10-minute drive from the main grounds. To stay in the historic hotel is to be in the center of everything (everything paranormal and ghostly, that is—wink, wink). Standard rooms are outfitted with handsome wood furniture, and beds are comfortable, with bright white sheets and soft blankets. Reserve rooms well ahead of a visit, especially if you have plans to arrive in October—the busiest month at the hotel. Room 217—the room Stephen King stayed in when he was inspired to write his book *The Shining*—usually books up for October 31 several years in advance. Pets are not allowed in the hotel, but are treated like royalty in the lodge next door to the hotel, which has a Preferred Pooch Program for dogs 50 pounds and less.

What would an old lodge be without a few quirks? At **The Historic Crags Lodge** (300 Riverside Dr., 970/586-6066, $270-305), the walls between rooms are on the thin side, and shower temperatures can vary wildly. Still, the elegance of this lodge overrides any minor inconveniences caused by its structural age. Opened in 1914, much of the furniture on the lower level is original and in surprisingly good condition.

The dining room is home to an upscale restaurant, **The View** (970/586-1087, 5pm-9pm Thurs.-Sun. winter, 5pm-9pm daily summer, $14-31), that features exceptionally prepared food and is the loveliest spot on the grounds. One wall of the restaurant is made up of French pane windows and has two private balconies that scream "date night." Outside the lodge, find a heated pool and a hot tub.

Reservations for Crags Lodge can be made through **Diamond Resorts International** (800/438-2929, www.diamondresorts.com) or check VRBO (www.vrbo.com) for openings.

The beauty of Lake Estes pales in comparison to any body of water found in Rocky Mountain National Park, but what it has that the park doesn't is a wide variety of boats available for rental. Guests of **The Estes Park Resort** (1700 Big Thompson Ave., 970-577-6400 or 855/377-3778, www.theestesparkresort.com, summer, $299-349) have prime access to the lake's marina and various watercraft (rental fees separate). Other amenities include spa services and an on-site restaurant/lounge. Rooms are comfortable and tastefully decorated in earth tones. Be aware that weddings are extremely popular at the resort, especially in the prime summer months.

Camping

PUBLIC CAMPGROUNDS

Two public campgrounds are located within Estes Park town limits. Prices for both campgrounds are $30/night for non-water and electric; $40/night for water and electric; $45/night for full-hookup sites. Reserve sites through **ReserveAmerica** (800/964-7806, www.reserveamerica.com); a two-night stay is required on weekends. The town's free **Estes Park Shuttle** (late June-mid-Sept.) serves both campgrounds.

Estes Park Campground at Marys Lake (2120 Mary's Lake Rd., 970/577-1026, www.evrpd.com, May 15-Oct. 15) has 120 spaces for tents and RVs, and features a swimming pool, a small store, flush toilets, potable water, and a playground. Some tent sites are partially shaded; mostly, tent campers and RVs can count on lots of sun exposure in this spot. The campground is close to the park and town, and just across the road from Mary's Lake. **Estes Park Campground at East Portal** (3420 Tunnel Rd., 970/586-4188, www.evrpd.com, May 15-Oct.15) grants easy access to the park's East Portal Trailhead and is on the same road as the YMCA. There is a playground, plus potable water, showers, and restrooms; ice and firewood are for sale. The 68 shaded sites at this campground may be occupied by tents or RVs 24 feet or less in length.

PRIVATE CAMPGROUNDS

There's no getting around the fact that the **Estes Park KOA** (2051 Big Thompson Ave., 970/586-2888, www.koa.com, May 1-Oct. 15, $39-150), is about as far from a nature experience as one gets. Still, this is a fun and cheerful place to stay, with tent- and RV-sites, cabins, and cottages available. Showers are piping hot, and the campgrounds owners go the extra mile to make your stay a positive one. Kids are kept entertained with a playground, basketball court, game room, and evening rides around the campground on a mini KOA "train." The KOA is situated directly next to busy and loud Big Thompson Avenue and across from the Estes Park Mountain Shop. For RVers, usage of the dump station is free for registered guests or for a fee by nonregistered guests.

Elk Meadow Lodge & RV Resort (1665 Hwy. 66, 970/586-5342, www.elkmeadowrv.com, May 1-early Oct., $39-125) has 169 RV sites—160 of which can accommodate big rigs up to 45 feet in length. Cabins, teepees, and tent-only sites can also be reserved. Elk Meadow is in a prime location just 0.5 mile from the Beaver Meadows Visitor Center; however, it has several shortcomings: the lack of shade and a feeling of being packed in like sardines. Amenities include a heated swimming pool and a hot tub; one pet per campsite is allowed. For RVers, usage of the dump station is free for registered guests or for a fee by nonregistered guests.

Spruce Lake Resort (1050 Marys Lake Rd., 970/586-2889, www.sprucelakerv.com, May 1-early Oct., $59-175) has 110 RV sites and four cabins on its property. Its namesake lake is stocked with rainbow trout, and a mini-golf course is a hit with families. Kids tear around on the grounds on their bikes all summer long, so drive slowly when you enter.

a lean-to at the Estes Park KOA

Yogi Bear's Jellystone Park of Estes Campground (5495 Hwy. 36, 970/658-2536, www.jellystoneofestes.com, early May-Sept., $40-140) is 5 miles southeast of downtown Estes Park, but has the most impressive list of family-friendly activities offered in the summer. You will feel like you are at summer camp all over again, with wagon rides, scavenger hunts, and movie nights. Accommodations include tent sites, RV sites, and cabins. Three RVs already parked on the property are also available to rent.

DISPERSED CAMPING

For a spot to pitch your tent with no amenities nearby, from the junction of Highway 34 and Highway 36 in Estes Park, drive 3.7 miles east of Estes Park on Highway 36, then head northeast on **Pole Hill Road.** The National Forest Boundary is about a mile from Highway 36; free, dispersed camping spots are located farther east down the road. A four-wheel drive vehicle is needed to navigate this rough terrain; trailers are not recommended. This is not a good option for people wanting to frequently pop in and out of downtown Estes Park.

TRANSPORTATION AND SERVICES

Car

From the Beaver Meadows Entrance Station, Estes Park is 3.6 miles east on Highway 36. Downtown Estes Park is very crowded in the summer. **Bumper-to-bumper traffic** creeps down Elkhorn Avenue and Moraine Avenue. Vehicles circle downtown parking lots like vultures. People swarm sidewalks. Estes Park's Board of Trustees has approved a multi-million dollar congestion-relief plan called the "Downtown Estes Loop," which will significantly alter (hopefully for the better) the flow of traffic downtown. However, construction is not expected to start until 2021, so for the time being travelers will have to wrestle with issues of getting around.

ALTERNATE ROADS

If you are traveling from the south—Denver, Boulder, or Allenspark—and your primary destination is the Beaver Meadows Entrance Station for Rocky, it is possible to avoid downtown Estes Park altogether. In the town of Lyons, take Highway 7 toward Allenspark and Estes Park, turn left at **Marys Lake Road** to cut over to Highway 36, and then proceed west to the park entrance. You can use this two-way road for the return trip, too.

The **Highway 34 Bypass route** also avoids busy Elkhorn Avenue, and runs east to west to the Fall River Entrance Station. In addition, the bypass provides access to lodges and cabins along Fall River Road.

Riverside Drive is especially handy midmorning and late afternoon when traffic on Highway 36 heading to and from the Beaver Meadows Entrance Station is heaviest. The road also enables drivers to avoid one of the busiest sections of Elkhorn Avenue. Riverside Drive runs parallel to Highway 36/Moraine Avenue and the Big Thompson River to the south, between Marys Lake Road and Elkhorn Avenue.

Moccasin Circle Drive is yet another option for steering clear of downtown traffic. Moccasin Circle connects with Riverside Drive on the western end, and on its eastern end turns into Fir Avenue, then Prospect Avenue, and finally Stanley Avenue before connecting with North St. Vrain Avenue or South St. Vrain Avenue.

PARKING

Free parking lots in town fall into three categories: unlimited parking time, three-hour, and 30-minute parking. In the summer, it is worth the effort to print a downtown public parking map from the Estes Park website (visitestespark.com) ahead of your visit so that you know all of your options; otherwise, you might cruise through a few full lots downtown and just throw in the towel. Some parking lots are not immediately obvious, which is another reason to have a map. Naturally, spots in lots closest to Elkhorn Avenue shops and restaurants are the hottest commodities. A limited amount of RV and bus parking is available in the parking lot next to the **Estes Valley Library** (335 E. Elkhorn Ave.) and at the **Estes Park Visitor Center** (500 Big Thompson Ave.).

A source of major congestion in the summer is the **Stanley Village Shopping Center** (at the intersection of Hwy. 34 and Hwy. 36), where a big-box grocery store and numerous other shops and restaurants are located. Travel around these lots with patience and extra caution, and don't expect to secure front row parking.

CAR RENTAL

Estes Park Rent-A-Car (343 S. Saint Vrain Ave., #12, 970/577-9715, www.estesparkrentacar.com, 9am-4pm Mon.-Fri.) rents cars, trucks, and vans by the day or week. You can rent specialty vehicles, including ATVs, Jeeps, and Harley-Davidson motorcycles from **Backbone Adventure Rentals** (1851 North Lake Ave., 970/443-2538, www.backbonecycles.com, 8am-6pm daily Mar.-Oct.; phone reservations only 9am-5pm daily Nov.-Feb.). Vehicles are also available through the online service **Turo** (www.turo.com).

Shuttle

The **Estes Park Free Shuttle System** (970/577-9900, www.visitestespark.com, daily late June-early Sept.) operates a fleet of vans and a street trolley that make more than 60 stops throughout town. Locations include campgrounds, hotels, Lake Estes, restaurants, and the Beaver Meadows Visitor Center. Shuttles start as early as 8am and end around 10pm. Once in town, pick up a copy of the shuttle schedule and map from the visitor center (500 Big Thompson Ave.) or print a copy ahead from the website.

One option for getting from Estes Park to Rocky in the summer is to park at the **Estes Park Fairgrounds** (1209 Manford Ave.), where there are 400 parking spaces, then take the shuttle's Silver Route to the Estes Park Visitor Center. The Silver Route runs daily on the half-hour 8:45am-9:44pm. From the Visitor Center, hop on the park's free **Hiker Shuttle Express** (hourly 7:30am-11am, on the half-hour 11am-6pm, hourly 6pm-8pm) to the Park & Ride on Bear Lake Road. Another alternative is to seek out a parking spot at the Estes Park Visitor Center, though they are much fewer in number than those found at the fairgrounds. From the visitor center, take Rocky's free Hiker Shuttle Express into the park.

Taxi

Estes Park Taxi (970/372-9888, 7:30am-3:30am daily year-round, $4 pick-up charge and $1 for each additional person, plus $2.25/mile) offers local or airport travel. Call 2-3 days in advance for a ride to the airport; for local destinations, you can make same-day reservations. Don't count on an immediate pick-up; this is a one-person operation.

Services

VISITOR INFORMATION

The spacious and modern **Estes Park Visitor Center** (500 Big Thompson Ave., 970/577-9900, 9am-5pm Mon.-Sat., 10am-4pm Sun., extended hours in the summer) has a wealth of information about area attractions, accommodations, restaurants, and activities, and a friendly volunteer staff to help whittle down the choices. A small selection of local books is for sale, and visitors may help themselves to maps and brochures. This location also serves as a stop for the park's free **Hiker Shuttle Express** (www.nps.gov/romo) during the summer.

MEDIA AND COMMUNICATIONS

The town's oldest newspaper is the *Estes Park Trail Gazette* (Wed. and Fri.). *Estes Inside & Out*—a free supplement to the *Trail Gazette*—and *The Estes Park News* are also available at newsstands on Friday. For regional entertainment listings covering the Highway 7 corridor from Nederland to Blackhawk City, pick up a copy of the monthly *Mountain Music Arts & Culture*.

Estes Park has one **U.S. Post Office** (215 W. Riverside Dr., 970/586-0170, 8:30am-4:30pm Mon.-Fri., 10am-1pm Sat.). Other mailing services include **The UPS Store** (453 E. Wonderview Ave. #3, 970/586-1954, 8am-6pm Mon.-Fri., 8am-4pm Sat.), **Master Graphics Printing, Inc.** (191 W. Riverside Dr., 970/586-2679, 8am-5pm Mon.-Fri.) for UPS and FedEx, and **Estes True Value and Radio Shack** (461 E. Wonderview Ave., 970/586-3496, www.estestruevalue.com, 8am-9pm Mon.-Sun.), which ships UPS and FedEx.

CELL AND INTERNET SERVICE

Being connected to the digital world is iffy in the national park, but in Estes Park there are few issues. Cell phone coverage is comprehensive within town limits. However, signals become weaker in every direction—and in some cases nonexistent—once you leave town proper.

Free Wi-Fi is easy to find at local coffeehouses, hotels, and lodges. **Kind Coffee** (470 E. Elkhorn Ave., 970/586-5206, www.kindcoffee.com, 6:30am–6pm daily) is a favorite place to log on. The coffee shop has a large indoor seating area where you can surf the net and sip a cup of locally blended Joe. Another Wi-Fi hotspot exists at the **Beaver Meadows Visitor Center** (1000 Hwy. 36, 970/586-1206, www.nps.gov/romo, 8am-4:30pm daily winter, 8am-5pm daily spring and fall, 8am-6pm daily summer). **The Estes Valley Library** (335 E. Elkhorn Ave., 970/586-8116, www.estesvalleylibrary.org, 9am-9pm Mon.-Thurs., 9am-5pm Fri.-Sat., 1pm-5pm Sun.) has free Wi-Fi and a large telecommuter-friendly workspace on the second floor, with plenty of tables and outlets; a library card is not required. **The Estes Park Visitor Center** (500 Big Thompson Ave., 970/577-9900, www.visitestespark.com, 9am-5pm Mon.-Sat., 10am-4pm Sun.; extended hours in the summer) also has several computer terminals available for public use.

LAUNDRY AND SHOWERS

During peak season, **Dad's Maytag Laundry & Showers** (457 E. Wonderview Ave., 970/586-2025, 8am-3pm daily fall, winter, spring, 7am-6pm daily Memorial Day-Labor Day, showers $6 adults, $4 children) is teeming with grungy campers. Owner Heidi Custer hires extra staff in the summer to thoroughly mop out each of the six shower stalls, ensuring a sanitary and pleasant bathing experience for everyone. Basic toiletries are available for purchase. Laundry facilities include TVs and stacks of magazines, plus free Wi-Fi; but swapping yarns with fellow travelers is the best diversion. Dad's is busiest on weekdays and in the late afternoon.

Village Laundry (172-174 S. St. Vrain Ave., 970/586-9274, www.villagelaundryinestespark.com, 7am-9pm Mon.-Sat., 9am-9pm Sun., June-Aug.; 7am-8pm Mon-Sat., 9am-8pm Sun. Sept.-May, shower $5) offers laundry facilities, free Wi-Fi, and a kid-friendly TV viewing area with a selection of videos to borrow. The facility includes two standard shower rooms and a larger shower/bathroom combination ($6) that is wheelchair-accessible. An additional laundry facility, **Estes Park Laundracenter** (900 Moraine Ave. www.nationalparkvillage.com, 6am-midnight daily) is located next to the Country Market.

EMERGENCIES

In the event of an emergency inside or outside the park, dial 911. For non-emergency assistance contact the **Estes Park Police Department** (170 MacGregor Ave., 970/586-4000) police dispatch line. Medical emergencies are handled by two facilities: **Estes Park Medical Center** (555 Prospect Ave., 970/586-2317, www.epmedcenter.com, open 24/7) and **Timberline Medical Urgent Care** (131 Stanley Ave., 970/586-2343, 8am-5pm Mon.-Fri., 9am-1pm Sat.).

Grand Lake

Paleo-Indians are believed to have been the first people to camp along Grand Lake's shores thousands of years ago. Native American tribes—including Ute and Arapaho—later passed through or briefly settled in the area. Because of enduring Native American legends, an air of superstition has long hung over Grand Lake's waters.

One oft-told tale describes an ambush of a Ute Indian camp by Arapaho Indians. In the name of safety, Ute men gathered a group of women and children onto a raft and pushed them out onto the lake. However, the plan backfired when a gust of wind upturned the raft, drowning its passengers. This devastating event haunted Utes from then on. In mist that often rose—and still rises—from the surface of the lake, they saw the human forms of those who perished, and even purported to hear their last desperate wails emanating from beneath the ice in winter.

A Native American told this story to the first documented settler of the area, Judge Joseph L. Wescott, who arrived in 1867. Wescott subsequently penned a poem about the battle called "The Legend of Grand Lake."

A supernatural buffalo reportedly roamed these parts as well. The supposed evidence? Extra-large buffalo tracks—found on frozen-over Grand Lake in the winter—that only traveled to and from a hole in the ice. According the Arapaho, the mystical buffalo rose up from deep within the waters of the lake. It is this second tale that earned Grand Lake the moniker "Spirit Lake." The official name of the town and lake is more straightforward and comes from the Colorado River, which, until 1921, was named The Grand. Still others call Grand Lake "Red Lake" because of rosy hues that appear on the mountains and water during alpenglow.

Today, some Ute Indians still shun Grand Lake because of the Spirit Lake legend. However, early settlers to the area, including trappers and hunters, were not deterred by a history of spooky occurrences. In the late 1800s, gold and silver miners arrived in the area, hoping to discover valuable ore. Though they initially found a small quantity of silver in the area, their get-rich-quick hopes were dashed when heaps of any type of metal never materialized.

Hunting lodges appeared in Grand Lake in the 1800s and are considered the earliest form of tourism in the area. In the early 1900s, the town began to carve out a niche for itself as a recreation and leisure hub. Grand Lake is known as one of the oldest tourist destinations in Colorado. Today, visitors continue to favor the area for its sparkling blue lake, numerous outdoor activities, and rich history.

SIGHTS

★ Grand Lake

Grand Lake (Lake Ave.) is the deepest and largest natural lake in the state. The dimensions of this cobalt beauty: 1.5 miles long and 1 mile wide, with an estimated depth of 265 feet. The lake serves many purposes. It is the crown jewel for the town with the same name, and an important conduit in the Colorado-Big Thompson River Project, which diverts water to municipalities east of the park. Grand Lake is also a major recreation center for the people of Grand County and for vacationers. Boating, fishing, ice fishing, swimming, waterskiing, and stand-up paddleboarding (SUP) are some of the many ways that people enjoy these waters. A variety of wildlife thrives along the lake's margins. This is a resource that gives much to visitors, and in return receives admiration and appreciation. For the easiest access to the shores of Grand Lake, park in town and walk south on Garfield Street, Pitkin Street, or Hancock Street to **Lake Avenue. Point Park,** located on the channel between Grand Lake and Shadow Mountain Reservoir, is also a great place to take in the lake and gaze up at

Around Grand Lake

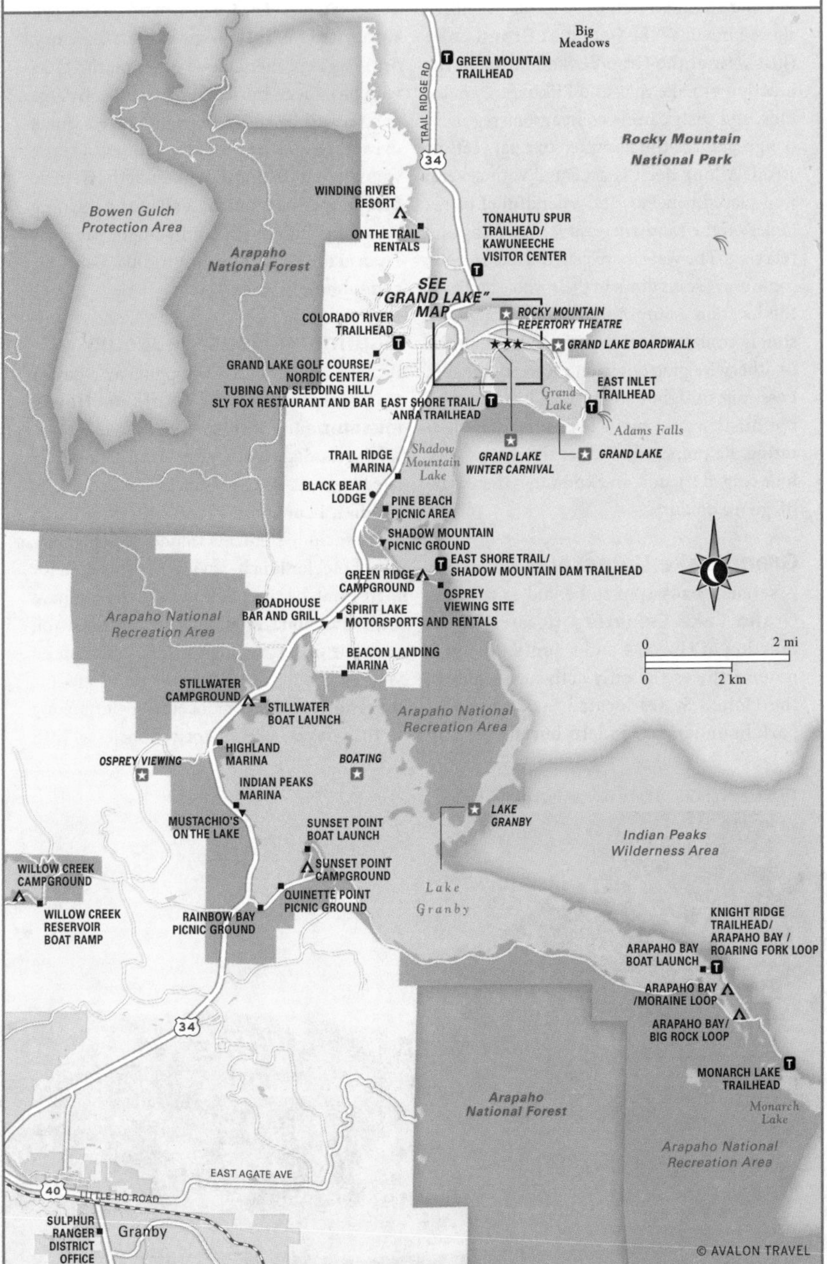

the most prominent mountain in the region: Mount Craig, also known as "Mount Baldy."

On a small stretch of sand on the north shore known as the **Beach at Grand Lake** (just west of the Grand Lake Marina at the junction of Lake Ave. and Pitkin St.), adults, kids, and their canine companions regularly congregate in the summer to chat, eat, or stroll. A long dock is accented with several well-placed benches, and a handful of picnic tables on the sand are great for lunching and relaxing. The waters are generally calm here; some brave souls dunk in their whole bodies at this location. Many other visitors, though, are simply content to wade in up to their ankles or otherwise plop down on a towel in the sun. Pessimists might call the lake bitterly cold; optimists would say it is positively invigorating. Be prepared to share the waters with four-legged friends, and know that there is no lifeguard on duty.

Grand Lake Cemetery

A serene, shady spot to be laid to rest, the **Grand Lake Cemetery** (located at the junction of Hwy. 34 and County Rd. 49) is noteworthy as the only active cemetery in the United States located inside national park boundaries. Modern burials are still accepted at this location. The cemetery dates back to at least 1875, and is operated by the Town of Grand Lake. The **Grand Lake Area Historical Society** (www.grandlakehistory.org) has kept meticulous notes on the folks who have been buried here, but the average person will be satisfied to just take a quick drive through the property. However, those who enjoyed visiting the **Holzwarth Historic Site** in the Kawuneeche Valley and learning about the Holzwarth family might pause, as I did, at the headstones of Virginia, Caroline, and Johnnie Holzwarth.

Kaufmann House Museum

Back in 1892, it cost a whopping $2 a day or $11 a week to stay at the **Kaufmann House Museum** (407 Pitkin Ave., 970/627-9644, www.grandlakehistory.org, 11am-5pm daily late May-Aug. and Sat.-Sun. in Sept., adults $5, children 12 and under free) with three meals a day included. Locals frequented this one-time hotel for lunch, paying 50 cents each for their meal, because Grand Lake did not have any stand-alone restaurants in those days. You can tour this early hotel-turned-museum on your own, but it is well worth it to pepper the museum's volunteer docents—who belong to the Grand Lake Historical Society—with

The Beach at Grand Lake has several picnic tables.

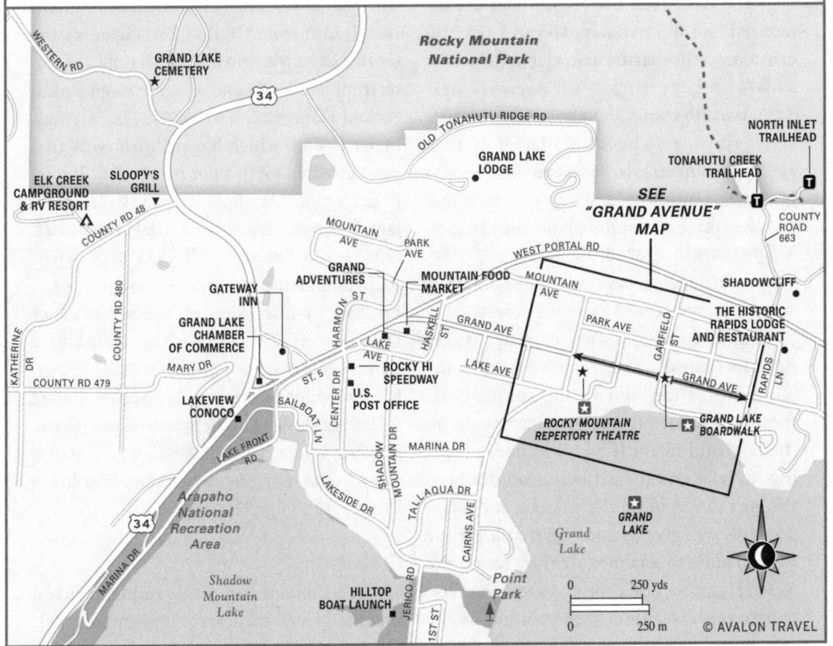

questions about the area, because they have plenty of fascinating answers. For example, you might learn about the history behind the four pots of geraniums that sit in front of the museum in the summer (they were grown from cuttings from original plants that grew at the hotel in 1906) or about the building's log architecture, which earned the house a spot on the National Register of Historic Places. Being a RMNP junkie of sorts, I was especially fascinated to learn about a remarkably preserved 1936 tourist map of the park, which is framed and mounted on a wall. Many permanent exhibits occupy the spaces of the museum, and the displays in one large exhibit room change once a year. A small selection of local history books is available for purchase.

SPORTS AND RECREATION

Boating and Water Sports

When Grand Lake is sun-soaked and dazzling, recreational boats of every variety bob in and glide along on the water. One of the easiest ways to get on the water is to visit or call ahead to **Grand Lake Marina - Boater's Choice** (on the waterfront at the Beach at Grand Lake, 970/627-9273, www.gl-marina.com, 8am-5pm daily Memorial Day-mid-June, 8am-7pm daily mid-June-Labor Day). Boater's Choice's various watercraft for rent include a chartered party boat for up to 30 passengers, pontoon boats, fishing boats, kayaks, and canoes. At the **Headwaters Marina** (on the Beach at Grand Lake, 970/627-5031, www.townofgrandlake.com/headwaters-marina, 10am-5pm Mon.-Thurs., 9am-5pm Fri.-Sun. late May-early Sept.), pontoon boats, paddleboats, runabouts, and fishing boats are rented. The marina offers scenic one-hour boat tours three times daily in the summer ($20 adults, $10 children 12 and under), and a one-hour sunset cruise for the same prices on Tuesday, Wednesday, Friday, and Saturday.

To reserve seats for these tours, call the day before.

If you have your own vessel and are interested in a slip rental on Grand Lake, you can contact the marina manager at the **Town of Grand Lake** (1026 Park Ave., 970/627-3435, www.townofgrandlake.com) to inquire about openings. The town offers both boat and kayak slip rentals, but it can take years to get off the waiting list and into your own slot. Another place to inquire about slips is **Trail Ridge Marina** (12634 Hwy. 34, 970/627-3586, www.trailridgemarina.com, 9am-6pm daily summer) on Shadow Mountain Reservoir.

Thanks to the mountains that rise up next to Grand Lake, boaters have some wind protection. But in the summer, afternoon thunderstorms can bear down on the lake and town. If bad weather is moving in, boat rental staff will head out onto the lake to round up their fleets, and when possible, will give a heads-up that it is time to skedaddle to anyone else they see on the water. However, don't count on someone else to give you a warning; keep your eye on the clouds and on the horizon to avoid getting caught in a bad situation. Also, keep in mind that Grand Lake's water is cold; even on a summer day, hypothermia can take hold rapidly if you were to capsize. Always wear a life jacket and make sure that your vessel has enough personal floatation devices for everyone, including little ones.

KAYAKING

Mountain Paddlers rents kayaks from their **Kayak Shak** (970/531-6334, www.mountainpaddlers.com, 8am-6pm daily Memorial Day weekend-Labor Day, $15-40 per hour) at the Headwaters Marina. **Trail Ridge Marina** (12634 Hwy. 34, 970/627-3586, www.trailridgemarina.com, 9am-6pm daily summer, $25-30 per hr) on Shadow Mountain Reservoir also rents kayaks.

STAND UP PADDLEBOARDING

At one time, stand-up paddleboarding (SUP) seemed like a passing fad in Colorado, but the skeptics have been disproved: SUP is here to stay. The sport is fun and offers a great workout. Several places in town offer board rentals for use on Grand Lake, including the **Grand Lake Marina** (on the Grand Lake waterfront south of Lake Ave., between Pitkin St. and Hancock St., 970/627-9273, www.gl-marina.com), which has paddleboards that can be rented for 1-4 hours ($28-70). Rental packages include a board, a paddle, and a life jacket. **Rocky Mountain SUP Colorado** (928 Grand Ave. #205, 970/364-8179, www.rockymountainsupco.com, 10am-4pm Mon.-Fri., 8am-6pm Sat.-Sun., Memorial Day-Labor Day) also has a fleet of 12 boards available for rent (1 hour is $25 pp, 2 hours is $40 pp). This family-owned business offers beginner-style SUP yoga classes taught by a local instructor. The best time to get on the lake with a SUP is early in the morning, when the water looks like glass and wind is less likely.

FISHING

Those who boat-fish on Grand Lake attest that the overall experience is phenomenal. If you have your own boat, or if you can rent or borrow a boat, get ready for great views and superb fishing. Boaters can tool all around Grand Lake and also access Shadow Mountain Reservoir via the Shadow Mountain Connecting Channel. Shore-fishing on Grand Lake, on the other hand, is extremely limited. While Grand Lake is not private, nearly all of the land surrounding it is. To shore-fish, you have two options: cast your line into the water from **Point Park** (located on the channel between Grand Lake and Shadow Mountain Reservoir) or from the town's docks. Point Park is wheelchair-accessible.

The main fish species in Grand Lake are brown trout and lake trout, both of which are self-sustaining, as well as rainbow trout and Kokanee salmon, both of which are stocked. Grand Lake's fish range in size from 1 pound to a robust 50 pounds.

A Colorado fishing license is required for individuals 16 and older to fish on Grand Lake or Shadow Mountain Reservoir; obtain one at **Rocky Mountain Outfitters** (900 Grand Ave., 970/798-8021, www.rkymtnoutfitters.com, 7am-6pm Mon.-Fri., 6:30am-6pm Sat.-Sun.), **Lakeview Conoco** (14626 Hwy. 34, 970/627-8252, 6am-9pm Tues.-Thurs., 6am-10pm Fri.-Sat.), or online at the **Colorado Parks & Wildlife** (www.cpw.state.co.us). Rocky Mountain Outfitters also offers equipment rentals and guided fishing trips, and will dispense great advice about fishing in the area. **Fishing with Bernie** (970/531-2318, www.fishingwithbernie.com, $300/4 hours), out of Granby, also guides on Grand Lake.

For boat rentals, head to the **Grand Lake Marina** (Grand Lake waterfront, 970/627-9273, www.glmarina.com, 8am-5pm daily Memorial Day-mid June; 8am-7pm daily mid-June-Labor Day).

Hiking

Tiny as it may be, Grand Lake is rich in history. The **Grand Lake Historical Walking Tour** (late May-Oct., free) is a great way to learn about the town's colorful past on your own time schedule. This self-guided tour is just over 1 mile in length and starts at the Beach at Grand Lake, with 25 stops outside or inside various businesses and homes. The tour ends at the Kaufmann House Museum. A tour brochure is available for a nominal fee at the **Grand Lake Visitor Center** (West Portal Rd. and Hwy. 34, 970/627-3402, www.grandlakechamber.com, 10am-4pm Memorial Day-Labor Day; 10am-2pm Mon.-Fri., 10am-4pm Sat.-Sun. winter, spring, and fall). Or, print a map and a guide from the **Grand Lake Area Historical Society** (www.grandlakehistory.org). Allow at least 1.5 hours to complete the entire tour at a leisurely pace.

Hikers can enjoy 15 miles of trails that are part of the **Grand Lake Metropolitan Recreation District** (970/627-8008, www.grandlakerecreation.com, late May-Oct.), west of downtown. To get to the trailhead, venture west of downtown Grand Lake on County Road 48/Golf Course Road. Travel for 1 mile on County Road 48 to the Colorado River Trailhead parking lot. No usage fee or parking fee is required. Dogs are allowed on all trails.

Biking

ROAD BIKING

Starting at the Grand Lake Entrance Station, you can pedal north along Highway 34/Trail Ridge Road and ride as far as your quads will allow. Heading south out of Grand Lake is another option, with possible destinations of Granby (16 mi), Tabernash (26 mi), Fraser (31 mi), or Winter Park (36 mi). All are located off of Highway 40.

MOUNTAIN BIKING

In the summer, the **Grand Lake Metropolitan District** (970/627-8008, www.grandlakerecreation.com) opens up 15 miles of intermediate-to-advanced trails for use by mountain bikers and hikers. The main access point for this network of trails is the Colorado River Trailhead (not to be confused with the trailhead that goes by the same name within Rocky) and is reached by heading west from Grand Lake on County Road 48/Golf Course Road. Travel for 1 mile on County Road 48 to the trailhead parking lot. There is no fee to use the trails in the summer.

Intermediate mountain bikers enjoy riding the **Wolverine Trail** (4.8 mi) and the **Gilsonite Trail** (4 mi) west of Grand Lake. The Wolverine Trail is a nonmotorized trail that transects the Bowen Gulch Protection Area in the Stillwater Pass area of the Arapaho National Forest. The trail can be accessed via the **North Supply Trailhead.** From Grand Lake, travel north on Highway 34 for 1.5 miles, then head west on County Road 491 for approximately 6.5 miles to the North Supply Trailhead. You can also access the Wolverine Trail from the Gilsonite Trail. The Gilsonite Trail is accessed from Stillwater Pass Road (NFSR 123). Gilsonite is a multi-use, single track trail where motorcycles and mountain bikes are welcome, but not ATVs. Logging operations might be occurring in these areas; call the U.S. Forest Service Sulphur Ranger District office (970/887-4100) for information.

BIKE RENTALS

Rocky Hi Speedway (510 Center Dr., 970/627-9595, www.rockyhispeedway.com, 11am-8pm daily Memorial Day-Labor Day, but hours vary seasonally, $15) rents mountain bikes, road bikes, and cruiser bikes for 2-8-hour increments. **On the Trail Rentals** (1447 County Rd. 491, 970/627-0171, www.onthetrailrentals.com, late May-Nov., $15) rents mountain bikes, Tag-a-Longs, and kid trailers.

ATV Riding

A vast network of ATV trails is located west of Grand Lake—the same region that is popular in the winter with snowmobilers. All told, there are more than 130 miles of terrain on which to bump along. A motor-vehicle use map for the Arapaho National Forest and the Sulphur Ranger District National Forest can be obtained at ATV rental outlets in town and from the **U.S. Forest Service Sulphur Ranger District office** (9 Ten Mile Dr., Granby, 970/887-4100). The map specifies the areas in which ATVs and off-highway vehicles (OHVs) are allowed. While snowmobilers are welcome almost everywhere around Grand Lake—even downtown—ATV riders are not. Vehicles must be towed on a trailer to an ATV-friendly trailhead.

Spirit Lake Motorsports and Rentals (10438 Hwy. 34, 970/627-9288, www.spiritlakerentals.com, 9am-5:30pm Tues.-Sat. summer and winter) and **On the Trail Rentals** (1447 County Rd. 491, 970/627-0171 or 888/627-2429, www.onthetrailrentals.com, 8am-5pm daily) both rent ATVs. On the Trail Rentals is located next to the Arapaho National Forest, with no ATV trailers necessary to head directly in.

Trails typically open in mid-June and are busy with ATVs until late fall.

Hunting

In the late summer and early fall, many hunters in Colorado unearth camouflage and blaze-orange clothing from their closets, and turn their thoughts to filling a freezer with elk or deer meat. Though Rocky prohibits hunting, hunting is allowed in the Arapaho National Forest. The Kawuneeche Valley's Bowen/Baker Trailhead serves as an access point for hunting areas northwest of Grand Lake. To gain information about local hunting opportunities and game-management units, contact the local **Colorado Parks & Wildlife Office** (CPW, 970/725-6200, Hot Sulphur Springs, www.cpw.state.co.us). A current hunting license is required and can be purchased from the CPW.

Spirit Lake Motorsports and Rentals has ATVs.

Golf

Visitors and locals love the **Grand Lake Golf Course** (1415 County Rd. 48, 970/627-8008, www. grandlakerecreation.com, mid-May-Oct., $40-70) for many reasons, including its views of the surrounding mountains and curious local wildlife—such as fox, squirrels, and moose—that are known to unwittingly poke their heads in on a game. Lessons are offered at the course; a pro shop sells golfing essentials. **The Sly Fox Restaurant & Lounge** (food served 7am-4pm, bar open until 6pm late May-end Sept., $5-12) serves breakfast and lunch to golfers, and the restaurant's bar is well-stocked for happy hour. In the winter, this sprawling, 18-hole, par-72 championship golf course is blanketed with snow and makes up a small portion of the Grand Lake Nordic Center's cross-country ski-trail system.

Geocaching

Geocaching—which is searching for virtual and physical caches with the assistance of a Global Positioning System (GPS) unit—is a popular activity in Rocky and in both of the park's gateway towns. At the **Grand Lake Visitor Center** (West Portal Rd. and Hwy. 34, 970/627-3402, Grand Lake, www.grandlakechamber.com, 10am-4pm daily Memorial Day-Labor Day, 10am-2pm daily Sept.-May) ask for information and a leaflet for the **Across the Divide GeoTour,** which takes GPS-toting adventurers to fun and scenic area locations. The official geocaching app can be found at www.geocaching.com.

Winter Sports

CROSS-COUNTRY SKIING AND SNOWSHOEING

An impressive system of snowy trails is revealed in the winter at the **Grand Lake Nordic Center** (1415 County Rd. 48, 970/627-8008, www.grandlakerecreation.com, $16 pp, $6 pp for 6 years old and under); 35 kilometers of them, to be exact. Meant for cross-country skiing and skate skiing, these groomed paths include a nice mix of easy, intermediate, and advanced terrain to satisfy any level of skier. For those who can't bear to ski without the company of their four-legged companion—which is not an option in the national park—there are 5.5 kilometers of trails designated Fido-friendly. The Nordic Center also maintains a smaller selection of snowshoe trails. Rental equipment is available on-site and lessons for both classic- and skate-skiing are offered. For après ski, relax in the **Sly Fox Restaurant** (970/627-3922, www.grandlakerecreation.com, 10am-4pm daily Dec.-Mar.) with a bowl of soup and an adults-only, hot apple cider spiked with Tuaca. The fireplace is crackling every day during the winter. A full-moon ski takes place each month and includes a campfire with hot cocoa and marshmallows.

SNOWMOBILING

When fat flakes start falling in Grand Lake, people's attention quickly turns to snowmobiling. In Grand Lake (which is marketed as the "Snowmobile Capital of Colorado"), the Arapaho National Forest, the Roosevelt National Forest, and the Bowen Gulch Recreation Area, there are more than 300 miles of motorized snow travel trails. Snowmobilers can zip around groomed and un-groomed trails, and in designated "snow play" areas. It's even normal and perfectly legal to sled along Grand Avenue, in the heart of town, to grab a cup of coffee. Visitors are advised to keep their snowmobiles off the lakes due to potentially unstable ice, but you will see it done anyway—mostly by people who are ice fishing and need a means to get to a good spot. To recap: this is a snowmobile-loving town. If snowmobiles aren't your thing, it is best to keep your opinions to yourself in these parts.

Grand Lake Trail Groomers (www.grandlaketrailgroomers.com) provides one of the best status reports of area trails and conditions. The **Colorado Snowmobile Association** (www.snowmobilecolo.com) is another resource for trail status reports and area information. Snowmobile rentals are available at **Grand Adventures** (304 West Portal Rd., 970/627-0218, www.

grandadventures.com), **Spirit Lake Lodge** (829 Grand Ave., 970/627-3344, www.spiritlakelodge.com), **Lone Eagle Lodge** (712-720 Grand Ave., 970/627-3310, www.loneeaglelodge.com), and **On the Trail Rentals** (144 County Rd. 491, 970/627-0171, www.onthetrailrentals.com).

A free snowmobile trail system map (www.grandlaketrailgroomers.com) is available online and at various locations in town.

SLEDDING

Kids and adults love slipping and sliding on inner tubes, sleds, and saucers at the **Grand Lake Nordic Center Tubing and Sledding Hill** (1415 County Rd. 48, 970/627-8008, www.grandlakerecreation.com) in the winter. The hill is free to use and the center has a handful of tubes that can be borrowed if you do not have your own. Afterward, grab a bite and get warm in the Nordic Center's on-site **Sly Fox Restaurant** (970/627-3922, www.grandlakerecreation.com, 10am-4pm daily Dec.-Mar.).

Ice fishing is a popular winter activity.

ICE SKATING

From mid-December through mid-April, a corner of the **Grand Lake Town Park** (1026 Park Ave.) is transformed into an ice rink; access is free. No skates? No problem. Just head to **Rocky Mountain Outfitters** (900 Grand Ave., 970/798-8021, www.rkymtnoutfitters.com, 7am-6pm Mon.-Fri., 6:30am-6pm, Sat.-Sun.) to borrow a pair at no charge.

ICE FISHING

Attempting to catch fish that swim beneath a frozen lake surface in the winter seems like a silly thing to do; at least that's what I thought until I tried it. Actually, it is quite enjoyable to hang out in a nylon hut all bundled up, keeping close watch on a Fish Finder, and hoping for a big one. Ice fishing is as much a social experience as it is recreational; pack a few friends into a hut with some good food and drink, unload a few good stories, and let the bonding begin. If you are addicted to summertime fishing, consider trying out the winter version at least once. For guided ice-fishing trips on Grand Lake, contact **Rocky Mountain Outfitters** (900 Grand Ave., 970/798-8021, www.rkymtnoutfitters.com, $250/up to 3 people for 4 hours). Hundreds of fishing enthusiasts show up for the **Grand Lake Annual Catch & Release Ice Fishing Contest** (970/627-3402, www.grandlakechamber.com) that happens each March.

ENTERTAINMENT AND SHOPPING

Watering Holes

Want to get your drink on after a long day of play? There are a few good places to do so. **Grumpy's** (913 Grand Ave., 970/627-0123, 11am-2am daily) is family-friendly up until 9pm, and has an adjoining arcade where young people like to play Pac-Man and hang out. On the weekends, DJ dancing is the norm, with country/swing music on Fridays and dance/hip-hop music on Saturdays. The divey **Lariat Saloon** (1121 Grand Ave., 970/627-9965, 11am-2am daily) is dimly lit and comfortably cluttered with

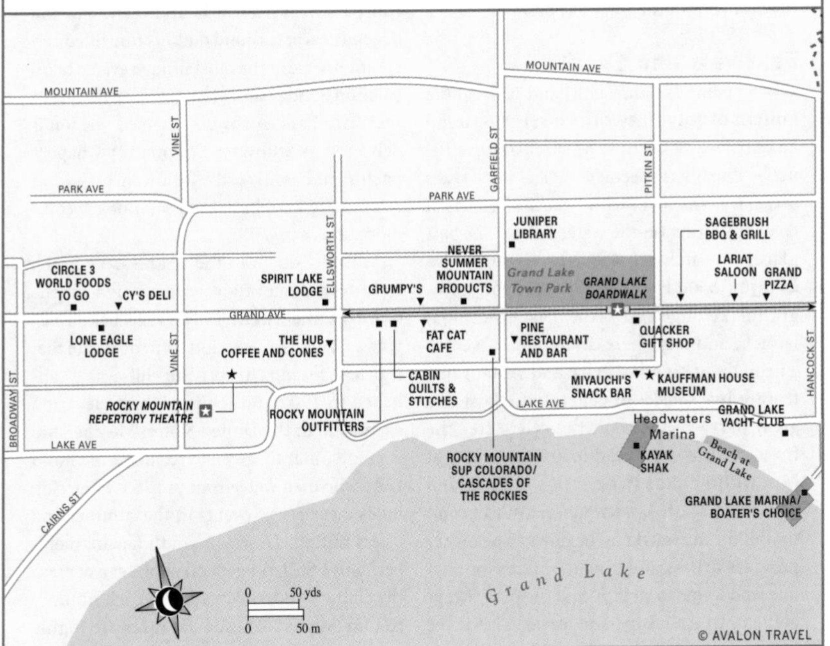

old signs and other memorabilia. The bar regularly hosts live musical acts and is a favorite spot for locals. Food is also served. The **Roadhouse Bar and Grill** (10188 Hwy. 34, 970/627-9300, 11am-10pm daily winter, 11am-11pm daily summer) is worth the short drive south on Highway 34. There is a nice, long, wooden bar, a pool table, and plenty of TV screens for watching sports for hours on end. The **Sagebrush BBQ & Grill** (1101 Grand Ave., 970/627-1404, www.sagebrushbbq.com, 7am-10pm daily), a central gathering place in town, is a great place to tip back a beer. You can find live music at the restaurant on a regular basis. **Pine Restaurant and Bar** (1000 Grand Ave., 970/798-8198, www.pinegrandlake.com, 11am-2am Wed.-Mon.) has wine, beer, and spirits, and a fun outdoor bar area.

★ Rocky Mountain Repertory Theatre

The **Rocky Mountain Repertory Theatre** (800 Grand Ave., 970/627-3421, www.rockymountainrep.com, June-Sept., $35-45 adult, $25-35 youth 13-18, $15-25 youth 12 and under) might look unassuming from the outside, but the musical productions that happen inside are absolutely top notch. Actors hailing from all over the United States take the stage here, performing Broadway musicals such as *Les Miserables* and *42nd Street.* It is hard not to be impressed with every aspect of a production here, from the set design to the costumes to the musicians. At the height of summer, a performance occurs on most nights. The schedule tapers off in September (one show Thurs.-Sun.); in the winter months the venue is used for holiday events. Actors are housed in Grand Lake during the performance season; their presence in town brings a sense of vibrancy and culture that is hard to come by in other mountain towns of a similar size. Tickets can be purchased online, over the phone, or through the theater's box office

(10am-4pm Mon.-Fri.). Refreshments are sold inside. Booster seats are provided to give kids the best view of the stage as possible.

Festivals and Events

When people exclaim "ooh" and "aah" at the **Fourth of July fireworks** display in Grand Lake, there is no hint of sarcasm or silliness—it really is spectacular. The show takes place over the lake, with beautiful bursts of color reflecting on the water below. The best places to watch are from the **Grand Lake Lodge** (15500 Hwy. 34, 970/627-3967, www.grandlakelodge.com), the East Inlet boat launch, and anywhere along Lake Avenue. Throughout the day, bars and restaurants feature live music; in general, it is just one great party in town on the 4th. After the fireworks are over, head to an after-party at **Mountain Lakes Properties** (1126 Grand Ave., 970/627-3103, www.mountainlake.com) to wait for the traffic to die down. The owner provides drinks and hors d'oeuvres for anyone who wants to stop in, and the party keeps going until the last person leaves. This is the busiest day of the year in Grand Lake, so book accommodations well in advance.

Constitution Week (970/627-3402, www.grandlakechamber.com, mid-Sept.) is a newer addition to the town's yearly lineup of events, and attracts more of a niche audience. The event largely consists of guest speakers who talk at venues around town each afternoon or evening, plus movie screenings and a Constitutional trivia contest. Everything on the schedule, of course, is designed to celebrate that landmark event that took place on September 17, 1787. The last day of Constitution Week features a 5K run, airplane flyover, parade, bingo, and fireworks—plus plenty of flag waving and displays of red-white-and-blue pride. All events are free; donations are appreciated.

Grand Lake Buffalo BBQ (970/627-3402, www.grandlakechamber.com, mid-July) is a major tradition in Grand Lake and is the town's second-busiest weekend of the year. Grilled buffalo and more grilled buffalo are on the menu for two days; a jam-packed schedule of events, including a pancake breakfast, 5K run, parade, Western arts-and-crafts fair, and live musical acts round out this fun-filled celebration. One of the most unique events takes place on Sunday morning: Cowboy Chapel in the Town Park. A cowboy-themed sermon is delivered by Stillwater Community Chapel's pastor and is directly followed by—what else—more BBQ buffalo to eat. Book accommodations early.

Walking down to the Grand Lake beach from town, you might notice a sign for the **Grand Lake Yacht Club** (1128 Lake Ave., www.grandlakeyachtclub.com) on a gate that is often closed. This private club was established in 1902 and is the highest-elevation yacht club in the United States. Membership is predominantly given to residents of Grand Lake who own waterfront property. The club holds a variety of events in the summer and offers sailing classes for youth (again, members only). Still, the general public can observe the club's **Regatta Week** held each summer in mid-August. These boat races are highly entertaining to watch from the shores of the Beach at Grand Lake.

The one-day **Spirit of the Lake Regatta and Brewfest** (www.spiritlakeregatta.com, mid-Aug.) features canoe/kayak and SUP races on the lake in the morning. Beer tasting and music are the main attractions at Gene Stover Lakefront Park (a small park next to the Beach at Grand Lake) that afternoon.

★ WINTER CARNIVAL

There's no such thing as a mid-winter slump in Grand Lake. At a time of year when the novelty of snow starts wearing off for some people, this town is more jubilant than ever about the white stuff. I am a sucker for Colorado's funky mountain town celebrations, and the **Winter Carnival** (970/627-3402, www.grandlakechamber.com, early Feb.) does not disappoint. All kinds of snowy shenanigans ensue during this one-day event, like teapot curling contests and snow golf. Shopkeepers build elaborate and colorful (food-coloring-dyed) snow sculptures such as castles and frogs, and several hundred people line the streets for a parade and bed-sled races. If you ever feel you've run out of things to do in the snow, look to this event for ideas. The carnival culminates with a fireworks show over frozen Grand Lake. Some events are free, while others require a small fee.

Shopping

★ GRAND LAKE BOARDWALK

Magnets, mugs, moose memorabilia—yes, you can find all kinds of knick-knacks in the souvenir shops in downtown Grand Lake. Somehow, even the most inexpensive souvenirs seem more desirable because **Grand Lake's Boardwalk** (Grand Ave., between Ellsworth St. and Hancock St.) is so quaint. The wood-plank boardwalk has an Old Wild West look and feel, and each storefront is attractive. Because most of the town's restaurants, coffee shops, and watering holes are located along the boardwalk, you will no doubt find yourself walking up and down this stretch multiple times during your stay and poking your head into a shop or two. In addition to souvenirs, you'll find jewelry, home furnishings, and antiques.

Quacker Gift Shop (1034 Grand Ave., 970/798-8014, www.quackergiftshop.com, 10am-7pm daily Memorial Day-Labor Day, 10:30am-4pm Tues.-Fri., 10:30am-5pm Sat. winter) is filled with rubber ducks of nearly every imaginable variety. Browse through Hippy Ducks and Viking Ducks and EMS Ducks, and eventually you might find something that strikes your interest—perhaps a Buddha Celebriduck? Even if ducks are totally not your thing, there are two other reasons to stop in to Quacker: fragrant, locally-made bath and body products, and melt-in-your-mouth homemade fudge. The latter is sold as thick squares and goes down the hatch all-too-easily. The gift shop features an unusual assortment of goods under one roof, but it somehow works, and is all sourced or made by the same husband-and-wife team.

For outdoor essentials, head to **Never Summer Mountain Products** (925 Grand Ave., 970/627-3642, www.neversummermtn.com, 8am-8pm daily mid-June-mid-Sept., 9am-5:30pm daily fall-winter). The shop stocks clothing, hiking and camping gear, maps and books, kayaks, and stand-up paddleboards. Summer- and winter-sport rentals are also available. The staff and owners at Never Summer are longtime locals, friendly and brimming with regional knowledge.

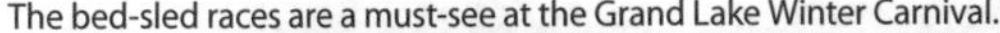

The bed-sled races are a must-see at the Grand Lake Winter Carnival.

If sewing is in your blood, **Cabin Quilts & Stitches** (908 Grand Ave., 970/627-3810, www.cabinquiltsnstitches.com, 10am-5pm Sun.-Fri., 10am-6pm Sat.) will be right up your alley. The shop is chock-full of yarn, sewing patterns, sewing kits, and, of course, attractive fabric. The shop also stocks a nice selection of high-quality children's clothing and gifts.

A whole lot of goodies are packed into the small space of **Cascades of the Rockies** (928 Grand Ave., 970/627-8166, www.grandlakebookstore.com, 10am-5pm daily Memorial Day-mid-Oct.; hours vary the rest of the year). Though it is known as Grand Lake's only bookstore, there might be more gifts than books inside; that's certainly up for debate. Local owner Avis Gray has shelves dedicated to geology, geography, critically acclaimed books about the American West, "women's good reads," and more. The children's and cookbook sections feature the largest quantities of selections. One nook of the store is dedicated to used books for sale. Gifts include cards, packaged gourmet food items, adult coloring books, and many other items.

FOOD

Breakfast and Lunch

If you flip through the guest book at the ★ **Fat Cat Cafe** (916 Grand Ave., 970/627-0900, 7am-11am Mon., 7am-2pm Wed.-Fri., 7am-1pm Sat.-Sun. summer, 7am-2pm Thurs.-Fri., 7am-1am Sat.-Sun. winter, $8-15), you will find numerous comments from people who arranged their Grand Lake vacation itinerary around a visit to the restaurant. The breakfast fare is that scrumptious: specifically, the all-you-can-eat brunch offered on Saturdays and Sundays. A great spread of food is set out on several low tables, and the one that immediately catches your eye is the desserts: many mouthwatering pies, chocolate cake, strawberry shortcake, and bread pudding—all made from scratch in-house (one of the owners routinely bakes at the café at 3am). But first, indulge in delicious vegan salad, chili, Scotch eggs (hard-boiled eggs wrapped with sausage, then breaded and cooked), corned-beef hash and thick wedges of French toast. It's easy to go back for thirds and even fourths. The dining room is casual, with booths, simple wooden tables, cat-themed décor, and colorful Tiffany lamps hung from the ceiling. Being called "darlin'" by the hostess when you pay your bill gives this place a homey feel. On Friday and Saturday nights in the summer, at the owner's discretion, fish and chips are cooked up for to-go only.

The first time I visited **Cy's Deli** (717 Grand Ave., 970/627-3354, www.cysdeli.com, 7am-5pm daily mid-May-mid-Oct., $6-9.50), I was so pleased with my sandwich that when lunchtime rolled around the following day, I made a return trip (and ordered the same sandwich: The Number One Melt with bacon added—Yum with a capital *Y*). Cy's sandwich ingredients taste very fresh, the coleslaw on the side has the perfect amount of tang, and best of all, food at this casual restaurant is delivered fast—even when there is big line at the counter, which is often. A small amount of seating is found inside, but most people gravitate toward the large patio with umbrella-shaded tables. Other menu items include breakfast burritos, soups, and baked goods.

A perfect few hours at the Beach at Grand Lake involves a requisite stroll over to **Miyauchi's Snack Bar** (1029 Lake Ave., 970/627-9319, 10am-8pm daily, Memorial Day-Labor Day, $3-8) for a sweet treat. Ice cream served up at this lakefront fast-food stand is rich and homemade, with flavors like Chocolate Peanut Butter Wonder and Georgia Peach Cobbler. Choose from cones, malts, shakes, and sundaes. The stand also prepares burgers and other snacks. Plenty of umbrella-shaded tables are available for seating, or take your food to go.

Bar and Grill

Sometimes it's a dubious proposition to stop at the first restaurant that you see after you leave a major attraction—such as a national park—but **Sloopy's Grill** (Hwy. 34 and Golf Course Rd., 970/627-8182, www.sloopysgrill.com,

11am-7pm Thurs.-Tues. June-Sept., 11am-7pm Thurs.-Tues. winter, $3-7) is a perfectly good place to grab a bite after a trip over Trail Ridge Road. "Sloopy" is a long-standing nickname for Richard Schliep, the husband half of the friendly husband/wife team that runs this spot (Jennie is the wife half). Sloopy's fare is mostly focused on meat—think hotdogs, hamburgers, and fried chicken—but a vegan burger, salad, and soup are on the menu for meat-free folks. A small selection of breakfast items is also available. The Schlieps have decorated their restaurant with family collectibles, the most interesting of which are beautiful wooden Rocky Mountain National Park retirement plaques for Jennie and Richard's fathers, who both retired the same year.

Even in Grand Lake's shoulder seasons, the **Sagebrush BBQ & Grill** (1101 Grand Ave., 970/627-1404, www.sagebrushbbq.com, 7am-10pm daily, $7-26) is reliably open for locals and tourists when most other establishments have hung the Closed sign on their front door. Year-round, the restaurant serves up a menu of satisfying, Western-style favorites, including ribs, burgers, steaks, and sandwiches. A bucket of peanuts is complimentary at each table, and patrons are invited to brush their shells onto the floor. The Sagebrush is located on the site of the original Grand County jail; in the front dining room, part of the décor features cell bars dating back to the late 1800s.

Pine Restaurant and Bar (1000 Grand Ave., 970/798-8198, www.pinegrandlake.com, 11am-2am Wed.-Mon., $10-24) is a relatively new kid on the Grand Lake boardwalk. Upon opening its doors in 2016, it was instantly welcomed by locals and visitors. An elegant and modern indoor dining room appeals to couples and groups of adults more so than families, though there are kid-friendly food options available. Outside, the large beer garden—complete with a bar, picnic tables, and several low-slung couches—is a fabulous place to swill beers and munch on a cheese-stuffed burger and homemade potato chips on a sunny afternoon. Pine whips up "creative American cuisine," and its menu of small plates, sandwiches, salads, and entrées changes with the seasons. The drink menu features an amalgam of hand-crafted infused cocktails, wine, and beer. In the summer, a taco to-go window (11am-9pm Wed.-Mon.) invites passersby to indulge in a nosh.

Pizza

The folks at **Grand Pizza** (1131 Grand Ave., 970/627-8390, www.grand-pizza.com,

Miyauchi's Snack Bar has homemade ice cream, a refreshing summer treat.

11:30am-9pm daily mid-June-Labor Day, closed Nov., 11:30am-8pm Sat.-Sun. winter, 11:30am-8pm Wed.-Sun. spring, $10-29) know how to do crust right. Their standard crust is hand-rolled on the edges, and just looks like it has been made with love and care, never mind its yummy flavor. Pies are intended for those with hearty appetites and can be topped with a long list of goodies, including bacon, green chili strips, and andouille sausage. Also on the menu are calzones, pasta, and salads, and—for lunch—submarine sandwiches and paninis. Soft drinks are bottomless. This small restaurant is hopping with groups of friends and families during the busy season, and popular with the take-out crowd. The décor isn't anything to write home about—some random, wine-themed artwork adorns the walls—but that is a moot point when the food is this good.

Grand Pizza makes delicious pies.

Fine Dining

When a special occasion is on the calendar, **The Historic Rapids Lodge and Restaurant** (210 Rapids Ln., 970/627-3707, www.rapidslodge.com, dinner served at 5pm daily late May-Labor Day, dinner served 5pm limited days during early May, lunch served 11am daily late June-Labor Day, lunch served limited days in May-early June) delivers. The rather dimly lit (perfect for romance!) dining room in this historic hotel is comfortable and attractive, with an original stone fireplace from the early 1900s and large windows showcasing the Tonahutu Creek just outside. The dinner menu features a variety of game, seafood, and poultry dishes that are impeccably prepared and presented. A great way to experience the ambiance of The Rapids without breaking the bank is to stop in for lunch (summer only) rather than dinner, when prices are friendlier on the pocketbook. On sunny days, patrons can sit riverside on the patio.

Groceries

Big-box grocery stores haven't edged their way into quaint Grand Lake; shopping options consist of just two mom-and-pop markets located in town. The most charming and well-stocked is the **Mountain Food Market** (400 Grand Ave., 970/627-3470, 9am-7pm Mon.-Sat., 9am-5pm Sun.). Here you will find a fantastic mix of vacation essentials: canned goods, a fresh meat counter, produce, small appliances, tent repair kits, and night crawlers. The walls are decorated with reusable shopping bags that have been brought to the owners from all over the world. **Circle 3 World Foods To Go** (701 Grand Ave., 970/627-3210, 7:30am–8pm Sun.-Thurs., 7:30pm–9pm Fri.-Sat.) is smaller and carries snacks, drinks, sundries, and rental movies. Otherwise, the largest chain store in the vicinity is a 20-minute drive away in Granby.

ACCOMMODATIONS

Just as in Estes Park, Grand Lake's cabins and hotel rooms routinely sell out during the prime summer months. Get researching early. Second homeowners claim 80 percent of Grand Lake's residences, which means that plenty of VRBO (www.vrbo.com) options are available—more than 200 of them.

$100-150

The atmosphere at **Gateway Inn** (200 West Portal Rd., 970/627-2400, www.gatewayinn.com, $129-159) is laidback, as indicated by a sign in the main sitting area: "Cowboys Scrape Shit Before Entering." Rooms are simple but attractive, with custom log furniture and soft, comfortable linens on the beds; some rooms include a gas fireplace. High ceilings give the accommodations an extra sense of spaciousness. Amenities at the hotel include continental breakfast, s'mores, assorted board games, a putt-putt golf course, shuffleboard, a weight room, an outdoor hot tub, and a sauna. Rates can fluctuate from high season to low season literally overnight, depending on whether Trail Ridge Road is temporarily closed due to snow. During football season, the hotel's lounge is a great place to watch a game.

The nicest lodge in Grand Lake is bordered on three sides by Rocky, and features a stop-you-in-your-tracks view of the lake. The **Grand Lake Lodge** (15500 Hwy. 34, 970/627-3967, www.grandlakelodge.com, late May-Oct. 1, $150) has served guests since 1920, though not consistently. One of its long periods of closure came after a devastating kitchen fire in 1973; if you step onto the hotel's front deck, you can still see char marks on the underside of the roof. The lodge is listed on the National Register of Historic Places and was once a vacation spot for Henry Ford, the founder of Ford Motor Company. The cabin he stayed in—one of 70 on the property—is aptly named the "Ford Cabin," and has some of the nicest furnishings of any of the accommodations. A beautiful outdoor swimming pool is located in front of the main lodge. Other on-site recreational pursuits include horseshoes, volleyball, table tennis, and billiards. Breakfast, lunch, and dinner are served seven days a week. Cabins can book up a year in advance for summer weekends.

If you are serious about preserving the environment, forgo traveling to Grand Lake by RV or car and instead arrive on foot via the Continental Divide National Scenic Trail (CDT). Then check into **Shadowcliff** (405 Summerland Park Rd., 970/627-9220, www.shadowcliff.org, Memorial Day-mid-Sept., $75-120)—an Earth-loving lodge, from its compact fluorescent bulbs to its low-flow showerheads. The Shadowcliff, which is indeed perched on a cliff and located up a steep driveway, is removed from Grand Lake's busy downtown scene and has sublime views of the lake. CDT thru-hikers love the reasonably priced hostel rooms ($25) and the camaraderie that comes with communal lodging. The facility also offers lodge rooms ($70-80) and private cabins ($120). A large meeting room contains plenty of seating, a fireplace, games, puzzles, and reading material. If you don't know anyone when you arrive, just settle into a chair and start up a conversation with someone; the vibe here is friendly and welcoming. Staff members serve meals from a "compassionate" kitchen, in which local and organic foods are favored over their conventional counterparts. Meals are available for groups that have pre-paid and occasionally for the general public. The only downside of this lovely place is its inaccessibility to individuals who use wheelchairs. Consider calling the Shadowcliff for last-minute lodging; I was able to get a bed in the women's hostel on the Saturday evening of Grand Lake's Buffalo BBQ Weekend, when many area campgrounds and hotels were sold out.

A single lodging destination faces challenges if it wishes to appeal to a wide range of visitors, but ★ **The Historic Rapids Lodge and Restaurant** (210 Rapids Ln., 970/627-3707, www.rapidslodge.com) nails it. The 100-plus-year-old lodge consists of a collection of offerings—cabins ($132-147), condos ($121-243), guest rooms ($60-156), and pet-friendly suites ($65-89)—that are enjoyed by every demographic. Each property has a unique decor, ranging from a contemporary, snow sports-themed cabin to lodge rooms adorned with vintage items. The "Tonahutu" guest room is a favorite with visitors because it has large windows and is the only lodge room with a king bed. Another people-pleaser is the Treehouse Suite, a cozy retreat with raspberry-hued carpeting that takes up the entire top floor of the main building. The lodge is adults-only; all cabins and some suites are dog-friendly. Many people traveling over from the west side of the park (via the Flattop Mountain and North Inlet Trails) stay here, since the location of the North Inlet Trailhead is conveniently located less than a half-mile north of the lodge. The **Rapids Restaurant** (dinner 5pm-close daily late May-Labor Day, lunch 11am daily late June-Labor Day) is located on-site.

The Historic Rapids Lodge and Restaurant

$150-200

If your goal is to be as close to Grand Lake's waters as possible, it's time to call up the **Western Riviera** (419 Garfield St., 970/627-3580, www.westernriv.com, $150-450; 2-night minimum). The hotel has five lakeside options to choose from: a motel with 16 rooms (the most budget-friendly option), a condo, two cabins, a "tree house," and a "lake house." Access to on-lake activities and Grand Avenue are the best perks of these units. One room in the hotel looks different from all of the rest; unit 6 (a queen double room) was made over by the Travel Channel's *Hotel Impossible* show, and has extra rustic flair. The Western Riviera also runs the Courtyard Cabins in town; some wheelchair-accessible units are available.

TRANSPORTATION AND SERVICES

Car

In summer, many visitors cross Trail Ridge Road from the east side of the park to reach Grand Lake. However, Trail Ridge Road is impassable in winter due to snow. When Trail Ridge Road is closed, visitors can bypass Estes Park and travel directly to Grand Lake from Denver.

From the intersection of I-70 and I-25 in downtown Denver, travel west on I-70 for 40 miles. Take the exit for U.S. 40 to Empire/Granby and continue 45 miles to the town of Granby. Once in Granby, take Highway 34 east for 14.5 miles to Grand Lake. Note that U.S. 40 is a high mountain pass; it can get snowy and icy in winter, and road closures are possible.

PARKING

Finding a spot for your car in Grand Lake isn't nearly the dilemma it is in Estes Park. Free parking is available in and around the main strip of Grand Avenue, and businesses and lodges in town generally have ample parking for their customers. In the winter, you will see snowmobiles parked in front of businesses, which is perfectly legitimate.

CAR RENTAL

The spot nearest to Grand Lake from which to secure a set of wheels is in Granby: **Avalanche Car Rentals** (622 E. Garnet Ave., 888/437-4101, www.avscars.com, daily May 15-Oct., daily Nov. 15-Apr. 15, off-season appointments possible with advance notice) offers free delivery to any location in east Grand County, and primarily provides pick-up and delivery to visitors arriving via the Granby and Fraser Amtrak stations. Avalanche does not have a walk-up location; reservations are made by phone appointment only.

Shuttle

Mountain Transit Adventures (970/888-1227, www.mtagrandlake.com, open year-round) provides on-demand bus and shuttle service for visitors to Grand Lake. Rates are $125/hour for transportation by bus (each has a capacity of 40 passengers) and $80/hour for a shuttle via 12-passenger van. For individuals or small parties that need rides, prices start at $12 per person. MTA shuttles passengers around Grand Lake, RMNP, and beyond.

Taxi

Valley Taxi (970/726-4940, www.valleytaxi-inc.com) provides transportation throughout Grand Valley, including Grand Lake. However, the service is based out of Winter Park, so traveling anywhere comes with a steep base price of $60. Reserve ahead.

Services

VISITOR INFORMATION

The **Grand Lake Visitor Center** (West Portal Rd. and Hwy. 34, 970/627-3402, Grand Lake, www.grandlakechamber.com, 10am-4pm daily Memorial Day-Labor Day, 10am-2pm daily Sept.-May) is stocked with brochures and an information desk; its shaded outdoor balcony is perfect for poring over maps or just stopping to rest. The staff doesn't just provide ideas for what to do in the area—they will gently, but firmly, guide folks who are torn between spending an afternoon finding the best caramel apple in the vicinity or searching for a moose. There is a personal touch to the advice handed out here; instead of saying "This is a nice hike," you are likely to hear, "This is a hike my family enjoys doing on the weekend." Even though the town of Grand Lake is small, there is a lot going on in greater Grand County; the visitor center is one of the best places to learn about activity and lodging options.

MEDIA AND COMMUNICATIONS

Get your regional news fix twice a week—on Wednesday and Friday—with the *Sky-Hi News* (www.skyhidailynews.com), distributed in Grand Lake and in six other nearby towns. Grand Lake also has its own newspaper, *The Boardwalk*, published every other week, which comes out on Fridays and is distributed around town.

The **Grand Lake Post Office** (520 Center Dr., 970/627-3340, Mon.-Fri. 8am-4pm) is the one U.S. Post Office in town. There is no place in Grand Lake to ship UPS or FedEx packages; the closest full-service shipping center is **KopyKat** (461 E. Agate Ave., Granby, 970/887-3320, www.kopykatgp.com, 9am-5pm Mon.-Fri.).

CELL AND INTERNET SERVICE

For Verizon subscribers, cell phone coverage is good in and around Grand Lake. For those with other services, reception can be inconsistent. The **Juniper Library** (316 Garfield St., 970/627-8353, 10am-7pm Wed., 10am-6pm Thurs., 10am-4pm Fri., 10am-4pm Sat.) has first-come, first-served computers available for public use, plus free Wi-Fi. The library is clean, cheerful, and cozy, with a fireplace just past the front entry. Free Wi-Fi is also available at **The HUB Coffee and Cones** (830 Grand Ave., 970/627-5095, 6:30am-5pm daily year-round), which has comfy couch seating.

EMERGENCIES

Call 911 in case of emergency. If you have an emergency on the lake, such as a disabled boat motor to get towed in, call 911 or the marina from which you rented equipment. For non-emergency inquires to the police, contact the **Grand County Sheriff's Department** (970/725-3343). The closest hospital to Grand Lake is the **Middle Park Medical Center – Granby Campus** (1000 Granby Park Dr. South, 970/887-5800, www.mpmc.org, open 24/7). This medical center also provides a weekend care clinic (10am-4pm Sat.) for treating colds and flu, minor broken bones, and other non-life-threatening conditions.

Arapaho National Recreation Area

It is by no means hidden, but somehow the Arapaho National Recreation Area (ANRA)—known as "The Great Lakes" of Colorado—is one of the better-kept secrets in the state. The 35,000-acre region is located near the towns of Grand Lake and Granby, but doesn't feel overrun in the summer. The ANRA consists of five reservoirs, as well as numerous campgrounds and picnic sites.

Three of the ANRA's five reservoirs—**Willow Creek Reservoir, Shadow Mountain Reservoir,** and **Lake Granby**—play a critical role in the Colorado-Big Thompson Project, a massive water diversion effort that delivers water from the western slope of the state to Front Range municipalities.

The pine beetle epidemic of recent years hit hard in this region, and many infested trees have been removed. Others are still standing, but are needle-less and rather drab. Regardless, the region is still picturesque, with brilliant blue waters, shorebirds and wildlife going about their business, and mountains peaks in the not-so-far distance. For recreation, choose your own adventure: boating, waterskiing, fishing, camping, hiking, wildlife-watching, picnicking, or stand-up paddleboarding.

SIGHTS

Visiting the **Arapaho National Recreation Area** (ANRA, www.fs.usda.gov, $5 day-use) requires purchasing a pass from an ANRA fee station or from the **Sulphur Ranger District office** (9 Ten Mile Dr., Granby, 970/887-4100, 8am-5pm Mon.-Fri.). Buying a pass from one of the stations en route to a destination is the most convenient option for most day-trippers. Stations are clearly labeled "Pay Here" and are highly visible. For stays longer than a day, purchase a three-day pass ($10) or a seven-day pass ($15). An annual pass for the ANRA is available for $30, and a pass for the RMNP and ANRA can be purchased for $70.

★ Lake Granby

At the bottom of what is today **Lake Granby,** a dude ranch for the well-to-do once sprawled over 1,500 acres. Financier Harry Knight was the brains and big bucks behind the Knight Ranch, which featured guest cabins, a miniature golf course, outdoor diversions such as hiking and hunting, and even a private airstrip for guests. The Colorado-Big Thompson Project forever changed this history-rich landscape with a dam and millions of gallons of water. Today, at 7,250 surface acres, Lake Granby is Colorado's second-largest body of water and still a popular recreation area—just in an entirely different capacity. Instead of ranch activities, the focal point for recreation now is fishing, waterskiing, boating, and picnicking. Today, the lake's guests come from all walks of life—not just the wealthy and elite. Along the water's edge, visitors can choose from three public **boat launches** (Stillwater, Sunset Point, and Arapaho Bay), more than 200 **campsites,** and numerous spots to enjoy a picnic lunch. In the winter, Lake Granby, especially, is a popular place for **ice fishing.**

From the intersection of Highway 40 and Highway 34 in Granby, travel northeast on Highway 34 for 5.4 miles to the junction of Highway 34 and County Road 6. If you continue 4.2 miles north on Highway 34, you will encounter several marinas, a restaurant, and Stillwater Campground. If you travel 9 miles east on County Road 6, you will find picnic spots and campgrounds located on the southern shore of the lake.

Shadow Mountain Reservoir

Grand Lake's neighbor to the southwest, **Shadow Mountain,** plays a key role in shuttling water from the Colorado River to Front Range reservoirs via the Alva B.

Lake Granby

Adams Tunnel (which runs underneath the ground in Rocky). This relatively shallow body of water (37 feet at its deepest, compared with Grand Lake's estimated depth of 265 feet) is also a prime spot for boating and fishing. Many visitors, however, are content to enjoy lake views from solid ground. The **Pine Beach** and **Shadow Mountain picnic areas** on the west side of the lake are popular places to congregate. For a fun day trip, rent a kayak from the **Trail Ridge Marina** (12634 Hwy. 34, 970/627-3586, www.trailridgemarina.com, 970/627-3586, 9am-6pm daily summer) and travel near the small islands located on the south end of the reservoir. The islands are osprey-nesting areas, so be sure to abide by any posted closures or restrictions. Shadow Mountain Reservoir is also known for its pelicans, which, along with osprey, are only seen in the summer months. You might even witness a large mammal in these parts: moose are known to swim from the reservoir's Pine Beach Picnic Area to the islands.

Pay close attention to seasonal closure signs around the reservoir. A **no-fishing zone** exists below Shadow Mountain Dam mid-October-late December in order to allow Kokanee salmon to spawn. A closure to protect wintering bald eagles is in effect mid-November-mid-March, also on the southern portion of Shadow Mountain Reservoir.

To get to Shadow Mountain Reservoir, at the intersection of Highway 40 and Highway 34 in Granby, travel northeast on Highway 34 for 5.4 miles to the junction of Highway 34 and County Road 6. Continue on Highway 34 heading north for 11.7 miles to Shadow Mountain Reservoir.

Monarch Lake

Monarch Lake (off County Rd. 6) provides access to trails leading into the Indian Peaks Wilderness, which makes it an attractive jumping-off point for a long day hike or an overnight backpack. Most people just enjoy strolling around the lake on the 4-mile loop trail, often with a leashed pup in tow. Keep your eyes out for moose, which sometimes browse the marshier areas of the lake. Monarch is also a popular spot to kayak and canoe; folks paddling around on the water set an idyllic scene. The parking lot is on the small side, and fills up on nice weather weekends.

From the intersection of Highway 40 and Highway 34 in Granby, travel northeast on Highway 34 for 5.4 miles to County Road 6/ National Forest System Road (NFSR) 125. Follow County Road 6 for 9.6 miles to the trailhead.

Willow Creek Reservoir

Willow Creek Reservoir (off County Road 4) is a well-loved spot for camping and fishing. In the summer, locals and visitors alike trek to the campground, which is a short stroll from the lake's shoreline and features a beautiful grove of aspen trees. Nonmotorized watercraft—such as float tubes, canoes, and kayaks—are allowed at this spot, and there is a boat ramp for that purpose. Cast a line in the

The Alva B. Adams Tunnel

The 13.1-mile Alva B. Adams Tunnel is a critical piece in the **Colorado-Big Thompson Project,** an elaborate water collection and diversion system designed to bring water to homes, farms, and ranch lands in eight counties east of the Continental Divide. The tunnel, at its deepest point, lies a whopping 3,800 feet underground.

The tunnel starts at Grand Lake, delivering water from reservoirs on the west side (Lake Granby, Willow Creek, and Shadow Mountain in the Arapaho National Recreation Area; and Windy Gap, outside the ANRA) to the East Portal on the east side of the park. The water is further diverted to east-side reservoirs, including Marys Lake and Lake Estes. All told, the Colorado-Big Thompson Project features 35 miles of tunnels, 95 miles of canals, 7 hydroelectric power plants, and 700 miles of transmission lines.

Water first gushed through the Alva B. Adams Tunnel on June 23, 1947—seven years to the day after work began on the project—and has been operational ever since. On the way to the **East Inlet Trailhead,** there is a pullout where you can get out and stand in close proximity to the start of the tunnel—though, in truth, there is really not a whole lot to see. You just have to use your imagination to envision the methodical boring and blasting that went on day after day to make this water diversion project a reality.

water and you might get a tug from a brown trout, rainbow trout, or salmon. In the winter months, you can enjoy ice fishing here.

From the intersection of Highway 40 and Highway 34 in Granby, take Highway 34 5.1 miles northeast to County Road 40. Turn left (west) on County Road 40 and drive approximately 3 miles to the lake.

Meadow Creek Reservoir

When you feel the urge to liberate yourself from crowds, computers, cars, and civilization in general, consider **Meadow Creek Reservoir** (off County Road 84) your happy place. This is the most remote ANRA reservoir, located 30-40 minutes from Highway 40. There is no established campground, just dispersed camping at no cost along United States Forest Service (USFS) Road 129 near the reservoir. Just south of the reservoir, the Junco Lake Trail leads into the Indian Peaks Wilderness. Meadow Creek is also a great place to fish. Vault toilets are on-site.

From south of the town of Tabernash on Highway 40, turn right (east) on County Road 83 for 0.4 mile. Turn left on USFS Road 129/County Road 84 and travel 8.2 miles east to the reservoir.

★ Osprey Viewing

Ospreys are a big deal around the ANRA; more than 50 breeding pairs of these birds of prey spend their summer (**May-Sept.**) here. The area's osprey nests are well-established and visible from the road. Ospreys, which almost exclusively subsist on fish, build their large nests on the tops of trees and on power line poles. Wooden platforms have been built on certain utility poles in the ANRA to protect them from electrocution. Three self-guided osprey tours are available for avid bird watchers: two can be done as driving or biking tours; the other is a boating tour. The **Willow Creek Driving/Biking Tour** takes viewers to Willow Creek Reservoir—the site of two nests—while the **Arapaho Bay Driving/Biking Tour** travels north from Granby along Highway 34, then heads east on County Road 6/Forest Service Road 125. Multiple nests are located along the latter route. The Shadow Mountain Islands Canoe/Kayak Tour starts at either the Pine Beach Picnic Area or the Shadow Mountain Picnic Area. To be certain of each nest's location, download the **self-guided tour maps** (www.fs.usda.gov) before embarking on any of these tours.

Don't have time for a tour? Pay a visit to the

ANRA's **Osprey Viewing Site**, which has interpretive signs, a viewing platform and telescopes (including one positioned at a height accessible to wheelchair users) at the ready. To get there, take Highway 34 to County Road 66 and drive approximately 1.5 miles east to the gate. There are no other services at the viewing site.

SPORTS AND RECREATION

★ Boating

When the sun is shining, figuring out what to do around the ANRA is a no-brainer: get afloat, whether it's on a two-seat catamaran or a multi-seat pontoon boat. Only small, human-powered watercraft like canoes and kayaks are allowed on the ANRA's smaller reservoirs—Willow Creek, Monarch Lake, and Meadow Creek Reservoir—while both motorized and nonmotorized boats are welcome on Lake Granby and Shadow Mountain Reservoir.

Unlike Grand Lake—which is somewhat sheltered—boats on wide, open Lake Granby are vulnerable to windy conditions. In general, morning is an ideal time to get on the lake; conditions are pleasant and boaters have a decent chance of spotting wildlife. Early to late afternoon—when the wind can pick up and thunderstorms often roll in—is a great time be off of the water, taking a siesta or grabbing a bite to eat. After 5pm, any blustery conditions that presented themselves in the afternoon tend to have settled down. Evening is another good time to spot animals.

The numerous inlets and bays of Lake Granby are fun for boaters to explore. Columbine Bay—which runs along the western border of RMNP—is considered one of the most scenic bays of the ANRA.

While you are out on Lake Granby exploring, take a moment to look southeast to the Indian Peaks Wilderness. A spot-on resemblance of President Abraham Lincoln lying on his back can be seen on the ridgeline.

If you have any intention of getting in the ANRA's lakes, consider donning a wetsuit; water temperatures are chilly.

MARINAS

Around Lake Granby, three marinas serve boaters: the **Beacon Landing Marina** (1026 County Road 64, Grand Lake, 970/627-3671 or 800/864-4372, www.beaconlanding.com, 7am-7pm daily summer), **Highland Marina** (7878 Hwy. 34, 970/887-3541, www.highlandmarinaonlakegranby.com, 7am-8pm Fri.-Sat.,

The Arapaho National Recreation Area's Osprey Viewing Site has a wheelchair-accessible telescope.

7am-6pm Sun.-Thurs. Memorial Day-Labor Day), and **Indian Peaks Marina** (6862 Hwy. 34, 970/887-3456, www.indianpeaksmarina.com, 8am-5pm Mon.-Thurs., 8am-6pm Fri.-Sun. May 15-Oct. 15). At all three spots, you can rent boats, chat up employees about where the fish are biting, and purchase boating supplies. Boat storage is available at each location, but expect a waiting list.

Trail Ridge Marina (12634 Hwy. 34, 970/627-3586, www.trailridgemarina.com, 970/627-3586, 9am-6pm daily summer) serves visitors of Shadow Mountain Reservoir. In addition to renting boats, the marina offers a two-hour, guided boat tour (10am-noon Tues. and Thurs., $40 pp) of the reservoir. While the tours are intended for groups of 12 people, it is sometimes possible for smaller parties to join another group on a non-full boat. Call ahead for details and reservations.

BOAT LAUNCHES

Lake Granby has three public launches for motorized boats: **Arapaho Bay** (located 10 mi east of Hwy. 34 on County Rd. 6), **Sunset Point** (located 1.5 mi east of Hwy. 34 on County Rd. 6), and **Stillwater** (located 6 mi south of Grand Lake, just off Hwy. 34).

For boat access to Shadow Mountain Reservoir, motorized vessels can launch from **Green Ridge Campground** (take Hwy. 34 12 mi north from Granby to County Rd. 66; travel 1.4 mi east on County Rd. 66); nonmotorized boats only can launch from **Hilltop boat launch** (located on Jericho Rd. at the north end of the reservoir, just south of the connecting channel between Grand Lake and Shadow Mountain Reservoir).

A boat ramp for nonmotorized boats is located at **Willow Creek Reservoir**. A $5 day-use fee is required to use ANRA boat ramps; payment stations are prominently displayed.

JET SKIING

Jet skiing and waterskiing are allowed on **Lake Granby** and **Shadow Mountain Reservoir,** but recreationists must provide their own equipment; rentals are not available in the area. Also, for liability reasons, the marinas do not rent out towables (such as inner tubes); those must be purchased ahead of a visit.

Fishing

Where there's water, there's fish—and the ANRA has plenty of both. Fishing enthusiasts can drop a line into any ANRA reservoir, as long as they hold a current fishing license (required for age 16 and older). The best fishing in the ANRA is from fall to early summer.

Lake Granby is the crown jewel of all five reservoirs, and considered by many to be the most underrated brown trout fishery in the state. Lake trout and rainbow trout are also found in the lake; if you get lucky, you might catch a Kokanee salmon. Though Kokanee are stocked, for a variety of reasons they do not thrive in the lake and are rarely caught. **Monarch Lake** and **Meadow Creek Reservoir** are stellar settings for fishing; both are full of brookies. At **Willow Creek Reservoir,** you can set your sights on catching rainbow trout, Kokanee salmon, or brown trout. **Shadow Mountain Reservoir** is full of brown trout, and also has quite a few rainbows.

Beacon Landing Marina (1026 County Road 64, 970/627-3671, www.beaconlanding.com) offers guided fishing on Lake Granby and Shadow Mountain Reservoir, and **Fishing with Bernie** (970/531-2318, www.fishingwithbernie.com) offers guided fishing on Lake Granby.

Ice Fishing

In the winter, ice-fishing huts (small, portable tents in which ice fishers stay warm) regularly decorate the frozen surfaces of Shadow Mountain Reservoir and Lake Granby. Ice fishing is a popular wintertime endeavor for locals and visitors, as indicated by not one, but two well-attended ice fishing contests held in the area. **The Three Lakes Ice Fishing Contest** (800/325-1661, www.granbychamber.com) takes place every January, and neighboring Grand Lake holds its **Grand**

Lake Annual Catch & Release Ice Fishing Contest (970/627-3402, www.grandlakechamber.com, Mar.). In Grand Lake, where there are a mere 1.2 fish per surface acre, every fish that is caught in their contest is tagged and tracked for future observation purposes. In Lake Granby, where there is an overabundance of lake trout—to the tune of 17 fish per surface acre—the Three Lakes Ice Fishing Contest helps to thin out a small portion of the population.

Ice-fishing season generally runs late December-April; all types of fish are caught, including lake trout, rainbow trout, and brown trout. **Beacon Landing Marina** (1026 County Road 64, 970/627-3671, www.beaconlanding.com, $375/1-2 people for a half-day) and **Fishing with Bernie** (970/531-2318, www.fishingwithbernie.com, $300/half-day with 1 guide) offer ice-fishing trips on Lake Granby.

ACCOMMODATIONS

Visitors to the ANRA have numerous options for overnight accommodations: hotels, lodges, or campgrounds in Grand Lake or Granby; ANRA campgrounds; and a handful of lodges nestled around the ANRA's lakes.

Located on the west side of the highway from Shadow Mountain Reservoir, **Black Bear Lodge** (12255 Hwy. 34, 970/627-3654, www.blackbeargrandlake.com, $90 and up) is close to Grand Lake and the ANRA. Room furnishings are understated, with surprisingly cozy beds and pillows. The continental breakfast often includes moist, homemade baked goods in addition to the requisite dry cereal options and java. An outdoor swimming pool is open in the summer; a sauna and an indoor hot tub are available to guests year-round.

There's plenty to love about the **North Shore Lodge** (928 County Road 64, Grand Lake, 970/627-8448, www.grandlakerentals.net, $99 and up, year-round), including its views of Grand Lake and watercraft (a canoe, kayaks, and a paddleboat) that guests are free to use during their stay. Each unit includes a private bath and kitchenette and features casual mountain furnishings and décor. Dogs are welcome; just make sure yours are well-behaved as extra charges may be tacked on to your bill at the end (a fee schedule is listed on the website). Additional on-site activities include volleyball, horseshoes, and croquet; guests regularly gather around a large fire pit in the evenings. The water levels change in Lake Granby—thus so do the views and access to the water from this property.

Black Bear Lodge is located across from Shadow Mountain Reservoir.

CAMPING

Campers staying in the ANRA must pay a **day-use fee** ($5/1 day, $10/3 days, $15/7 days), or hold an ANRA annual pass, in addition to any campground fees. Day-use fees can be paid at pay stations located at each campground or at the Sulphur Ranger District office (9 Ten Mile Dr., Granby, 970/887-4100, 8am-5pm Mon.-Fri.).

A **campfire program** (Memorial Day-Labor Day) is occasionally offered at the Stillwater Campground or Green Ridge Campground by a ranger from the Sulphur Ranger District office. The program features information about the area's lakes and rivers, local wildlife, wildlife management, or other topics. Some summers, staffing issues have prevented the program from occurring at all; call the district office (970/887-4100) for information.

Green Ridge Campground

Green Ridge Campground

Green Ridge Campground (County Road 66, 877/444-6777, www.recreation.gov, mid-May-late Sept., $19 singles, $38 doubles) is located on the south shore of Shadow Mountain Reservoir and next to the Colorado River. Seventy-eight sites for tents and RVs are available. Amenities include a boat ramp, water, restrooms, and picnic tables. To reach the campground, take Highway 34 12 miles north from Granby to County Road 66, then travel 1.4 miles east on County Road 66.

Arapaho Bay Campgrounds

If you haven't grown fond of Lake Granby while driving by it on Highway 34, you will when you venture 9 miles down the dirt road that leads to **Arapaho Bay Campgrounds** (County Rd. 6, 877/444-6777, www.recreation.gov, reservations late May-early Sept., first-come first-served early Sept.-mid-Oct., $19 singles, $38 doubles). County Road 6 hugs the edge of the lake and offers a gorgeous view of the water. The campground sits at the southeast end of the lake and feels secluded—being so far off the main highway—with three great loops to choose from. The Big Rock Loop is closest to the campground's entrance and has nice sites, but no lakeside spots. Moraine Loop is the middle loop and features a handful of waterfront sites. The Roaring Fork Loop also has waterfront sites and the closest access to a boat ramp, as well as access to trails leading into the Arapaho National Forest. In total, there are 84 sites—singles and doubles—that are available to tents, trailers, and RVs. The campground has water and vault toilets, and each site has a tent pad, picnic table, and fire pit. In the winter, seven sites at Big Rock are open to RV campers only. A campground fee is not charged, but visitors must pay the ANRA's day-use fee of $5. The sites are not plowed out, so you have to be motivated to roll up your winter jacket sleeves and shovel out a space. No campsite amenities—such as restrooms and water—are available in the winter.

Stillwater Campground

The largest of all the campgrounds in the area, **Stillwater Campground** (Hwy. 34,

877/444-6777, www.recreation.gov, May-Sept., $22-25 tent site, $27 site with hook-ups, $44 double site) is situated on the northwest corner of Lake Granby. Choose from 129 sites, both electric and nonelectric. Tents, RVs, and trailers are welcome. Amenities include a boat ramp, dock, restrooms, potable water, and trash service. There is also a dump station on-site. The pine beetle epidemic resulted in the removal of trees from this campground—which gives it a feeling of less privacy. On the plus side, views of Lake Granby are unobstructed. The campground includes a mix of reservable and first-come, first-served sites. Eleven campsites outside the main gate are available for winter camping, with the purchase of a day-use pass ($5).

Stillwater Campground is the only campground within the ANRA that has **showers;** you must be staying at the campground to use them. There are no other public shower facilities in the area. The campground is located 6 miles south of Grand Lake off Highway 34; turn left (east) into the campground.

Willow Creek Campground

Located at the Willow Creek Reservoir west of Lake Granby, **Willow Creek Campground** (County Rd. 40, Granby, www.fs.usda.gov, late May-mid Oct., $19) has 35 sites for tents, RVs, or trailers. Sites feature a tent pad, grill, and picnic table. Amenities include potable water and vault toilets, and firewood for purchase. Nonmotorized watercraft are allowed on the reservoir and there is a boat launch. This is also a popular spot for anglers. All sites are first-come, first-served except for one **group campsite** that must be reserved (877/444-6777, www.recreation.gov, $75).

Sunset Point Campground

Twenty-five first-come, first-served nonelectric campsites are found at **Sunset Point Campground** (www.fs.usda.gov, $22-44), which is located on the south shore of Lake Granby. From Grand Lake take Highway 34 south for 9 miles; turn left (east) on County Road 6 and travel 1.5 miles to the campground. There is a boat ramp at this location, as well as bathrooms and potable water.

Dispersed Camping

Free first-come, first-served camping is available along USFS Road 129 leading to **Meadow Creek Reservoir;** keep a look out for primitive fire rings. Camping right on the banks of the reservoir is not allowed.

At **Lake Granby,** dispersed camping is available on the northeast shores of the lake for people traveling by boat. Visitors must camp on ANRA land, not in the adjacent national park. Camping on any of the lake's islands is prohibited. For more information about dispersed camping sites, contact the U.S. Forest Service's Sulphur Ranger District office (970/887-4100).

FOOD

Italian hats are kind of a "thing" at **Mustachio's on the Lake** (6732 Hwy. 34, 970/531-4002, www.mustachiosonthelake.com, 5pm-9pm Wed.-Sun late May-mid June, 5pm-9pm daily mid-June-early Sept., 5pm-9pm Thurs.-Sat. Dec.-Mar., closed Nov. and Apr., $14-26) The restaurant's logo features a hat, the wait staff wears them, and if you are feeling sassy, you can borrow one to wear during dinner and return it when you're ready to leave. The real reasons to come here, though, are the pasta dishes made with family recipes and the views of Lake Granby off the deck in the summertime. The owners operate a year-round lodge upstairs, and the restaurant sees plenty of foot traffic from those folks as well as recreationists of all ages. If you are hankering for something hearty and delicious, sink your teeth into Mustachio's delicious sausage rolls, lasagna, or lobster ravioli. Mustachio's on the Lake is located on Highway 34, approximately 7.8 miles south of Grand Lake.

No need to put on your fancy duds for the **Roadhouse Bar and Grill** (10188 Hwy. 34, 970/627-9300, 11am-11pm daily summer, 11am-10pm daily winter, $8-21); most of the time this is a jeans-and-flannels kind of establishment (unless its Halloween or Fat Tuesday, when you'd best get in the spirit of things). There is always something going on at this spot, whether it's a band jamming on the outside patio, a lively game of billiards, or a group of friends taking shots at the expansive bar. While the bar and its many liquors are the centerpiece of the Roadhouse, this is still a fine place to take the kids out for a burger and fries. The menu contains a variety of fare, including steaks, sandwiches, and fish. Roadhouse Bar and Grill is located on Highway 34, about 4.5 miles south of Grand Lake.

Picnicking

Picnicking on a warm summer day is even better when there's a sparkling body of water nearby. For an enjoyable outing, slap together some sandwiches and head to one of the ANRA's picnic sites for lunch. **Pine Beach Picnic Area** (from Granby, drive 12 miles north; the picnic ground is on the east side of the highway), on the shore of Shadow Mountain Reservoir, is one of the most sought-after spots to dine outdoors, with great wildlife-watching opportunities. From this location, visitors have a nice view of Shadow Mountain's small islands.

Nearby **Shadow Mountain Picnic Ground** (drive 12 mi north from Granby on Highway 34 to County Rd. 66; then drive 0.5 mi east to your destination) also offers great views and shade trees. On Lake Granby, **Rainbow Bay Picnic Ground** (drive 6 mi north on Hwy. 34 from Granby; take County Rd. 6 east for 400 ft) and **Quinette Point Picnic Ground** (drive 6 mi north on Hwy. 34 from Granby; take County Rd. 6 east 0.6 mi) are beautiful spots to eat al fresco. The use of any picnic area requires a $5 day-use pass for the ANRA; purchase a pass from one of the prominently displayed fee stations.

TRANSPORTATION AND SERVICES

Car

The ANRA is convenient to visitors staying in both Grand Lake and Granby. A private vehicle is ideal, since few public transportation options are available in the area. Highway 34 is the main artery for the area, running along the west side of Shadow Mountain Reservoir and Lake Granby. Access to some of ANRA's reservoirs, picnic areas, and campgrounds is via county or Forest Service roads to the east or west of Highway 34. Parking lots are located at all major attractions.

For roadside assistance and towing, call **Pete's Towing and Mobile Repair** (970/887-0066) in Granby.

RV

RV travelers have no problem traveling along the area's county or Forest Service roads. But if you are interested in traveling extensively off the main highway in an RV, it's wise to scope out roads with a smaller vehicle first; then make a judgment call based on the size of your vehicle and on your comfort level with driving. Dump stations are located at the **Stillwater Campground** (8 mi north of Granby off Hwy. 34; turn right into the campground) and **Shadow Mountain Picnic Ground** (12 mi north of Granby, take Hwy. 34 to County Rd. 66 and drive east 0.5 mi).

Winter Travel

Chains and snow tires are not required in the area; however, visitors and residents should be prepared for snow or icy road conditions. Outfitting your vehicle with snow- or all-terrain tires is the safest bet for winter travel. Highway 34 is regularly plowed in the winter, during and after snowstorms. Some of the area's county roads are only plowed to the place where residences end. Meadow Creek is only accessible by snowmobile in the winter. To go to Monarch Lake in the winter, you can only get as far as the Arapaho Bay Campgrounds in your car; that is where the snow plowing ends. From that location, it is approximately another mile to walk, snowshoe, or cross-country ski to the lake.

Taxi and Shuttle

To reserve a private shuttle bus for your group,

contact **Mountain Transit Adventures** (970/888-1227, www.mtagrandlake.com, year-round). **Valley Taxi** (970/726-4940, www.valleytaxiinc.com, year-round), a one-man operation based in Winter Park, also provides transportation within Grand County.

Services

For information about the ANRA, call or visit the **Sulphur Ranger District office** (9 Ten Mile Dr., Granby, 970/887-4100, 8am-5pm Mon.-Fri., closed holidays). Staff are on hand to answer questions about the area. The center also sells hiking and hunting maps, field guides, and hiking guides. Videos about the region and local wildlife can be viewed on-site. Various free handouts are available for the taking, and the office sells federal lands passes.

Alternatively, stop in the **Grand Lake Visitor Center** (West Portal Rd. and Hwy. 34, 970/627-3402, www.grandlakechamber.com, 10am-4pm daily Memorial Day-Labor Day, 10am-2pm daily winter, spring, and fall), where free leaflets and maps about the ANRA can be obtained. The staff are knowledgeable about recreational opportunities in and around the ANRA.

Purchase firewood and ice from the **Indian Peaks Marina** (6862 Hwy. 34, Granby, 970/887-3456, www.indianpeaksmarina.com), **Highland Marina** (7878 Hwy. 34, Granby, 970/887-3541, www.highlandmarinaonlakegranby.com), or **Beacon Landing Marina** (1026 County Road 64, Grand Lake, 970/627-3671, www.beaconlanding.com).

Background

The Landscape

GEOGRAPHY

The Continental Divide of the Americas

Geologic uplift of the earth created the Continental Divide of the Americas, which is more commonly referred to as simply "the Continental Divide." The Continental Divide in its entirety runs a meandering path north to south—from Alaska to Nicaragua—and creates two separate water drainages. On the west side of the Continental Divide, streams and rivers flow to the west toward the Pacific Ocean, and on the east side, water—you guessed it—drains eastward toward the Atlantic Ocean. Any good map has the Continental Divide's course plotted with a line. You can travel on top of it, though not always on a defined hiking trail or road. The Continental Divide National Scenic Trail (www.continentaldividetrail.org) attempts to get hikers on, or as close as possible to, the Continental Divide. In Rocky, the best places for straddling the two drainages are La Poudre Pass, Milner Pass, and Flattop Mountain. You can also travel along the Divide on a 4-mile (one-way) hike that starts north of Poudre Lake on the Ute Trail and ends at Mt. Ida.

GEOLOGY

Hundreds of thousands of natural events—large and small—have chiseled Rocky's landscape over millions of years, making it the picturesque place it is today. But the park's majestic peaks and wide-open valleys most certainly would not exist without fire, pressure, and ice.

Rock

Billions of years ago, sedimentary rocks—including shale, siltstone, and sandstone—were located in and around Rocky. With repeated tectonic activity, the rocks were transformed by heat and pressure into metamorphic rocks: **gneiss** and **schist.** Today, visitors can see gneiss and schist all around the park. The two types of rocks are made up of layers of compressed minerals. Gneiss is characterized by light bands of minerals, while schist typically features layers of darker minerals.

A third type of rock—**granite**—is also abundant in Rocky. Granite is gray or pink in color, and formed when molten rock becomes hardened. With repeated erosion, granite can appear rounded or dome-shaped. Its surface is speckled with minerals. Bear Lake—among many other places in the park—is a great place to see gneiss, schist, and granite. The many bumps, lumps, and domes of Lumpy Ridge are made up entirely of granite.

A fourth type of rock found in the park—**volcanic rock**—is considered young in comparison to granite, gneiss, and schist. As a result of geologic uplift, the peaks of the Never Summer Mountains spewed molten rock (magma) between 24 and 29 million years ago. Consequently, deposits of volcanic material—including ash, mud, and rock—made a permanent home in several areas of the park, including the Lava Cliffs next to Trail Ridge Road, and Specimen Mountain, located north of Milner Pass. The Never Summer Mountains, therefore, are not just mountains, but extinct volcanoes.

Uplift

The landscape of Rocky in Proterozoic times (2.5 billion-541 million years ago) was originally mountainous, but millions of years of erosion wore down ancient

Previous: male elk in a "bachelor" herd; butterfly on the the Fern Lake Trail.

Colorado Regions

A handful of geographic references are used often in Colorado; it is helpful to know them before you arrive:

THE FRONT RANGE

The range of mountains farthest east along Colorado's Rocky Mountain range is referred to as the "Front Range." The name is also used to describe an urban corridor that runs from the Colorado/Wyoming state line to the town of Pueblo. Colorado's population is at its densest along the Front Range, which includes the towns of Fort Collins, Boulder, Denver, and Colorado Springs. The western border of the Front Range is the Continental Divide.

WESTERN SLOPE

Communities located on the west side of the Continental Divide are part of the "Western Slope." Durango, Montrose, and Grand Junction are three well-known Western Slope towns. The Western Slope ends at the Utah border.

THE MOUNTAINS

If you live anywhere along the Front Range, your weekend plans often include "heading to the mountains." This reference generally includes mountains 8,000 feet or higher located in Colorado's designated wilderness areas, on U.S. Forest Service land, on Bureau of Land Management land, or within Rocky Mountain National Park (RMNP). "The Mountains" can also generally refer to a town or community at high elevation, such as Aspen, Breckenridge, or Crested Butte.

EASTERN COLORADO

A good number of Western Slope and Front Range residents never venture to the eastern part of the state, and do not discuss this area with as much frequency as The Mountains. Largely consisting of farmland—and also known as "The High Plains"—Eastern Colorado is not considered so much a tourist destination as it is a place to make an honest living. The region starts just east of the Front Range and stretches to the Kansas border.

mountains to nearly flat ground. Five hundred million years ago, seas, surprisingly, were a dominant feature of the area. Mountains were formed yet again by a major collision of two tectonic plates called the Pacific Plate and the North American Plate. The collision commenced somewhere around 130 million years ago. It took somewhere in the neighborhood of 60 million years for this major geological event to have a marked effect on Rocky. Vertical displacement of the earth's crust gave dramatic shape and definition to the land, and also spurred volcanic activity in the Never Summer Mountains. Though Rocky's mountains might appear to have distinct, "permanent" shapes, they are in a constant state of change, thanks to erosion.

Glaciers

Major touches of beauty were bestowed on Rocky by ice. Approximately 1.6 million years ago, the area first experienced the effects of the Ice Age. During this time, massive sheets of frozen water dominated the Northern Hemisphere. Ice has come and gone from the area of the park numerous times, and some periods of glaciation remain largely unknown—and therefore unnamed. However, the effects of the Bull Lake Glaciation (127,000-180,000 years ago) and the Pinedale Glaciation (12,000-35,000 years ago), which have been well-researched and documented, were critical land-shapers for Rocky: ice scraped the surface of the land, sculpting peaks, and thrusting rocks and sediment into large piles called moraines.

Glaciers began to disappear somewhere around 15,000 years ago. Today, there are just six small glaciers still present in the park: Tyndall Glacier, Sprague Glacier, Rowe Glacier, Moomaw Glacier, Andrews Glacier, and Mills Glacier. Andrews Glacier can be hiked to from the Glacier Gorge Trailhead or Bear Lake Trailhead. Tyndall Glacier, located between Hallett Peak and Flattop Mountain, is easily viewed from the shores of Sprague Lake; you can also see it while driving on Bear Lake Road (past the Park & Ride turnoff) and hiking on the Flattop Mountain Trail.

There are also roughly 30 permanent snowfields in the park. Many people are unsure if they are looking at a glacier or a snowfield. Even if you know the difference scientifically, sometimes it can still be impossible to discern with the naked eye. The key difference between a glacier and a snowfield is movement. Glaciers are always moving or flowing downhill (often at a snail's pace), while snowfields stay put. Rocky's glaciers advance no more than three feet annually. Late summer and early fall are the best times to observe snow features around the park; after the rest of the previous winter's snow melts off, only glaciers and snowfields remain.

CLIMATE

Seasons

Four seasons, each one glorious in its own right, present themselves in Rocky. Winter (late Dec.-late-Mar.) is typically snowy, cold, and windy. Spring (late Mar.-mid-June) can be a mixed bag of conditions, with warm temperatures in the 60s one day, and snow stacking up on the ground on the next day. Summer (mid-June-late-Sept.) sees plenty of sunshine, but unpredictability is still the name of the game in this season. Even in July, it can snow. In mid-summer, afternoon thunderstorms are more the rule than the exception. Fall (late Sept.-late Dec.) is defined by crisp, cool air, sunshine, and—as always—the possibility of white stuff falling.

East Side vs. West Side

Some park staff members playfully refer to the west side of Rocky as the "better, wetter side of the park." According to studies, Grand Lake typically receives more rain and snow than Estes Park does year after year—approximately 19 inches of precipitation yearly, compared with Estes Park's 13 inches. A rain shadow effect is the explanation for this disparity. The entire western slope of Colorado in general is wetter that the east side. As

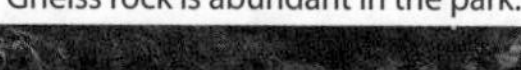
Gneiss rock is abundant in the park.

Glacial Vocabulary

MORAINES

As large glaciers moved into valleys, they brought all kinds of rock, gravel, and dirt along for the ride. This debris was pushed into giant mounds by the movements of the glaciers. When the glaciers eventually retreated, the mounds—or "moraines"—remained. There are two types of moraines: lateral moraines form along the sides of glacier, while terminal moraines form at the endpoint of a glacier. If you did not know better, you might look at a moraine and call it a mountain. In Rocky, moraines are evident in numerous locations in the park, including around Moraine Park and Horseshoe Park, near Lake Bierstadt (Bierstadt Moraine), and next to the East Longs Peak Trail (Mills Moraine).

U-shaped Kawuneeche Valley

CIRQUES AND TARNS

A cirque is a bowl-shaped amphitheater carved into a mountain by a glacier. A tarn is a lake that fills a glacial cirque. Some tarns in the park are actually named "tarn," such as Andrews Tarn—which pools up at the base of Andrews Glacier. Others, such as Chasm Lake, are not named as such, and are identifiable as tarns by their location and geologic characteristics.

GLACIAL ERRATIC

At times, you will run across a large boulder in the park that looks totally out of place. The other rocks in the vicinity are, in comparison, much smaller in size, or perhaps there are no other rocks nearby at all. These boulders are called glacial erratics—rocks that were pushed along the land by a glacier and then left in place once the glacier retreated. An erratic, by definition, must have different physical characteristics from the bedrock on which it is sitting. Glacial erratics can be a variety of sizes, but the biggest, most unusual ones get the lion's share of attention. Cub Lake is a great place to spot erratics, as is Old Fall River Road.

U-SHAPED VALLEY

To understand the characteristics of a U-shaped valley, you must first start with its close cousin, the V-shaped valley. When the earth rises up steep and straight on both sides of a classic river valley, a *V* is formed. A U-shaped valley is a V-shaped valley that has been widened—and its sharp edges softened and rounded—by a glacier. As you look across the valley, you can see a *U* on the landscape. Kawuneeche Valley is a U-shaped valley, and there are others around the park.

prevailing westerly winds go up and over the mountains, moist air becomes drier on the other side, producing less precipitation.

Wind

When wind is tossing grit into your eyes, and your hair is twisting into a wild bird's nest, figuring out what *type* of wind is occurring is usually not of primary concern. But not all wind is the same, and in Rocky, two types are most prevalent: Chinook and Bora. Chinook winds are often referred to as "snow eater" winds, and if you have ever seen Chinooks in action you know that this is an accurate descriptor. Chinook winds only occur on the lee (east) side of the Continental Divide and come

Wind Precautions

Wind is common in the park and can wreak havoc on the best-laid plans. In the winter, wind combined with snow can create ground blizzards, obscure snowy trails, and cause low-visibility driving conditions. At any time of the year, wind can more quickly fatigue and dehydrate a hiker. The impacts of wind on people—and the landscape—are many.

If you plan on hiking in Rocky—and especially if you are heading above the tree line—be prepared with extra water, good eye protection, a windbreaker, trekking poles for stability, a snug-fitting hat, and a thin Buff or neck gaiter. Wind is a very real reason to turn around on a hike. Once, while attempting to hike to Chasm Lake, wind pressed up against my body with such brutal force and intensity that I made the decision to head back to the trailhead. Below the tree line, the wind was negligible, and on the trail I bumped into a man who was incredulous that I had not reached my destination. He stated he had "never turned around on a hike because of wind." My words of advice to him and anyone who hikes in Rocky are to not underestimate the power of this invisible force. On the summit of Longs Peak, winds can top 100mph and can make travel on exposed terrain extremely dangerous. Always take note of the wind portion of the daily forecast and plan accordingly.

in warm, dry, and fast from the Pacific. They are caused by low air pressure and can sweep down eastern mountainsides with amazing velocity. In the process, piles of snow are "eaten up" and quickly transformed into small rivers of water trickling down the mountainside. By the next day, a wintery landscape can look decidedly springlike. Bora winds are dry and icy cold, originating from the Artic and Canada. You can especially see their mark on the earth at the tree line; they are the primary shapers of Rocky's flag-shaped "krummholz" trees.

ECOSYSTEMS

An ecosystem is a biological community in which specific types of animals, plants, and organisms thrive, interact with one another, and affect one another. Rocky has four ecosystems: montane, subalpine, alpine, and riparian. It is possible to visit all four ecosystems in one day, either on a long hike, bicycle ride (on roads only), horseback ride, or on a drive from one of the park entrance stations up to the top (or near the top) of Trail Ridge Road. Though three of Rocky's ecosystems are based on elevation, an altimeter or Global Positioning System (GPS) is not necessary to figure out what ecosystem you are in; simply look to the environment for clues.

Montane

You will breathe the easiest in Rocky's montane ecosystem, which is found in elevations ranging from 5,600-9,500 feet. Rocky's wide-open meadow valleys are classified as montane, including Horseshoe Park, Moraine Park, and the Kawuneeche Valley. Here you will find abundant grasses, shrubs, and wildflowers. Tree species include lodgepole pine, ponderosa pine, Douglas fir, and Engelmann spruce. Wildflowers are copious in this ecosystem. Many different types of wildlife—including mule deer and coyotes—call montane areas "home."

Subalpine

The air is starting to get a lot thinner in these parts, since the subalpine ecosystem falls between 9,000-11,000 feet. Plants and animals must stand up to a more difficult living environment. Subalpine fir, Engelmann spruce, and limber pine grow in this ecosystem, and at the transition point between subalpine and alpine, krummholz—trees shaped by fierce winds—can be spotted. Many varieties of wildflowers and types of animals thrive here. Dozens of popular hiking destinations in Rocky arrive at subalpine environments, such as Mills Lake and Emerald Lake.

Alpine Tundra

It's official: you are in the highest region of the park now, where the air is markedly less dense than at sea level. Approximately one-third of Rocky's acreage falls within the alpine tundra, which consists of terrain located at 11,000 feet and above. The environment here is unforgiving, and animals and plants must adapt to wind, precipitation, and fluctuating temperatures. The first clue that you are in the tundra is that the trees, after getting smaller and smaller as the elevation increases—disappear altogether. Rocks are often given extra texture and color with a layer of lichen. Wildflowers still exist, but many grow low to the ground to stay protected from the wind. The tundra is rocky, and in places, snow clings to the surface into the summer months. Only the hardiest of mammals—such as snowshoe hares and pikas—live year-round on the tundra. In addition to making up a significant part of the scenery along Trail Ridge Road, the tundra can be viewed on many different hikes, including Chasm Lake, Flattop Mountain, and Longs Peak.

Riparian

Elevation does not define a riparian ecosystem. You will know you are there if you find yourself near a body of water—whether it be a stream, river, lake, or pond. Riparian ecosystems are found within montane, subalpine, and alpine tundra ecosystems. In lower elevations, alder, birch, and spruce trees grow in riparian environments. Animals that thrive in water—like muskrats and frogs—can also be found here. The soil is moist and the vegetation is lush. A few great places to explore riparian areas are the Colorado River along the Coyote Valley Trail on the west side, and the Big Thompson River on the east side.

ENVIRONMENTAL ISSUES

Beetles

A statewide pine beetle epidemic that started in 1996 has ravaged the trees of Rocky, as well as trees located on National Forest land nearby the park. Today, pine beetles are still active and causing destruction in the park. Beetles do their damage by burrowing into trees, laying eggs, and producing more beetles, which chow down on and destroy the bark. The result is a weakened or dead tree, identifiable by a pockmarked trunk; saggy, limp, gray branches; and needles that have turned from verdant green to a sad shade of rusty brown. Bark beetle-assaulted trees

Bierstadt Lake is a subalpine lake.

Krummholz Trees

There is an upper limit to the kind of environmental conditions that trees can withstand. At elevations above 11,000 feet, fierce winds, cold temperatures, and other environmental factors cause trees to disappear from the landscape altogether.

But as you drive above the tree line on Trail Ridge Road or hike from a subalpine to alpine ecosystem in another area of the park, you will notice that towering spruces and pines do not just vanish abruptly. There is a transitional zone where various species of trees become smaller and smaller, their trunks contorted and limbs twisted. These trees are called krummholz, which is the German word for "crooked wood."

Some krummholz trees look like shrubs. Others resemble flags waving in the wind, their leafless limbs thrust in one direction. These trees survive because some part of them is protected from the wind, whether by rocks, other krummholz trees, or other natural objects. The height of krummholz trees is often very small, ranging from approximately 1-8 feet.

are aesthetically a big bummer for camera-wielding tourists. More important, affected trees pose a real danger: they can topple over and cause injury or even death. Workers have removed scores of dead trees from the park, while trees in some high-use areas of Rocky—such as campgrounds—are sprayed with insecticide and are identifiable by a large blue dot located at the base of the tree. When insecticide application is in progress, visitors are made aware through signage.

Air Quality

It is reasonable to assume that Rocky's air quality is quite good, based on the fact that a dense, yellow/brown haze isn't constantly hovering over the park. One might also expect that the park's air quality is good because Rocky is a designated wilderness area, or simply because it is a national park. In truth, Rocky sees its fair share of air quality problems, high ozone among them. Ozone—which is a colorless, odorless gas—can be problematic for human health. Car exhaust that comes from visitors' vehicles and from automobiles from nearby Front Range communities is a primary cause of high ozone in Rocky, which occurs most commonly during the hot summer months. For visitors who have preexisting health conditions that are affected by air quality, such as asthma, there are several ways to check on ozone levels during or before a trip. If levels are especially high, the park will post notices at the entrance stations, visitor centers, and on social media (www.facebook.com/RockyNPS or www.twitter.com/RockyNPS). Current information about Rocky's air quality is also posted on www.nature.nps.gov/air.

Nitrogen deposition is another air quality issue for the park, particularly on the east side. High levels of nitrogen deposited in Rocky can adversely affect trees, soil, plants, and water. People are to blame for this problem: excess nitrogen that ends up in the park comes from many human-made sources, including power plants, landfills, vehicles, and agricultural processes. Effects already noted from excessive nitrogen deposition include changes in alpine and aquatic plant species and an uptick in weedy lichen species. The Rocky Mountain National Park Air Quality Initiative (www.colorado.gov) works to reduce air quality problems in the park.

Flooding

Flooding is a familiar foe in Rocky. In 1976, unrelenting rains caused flooding along the upper portion of the Big Thompson River, which resulted in the destruction of homes and businesses and the loss of 145 lives. This natural disaster is known as the Big Thompson Canyon Flood. Almost six years later to the date, a failed dam at Lawn Lake triggered the Flood of 1982, which unleashed more than 300 million gallons of water down the Roaring River. The debris that floated downriver and finally settled is now a major park attraction, the Alluvial Fan. Three people died in the Flood of 1982.

A real doozy of a natural disaster caused significant damage on the east side of the park in 2013. The Colorado Flood of 2013—a 100-year flood—most notably closed Old Fall River Road for almost two years. Numerous bridges were destroyed during the event, and trails along the east side of the park were damaged. The visible effect of a huge landslide on the Twin Sisters mountains is one of the many reminders of the disaster. No lives were lost within the park boundaries, but four individuals in the region succumbed in the flood.

Overcrowding

Annual visitation to Rocky shows no signs of declining, and in some respects this is a good thing. For one, it indicates that people still find enjoyment and value in being surrounded by nature, even in our increasingly technology-driven society. But park officials must constantly refer to Rocky's mission to decide how much growth is too much. The park's mission states: "The purpose of Rocky Mountain National Park is to preserve the high-elevation ecosystems and wilderness character of the southern Rocky Mountains within its borders and to provide the freest recreational use of and access to the park's scenic beauties, wildlife, natural features and processes, and cultural objects." When more than 13,000 visitors travel into the park on a pristine fall day—as has been known to happen—is Rocky's "wilderness character" being sacrificed? Is significant harm coming to Rocky's wildlife, plants, or air? These are tough questions to answer, and park officials must always walk a razor's edge of two directly competing purposes: preservation and recreational use. Even the park's shuttle system—which positively impacts Rocky by reducing parking lot traffic jams and vehicle emissions—also creates a potential negative: burgeoning crowds on popular trails. Park officials have yet to place a cap on annual or daily visitation to Rocky, but the idea has been considered. In the summer of 2016, the park instated temporary road closures to heavily visited areas—including Bear Lake, Old Fall River Road, and Wild Basin—during peak hours (when parking lots and roads had reached capacity) to alleviate congestion.

Climate Change

The decline of Arctic sea ice is the unfortunate posterchild of climate change in the Northern Hemisphere. In Glacier National Park, the disappearance of more than 100 glaciers since 1850 is one of the most telling signs that the Earth's temperature has unnaturally warmed due to human activities. In Rocky, the timing of snowmelt is an important indicator of climate change. Park managers have noted that over a more than 30-year period, snowpack has consistently started its annual melt two to three weeks earlier than it did prior to the 1970s. Overall, Rocky and its surrounding areas have experienced a warming trend during the past 100-plus years. In the 20th century, a seemingly small but significant increase in the park's average temperature, 3.4 degrees Fahrenheit, has been documented.

What happens when the park is warmer and the snow melts faster? Plant growing cycles are affected; if thrown off drastically, they can, in turn, affect the feeding habits of everything from insects to mammals. Also, pine beetles thrive in warmer climes. Park officials count climate change as a strong contributing factor in the most recent pine beetle epidemic. Longer summers translate into increased reproduction of beetles, and dry or dead trees are more prone to penetration by beetles.

Scientists predict that over time, rising temperatures could affect many aspects of the tundra. The tundra ecosystem—which supports the hardiest of creatures and plants—could dramatically shrink. With warming temperatures, the tundra might also become a more welcoming place for trees and animals that now only thrive in subalpine environments. The tree line as we know it now could creep up higher on the mountain (if the climate is warmer, trees will be able to survive at higher elevations), and high-elevation mammals and plants might be forced out of their existing territory. Researchers are keeping a close watch on mammals that thrive above the tree line, including pikas, marmots, and white-tailed ptarmigans.

Surprisingly, Rocky's glaciers remain unaffected by climate change, since they are small and uniquely positioned in high-elevation areas that are sheltered from the sun. For now, at least, the disappearance of glaciers in the park is not a top concern of climate change researchers.

Plants and Animals

PLANTS

Wildflowers

Each summer, a radiant display of wildflowers appears in the park. A particularly wet spring season means more blooms; drier conditions bring less. Regardless of the amount, wildflowers always appear in a progression, with a strikingly different palette of blooms dotting the landscape from one month to the next. The first flowers start to appear as early as late March. The wildflower season really gets rolling around mid-June, and continues until early- to mid-August. Flowers typically bloom above the tree line for only four to five weeks. Abundant beauties like golden banner and Colorado columbine are popular with visitors, but it can also be fun to seek out more obscure varieties like the brownie lady's slipper—which often gets overlooked due to its muted color scheme—or the uncommon wood lily. Bring a field guide with you on hikes and identify flowers on your own, or join a ranger-led program to gain more in-depth knowledge about the subject. Do not pick wildflowers or remove them from the park; both acts are illegal.

Berries

Berry bushes are found all over the park, and visitors can—at their own risk—take a taste of the fruit if they wish. However, filling any type of container with fruit is not allowed. As one longtime ranger regularly advises her groups, "You can go down to the store and buy some raspberries, but the bears can't." The boulder raspberry bush is an especially showy

Wildflowers bloom along the Mummy Pass Trail.

Where to Find Wildflowers

Visitors don't have to venture far—or even leave their vehicles—to see wildflowers in the summertime. Many varieties, like locoweed (May-June) and golden banner (May-July) spring up right along the edge of the curb on major park roads. But the best way to see flowers, naturally, is up close. Identify them, photograph them, smell them, and otherwise take in their beauty at these great spots:

The wheelchair-accessible loop around **Lily Lake** is home to a wide variety of blooms. In this transitional zone at 9,000 feet, varieties specific to both montane and subalpine ecosystems are present. On the north side of the lake, find montane flowers: blanketflower (July-Aug.), yellow salsify (June-July), wild geranium (May-Aug.), and one-sided penstemon (June-July). On the south side of the lake, in the subalpine zone, keep your eyes peeled for Colorado columbine (June-July) and mountain iris (May-July). Some flowers cross over into both the montane and subalpine environments, including the pearly everlasting (July-Sept.) and wild rose (June-Aug.).

To see pasque flowers (Apr.-May)—some of the first wildflowers to emerge in the spring—take a leisurely stroll on the **Moraine Park Discovery Center Nature Trail.**

Amble along the **Tundra Communities Trail** and discover low-lying beauties like alpine avens (June-Aug.) that somehow survive, despite being whipped by fierce winds and pummeled by rain, hail, and snow. To detect the sweet scent of alpine forget-me-nots (June), it is necessary to get down on all fours and take a whiff. In the summer, enjoy large alpine sunflowers (June-July), which turn their faces slowly throughout the day in order to follow the movement of the sun. The appearance of the arctic gentian (Aug.) signals that winter is just around the corner.

In the northwest corner of the park—on the **Mirror Lake Trail**—find a riot of wildflowers leading up to the lake, including Parry's primrose (June-Aug.) and rosy paintbrush (July-Aug.).

On the west side, hike from the **Colorado River Trailhead** to **Lulu City** to view a wide variety of subalpine wildflowers. Colorado columbine (June-July) is abundant along this trail, as are little pink elephants (July). Keep your eyes peeled for wood nymphs and elephant heads.

The **East Inlet Trail** should also be explored in the Kawuneeche Valley. Bursts of color are found along the path, and flowers blanket a pretty mountain meadow that opens up within a mile after hiking east from **Adam Falls.** Look for paintbrush (July-Aug.) and little pink elephants (July). Find the green gentian along the Kawuneeche Valley's roads and in its meadows.

The relatively rare Brownie lady's slipper and calypso orchid (or "fairy slipper") can be found on the **Green Mountain Trail** and **Onahu Trail.**

plant that displays broad white flowers in the spring before bearing fruit from mid-summer until early September. Also called the delicious raspberry, this fruit can be quite bitter to the taste buds. Look also for wild strawberries and chokecherries along the trails.

Rare and Endangered Plants

Ute ladies'-tresses and the Colorado butterfly plant are included on the U.S. Fish and Wildlife Service's threatened and endangered species list. The two species fall into the threatened category. Neither plant blooms in Rocky, but because they are found in the nearby counties of Boulder and Larimer, park officials keep tabs on them.

Poisonous Plants

Of the many things that can go awry while hiking through the park, stumbling upon a patch of poison ivy is not one. Rocky's high elevations are inhospitable to both poison ivy and poison oak. Stinging nettles, another plant that can cause terrible discomfort to the skin, is also mostly absent here. A plant to just admire—never to eat—is golden banner. This delightful yellow flower which blooms in profusion at the beginning of the summer season and is pretty to look at contains seeds that are poisonous to humans and animals. Several different types of mushrooms found in the park can also cause illness or death if they are ingested, so do not put mushrooms of any kind in your mouth (in addition, they are illegal to pick). To learn more about edible and inedible plants of the Rocky Mountain region, considering picking up a copy of Liz Brown Morgan's *Foraging the Rocky Mountains: Finding, Identifying and Preparing Edible Wild Foods in the Rockies.*

Invasive Plants

Some rather eye-catching varieties of flowers found in the park—like yellow toadflax—are invasive exotic species: plants that did not originate in Rocky. These blooms and more than 100 other types of invasive plants and grasses in the park have the ability to displace native plants. More than 30 types of non-natives are considered significant threats to park resources, and officials follow a multi-pronged management plan to control their growth. Aggressive cheatgrass—which originated in Europe—is a special concern of park staff during fire season due to the grass's exceptional flammability.

Trees

Rocky's trees fall into one of two categories: conifers (spruce, pines, and firs) and deciduous (cottonwood and aspen). Aspen trees are easy for most people to spot. Identifying characteristics include brilliant green leaves that quiver on their stems, eye-shaped knots on a white bark trunk, and, in the fall, beautiful golden leaves. Identifying trees that come from the conifer family—well, that's another story. When walking through a dense green forest, it can be difficult to discern an Engelmann spruce from a Douglas fir or from a ponderosa pine. It takes practice and discipline to examine a tree's bark, cones, overall shape, branch structure, and needle shape. *Rocky Mountain Tree Finder* by Tom Watts and Bridget Watts is a helpful pocket guide that leads readers to the correct tree type through a series of pointed questions.

As you examine Rocky's trees, you will quickly notice which ones are in good health and which ones are not. Some have been decimated by fire, others ravaged by mountain pine beetles. Dead, dying, and downed trees present a constant challenge for park officials. Still, even trees that don't look robust play an important role in Rocky's complex ecosystems, often serving as dwellings for birds or other critters.

ANIMALS

Elk

Elk (also known by the Native American name wapiti) are majestic, charismatic, and entertaining members of the ungulate (hoofed mammal) family. Elk reside in the park year-round. In the summer, when the elk population is at its highest, the animals will forage all over the park, including above the tree line. In the winter, the elk population in the park becomes smaller as the animals widen their search area for food to include lower-elevation locations.

With stately racks of antlers that can weigh up to 40 pounds and have 6-8 points, male (bull) elk get the most attention from visitors. For most of the year, males typically travel around the park solo or in a small bachelor herd. Female elk, or "cows," move about in larger herds with their young. Females choose privacy over the company of their pack only in the spring or early summer, when they bear their babies. Then, they retreat to a secluded wooded area to give birth. Bull elk can weigh up to 900 pounds while females can reach up to 600 pounds; a newborn elk can weigh up to 35 pounds.

During the fall "rut" or mating season, when males are hot-and-bothered from a sharp surge in testosterone, their behavior is most fascinating. During this time, mid-September-mid-October, bull elk abandon their bachelor herd and proudly acquire a harem of up to 60 cows. Males rest and eat very little during this time; all of their attention is focused on winning over females, mating, and fending off competition from other bulls. Once the rut is over, males befriend their competition once again.

The diet of elk consists exclusively of vegetation; they consume grasses, forbs (herbaceous flowering plants), shrubs, and tree bark.

Keeping Elk Numbers in Check

The elk population in the park and the Estes Valley has waxed and waned dramatically in the last two centuries. Before Euro-American settlers came to the region, elk generally flourished. But by the late 1800s, elk were overhunted by early homesteaders. When the early 1900s dawned, the population had dwindled. So in 1913 and 1914, a group of individuals from Estes Park decided to fix this sad state of affairs by traveling up to Yellowstone National Park, loading up elk into the back of trucks, and giving them a new home in the Estes Valley. During this time the local grizzly bear and gray wolf population had also dwindled due to hunting—which largely eliminated the elk's main predators. As the newly introduced elk thrived and multiplied, concerned citizens patted themselves on the back. But this was actually far from a happy ending, because the elk population grew and grew. As the 1960s rolled around, now too many elk roamed the area, causing vegetation to be impacted. A number of the elk were culled by rangers, which caused significant pushback from community members who felt that killing animals was a callous act. Over time, the elk inevitably multiplied again. Depletion of vegetation around the park—particularly willow trees and aspen trees—that other animals also relied on for food once again became a critical concern. Finally, in 2008, park officials launched a long-range, comprehensive strategy to control the elk population called the Elk and Vegetation Management Plan. The plan extends 2008-2028 and includes a variety of methods to maintain healthy ecosystems in the park, including fenced-off areas called "exclosures," vegetation restoration techniques, culling, and redistributing elk to other areas, to keep the winter herd at an ideal size—600-800. The plan has been criticized by animal rights activists, hunters, and community members, who have introduced their own ideas for how the elk population could be controlled. Those ideas, which have not been adopted, include public hunting and reintroduction of wolves to the area.

Mountain lions are the main predator of elk. In the past decade, a small number of elk in Rocky have been identified as having chronic wasting disease.

Moose

Here's a great reason to head to the west side of the park: the moose. Up to 30-50 moose have taken up residence in Rocky, and they are most commonly seen in the Kawuneeche Valley. These members of the deer family favor rivers and lakes as hang-out spots; they like to eat aquatic plants and the leaves, bark, and stems of willows and aspens. Because of their sheer size—bulls can weigh up to 1,500 pounds—visitors are wise to keep their distance. While often mild-mannered, moose may behave unpredictably and are known to charge humans when threatened. Moose are also witnessed on the east side of the park, but considerably less often than they are seen in the Kawuneeche Valley.

Historical evidence from the 1800s indicates that moose dipped in and out of Colorado from Wyoming, and the occasional moose crossed through the region known today as Rocky. Because they are native animals, they are allowed in the park. But the moose population hasn't always been as large as it is today. In an effort to bolster moose numbers statewide, Colorado Parks and Wildlife initiated a handful of moose reintroductions starting in 1978. The first reintroductions involved bringing 12 moose from Utah and 12 moose from Wyoming a year later into North Park, a region of Colorado that is northwest of the national park. Within five years, Rocky saw its first moose appear as a result of that reintroduction. Moose will go where they want to go, and they clearly found great habitat in Rocky—especially on the west side—with its willows and wetlands. Since 1978, multiple other reintroductions have taken place in the state, which have resulted in a population of approximately 2,300 moose in Colorado.

Bighorn Sheep

The bighorn sheep is the official animal of the park, and more than 350 of them live here in distinct herds. Numerous sheep spend their winter on Specimen Mountain and in the park's Mummy Range. One herd sticks fairly close to the Fall River Visitor Center in the cold months. In the warmer months, sheep will travel to lower-elevation areas. Male sheep have impressive, curled horns, while females possess shorter, pointier horns. The horns are used as defense against predators, and—for males—serve as a form of weaponry during the fall mating period. Neither male nor female horns are shed at any point during a sheep's lifetime. A sheep's diet consists of grasses in the summer and shrubs in the fall and winter. In addition, sheep seek out mineral-rich soil called mineral licks. Sheep Lakes is a mineral lick, and in the spring and early summer, this location is often frequented during daytime hours by bighorns. Bighorns are also commonly seen along Trail Ridge Road.

Black Bears

Bruins are alive and well in the park; if you spot one, count yourself lucky. These mammals are fascinating to observe, and can exhibit especially adorable, childlike behavior when chowing down in a berry patch or munching on other foliage. To witness a mama bear and her cubs traipsing around in the springtime is an unforgettable experience. Cute as they may be, bears are not to be messed with. Especially when food is involved, a close encounter with a full-grown adult bear—weighing 200-600 pounds—can be life-threatening or even fatal.

Most recent estimates place the park's bear population at 20-24 animals. Only black bears—not grizzlies—are found in Rocky. Black bears are omnivores, with roughly 90 percent of their diet consisting of vegetation and insects; the other 10 percent of their meals is composed of fish or small mammals. There is quite a bit of variety in the coloration of black bears. The shade of their fur can be tan; light brown; a rich, dark brown; or black. Mamas give birth every other year, and can bear from one to five sows.

In the fall, bears gorge themselves in preparation for hibernation. During this stage of increased hunger and excessive eating, known as hyperphagia, they can consume as many as 20,000 calories in a single 24-hour period.

Do Bears Hibernate?

Depending on the person with whom you talk, bears either "hibernate," "den," "go into winter sleep," or "go into winter lethargy," during the cold months. In the scientific community, a debate is ongoing as to whether the long-favored term "hibernation" most accurately describes bears' period of winter inactivity. *Merriam-Webster* defines hibernation as "passing all or part of the winter in an inactive state in which the body temperature drops and breathing slows." However, some scientists counter that bears don't actually hibernate in the same way that other animals do, because the bears can be aroused easily, and because their body temperatures are not as drastically reduced as those of some other hibernators. What is not up for debate is the fact that bears enter a long period of inactivity in the winter. They do not eat, drink, or pass waste for months, and must survive off of a fat layer built up in the summer and fall. Both male and female black bears enter their dens in late October or early November, when snow and other signs of winter start to appear. In the spring, males emerge in March, while mamas stay put with their cubs until sometime in April. Hibernation, or a long winter nap? You decide.

Mountain Lions

If you find yourself in an area inhabited by deer or elk, chances are fairly good that a mountain lion is lurking somewhere nearby. These two mammals are main food sources for mountain lions (also called cougars). Some people call mountain lions "ghost cats" because they are so rarely seen, but their presence is often felt and solid evidence exists that they are around. Mountain lion scat is an indicator, as are carcasses of deer or elk, and the rare sighting by a visitor or ranger. In the history of the park, there has been one human fatality from a mountain lion; a 10-year-old boy was attacked in 1997 on a hiking trail on the west side of the park. Mountain lions are thought to number 20-30 in Rocky.

Coyotes

One of the many perks of being in Rocky at dawn or at dusk is hearing coyotes' "yips" and "yowls." It is a symphony that happens often, as coyotes have a presence throughout the park. Visitors sometimes note that Rocky's coyotes look "very big," and occasionally mistake them for wolves. While wolves once roamed these lands, they were hunted to extinction around the turn of the 20th century. Rocky's coyotes are presumed to be on the larger side simply because a staple of their diet—small mammals, including ground squirrels, rabbits and chipmunks—are especially abundant in the park. Coyotes typically travel in larger packs, but naturalists have noted that the park's coyotes tend to stick close just with their core family unit. If you are fortunate to spot a whole family of coyotes, it can be great fun to watch their behavior. Moms and dads will teach their young, in very entertaining ways, how to do everything from hunt to howl. The park's many meadows are great places to look for coyotes.

Deer

Mule deer—named for their large ears that resemble those of an actual mule—are found in forests and meadows on both the east and west sides of the park. In the summer, mule deer have red-tinged fur; in the winter, their fur takes on a duller, grayish-brown tone. Year-round, each deer has a black-tipped tail and a white bottom. Only male deer, called bucks, grow antlers. Though deer nearly disappeared from the park in the early 20th century due to overhunting and predation, today, their population hovers around 500 animals. Deer often travel in packs—females and their young group together—and males form their own bachelor packs or travel alone. Much is said about the elk rut in Rocky, but the deer rut—which follows in the late fall—is also quite exciting, with males vying for a female's attention in some of the same ways that elk do, minus the bugling.

Beavers

Though a handful of Rocky's features are named after North America's largest rodent, today, these creatures are largely absent from the park's rivers, streams, lakes, and wetlands. A handful of active beaver lodges have been identified in the Wild Basin area of the park; otherwise, sightings of these toothsome creatures are few and far between. The beaver population is now considered to be in the dozens, not in the hundreds (as it once was). The main reason for the decline: over time, the park's large population of elk have overbrowsed willows, aspens, and other streamside vegetation that are essential parts of the beaver's diet and building material supply. Beavers have a significant impact on the health of entire ecosystems, and their exodus from Rocky over the past 50 years concerns officials. The park staff continues to monitor the local beaver population and is working to restore its wetland habitats.

Pikas

The American pika—which lives only above the tree line in rocky areas—is mouselike in appearance, with rounded ears and grayish-brown fur. Throughout the summer, pikas can

Pikas and Climate Change

Scientists who study climate change are looking closely at pika behavior in Rocky and in seven other national monuments and national parks. The scientists' formal evaluation, called Pikas in Peril, started in 2010. The connection between pikas and climate change becomes crystal clear when you consider that these members of the rabbit family will not survive when exposed to temperatures above 70 degrees Fahrenheit. On hot days, pikas will perish if they cannot quickly find shelter from the heat. However, seeking cooler temperatures means that the animals must temporarily halt their vital food collection and storage activities, which can affect their ability to survive throughout a long winter. Researchers predict that as global temperatures become warmer, pikas will climb higher and higher in the mountains, searching futilely for colder habitat. In a worst-case scenario, warmth could mean extinction for these disarmingly cute, temperature-sensitive creatures. Teams of individuals are closely monitoring common pika habitat and specifically tracking where fecal matter and food piles are found. Evidence from the study is indicating a general decline in pika activity in the park's tundra areas.

be seen scurrying around with a great sense of purpose, often with large amounts of plant material stuffed in their mouths. Pikas must collect food to last them an entire winter, and much of their summertime activity is focused on seeking out and transporting plants. The plants that they collect are gathered into "hay piles," where they dry out in the sun, and are eventually brought into an underground den for storage. When all is said and done, pikas accumulate several pounds of grasses, sedges, and wildflowers to last them throughout the snowy months. The pika is a vocal creature, and frequently emits a high-pitched "eek" noise when a threat is perceived. If you are exploring around Forest Canyon Overlook or at Rock Cut on Trail Ridge Road, chances are good that you will see—or at least hear—a pika. In the winter, pikas thrive below ground in their snow-covered dens, as long as they are amply prepared.

Yellow-Bellied Marmots

Marmots are mostly red-brown in color, with a patch of yellow fur on their front. Like pikas, marmots live in high-elevation areas, including meadows and rock piles. Many people find these members of the squirrel family to be quite endearing, though there are stories of hikers and climbers who have set down their backpacks, hiking boots, or clothing, only to later find them chewed apart by the little guys: they are attracted to the salt in human sweat and urine. Otherwise, the diet of the marmot consists of insects, flowers, and grasses. Marmots plump up before winter, since they are hibernators that spend in the neighborhood of 200 days hunkered down in underground burrows.

Fish

A variety of fish are found in the park, including brook trout, brown trout, rainbow trout, greenback cutthroat trout, Colorado River cutthroat trout, suckers, and sculpin. Fish stocking occurred regularly in and around Rocky from the late 1800s until the mid-1930s, and included depositing fish non-native to the area in the park's waters for recreational purposes. Stocking for recreation finally ceased in 1968; since that time, park managers have focused on preserving and protecting native species.

Birds

Birds are everywhere in Rocky; their delightful chirps, trills, and liquid songs fill the air. More than 280 species of birds have been observed in the park, from delicate hummingbirds to plump wild turkeys. Visitors are often on the lookout for magpies and Steller's Jays, both of which are common in the park—as well as Clark's Nutcrackers. The latter birds have long bills that look sharp enough to open a tin can.

PTARMIGAN

White-tailed ptarmigan are beautiful, but often hard to see unless you carefully scan the landscape. The birds are like feathered Houdinis that masterfully conceal themselves from their predators. In the summer, ptarmigan are gray, white, and brown in appearance, which allows them to blend in with rocks and shrubs. In the fall and spring, ptarmigan plumage is a mixture of mottled brown feathers and white feathers. In the dead of winter, their feathers are snowy white. Ptarmigan live at or above the tree line and must protect themselves from a variety of predators, including raptors and foxes. Rarely will you see ptarmigan airborne; they prefer walking over flying, which makes their ability to hide all the more important. White-tailed ptarmigan mostly subsist on seeds, leaves, insects, buds, and flowers.

BIRDS OF PREY

To witness a bird of prey soaring through the air with its talons gripped tightly around "dinner"—typically a small mammal or fish—is an unforgettable moment. Raptors are alive and well in the park, especially red-tailed hawks, prairie falcons, golden eagles, and peregrine falcons. The park is also home to ospreys, kestrels, and vultures. Each year, the park strictly enforces a bald eagle closure mid-November-mid-March in the vicinity of the Colorado River on the west side of the park to protect birds during their mating and nesting periods. In addition, the park implements raptor-nesting closures along Lumpy Ridge March 1-July 31 each year. Owls also thrive in the park, including boreal owls, great pygmy owls, and great horned owls. In recent years, great horned owls have taken to nesting around the former Cascade Cottages property just inside the Fall River Entrance Station.

Steller's Jay

Butterflies

An extensive research study called the Rocky Mountain Butterfly Project was conducted in the park 1995-2011, during which time 55 volunteers painstakingly inventoried and monitored the activities of regional butterflies. A total of 140 species were identified as existing in Rocky's life zones. Ninety-four of those species are considered permanent residents of the park, while the rest arrive via classic or partial migration. Visitors can spot butterflies at any time of the year in Rocky, but mostly in the summer. Many trails provide a good opportunity for visitors to spot butterflies. Among them are Fern Lake Trail, Cow Creek Trail, Coyote Valley Trail, Lily Lake Trail, and the East Shore Trail below Shadow

Birding Basics

Observing birds' nesting, mating, and feeding activities—and listening to their conversations (sometimes cheerful; other times snarky)—can be fascinating. Following are some tips for newcomers to this popular pastime:

- **Purchase binoculars.** These are an essential investment, and not just any pair will do. Enlist the help of a reputable sporting goods store to make your decision, or consult with Audubon's online bird watching guide (www.audubon.org/birding) for a great list of purchasing pointers.
- **Join a bird walk.** The park regularly offers free, ranger-led bird walks; these programs are a great introduction to the activity. Check the park's newspaper for specifics. Rocky Mountain Conservancy's Field Institute (www.rmconservancy.org) also offers bird programs led by naturalists. The enthusiasm exhibited by seasoned bird watchers is contagious.
- **Pack a birding guide.** Two excellent guides are *The Sibley Field Guide to Birds of Western North America,* by David Allen Sibley, and National Geographic's *Field Guide to the Birds of North America,* by Jon L. Dunn and Jonathan Alderfer. Numerous other regional guides are also available.
- **Download a birding app.** What better way to learn birdcalls than by listening to them over and over? Sibley Guides (www.sibleyguides.com) and Audubon (www.audubon.org) both have birding apps that feature extensive audio recordings.
- **Track your sightings.** Jot down notes about bird sightings on a notepad for future reference. Bird watching checklists can also be purchased at the park's visitor centers.
- **Cup your ears.** Forming a "cup" shape with your hands around the backs of your ears can help you to discern birdcalls.
- **Stay put and be patient.** Tempting as it might be to walk mile after mile looking for birds, a better strategy is to park yourself in one spot. Get to high ground, peer across a tree canopy, and look for birds flitting about. Pay close attention to cavities in dead trees, where nests are commonly built. Listen for peeps and chirps. Sit on a bench near a stream or lake. Wait and they will come.

Mountain Reservoir. Around Rock Cut and on the Tundra Communities Trail, an elusive butterfly called the Magdalena Alpine can be spotted. The Mormon Fritillary is the most common butterfly species seen in Rocky.

Snakes and Spiders

Garter snakes are the only type of snake found in the park. Visitors occasionally mistake Rocky's garters for water moccasin snakes—which are poisonous—because they slither in and out of the water to keep their skin moist. Garters are not poisonous.

Dozens of species of spiders live in Rocky, including wolf, brown recluse, and black widows. Despite their large size and menacing look, wolf spiders are not dangerous. Brown recluse and black widow spiders, however, deliver venomous bites that can result in a myriad of unpleasant symptoms.

History

ENOS MILLS

Enos Mills (1870-1922) is widely credited as the "Father of Rocky Mountain National Park," and deservedly so. The naturalist, author, businessman, and longtime resident of Estes Park had incredible foresight in realizing that one small section of the Rocky Mountain Range was a national treasure that should be conserved. He campaigned tirelessly, more than anyone, to secure federal protection for the land's wildlife and natural resources.

However, Mills did not alone build a case for safeguarding the region's assets. A nationwide focus on conservation—which started in earnest in the mid-1800s and gathered considerable momentum in the early 1900s—laid a solid foundation for his cause. In addition, numerous individuals along the way lent Mills their support, which was essential to the creation of Rocky. As the saying goes, it takes a village to raise a child. It also takes a village to create a national park.

AMERICAN CONSERVATION MOVEMENT

The American Conservation Movement (1847-1920) involved the efforts of many people, including artists, writers, poets, naturalists, activists, and political figures—each of whom recognized the need to protect our nation's most valuable natural assets. Before the movement picked up steam, conservation efforts were haphazard. To most individuals, a seemingly limitless supply of natural resources existed, including water, land, fertile soil, animals, and timber. As early homesteaders migrated west, their thoughts were centered more on abundance and wealth, less or not at all on safeguarding the earth for future generations.

Still, conservationists enjoyed successes. The creation of the American Forestry Association in 1875—with its mission of protecting forests—was one of them. The

Few signs of early homesteads and guest lodges remain around Rocky.

establishment of Yellowstone National Park in 1872 by President Ulysses S. Grant was another.

When Theodore Roosevelt became president in 1901, issues of resource management gained a strong champion. The environment was a cause about which he was passionate and is still remembered for today. While in office, Roosevelt formally protected a staggering 230 million acres of public lands. In 1905, he granted early, limited protection for the region now known as Rocky by including it in what was then called the Medicine Bow Reserve—a large region that included land in both Wyoming and Colorado. However, regulations for Forest Reserves—including the Medicine Bow Reserve—were only loosely enforced, and people still felt largely entitled to the resources on these lands. Minerals, timber, and water were still taken and used at will.

The creation of the United States Forest Service (USFS) in 1905 tightened regulations for Forest Reserves (which were now called National Forests), but the overall management plan for the reserves still wasn't focused enough on conservation to satisfy the desires of Enos Mills and other locals. A body of concerned citizens formed in 1906—The Estes Park Protective and Improvement Association, which would later be instrumental in promoting Rocky.

THE ROCKY MOUNTAIN NATIONAL PARK ACT

In 1908, Enos Mills began advocating for a national park. By that time, he had spent the better part of the last quarter of a century recreating in, studying, observing, writing about, and working in the region that is now known as Rocky. He came up with an ambitious plan to create a game refuge that encompassed 1,000 square miles of land. From then on, Mills directed his energy toward making the refuge a reality. He spoke passionately to audiences, lobbied Congress, and wrote thousands of letters urging people's support. Mills had his work cut out for him, since his plans were met with a good deal of opposition. Some members of the Forest Service weren't keen on the idea of a game refuge, nor were other groups of individuals, who felt that Forest Service regulations already in place sufficed.

Even so, along the way, Mills gained support from a wide variety of people, both locally and across the nation. F. O. Stanley, proprietor of Estes Park's Stanley Hotel, was a good friend of Mills and advocated for the game refuge. Renowned naturalist John Muir, Mills's longtime mentor and friend, also backed him. James Grafton Rogers, founder of the Colorado Mountain Club, promoted the park. Mary Belle King Sherman, a National Federation of Women's Clubs member, had great influence and spoke to women's clubs all over Colorado about the proposed refuge.

In 1910, a bill for the Estes Park National Park and Game Preserve was created. The bill underwent multiple revisions before it was presented to Congress in 1913, and more revisions thereafter. In 1914, after numerous complex issues were ironed out, one last bill was created—and this one was a winner. Congressman Edward Taylor shepherded the bill through the House and Senate, and President Woodrow Wilson officially signed The Rocky Mountain National Park Act into law on January 26, 1915. The 10th national park (and the second national park in Colorado, after Mesa Verde National Park in 1906) was born. In the final bill, the acreage of the park had been whittled down to a mere fraction of what Enos Mills had envisioned. Instead of 1,000 square miles, the new park was to encompass 358.5 square miles. Nonetheless, its passage was considered a triumph for Mills, The Estes Park Protective and Improvement Association, and the bill's many other supporters across the nation. On September 4, 1915, several hundred individuals attended a drizzly ceremony in Horseshoe Park to dedicate Rocky, at which Mills served as the master of ceremonies.

In its first year, visitors could still variously interpret the meaning of a "national park." People could boat, fish, shoot animals, and light a campfire wherever they pleased. In

Rocky's Wilderness Designation

National Parks enjoy a good deal of government protection, but for conservationists, a true sense of security came about in 2009, when 94 percent of Rocky became official designated wilderness. Getting to this point took decades of work. It all started with the Wilderness Act of 1964, which recognized wilderness as "an area of undeveloped Federal land retaining its primeval character and influence without permanent improvements or human habitation, which is protected and managed so as to preserve its natural conditions." From this point, a long and lively discussion/debate/conversation ensued among individuals who were passionate about the park. While some people desired completely pristine and protected land, others found certain human activities and pastimes acceptable for Rocky. President Nixon eventually recommended wilderness protection for the park in 1974. Specifically, he recommended to Congress that 239,835 acres of the park receive wilderness protection under the Wilderness Act of 1964. Though his legislation was not immediately accepted, from that point, park officials managed the land in a manner that was consistent with wilderness protection. Over the years, critical details were ironed out regarding park boundaries and private land ownership.

In 1980, the park acquired a small amount of wilderness through a boundary adjustment. The park's original, legal boundaries were established along section lines—boundary lines that are used in land surveying. If you look at maps from 1915, the park's boundary lines on the north and south went straight across. After Congress approved the boundary adjustment in 1980, the north and south boundaries from there forward were more fluid, following natural features. The park acquired 2,917 acres of land from the U.S. Forest Service on its south end that was designated wilderness.

Closure on the park's proposed (not inherited) wilderness finally occurred March 30, 2009 when President Obama signed the Omnibus Public Lands Management Act, which officially gave Rocky wilderness designation and also protected hundreds of thousands of acres of lands in states across the United States. Today, 252,085 acres of the park are designated wilderness and 360 acres are being considered as potential additions.

1916, President Woodrow Wilson signed into law the National Park Service (NPS), which provides unified management for each one of the national parks, including Rocky.

Over time, many sections of Rocky's land on which people had previously built (predominantly guest lodges and homesteads) were returned to conditions as close as possible to their natural state. From 1933 to 1942, the Civilian Conservation Corps (CCC) worked to improve the park by undertaking a number of projects, including constructing visitor centers, restrooms, and trail systems. Over the years, staff have thoughtfully (but not without controversy) established guidelines for managing wildlife in the park. Today, Rocky is closer to "pristine" than ever, and with the addition of an official wilderness designation for 250,000 acres of the park in 2009, the park is enjoying its highest level of protection in history.

In our ever-changing world, many visitors gain comfort from the consistency that they find year after year in Rocky. They can all but count on spotting elk, and they are reassured that they can enjoy the same mountain views from Moraine Park from one summer to the next. They know that high-rises are never going to crop up along Trail Ridge Road in the Kawuneeche Valley. While Rocky is impeccably preserved, change is still occurring all of the time: in nature and in the park's governance. Preserving and protecting the park's assets will forever be a challenge, but for Rocky's team of employees and supporters, it is a fight worth fighting. If Enos Mills were alive today, surely he would be proud of how far his idea has come.

National Park Service Director Jon Jarvis spoke at Rocky's centennial celebration in 2015.

CENTENNIAL YEAR AND RE-DEDICATION

When Rocky's 100th birthday rolled around in 2015, park officials marked the anniversary with a 365-day celebration. Visitors acknowledged the milestone by plastering their vehicles with Happy Birthday messages, penning love letters to the park on an old typewriter at the Fall River Visitor Center, and uploading thousands of favorite personal snaps to the photo-sharing website Instagram. A birthday party was held on January 26, the anniversary of the date on which Rocky was signed into law as an official national park. The year culminated with a larger rededication ceremony, held at Glacier Basin Campground on September 4. Hundreds of supporters came to hear speakers wax poetic about the park and discuss issues park staff faced going forward. More than once, speakers addressed the need to attract and engage younger visitors. Climate change and the pine beetle epidemic were cited as other areas of concern for the future. Mostly, though, a lighthearted vibe prevailed at the celebration, which included a jovial singalong to "Rocky Mountain High," and generous slices of cake for all who attended.

Shortly after the ceremony ended, the meadow was transformed from a formal-looking event site back into wilderness once again; sprinkles fell from ominous-looking skies and a single elk appeared from nowhere, checking out the scene as people dispersed. Attendees left feeling inspired by the park's many treasures, and assured that Rocky was a gift that would keep on giving: so long as its visitors, volunteers, staff, and financial supporters keep giving back.

Essentials

Getting There

SUGGESTED DRIVING ROUTES

From Denver to Estes Park

HIGHWAY 36
58 MILES / 1.5 HOURS

Highway 36 is the shortest route to the park from downtown Denver. Starting at the junction of I-70 and I-25 in Denver, take I-25 north for 3.2 miles and exit on Highway 36. Travel northwest on Highway 36, passing by several suburbs before arriving in the town of Boulder (20 mi). In Boulder, the highway becomes 28th Street, and is lined on both sides with housing, shops, and hotels. As the road heads farther north, the bustle of big city living is left behind and a rural landscape unfolds. There are fewer cars on this stretch (15 mi) to the small town of Lyons, but often many bicycles. Keep a close watch for cyclists and take good care while passing them. From Lyons—which made national news in 2013 for being heavily impacted by the region's 100-year flood—it is 20 more miles on Highway 36 to Estes Park. (From Lyons you can also take Highway 7 to Estes Park; the route parallels the St. Vrain Creek and is quite scenic, but several miles longer.) From downtown Estes Park, Highway 36 continues for 3.9 miles to the Beaver Meadows Entrance Station and ends at Deer Ridge Junction inside the park. This spot is the westernmost point of the highway, which spans 1,414 miles from Colorado to Ohio. The drive time for this 58-mile, one-way route is 1.5 hours with no traffic or weather delays.

HIGHWAY 66
68 MILES / 1.5 HOURS

Highway 66 is another option for traveling to Estes Park from Denver. From the intersection of I-70 and I-25 in downtown Denver, take I-25 north for 29.8 miles, then drive west on Highway 66. For part of the drive along Highway 66, you will travel along the northern boundary of the city of Longmont. The scenery is otherwise mostly rural. At approximately 14.4 miles, in the town of Lyons, Highway 66 turns into Highway 36. Continue 20 more miles west from Lyons to downtown Estes Park, then another 3.9 miles to the Beaver Meadows Entrance Station. This route is approximately 68 miles one-way. The views along the major thoroughfare of I-25 are less appealing than that along Highway 36, but the I-25 speed limit is higher. Travel time to the park on this route is around 1.5 hours with no delays.

PEAK-TO-PEAK SCENIC BYWAY
93 MILES / 2 HOURS

If you are in no particular hurry to get to the park, the hour-and-a-half drive along the 55-mile Peak-to-Peak Scenic Byway—Colorado's oldest scenic byway—is a real gem. As a one-time resident of the town of Boulder, I dipped in and out of this highway many times for outdoor adventures. But it wasn't until much later that I drove the whole road from tip to tail and discovered how many interesting spots there are to explore. The road is fun to drive, with lots of wide curves and great views, but be sure to keep your speed in check; the limit mostly fluctuates between 35 mph and 45 mph.

From the junction of I-70 and I-25 in Denver, drive approximately 12 miles west on I-70 to Highway 6. Take Highway 6 for 4 miles northwest to Golden; then continue an additional 11.5 miles west on Highway 6 to Highway 119. Once on Highway 119, drive approximately 7.2 miles northwest to Blackhawk/Central City. The Peak-to-Peak

Previous: a birthday cake for Rocky's centennial celebration; Union Station in Denver.

Scenic Byway officially begins in Black Hawk/Central City, two adjoining historic towns that are full of gambling spots. Heading farther north, approximately 5 miles from the casinos, you will pass Golden Gate Canyon Road, which provides access to Golden Gate Canyon State Park (located to the east). Gap Road, which is 3.2 miles farther north on Highway 119, also provides access to Golden Gate Canyon State Park, which is a great spot for camping and hiking. In 5 miles, don't blink, or you might miss the tiny community of Rollinsville, which has a population that hovers around 200. If you are interested in an aerobic warm-up before getting to Rocky Mountain National Park (RMNP), head 8 miles west on County Road 16/East Portal Road in Rollinsville to the East Portal Trailhead, which leads to a handful of enjoyable and challenging hiking trails. Next up, in approximately 4.8 miles, arrive at laidback and funky Nederland, which has a quaint downtown and several lodging options. Eldora Mountain Resort, a great small ski mountain, is 4.2 miles west of Nederland (take Hwy. 130 to Shelf Rd.). To keep traveling along the Peak-to-Peak without a detour, continue north on Highway 72; in approximately 11 miles you will reach the old gold mining town of Ward. For another side trip, consider driving 4.6 miles west on Brainard Lake Rd. to the Brainard Lake Recreation Area. The area is a snowshoeing/cross-country ski destination in the winter and a hiking hot spot in the summer. Otherwise, take Highway 72 for another 10.6 miles to Highway 7, then travel west for 4.3 miles to the community of Allenspark. Approximately 15 miles later you will arrive at the junction of Highway 7 and Highway 36 in Estes Park, which is the end point of the Peak-to-Peak Byway.

From Denver to Grand Lake
102 MILES / 2-3 HOURS

The trip from Denver to Grand Lake, which is 102 miles long, can take more time than you might expect. In the winter, and especially on weekends, I-70 routinely becomes clogged with traffic because it is the main thoroughfare for many of Colorado's ski resorts. In the summer, when urbanites flock to the mountains for weekend getaways, westbound traffic on I-70 can be slow moving on Friday night and Saturday morning; eastbound traffic to Denver on Sunday afternoon and evening can be equally heavy.

This route begins in downtown Denver at the intersection of I-70 and I-25. Travel west on I-70 for 41 miles—past the old gold mining town of Idaho Springs—before taking the exit for US 40 to Empire/Granby. After passing the tiny town of Empire, the route, which is also known as Berthoud Pass, starts to become windy and climbs in elevation, with numerous switchbacks. In the winter, the road can become slick with ice, and avalanches are also possible. Closures or restrictions may be in effect on the road; it is smart to check in with the **Colorado Department of Transportation** (CDOT) (www.cotrip.org) before embarking on this route.

With an abundance of backcountry skiing located in the mountains around US 40, in the winter you are likely to see skiers or snowboarders on the side of the road hitching rides back to their cars after a run. In all seasons, the views up this high—11,307 feet at its uppermost point—are incredibly scenic. Fourteen miles north on US 40, you will reach the Berthoud Pass Trailhead, which is located on the Continental Divide. This area is popular for hiking in the summer and backcountry skiing in the winter. Continue north, and you will arrive at Winter Park Ski Resort, 24 miles up US 40. In another 5 miles, after driving through the town of Fraser, leave the busy ski resort scene behind and travel 4 miles to another speck of a community, Tabernash, before heading on to Granby. From Granby, it is another 14.5 miles (about a 20-minute drive) to Grand Lake and the west-side entrance of the park. Total drive time for the entire route, one-way, is two hours in optimal conditions.

TRAVEL HUB: DENVER

Air

The majority of people traveling to the Denver area by plane fly into **Denver International Airport** (DEN, 8500 Peña Blvd. 303/342-2000, www.flydenver.com). The airport, commonly referred to as DIA, is served by 18 airlines and features many restaurants, shops, and services. On-site is the 519-room, 35-suite **Westin Denver International Hotel** (8300 Peña Blvd., 303/317-1800, www.westindenverairport.com, starting at $300), as well as a rail station that transports passengers to Denver's downtown transit hub, Union Station (1701 Wynkoop St., www.unionstationindenver.com). The most reasonable options for traveling to RMNP from the airport are (1) renting a car at the airport, (2) scheduling a pick-up by the Estes Park Shuttle, or (3) scheduling transportation to Grand Lake with Home James shuttle. The distance from the airport to Estes Park is 75 miles, which translates to approximately 1.5 hours of driving. The distance from the airport to Grand Lake when Trail Ridge Road is not open is 126 miles, or approximately 2 hours and 40 minutes of driving. When Trail Ridge Road is open, it is 122 miles to Grand Lake via Estes Park (2 hours and 25 minutes of driving).

Train and Bus

At Denver's **Union Station** (1701 Wynkoop St., www.unionstationindenver.com), you can catch a *California Zephyr* **Amtrak** (800/872-7245, www.amtrak.com, from $36 one-way) train and ride it to the Amtrak Station in Granby (438 Railroad Ave.). The train leaves Denver once daily at 8:05am and arrives in Granby at 10:37am. For the return trip to Denver, catch the Amtrak in Granby at 3:12pm and arrive in Denver at 6:38pm. There is no Amtrak service to Estes Park.

Greyhound (1055 19th St., Denver, 800/231-2222, www.greyhound.com, starting at $21 one-way) offers bus service from Denver to Granby once daily, with no transfers. The bus departs at 9:35am, arriving at a Shell gas station (516 E. Agate Ave.) in Granby at 11:45am. Trips from Granby to Denver leave the Shell station once daily at 5:25pm, arriving in Denver at 7:35pm. From Granby, you will need to arrange transportation to Grand Lake and the park. Greyhound does not operate buses to Estes Park.

To get to Grand Lake from Granby, you can rent a car from **Avalanche Car Rentals** (888/437-4101, www.avscars.com), or arrange a pick-up with **Valley Taxi** (970/726-4940, www.valleytaxiinc.com). The taxi service provides transportation throughout Grand Valley, including Grand Lake. Call at least 24 hours ahead to make a reservation.

Shuttles

The **Estes Park Shuttle** (1805 Cherokee Dr., Estes Park, 970/586-5151 www.estesparkshuttle.com, year-round, $85 round trip; $45 one-way; children 2 and under are free) offers transportation between Estes Park and Denver International Airport (DIA). The shared-ride shuttle takes people to their destination of choice in Estes Park. (The service also provides pick-ups and drop-offs at the Amtrak and Greyhound stations in Denver during non-rush hour times). In the high season—May 1-Oct.1—departures from Estes Park are at 5am, 7am, 10am, 1pm, 4pm, and 7pm; departures from the airport are at 8am, 10am, 1pm, 4pm, 7pm, and 10pm. In the low season—Oct. 2-Apr. 30—departures from Estes Park are at 7am, 10am, 1pm, and 4pm; departures from the airport are at 10am, 1pm, 4pm, and 7pm. Passengers who wish to leave at other times can arrange for a charter, but the price is steep, starting at $165; private four-hour tours of RMNP can also be arranged with the service for $59 per person. Shuttles consistently book up in the summer. However, in arranging shuttles for family members, I have learned that cancellations happen often. If you need a ride, it is worth calling back several times to see if a seat has freed up at the last minute.

Home James (800/359-7536, www.homejamestransporation.com, $95 pp adults, $47.50 pp children 11 and under) shuttles visitors from Grand Lake to DIA (and the other way around) year-round. In the summer, shuttles depart three times a day from Grand Lake (5:45am, 8:45am, 12:45pm). In the winter, there is one departure each day from Grand Lake (8:45am). Advance reservations are recommended.

Tours

If Denver or Boulder will be your home base during a visit, a handful of tour operators offer day or overnight trips.

DENVER

The **Colorado Sightseer** (7290 Samuel Dr., Suite 150, Denver, 303/423-8200, www.coloradosightseer.com, departs downtown Denver daily at 8:15am Memorial Day-mid-Oct., $95 pp age 5 and up, mid-Oct.-Memorial Day, $85 pp age 5 and up, children under age 5 ride for free year-round) offers 8-hour bus tours to Rocky year-round. The summer tour includes a trek up Trail Ridge Road.

Grayline Tours (1835 Gaylord St., Denver, 800/472-9546, www.grayline.com, starting at $125 pp) takes visitors from Denver to the west side of the park for sightseeing tours four days a week, from the end of May through the end of September.

BOULDER

For active-minded individuals, **The World Outdoors** (2840 Wilderness Pl., Suite D, Boulder, 800/488-8483, www.theworldoutdoors.com) has two excellent tour options. The five-day, four-night Rocky Mountain Hiker ($1,998 pp) trip features four days of hiking in the park and includes accommodations in Grand Lake and Estes Park. The Rocky Mountain Multisport ($2,398 pp) tour includes two days of hiking in the park, as well as biking, rock climbing, and rafting in nearby locations; overnight stays at lodges and inns are part of the package. Both tours depart from Boulder.

Colorado Wilderness Rides and Guides (4865 Darwin St., Boulder, 720/242-9828, www.coloradowildernessridesandguides.com) offers full-day, educational sightseeing trips ($165 pp) on the east side of the park. Pick-up locations are in Denver, Boulder, and Estes Park. The tour operator also offers hiking day trips to a variety of locations in Rocky ($120 pp).

Car Rental

Ten car rental companies are located at Denver International Airport: **Advantage** (720/324-2260, www.advantage.com), **Alamo** (877/222-9075, www.alamo.com), **Avis** (303/342-5500, www.avis.com), **Budget** (800/537-0700, www.budget.com), **Dollar** (303/317-0598, www.dollar.com), **E-Z** (800/277-5171, www.e-zrentacar.com), **Enterprise** (800/261-7331, www.enterprise.com), **Fox** (800/225-4369, www.foxrentacar.com), **Hertz** (800/654-3131, www.hertz.com), **National** (877/222-9058, www.nationalcar.com), **Payless** (800/729-5377, www.paylesscar.com), and **Thrifty** (800/367-2277, www.thrifty.com).

Enterprise, Avis, and **Budget** also have outlets in Boulder. **Avalanche Car Rentals** (888/437-4101, www.avscars.com) will deliver a rental car free of charge to any location in east Grand County.

RV Rental

Numerous RV rental agencies are located in Denver. Family-owned **B&B RV, Inc.** (6960 Smith Rd., 303/322-6013, www.bb-rv.com), is the closest to the airport at roughly 20 minutes away, and has a fleet of more than 65 vehicles for rent. RVs run $260-350 per day. No vehicle in the fleet is more than three years old. **Cruise America** (8950 Federal Blvd., 877/784-3733 or 303/650-2865), also in Denver, has approximately 160 vehicles in its fleet. Cruise America's RVs—which are particularly popular with international travelers—are commonly seen around the park. On **RVShare** (www.rvshare.com), private RV owners rent out their rigs.

Equipment Rental

Outdoors Geek (4431 Glencoe St., Denver, 303/699-6944, www.outdoorsgeek.com)

is located about 20 minutes from Denver International Airport, just south of I-70. The shop's rental inventory includes name-brand backpacking and camping gear in pristine condition, with the option to buy what you fall in love with, and return what you don't. The shop will also ship via UPS to lodges and hotels, but just make sure that whoever you ship the gear to is aware of your plans. Shipping to a UPS store is another option, but sometimes the store will tack on an extra charge for package pick-ups. Again, call ahead so that there are no surprises. Outdoors Geek also rents bear canisters—which are required for camping at any of Rocky's wilderness campsites located below the tree line during the summer—and is the only place I have found in the Denver/Boulder area that rents Global Positioning System (GPS) units.

TRAVEL HUB: GRAND JUNCTION

While there are no luxury hotels in Grand Junction, there are plenty of moderately priced, comfortable hotels, inns, and bed-and-breakfasts from which to choose. **The Historic Melrose Hotel** (337 Colorado Ave., 970/242-9636, www.historicmelrosehotel.com, $30) is the thriftiest lodging option; a bed in the hostel section of the hotel is a favorite place for Amtrak travelers to crash. Downtown Grand Junction also has a number of restaurants and cafés.

Car

Grand Junction is the biggest city in western Colorado. The drive from Grand Junction to Grand Lake is approximately 256 miles long and takes roughly 4 hours and 20 minutes in normal traffic conditions. From downtown Grand Junction, take I-70 east. Here you will stay for 169 miles, minus any detours of your choosing. If you have time, a stop-off in Palisade—just 15 miles east of Grand Junction—is worthwhile; the town is known for its spectacular peaches in the summer and numerous family-run wineries. Eighty-eight miles from Grand Junction, Glenwood Springs—home to the world's largest hot springs pool (www.hotspringspool.com)—is also worth exploring. Otherwise, after passing the town of Frisco on I-70, take exit 205 toward Silverthorne/Dillon and head northwest on County Road 9 for 37 miles to the town of Kremmling. Then, take U.S. Highway 40 for 26.6 miles into Granby. Driving 14.5 miles northeast on Highway 34 will take you to Grand Lake.

Air

The **Grand Junction Regional Airport** (GJT, 2828 Walker Field Dr., Grand Junction, 970/244-9100, www.gjairport.com) is served by Allegiant Air, American, Delta, United, and US Airways.

Train

There is no direct route from Grand Junction to Rocky via train, but traveling by **Amtrak** (800/872-7245, www.amtrak.com) to Granby will get you close. The eastbound *California Zephyr* departs daily from the Grand Junction Station (339 S. 1st St.) at 10:23am and arrives in Granby (438 Railroad Ave.) at 3:12pm, barring any delays (delays are common). Granby is approximately 20 minutes away from the west entrance of the park, so additional transportation (taxi or car rental) must be arranged.

Bus and Shuttles

Greyhound (230 S. 5th St., Grand Junction, 800/231-2222 or 970/242-6012, www.greyhound.com) travels from Grand Junction to Granby, which is approximately 20 minutes away from Grand Lake. The journey is long: 9.5 hours with a two-hour stopover in Denver. Be prepared for anything when taking the bus, including cancellations and delays. It is always best to adopt a 'go with the flow' attitude when taking the bus. After arriving in Granby, you can take **Valley Taxi** (970/726-4940, www.valleytaxiinc.com) to Grand Lake, or rent a car from **Avalanche Car Rentals** (888/437-4101, www.avscars.com), which will deliver your car free of charge.

Northwest Colorado 360-Mile Loop Tour

Rocky Mountain National Park, Estes Park, and Grand Lake are part of an established driving tour that highlights the best of Northern Colorado. The tour includes three scenic byways: **Trail Ridge Road Scenic Byway** (48 mi), **Cache la Poudre – North Park Scenic and Historic Byway** (101 mi), and the **Colorado River Headwaters Scenic and Historic Byway** (69 mi). The Cache la Poudre River National Heritage Area (45 mi) is also part of the loop. The driving tour takes 2-3 days to drive, and that is without extended stopovers. If you have time on your hands, an itinerary of one or many weeks can be created using this route as the framework. Start the tour in any town, and travel either clockwise or counterclockwise around the loop. A map of the tour and suggestions for what to do along the way can be found at www.northcoloradolooptour.com.

American Spirit Shuttle (970/523-7662, www.americanspiritshuttle.com) provides transportation from Grand Junction to Grand Lake. The shuttle service has a variety of vehicles—including Suburbans, vans, and buses—to accommodate groups of various sizes. Rates vary depending on the group size, vehicle, and requested itinerary. For multi-day trips, in addition to paying a day rate, passengers might be requested to cover the cost of a hotel room for the driver.

Car Rental

Most major car rental companies have one or more locations in Grand Junction. At the airport, find **Alamo** (970/243-3097 or 800/462-5266, www.alamo.com), **Hertz** (970/243-0747 or 800/654-3131, www.hertz.com), **National Car Rental** (970/243-6626 or 800/227-7368, www.nationalcar.com), **Enterprise** (970/254-1700, www.enterprise.com), and **Avis/Budget** (970/244-9170 www.avis.com, www.budget.com). Avis and Budget have secondary outlets at the **Sears Auto Center** in the Mesa Mall (2424 Hwy. 6 and Hwy. 50).

RV Rental

Family-owned **Funshares RV and Sport Rentals** (2583 Hwy. 6 and Hwy. 50, Grand Junction, 970/241-2702, www.funshares.com) has a dozen motor homes and camper trailers to rent at any given time; units vary in size and amenities and start at $130 a day. A second option is to rent a privately owned RV or trailer through **RVShare** (www.rvshare.com).

Equipment Rental

Colorado Mesa University's Outdoor Program (1100 North Ave., Grand Junction, 970/248-1428, www.coloradomesa.edu/op, daily, 9am-5pm) has a superb inventory of outdoor equipment that can be rented by the general public. Sleeping bags, camp kitchen supplies, tents, backpacks, and more are all reasonably priced and rented by the day. The program also rents out climbing and boating gear, snow sports equipment, and bikes. Reservations are recommended for equipment; a $5 fee to hold gear is deducted from the total bill. Various other outdoor retailers in the area rent bikes, boats, and snow sports equipment, but the university is the best one-stop shop.

Getting Around

CAR

The speed limit on park roads ranges 25-35 mph, with the exception of one-way Old Fall River Road, which has a posted speed limit of 15 mph.

Most park roads are open and plowed year-round. Trail Ridge Road closes from the Colorado River Trailhead on the west side of the park to Many Parks Curve on the east side of the park mid- to late October-Memorial Day weekend each year. Old Fall River Road is only open to vehicles early July-mid-October. Sometimes, Old Fall River Road will close early for the season if maintenance needs to be performed.

Other winter road closures on the east side include Upper Beaver Meadows Road, a portion of Fern Lake Road (starting at the Fern Lake Bus Stop and ending at the Fern Lake Trailhead) and the Twin Sisters Trailhead access road. Wild Basin Road is unplowed for a 1-mile stretch: from the winter trailhead parking area to the summer trailhead parking lot. Endovalley Road closes at the West Alluvial Fan parking lot.

On the west side, the short access road to the Coyote Valley Trailhead is closed in the winter, but visitors can still get to the trailhead on snowshoes.

Some smaller service roads in the park might not be plowed immediately after a snowstorm.

In the summer, park officials will—at their discretion—temporarily close off access to several corridors when roads become too congested and parking lots become full. Closures can take effect on Bear Lake Road (near the William Allen White cabins), on Wild Basin Road at the winter parking area, and Old Fall River Road at the start of the road. To avoid getting turned around on the way to a trailhead, plan for an early start. Between 10am and 3pm is when the park sees its highest volume of visitors each day. Weekends are busier than weekdays.

Upper Beaver Meadows Road can close temporarily in the summer when there is an emergency; a helicopter landing pad in the vicinity is utilized by first responders.

Utility task vehicles (UTVs) and all-terrain vehicles (ATVs) cannot be used in the park.

All visitors to Rocky need to park their vehicles in designated parking spots only. The park has, in recent times, seen an uptick in people parking on vegetation, or making their own parking spot, which is strictly verboten. If you are driving a car, truck, or motorcycle, do not park in spots designated for RVs.

For information about road closures, check online (www.nps.gov/romo), or call the **Trail Ridge Road status line** (970/586-1222). The **Colorado Division of Transportation** (303/639-1111, www.cotrip.org) is useful when traveling to and from the park.

If you would like a preview of the traffic situation at Rocky on any given day, check out the park's **Fall River Entrance** and **Beaver Meadows Entrance webcams** (www.nps.gov/romo).

Driving Concerns

WEATHER

Even at the height of summer, winterlike weather can swoop in with little warning, and vehicle travel can become hazardous. On Trail Ridge Road, especially, drivers might find themselves challenged by high winds, whiteout conditions, hail, or heavy rain. If this is the case during your travels, consider temporarily stopping in a parking lot or pullout to wait out foul weather, as it could leave just as fast as it came. Travel in the park with plenty of gas in your vehicle, a good set of wiper blades, and a box stocked with emergency supplies. Do not count on having cell phone service, because it is intermittent and sometimes nonexistent in the park. A four-wheel drive vehicle or snow tires are recommended—but not required—for winter travel in and around Rocky.

WILDLIFE

Remember defensive driving from driver's education? You might need to call on those skills in Rocky. It is common for visitors to pull off to the side of the road with one swift (and often unexpected) movement in an attempt to gain a better glimpse of wildlife. Sometimes, in the excitement of spotting a furry creature, people will stop their vehicle right in the *middle* of a road, which is especially hazardous. Use caution in navigating around vehicles, and keep a close eye out for individuals who might dash across the road to snap a picture.

When attempting to view wildlife yourself, always consider the safety of people, bicycle riders, and wildlife in close proximity to you. Pull over slowly and carefully, use your turn signal, and use established pullouts. Stay at least 25 yards away from animals. Bears in particular should be given more space (100 yards is recommended).

If an animal is crossing the road, give it the time and space to get across (make sure the animal doesn't feel cornered by cars and/or people).

Strict "no stopping" rules apply on Highway 34 near Sheep Lakes on the east side of the park.

Also, from September 1 through the end of October, visitors are not allowed to venture off certain roadways or trails on foot during the annual elk rut. On the east side, during the elk rut, foot traffic is not allowed 5pm-7am around Horseshoe Park, Upper Beaver Meadows, and Moraine Park. On the west side, leaving the roadway 5pm-7am at Harbison Meadows or entering the meadow next to Holzwarth Historic Site is forbidden.

VAPOR LOCK

Vehicles in otherwise good condition sometimes go "kaput" on Trail Ridge Road, Old Fall River Road, and at other locations around the park. The culprit is a phenomenon called vapor lock. When the fuel line to a vehicle's engine becomes hot, gas can turn into vapor, causing the vehicle to stall. Older cars traveling at high elevations are especially prone to vapor lock, particularly on hot days. I experienced vapor lock on one occasion while driving a 1991 Toyota Land Cruiser over Trail Ridge Road on a summer day. My vehicle stalled at least once during the trip, and I felt like it might stop working altogether. After coming back down in elevation, I released the gas cap and droplets of fuel sprayed out forcefully for at least five seconds. It took some research to figure out what was the culprit.

To prevent vapor lock, setting off on your journey with a full tank of gas can help. If you feel like you are in trouble while driving around the park, you can pull over and release your car's gas cap (keeping your face and your entire body clear, in case of spray), or try restarting your car with your foot depressing the gas pedal all the way to the floor. Pulling off the road and turning your car off for 30 minutes or longer might help, too. In a worst-case scenario, a car that has been affected by vapor lock might need to be towed.

Gas

There are no gas stations within the park boundaries, so plan on filling up in Grand Lake or Estes Park. If driving to or from the park via Highway 7, note that between Estes Park and the town of Lyons, gas stations are nonexistent. There is a sign at the turnoff for Allenspark (along Highway 7) indicating that gas, food, and lodging are around the corner, but only the food and lodging parts are accurate. Plan accordingly.

Maps

Rocky's free park map—available at entrance stations, visitor centers, ranger stations, and online (www.nps.gov/romo) —clearly outlines major roads in the park and is sufficient for most travelers. For extended travel around Colorado, consider investing in a *Colorado*

Atlas and Gazetteer from DeLorme ($19.95). Outdoorsy Coloradans consider this map book essential for getting around; it offers excellent topographic maps and detailed information about hiking, biking, scenic drives, campgrounds, mountain passes, and natural features throughout the state.

SHUTTLE BUSES

From late June through October, three different shuttle bus routes provide transport around the heavily visited Bear Lake region of the park. One shuttle picks up passengers as far away as the Estes Park Visitor Center. The shuttle system is easy to use and reliable, and essential for getting to the always-packed Bear Lake parking lot in the busy summer months. Maps are posted at trailheads and visitor centers.

Hiker Shuttle Express Route

The **Hiker Shuttle Express Route** (7:30am-8pm daily late June-early Sept., 7:30am-8pm Sat.-Sun. mid-Sept.-early Oct.) stops at the Estes Park Visitor Center, the Beaver Meadows Visitor Center, and the Park & Ride. The bus runs hourly from 7:30am-11am and 6pm-8pm, and on the half-hour from 11am-6pm.

Moraine Park Route

The **Moraine Park Route** (7am-7:30pm daily late May-early Oct., every 30 min) stops at the Park & Ride, Glacier Basin Campground, Glacier Creek Stables, Hollowell Park, Tuxedo Park, Moraine Park Discovery Center, Moraine Park Campground, Cub Lake Trailhead, and the Fern Lake Bus Stop.

Bear Lake Route

The **Bear Lake Route** (7am-7:30pm daily late May-early October, every 15 min) serves the popular Bear Lake corridor. Stops include the Park & Ride, Glacier Creek Stables, Bierstadt Lake Trailhead, Glacier Gorge Trailhead, and Bear Lake.

RV TRAVEL

Millions of people each year take a recreational vehicle on the road for the quintessential family vacation. Pop-up trailers and motor homes are omnipresent in Rocky, and one only needs to witness dozens of them lined up at the **Elk Meadow Lodge & RV Resort** (1665 Hwy. 66, 970/586-5342, www.elkmeadowrv.com)—just 0.5 mile away from the Beaver Meadows Visitor Center—to understand how popular they really are. A few

Free shuttles transport visitors to Bear Lake in the summer.

considerations should be made before embarking on an RV trip.

Driving and Parking

Most of the park's 120 miles of road are suitable for RVs; however, they are not allowed on Old Fall River Road. RVs are allowed to travel the length of Trail Ridge Road, though navigating a bulky vehicle on this high-elevation, curving thoroughfare can be nerve-wracking, especially for those who have rented an RV and are still getting the hang of things. Parking lots for hiking trails fill up fast and do not have spaces large enough for RVs. At the park's visitor centers and the Park & Ride, a handful of RV parking spaces are available (though sometimes, people will park their cars in these spots, which can be frustrating). In the summer, visitors to the east side should consider parking their RV at the Estes Park Visitor Center (500 Big Thompson Ave.) and taking the Hiker Shuttle Express into the park.

If you plan on camping in the park or staying at an RV park in Estes Park or Grand Lake, tow a smaller vehicle to use when ease of travel is needed.

Campgrounds

RV and trailer length limits vary for the park's campgrounds. On the east side, Aspenglen's B and C loops have an RV and trailer length limit of 30 feet. On the west side, the maximum length limit for RVs at Timber Creek Campground is 30 feet. At Glacier Basin Campground, the RV and trailer length limit is 35 feet; the Glacier Basin Group Site does not allow RVs. Moraine Park can accommodate RVs and trailers up to 40 feet in length. RVs are not allowed at the Longs Peak Campground. Outside the park, numerous campgrounds in Estes Park and Grand Lake welcome RVs.

The park's RV sites do not have individual hook-ups, and some generator restrictions apply. At Aspenglen Campground, generators are allowed only in the C loop. At Moraine Park Campground, visitors cannot use generators in the D loop.

Dump stations and potable water hookups are provided at Moraine Park Campground, Glacier Basin Campground, and Timber Creek Campground. Numerous RV Parks in Estes Park and Grand Lake have disposal stations.

Recreation

CAMPING

Spending the night at one of Rocky's campgrounds is like temporarily moving into a new neighborhood, with new faces and new rules to abide by. To stay on good terms with those neighbors, consider following these guidelines:

- Keep bear box items clean and organized. Though you might find an empty bear box upon arrival, chances are that someone will be sharing it with you before you leave. Make sure that your cooler's drain valve is secured before stowing it, or you might unknowingly water-log your neighbor's (and your own) dry goods.
- As you travel back and forth from a shared bear box for each meal, take care not to tromp through your neighbor's outdoor living space. If you are arriving at a campsite late-night, stow items as quietly as possible.
- Random acts of kindness go far in the campground. I have been offered everything from next-to-new canvas camp chairs to bags of oranges from travelers who were flying home after a stay at a campground. If you have something leftover, consider offering it to your neighbor. One of the easiest ways to pay it forward is by leaving any leftover firewood stacked neatly near your fire grate.

- Know and observe rules regarding quiet hours, pets, and generator use.
- If you see someone dismantling their tent and you would like to take over their space for the next night, ask politely and then give them the time and space to finish packing. Their tent pad is theirs to occupy until noon, the standard check out time for all of Rocky's campgrounds.
- Leave your campsite looking better than you found it.
- Use the campground's restrooms. Every time. Enough said.

HIKING

As you enjoy the park, always remember that what you do in Rocky affects one or many people. Pay attention to park signs, take extra care to Leave No Trace, and keep your favorite music to yourself.

Trail Safety

HIKING IN GROUPS

Whenever possible, hike in a twosome or small group. On Rocky's 355 miles of hiking trails, anything can happen, and for safety reasons it is wise to use the buddy system. Should an injury or nasty weather event occur out on the trail, you will be grateful to have a set of helping hands. Studies have shown that wildlife rarely approach or attack groups of hikers, and groups naturally make more noise through conversation and footsteps to scare off wildlife than individuals do. If you do choose to hike alone, leave your earbuds and iPod behind. Don't be afraid to sing a song or talk out loud to alert animals of your approach.

Solo travelers might want to consider joining a ranger-led hike to establish safety in numbers. Times and dates for these hikes are listed in Rocky's newspaper, which is handed out for free at entrance stations and available at any visitor center. For more options, join a hike led by the **Rocky Mountain Conservancy** (48 Alpine Cir., 970/586-0108, www.rmconservancy.org), by a commercial guide service, or join a hiking group through **Meetup** (www.meetup.com).

CORSAR

Good health insurance is key in the event that you have an accident in the park. Coloradans who are highly active outdoors carry with them a **Colorado Outdoor Recreation Search and Rescue Card** (CORSAR). Should you become lost, stranded, or seriously injured in the park, a Search and Rescue (SAR) team will likely come to your aid. People who are rescued are not required to reimburse these teams for costs incurred in the SAR mission. Therefore, it is considered good karma—and good outdoor ethics—to buy a CORSAR card, which contributes to a fund that covers the expenses for rescuers. The fund does not pay for medical transport via helicopter or ambulance. Both visitors and residents of Colorado can purchase a CORSAR card online at www.colorado.gov. The card costs $3 for one year and $12 for five years.

COMMUNICATION

Let someone know your hiking itinerary, whether you are traveling solo or with someone else. Get in touch with a friend or family member while in cell phone range, or leave a note in your vehicle detailing your travel plans, along with emergency contact information. In the event that you become lost or injured in the park, someone will know that you haven't returned on schedule and can put the wheels in motion to figure out why.

Cell phone coverage in the park is spotty or nonexistent at times; however, many calls have gone through with persistence by the user. Become familiar with the location of Rocky's emergency phones: the Longs Peak Trailhead, Twin Owls at Lumpy Ridge, Cow Creek Trailhead, Lawn Lake Trailhead, Park & Ride, Bear Lake Trailhead, and Wild Basin Trailhead, as well as Timber Creek, Aspenglen and Glacier Basin Campgrounds.

Invest in a **SPOT satellite messenger device** (www.findmespot.com) so you can stay in contact with others while hiking in the park, and alert rescue teams in case of an emergency; cell phone service is not needed to use the device.

The Ten Essentials

A number of "ten essentials" lists exist and are used by hiking and scouting groups around the world. **The Mountaineers** (www.mountaineers.org) developed the first list in the 1930s, and I recommend the organization's updated version, which was released in 2003. The "ten essentials" were created with hiker safety in mind and address two questions: (1) are you equipped to respond to a backcountry emergency? (2) can you spend the night outside? The short answer to both questions is that you will be, if you carry the right equipment and—more important—know how to use it. Make some space in your daypack for these necessities:

- **Navigation:** A complimentary map is provided to visitors of the park. For greater depth and detail, consider purchasing a waterproof topographic map. If you know how to navigate with a compass, pack it. A Global Positioning System (GPS) unit with fully charged batteries can be very helpful but should not be considered a substitute for good navigation skills.
- **Sun Protection:** The sun in Rocky feels—and is—much more intense than what you will experience at sea level. Don a pair of sunglasses, and before any outing slather on sunscreen with both UVA and UVB protection. Those with extra-sensitive skin might want to purchase hiking clothes rated by ultraviolet protection factor (UPF), found at many outdoor retail shops. Top your head with a wide-brimmed hat or baseball cap.
- **Insulation:** Wear wicking, non-cotton clothes, and pack additional layers made of synthetic fabric. A sweat-soaked cotton shirt or pair of pants takes a long time to dry out, and under the right set of circumstances can contribute to a case of hypothermia (and can just be plain uncomfortable). Bring along a rain jacket, rain pants, a warm layer made of wool or fleece, a knit cap, and a spare pair of socks.
- **Illumination:** If dusk turns to night in a big hurry, you'll be glad you have a headlamp or compact flashlight. Keep it loaded with fresh batteries, and bring along some spares.
- **First-Aid Supplies:** Scrapes, blisters, and bee stings are just several minor medical events that can occur on a day hike. Be prepared for minor and major emergencies with a well-stocked first-aid kit. The **National Outdoor Leadership School** (NOLS) (www.nols.edu) has great ready-made kits in a variety of sizes ($14-85), or you can assemble your own. Know how to use everything in your kit, and consider taking a Wilderness First Aid or Wilderness First Responder course (offered by NOLS and other providers) if you plan to spend extended amounts of time in the wilderness.
- **Fire:** For an unexpected night out in the wilderness, a heat source is imperative. Carry matches in a waterproof case and a fire starter. Familiarize yourself about how to build a fire on the fly (and how to do so without igniting a whole forest); the **Rocky Mountain Conservancy Field Institute** (970/586-3262, www.rmconservancy.org) offers several survival courses with instruction about how to build fires in the summer and winter.
- **Repair Kit and Tools:** A multi-tool can be used for first aid (e.g., cutting moleskin into a donut-shape for a blister), food preparation, and a number of other trail-based scenarios. A bare-bones repair kit should contain duct tape and zip ties, both of which have surprising versatility. For overnight trips, bring along a tent repair kit.
- **Nutrition:** Always include plenty of food in your pack: meals for longer outings, and plenty of snacks for shorter ones. Nuts and nut butter, seeds, good old raisins and peanuts (GORP), beef jerky, fruit leather, and energy bars all pack a nutritional punch. Leave behind odiferous foods that could attract animals.
- **Hydration:** Travel with 2-3 liters of water in bottles or a hydration pack. Only drink water from streams or rivers if it has been filtered or treated with purification drops.
- **Emergency Shelter:** A thermal blanket is an economical emergency shelter, and when folded, takes up very little space. A large trash bag is a second option for shelter. Both can be used in lieu of a sleeping bag if you are stranded.

Cairns

When a hiking trail is so faded or rocky that route-finding becomes difficult, cairns are sometimes placed on the ground to mark a path. The word cairn is derived from the Scottish word *càrn* (pile of rocks). In Rocky, cairns are not as common as they are in other national parks, such as Bryce Canyon or Arches in Utah—where many slick rock and deep canyon routes are mostly marked with rock piles. A good majority of Rocky's trails are well-defined and marked with signs. But cairns are still found on certain trails (such as the Ute Trail). It's important to note that the park does not create or maintain cairns. Though they have been placed by well-intentioned visitors, by following them you are taking a calculated risk. If you find a cairn that is accurately placed, feel free to place another rock or pebble on the pile; do not, however, add any other marking material or decoration to a cairn.

Maps

The free park map (www.nps.gov/romo) is available at entrance stations, visitor centers, and ranger stations. It provides basic information about roads, restrooms, trails, and the park's topographical features. Free paper maps with basic line drawings of trails are also available at various trailheads, but are elementary in nature and should not be strictly relied on for navigation. For more detailed information, consider purchasing a National Geographic *Trails Illustrated* map bundle ($17.95) for Rocky Mountain National Park and Longs Peak. These two waterproof maps provide much greater detail about trails, landmarks, and wilderness campsites than that found on any of the free park maps.

Mountain Jay Media LLC also sells two maps of Rocky that are conveniently organized by west side and east side ($11.95 each). The level of detail in these maps, which are self-published, is superb. Many park volunteers swear by these maps, which are sold in the park's visitor centers.

The *Rocky Mountain National Park Hiking Map* by Trail Tracks ($11.95) is also a great resource (and serves as a stellar wall decoration). The map has aerial panoramic views of all the park's peaks and valleys. Distances are not to scale on the map, so this one should not be relied on for navigation. However, it is helpful for getting a better sense of the park's features.

Various books about RMNP hiking also include maps and can be handy trail companions, such as Lisa Foster's *Rocky Mountain National Park, the Complete Hiking Guide* ($27.95, Renaissance Mountaineering, LLC).

Relief maps located at the Beaver Meadows Visitor Center and the Kawuneeche Visitor Center are also useful for getting oriented to the park, and the wilderness offices have maps specific to wilderness campsites within the park. One wilderness office is located on the west side in the Kawuneeche Visitor Center; another wilderness office is located on the east side, adjacent to the Beaver Meadows Visitor Center.

Winter Hiking

FOOTWEAR

Trails considered easy to moderately difficult in the warm months can become treacherous when walloped with snow and slicked with ice. In the winter, plain old hiking boots aren't going to cut it; snowshoes, traction devices, or cross-country skis are essential to get around on many of Rocky's paths. Traction devices, which are sold by outdoor stores, fit over shoes and "grip" slick ground with spikes or metal coils. These devices are fairly lightweight and superb for walking across icy patches on a trail. In the late spring/early summer, you are still likely to need traction devices even on short hikes; always throw a pair in your pack, just in case.

An unpleasant and exhausting way of walking through deep snow is called "postholing." With each step, your foot and a good portion of your leg sinks deep into the snow. You might become temporarily stuck in the snow, your clothing can become wet and cold, and you are at risk of aggravating or causing an ankle or knee injury. Furthermore, terrain becomes uneven for the next person coming along, even if they are on skis or snowshoes. To avoid postholing, come prepared with snowshoes or cross country skis, and wear gaiters or waterproof snow pants over long underwear in order to keep your legs dry and warm.

NAVIGATION

Compared with traveling along dry trails, route-finding can become immensely more difficult in the snow. While hiking or skiing on a snowy trail, you could very well see orange plastic markers attached approximately eight feet up on the trunks of trees. These markers might appear to be a great navigational aid, but that is not the case. The park does not regularly maintain the markers; therefore, they are not dependable. The safest way to travel trails in the winter is with great awareness of your surroundings and with solid map and compass skills. A GPS unit can be immensely helpful—if used properly—but should not be your sole source of navigation. Following footprints is also no assurance that you are traveling in the right direction. In addition, snowfall can quickly obscure footprints—yours or someone else's. On one occasion, while hiking on the Emerald Lake Trail in February, I happened upon a couple who had been taking nature photos and who had become disoriented to the location of the trail (just a few dozen yards away) after ten minutes of moderate snowfall. Such confusion can happen quickly. Sometimes you will see a packed-out trail abruptly end, followed by multiple sets of footprints, ski tracks, or snowshoe tracks heading in various directions. This type of scenario can be disorienting as well. If you are unsure how to proceed, turn around.

HYDRATION

Tipping back a bottle of water is pretty easy on a warm summer day. But in the winter, people sometimes mistakenly neglect hydration because they are not thirsty and drinks are unappealing. A hike in cold, dry, windy air at a high elevation can deplete a person's water supply just as quickly as on a hot day in the summer. Pack water in insulated containers or hydration packs and sip often.

CONDITIONS

Checking trail status reports, weather reports, and avalanche conditions is imperative in the winter. The park regularly updates trail information online (www.nps.gov/romo), and a ranger at any one of the visitor centers can give you a good sense of potential hazards or trail closures. At the visitor centers, you can also learn about the day's weather forecast. The **Colorado Avalanche Information Center** (avalanche.state.co.us) provides valuable information about recent slides and avalanche potential in the near future.

BACKPACKING

Whether it is just for one night or for a multiday hike from one side of the park to the other, backpacking is a great way to experience Rocky. In the warm months, there are 267 wilderness campsites to choose from.

For backcountry camping dates that fall **May 1-October 31,** reservations can be made online (www.pay.gov) or in person at a park wilderness office March 1-October 28. Campsite reservations must be made at least three days in advance. A Wilderness Administrative Fee ($26) is charged, which covers multiple nights out and multiple people in your party. Visitors can camp in the wilderness for a maximum of seven nights June 1-September 30. Bring a bear canister for food storage if you are camping below the tree line.

For camping dates **November 1-April 30,** reservations can be made by phone (970/586-1242) or in person at a wilderness office October 1-April 30. On the east side of the park, a wilderness office is located next to the Beaver Meadows Visitor Center; on the west side of the park, the wilderness office is located inside the Kawuneeche Visitor Center. Visitors can camp in the wilderness for a maximum of 14 nights October 1–May 31.

In the winter and early spring, it is

Pooping in the Woods

A whole book has been written about going "number two" outside: *How to Shit in the Woods*, by Kathleen Meyer. But for those who want a down-and-dirty version of what to do, here it is:

- Choose a spot at least 200 feet away from a waterway, campsite, or hiking trail. Use a stick or small shovel to dig a 6-8-inch-deep hole in the dirt to hold fecal matter. Do your business. Then cover up the hole with dirt, and make things look as much as possible like they did before, scattering a few downed branches or rocks over the whole thing for good measure.
- Pack out—never bury—all toilet paper, tissues, wipes, and/or other sanitary products. Some visitors do not bother to bury their TP and leave it "hidden" behind a rock or a tree. Don't be that person.
- For little ones who can't wait for a hole to be dug, find a private spot for them to go, then dig a hole after the fact. Or, pick up waste matter off the ground with a plastic bag, tie it up and pack it out. I've learned from personal experience with this second method to deposit the bag well inside my pack so that the sun doesn't beat down on the bag and worsen the odor.
- Carry a small container of antibacterial gel or wipes in your backpack to keep hands clean post-poo.
- If backpacking, inquire about human waste bags at the park's wilderness office. The bags are made of a polymer that neutralizes smell. Bags must be discarded in the trash, not in pit toilets. "Wag bags," as they are sometimes called, are also available from a dispenser on the Black Canyon Trail in Lumpy Ridge.
- Use vault toilets at trailheads and wilderness pit toilets whenever possible.

possible to self-register for a backcountry trip at the following locations: Wild Basin Winter Trailhead, Sandbeach Lake Trailhead, Longs Peak Ranger Station, Dunraven/North Fork Trailhead, the Fall River Entrance Station, and the Beaver Meadows Entrance Station. However, registering in person or on the phone has its advantages: staff can provide valuable information about trailhead conditions and closures, weather, bear activity, and other factors that might affect the overall success of your trip. Planning ahead is advised, because backcountry permits are limited.

Wilderness office staff will do everything that they can to set up backpackers for a safe and successful trip, which means any or all of the following: reviewing logs of recent bear and mountain lion sightings; going over the current weather forecast; discussing possible hazards on trails and at campsites, including snow slides, wind gusts, and high water areas; and reviewing maps. In addition, you will be advised to camp well away from dead, standing trees.

Every wilderness camper is issued a pack tag and a tent tag for their trek, and a dash tag for their vehicle. Bivouac site permits are issued for wilderness campers who intend to do technical climbs.

In the winter, the park allows wilderness camping in 55 zones that are defined not by signs but simply by the walls of a canyon. As long as four inches of snow are on the ground, anything is fair game in a zone, provided that the selected space is 70 adult steps away from any water source, the same amount of steps away from a trail, and out of sight of other visitors. The wilderness offices encourage the use of human waste bags, which they distribute free of charge. At a number of wilderness campsites and off of some trails, visitors will also find basic pit toilets.

In the summer, some wilderness campsites are naturally more popular than others. Plan well ahead if you wish to camp at the following sites on the east side: Glacier Gorge, Andrews Creek, the Longs Peak Boulderfield,

Leave No Trace

Armed with knowledge, visitors can dramatically limit their impact on the park's landscape, and thus help to preserve fragile habitats for future generations to enjoy. The gold standard for personal responsibility in the outdoors comes from the nonprofit organization Leave No Trace and includes seven key principles:

- **Plan ahead and prepare.** Expect the unexpected and be well-prepared for your outing with proper footwear, foul weather gear, food, maps, and extra clothing. Break down large parties into small hiking groups to minimize trail impact.
- **Travel and camp on durable surfaces.** Only pitch your tent at established campsites in the park, and consult with rangers about campsite and trail closures. Hike on trails, snow, dry grasses, or gravel, and do not hike on the tundra in designated "Tundra Protection Areas." Resist the urge to cut switchbacks on a steep hike.
- **Leave what you find.** Admire flowers, rocks, pinecones, and other natural objects and leave them in their place. Teach children that everything found in the park must stay in the park. At historic sites, artifacts should be viewed, not be handled, unless noted otherwise.
- **Properly dispose of waste.** Utilize the park's established restrooms whenever possible. In the backcountry, do not bury toilet paper or feminine hygiene products. Pack out all refuse and food, and use the park's trash and recycle stations. Pick up microtrash, which includes tiny bits of paper, foil, plastic wrappers, and broken glass.
- **Minimize campfire impacts.** Use designated campfire rings, only with wood purchased or legally collected outside the park boundaries. Be aware of fire restrictions. Properly drown out fires.
- **Respect wildlife.** View wildlife from a distance of 25 yards or more, and rely on binoculars or telephoto lenses to see animals in greater detail. Store food properly and ignore hungry critters that beg for handouts. Respect raptor-nesting sites in the spring and other wildlife closures around the park.
- **Be considerate of other visitors.** Share the trails with other visitors, and step aside on a durable surface to let horses, pack animals, and other hikers pass. Keep conversations at a respectable volume and do not play music aloud on the trails.

For more Leave No Trace information, visit www.LNT.org. © Leave No Trace Center for Outdoor Ethics

and Thunder Lake. On the west side, be aware that Lake Verna, Timber Lake, July, and Renegade book out early.

You can check the park's website (www.nps.gov/romo) for a wilderness site availability calendar, which is updated daily (but not in real time). It is always worth checking in with a wilderness office if you need a site last-minute; if a party does not pick up its permit by noon on the day a trip is scheduled to start, that wilderness site will be freed up for other backpackers.

CLIMBING

Rock Climbing

Even visitors who are still clad in diapers find appeal in scrambling around on the park's rocks. For older youth and adults, there are hundreds of named climbing routes around the park to enjoy. Climbing is an exhilarating activity, to be sure, but only those with prior experience should consider attempting routes in the park without the expertise of a guide. Climbing accidents and fatalities are a reality in the park and can be attributed to many unpredictable factors, including loose rock, adverse weather conditions, improperly rigged gear, and the effects of altitude.

Before heading out on an adventure, climbers should familiarize themselves with the park's climbing etiquette and rules, listed online (www.nps.gov/romo). A park entrance fee must be paid to access some climbing spots, although one of the most popular climbing areas, Lumpy Ridge, is fee-free. Those who plan to embark on overnight climbing trips must obtain a **bivouac permit** from the park's wilderness office (970/586-1242). The permit is required for climbs that take place more than 3.5 miles from a trailhead and involve four or more technical pitches. Climbers should adhere to Leave No Trace ethics, and abide by raptor-nesting closures.

Traditional climbing (using only removable hardware along the climbing route) is allowed in the park. Sport climbing (climbing with bolts or hardware permanently affixed to rocks) is prohibited.

Several local guide services and outfitters on the east side of the park offer climbing instruction, and newcomers to the sport might consider signing up for a beginner's course. **Colorado Mountain School** (341 Moraine Ave., Estes Park, 800/836-4008, www.coloradomountainschool.com) offers an Intro to Rock Climbing course ($195 pp) and Half Day Fun Climbs ($90 pp) in Estes Park, as well as courses and outings for more advanced climbers.

In-depth information about climbing routes is not available on the park website. However, several well-researched books specific to climbing can provide visitors with some guidance, including *Rocky Mountain National Park: A Comprehensive Guide to Scrambles, Rock Routes, and Ice/Mixed Climbs on the High Peaks,* by Richard Rossiter, and Bernard Gillett's *Rocky Mountain National Park, The Climber's Guide: High Peaks.* Mountain Project's website (www.mountainproject.com) also lists many bouldering and rock-climbing routes. Like everything on the Internet, you will sometimes see widely varying opinions about routes and conditions and will need to use your own personal filter to decide what information is legitimate. The biggest value of this website is its many photos, which depict rock features, anchors, and other important visuals.

Ice Climbing

Come winter, climbers shift their attention from rock to ice. In the colder months, ice is in a constant state of change: forming and melting, forming and melting again. Ice climbing is popular in Rocky because the park has big, fat ice features with fairly simple approaches. Climbers are often hush-hush about where the good ice is, in the same way that backcountry skiers are tight-lipped about where the best powder stashes are. Still, information about ice in Rocky is available. Two websites are helpful: **Mountain Project** (www.mountainproject.com) and a public Facebook page called **Colorado Ice Conditions** (www.facebook.com/groups/iceclimbing). As with rock climbing, only those with experience and good physical fitness should attempt the sport. **Colorado Mountain School** (341 Moraine Ave., Estes Park, 800/836-4008, www.coloradomountainschool.com) provides introductory ice climbing courses from mid-December to the beginning of April. Popular ice climbing routes, such as Hidden Falls in the Wild Basin region of the park, can become crowded on the weekends, so consider arranging a weekday trip if possible.

BIKING

Bikes are allowed only on park roads, not on trails. There are no dedicated bike lanes anywhere in the park, so taking measures to be safe on your bicycle is imperative. Always wear a good helmet, don a brightly colored jersey or jacket, and constantly be on the lookout for distracted drivers. If it is dark out or if visibility is poor due to foggy or stormy weather, the park requires each rider to attach a white light or reflector to the front of his or her bike, and a red light or reflector to the back of his or her bike.

The park allows cyclists to secure their bike to a tree if a bike rack is unavailable, but takes no responsibility for stolen gear. If you choose to ride to a trailhead for wilderness camping, the wilderness office (970/586-1242) will require you to get a special tag to attach to your bike. Otherwise, if your bike is found without a tag, the park might remove it. Do not lock a bike to any pole or sign in the park, as you are likely not to see it upon your return.

Make sure your bike's brakes are in good condition before traveling around the park, and carry a tool kit with you.

HORSEBACK RIDING

If you choose to bring your own horse into Rocky, your options for exploring are many. Approximately 260 miles of trails are deemed horse-friendly. Some trails are permanently off-limits to horses, while others are closed temporarily due to flood, fire, or other environmental factors. Review online (www.nps.gov/romo) the current list of closures, as well as the park's horse and pack animal guidelines before you venture into Rocky. Many of the park's trails have hitch racks; otherwise, riders need to secure a padded rope between two trees and hitch their animals to the rope.

If you plan to stay overnight in the park with your horse, you must make arrangements with the park's wilderness offices (970/586-1242). Thirteen wilderness stock campsites in the park can be reserved, three of which are set aside for llamas only. Horses, ponies, mules, burros, and llamas are all allowed to travel on park trails.

FISHING

Individuals 16 and older who want to fish in the park must carry a current Colorado fishing license. Various shops in Grand Lake, Estes Park, and other locations throughout Colorado also sell fishing licenses; a list of retailers is posted on the **Colorado Parks and Wildlife** (cpw.state.co.us). Colorado residents can purchase a one-day license ($9) or an annual license ($26). Nonresidents can purchase a one-day license ($9), a five-day license ($21), or an annual license ($56). An annual pass ($1) for seniors is available to Colorado residents only. An additional, one-time, annual purchase of The Habitat Stamp ($10) must be made by license holders age 18-64. Fees collected for the stamp help fund a habitat-protection program.

horseback riders on the Storm Pass Trail

Tips and Tricks

Throw a dart at a map of Rocky and chances are good that you will land on a stream, river, lake, or somewhere near a stretch of water. The park, with its vast network of waterways, is simply a superb place to fish. Brown trout, brook trout, rainbow trout, and cutthroat trout are commonly caught in Rocky. Additionally, western longnose suckers, western white suckers, and mottled sculpin call the park home.

Each body of water presents its own set

Ready, Set, Goal

A park ranger friend of mine gives a talk to visitors that I find particularly inspiring. It's called "Trail Quest," and during the program he talks about his own personal quest to hike every trail in the park (a feat he completed in around three years). While weaving an interesting tale about his adventures on Rocky's trails, he encourages his audience to always have dreams and goals in life, no matter what age you are. Indeed, Rocky is a great place to press the reset button and think through "what's next." Many visitors, during their stay in Rocky, are inspired to create a goal or bucket list item that is centered on some activity in the park. Of course, if you live within easy driving distance of the park, the possibilities for goal-setting are virtually endless. A few that I love: a group of local women that are bound and determined to ice-skate on each lake in the park. Another Estes Park resident strives to hike every day of the year in Rocky, even if just for a short distance. Backcountry skiing the 50 highest peaks in the park is the aim of two men who live near Rocky. Some people aspire to climb Longs Peak one or many times, while others are on a mission visit every national park in their lifetime.

Any visitor can set a park-related goal and it doesn't have to be extreme. As you consider the time you have to spend in Rocky, think about what activities will lead to a great sense of satisfaction. Hiking on a new trail? Hiking to five lakes in five days? Finally setting your alarm early to watch the sun rise? Or perhaps it is attempting to fish a Colorado Grand Slam (catching a brook trout, brown trout, rainbow trout, and cutthroat trout all in the same day). Families might find fulfillment in discovering a certain number of geocaches during their stay, or by completing a Junior Ranger booklet from cover to cover. As you plan your visit to Rocky, consider setting a concrete goal, large or small. Then, go for it!

of opportunities and challenges. In many of Rocky's high alpine lakes, there are no species present because the water is too cold for fish to reproduce. Of the 147 lakes in the park, just 48 have reproducing populations of fish. Do your research before trekking 10 miles to a remote lake, so you do not carry along fishing gear all for naught. Steve Schweitzer's *A Fly Fishing Guide to Rocky Mountain National Park* is a great resource.

METHOD OF CAPTURE

Fly-fishing is the only type of fishing allowed in the park, with one exception: children 12 and under are allowed to use bait in the form of worms or preserved fish eggs in areas that are not designated as catch-and-release. These guidelines are in place to protect the park's fish populations. Fish that go for worms or preserved fish eggs tend to get hooked deeper than with an artificial fly or lure, which translates to a higher mortality rate. While there are children who fish in Rocky, the percentage is considerably smaller than adults, and therefore, their impact on the fish population is thought to be without major consequence.

FISH LIMIT

When you catch and keep 18 fish in one day, you should allow yourself a self-congratulatory fist-pump in the air, and maybe let out a few whoops and hollers while you are at it. You should also pack everything up and call it a day, because 18 is the park's cutoff for the number of fish caught. You will have reached the limit if you have caught (1) 18 "brookies," 8 of which are any size and 10 that need to be 8 inches or less in length; or (2) 16 brook trout, 6 of which are any size, and 10 that are 8 inches or less in length. You can add to that mix two additional trout species, just not greenback cutthroat trout.

AVERAGE FISH SIZE

Rocky's fish are modestly sized, on average, 12-15 inches. If catching The Big One in Rocky is your intent, then you may want to readjust your expectations.

THE COLORADO GRAND SLAM

If you would like a lofty but achievable goal for your outing, the "Grand Slam"—catching four different fish species in a single day—could be it. The Colorado Grand Slam consists of brook trout, rainbow trout, brown trout, and cutthroat trout.

Travel Tips

INTERNATIONAL TRAVELERS

Entering the United States

Travelers to the United States must have a valid passport and a valid visa to enter the country, though there are exceptions. For tourism or business visits of 90 days or less, international citizens from 38 countries can enter the United States with a valid passport and acceptance through the Department of Homeland Security's Visa Waiver Program. A complete list of countries and more information can be found at the **U.S. Customs and Border Protection** (www.cbp.gov) or **U.S. Department of State** (www.travel.state.gov). Individuals must complete an Electronic System for Travel Authorization application online to determine eligibility; approval takes 72 hours or less.

Canadian citizens traveling to the United States by air must possess a valid passport or NEXUS card. If traveling by land or sea, a Canadian passport, Enhanced Driver's License or Enhanced Identification Card, NEXUS, FAST/EXPRES, or SENTRI enrollment card is required for entry.

Customs

United States customs laws prohibit numerous items from being transported into the country. Among them are firearms and ammunition; most meat, poultry, pork, and egg products; certain fruits, vegetables, and plants; and illegal substances such as absinthe. Bear spray can be brought into the United States in a checked bag, but "bear bangers"—which are explosive devices—are not permissible. All travelers into the United States must fill out a customs declaration form and will be inspected by U.S. Customs and Border Protection officers upon entry. Failure to declare items might result in fines and penalties. More information can be found online at the **U.S. Customs and Border Protection** (www.cbp.gov).

Money and Currency Exchange

Though there are financial institutions in major cities that will exchange money for travelers, many banks—including those in Estes Park and Grand Lake—will only exchange foreign currency for customers with existing accounts. That said, travelers should consider exchanging money ahead of time in their home country to best be prepared for cash-only transactions immediately after arriving in the United States. Another option is to exchange money at the airport, though airports typically have the highest exchange rates. You can also locate a currency exchange service in the major city where you have arrived. Denver has a handful of currency exchange centers, including **Currency Exchange International** (Cherry Creek Shopping Center, 3000 East 1st Ave., Denver, 303/586-1144, www.denvercurrencyexchange.com) and **Travelex Currency Service** (950 17th St., Denver, 303/260-7433, www.travelex.com).

Alternatively, travelers can make purchases using debit or credit cards, or use ATMs to withdraw cash for their visit. Check with your bank ahead of time about international transaction and service charges, and plan to take out larger amounts of cash at a time to avoid multiple service fees. There are no ATMs within Rocky Mountain National Park, so plan to get cash before entering the park

Marijuana and the Park

In Lyons, Colorado, just 20 miles from Estes Park, the Bud Depot dispensary advertises itself online as "the closest legal cannabis store to Rocky Mountain National Park." That may be true, but just because recreational marijuana is legal in Colorado, it does not also mean that lighting up a joint in the park is allowed. Whether purchased for medicinal or recreational purposes, possessing and smoking the green stuff is forbidden on federal lands, including national parks, forests, and monuments. Do not assume that rangers will look the other way, because if they don't, the consequences are lousy: up to one year in jail and a fine of $1,000 for the first offense. To partake of recreational pot legally in the state, individuals 21 and older can purchase it from a licensed retail marijuana store and smoke it in a private location, such as a home. It is at the discretion of individual hotels whether they will allow marijuana in "smoking" rooms, which are primarily designated for those who smoke tobacco.

boundaries. Though many purchases—such as wilderness permits and gift shop items—can easily be made with a credit or debit card, cash is essential for tipping (horseback guides, for example), buying firewood and ice at campgrounds, and other incidentals. Traveler's checks—though much less used these days than in the past and not always accepted—can be purchased ahead of your trip, as added protection in the case of loss or theft of cash and/or ATM/credit cards.

ACCESS FOR TRAVELERS WITH DISABILITIES

An **America the Beautiful Access Pass** is offered at no charge to U.S. citizens who have a life-altering medical disability. The pass is good for lifetime entry to national parks and federal lands—including Rocky—and grants its holders 50 percent off of the camping fee at Rocky's five campgrounds. Obtain your pass at any park entrance station for free, or mail in an application for a $10 fee (www.nps.gov). Visitors with disabilities can obtain detailed information about accessibility from the park's website (www.nps.gov/romo) or from the **Disabled Traveler's Companion** (www.tdtcompanion.com). A brochure entitled *Access Rocky* can also be picked up at any of the visitor centers. Service animals compliant with the Americans with Disabilities Act (and secured on leash six feet or shorter) are allowed on trails, but therapy animals are not.

Most of the park's shuttles, which run in high season, are outfitted with wheelchair lifts. Three of the park's campgrounds have wheelchair accessible campsites: Moraine Park, Glacier Basin and Timber Creek. An accessible wilderness camp site available at Sprague Lake can accommodate groups of up to twelve, including five wheelchair users. The Sprague Lake site must be reserved ahead through the park's wilderness offices (970/586-1242).

The park will arrange for a sign language interpreter, but requires several weeks notice to do so. Call the park's main number (970/586-1206) to make arrangements.

TRAVELING WITH CHILDREN

Rocky is conducive to family fun, with plenty of kid-friendly activities to choose from. When traveling with little ones, always come prepared with extra layers of clothing, rain gear, spare shoes, and plenty of food and water. Unpredictability is often the name of the game in Rocky, meaning you might end up playing "I Spy" in the car while waiting out a hailstorm or, on the way to dinner, get waylaid watching a family of wild turkeys. Pad your schedule with extra time to allow for serendipitous moments.

Fourth-grade students can obtain a free,

one-year pass—good for themselves and their families to use on federal lands and waters—through the **National Park Foundation's Every Kid in a Park Program** (www.everykidinapark.gov). Starting on September 1 of each year, current third-grade students can complete online activities in exchange for a pass for their fourth-grade year.

Junior Ranger Program

Junior Ranger activity booklets for three different age categories are provided for free at each of the park's visitor centers. Upon completing part or all of the booklet—and after taking the Junior Ranger Pledge in the presence of an official park ranger—youth receive a badge and a certificate of achievement.

Ranger-Led Programs

Rangers present fascinating insight into the park's features, and do so in an enthusiastic manner that appeals to children. Ranger presentations often include cool props that can be touched, like animal skins, skulls, and horns. For kid-specific programs in the summer (late June-late August), visit the Junior Ranger Headquarters in Hidden Valley (from the Fall River Entrance Station, drive 6.3 mi west on Trail Ridge Road). Thirty-minute programs are offered four times a day (10am, 11:30am, 1pm, 2:30pm) seven days a week during those months. Many other ranger-led activities held throughout the park are appropriate for kids; checking the park's free newspaper is the best way to find programs. Evening programs held at park amphitheaters are always well attended by little ones, though some presentations do not start until 9pm in mid-summer and can last for an hour—making for a late bedtime.

Books

A handful of regional interest books have been created especially for kids and are available at a variety of local businesses. Among those to look for: *The Trail Ridge Road Adventure Sticker and Game Book* from Rocky Mountain Nature Association Publishers; *Exploring the Park Together: A Family Guide to Rocky Mountain National Park*, by Patricia P. Pickering and Patricia Y. Washburn; and *Lil' MacDonald Likes to Hike: A Rocky Mountain National Park Kid's Sing Along and Hiking Guide*, by Jennifer Taylor Tormalehto.

Junior Ranger backpacks at the Kawuneeche Visitor Center

Hiking

On the west side of the park, the best family-friendly hikes are **Coyote Valley Trail, Holzwarth Historic Site,** and **Adams Falls.** Each outing is less than a mile roundtrip. On the east side of the park, **Bear Lake, Lily Lake,** the **Moraine Park Discovery Center Nature Trail,** and **Sprague Lake** are ideal for little ones. Off of Trail Ridge Road, the **Tundra Communities Trail** is short and has minimal elevation gain—although a trek on this trail might leave your child (and you) breathless due to its starting elevation of 12,110 feet. **Lumpy Ridge** is also a great spot for kids, with many rocks and boulders to climb. Numerous other hiking possibilities in the park are available for families with older children, depending on stamina and level of interest.

Childcare

There are times when a challenging all-day hike in the park beckons, but parents are left scratching their heads about how to pull it off with little ones. Local preschool **Mountain Top Child Care** (1250 Woodstock Dr., 970/586-6489, www.mountaintopchildcare.com, 7am-5:30pm Mon.-Fri. year-round, $38/day) welcomes vacationing children on a drop-in basis; the experience is top notch. Husband-wife owners John and Jodi Ayotte are even-keeled, friendly, and organized, and put both parents and kids at ease. Children love the large and shady backyard play area, and healthy snacks and a lunch are provided. Holiday care is also available at a higher rate ($46/day). Reservations are required, and be prepared to provide your child's current immunization records.

Safety

In Rocky, many known and unknown variables in the environment mean that parents need to keep a close eye on children. At higher elevations, UV rays are extra harsh; protect your child's skin and eyes with sunscreen, a hat, and sunglasses. Always be vigilant around water features in the park, from placid lakes to roaring rivers, and exercise caution when climbing with little ones on large boulders. Make sure your kiddo is well-hydrated. A first-aid kit is essential gear on hikes and in your car's emergency kit.

Rocky's visitor centers can get crowded in the summer and the Trail Ridge Store next to the Alpine Visitor Center can become somewhat of a mob scene. Establishing a meeting spot with your children ahead of time—in case you accidentally get separated—is a smart move.

Diaper Changing Stations

If you are at one of the park's visitor centers, you will either find a diaper changing station, a family restroom, or an otherwise adequate space to change a diaper. However, many bathrooms at trailheads and campgrounds are basic pit or "vault" style toilets without the right amount of space or proper sanitary conditions for diaper-changing. If you are traveling with a baby, pack a changing mat to perform diaper changes on the fly. Diapers and wipes should be deposited in the trash, not in vault toilets.

SENIOR TRAVELERS

United States citizens ages 62 and over are eligible for a National Park Service **America the Beautiful Seniors Pass,** which guarantees lifetime free entry to the park. Obtain yours at any entrance station for a one-time fee of $10, or mail in an application for $20 (www.nps.gov). The pass also grants lifetime access to more than 2,000 federal recreation sites, including all other national parks. In Rocky, present the seniors pass to receive 50 percent off camping fees at any of the five campgrounds.

MILITARY TRAVELERS

Active-duty U.S. military and their dependents are eligible to receive a free annual pass—the **America the Beautiful Military Pass**—which can only be obtained in person at the park. Applicants must present a Common Access Card or Military ID (Form 1173).

TRAVELING WITH PETS

Pets are permitted in Rocky, but only in areas where vehicles are allowed—not on trails or in the wilderness. Acceptable areas for pets include parking lots, picnicking spots, campgrounds, and along the roadside. Pets must be kept on a leash six feet or shorter, and never left alone. These policies are in place to protect wildlife and vegetation, and are strictly enforced.

For a short period of time in the spring when Trail Ridge Road is closed to automobile traffic, leashed pets can be walked along the road. Additionally, when Upper Beaver Meadows Road, Twin Sisters Trailhead Access

Road, and Endovalley Road are closed to car traffic in the winter, they are open to leashed dogs.

Come prepared with waste bags, and always dispose of them in the trash, not in vault toilets. Be mindful about leaving furry friends locked in vehicles, even with the windows rolled down. Marked changes in the weather are common, and a storm-cloud-covered sky can easily give way to full sun—leading to rapidly rising temperatures in your vehicle and to possible devastating consequences for your pet. It is a finable offense if rangers have to rescue your pet from a hot car.

Formally trained service animals as defined by the Americans with Disabilities Act are allowed in the park and can accompany visitors with disabilities. Service animals must be kept on a leash six feet or shorter. Therapy dogs and service animals that are in training are not allowed.

Pet boarding is available in Estes Park at the following locations: **Estes Park Pet Lodge** (1260 Manford Ave., 970/586-9282, www.estesparkpetlodge.com), **Animal Hospital of the Rockies** (453 Pine River Ln., 970/586-4703, www.estesparkpetvet.com), and **Linda's Pet Care Services** (950 Comanche St., Unit C, 970/586-0340, www.lindaspetcareservices.com). In Grand Lake, there is one place to drop off pets: **Mountain Mongrels** (525 Grand Ave., 970/531-0837, www.mountainmongrels.com). **Four Paws Resort, Inc.** (443 County Rd. 631, 970/531-9293, www.fourpawsresortinc.com) is located in Granby and is a reasonable option for visitors to the Arapaho National Recreation Area (ANRA). All facilities will require your pet's immunization records.

Many hotels and lodges in Estes Park and Grand Lake also have pet-friendly rooms.

SPECIAL USE PERMITS

The park issues special use permits for activities such as weddings, parties, the scattering of ashes, and research. If you have plans to do something out of the ordinary in the park, err on the side of caution and check in with a visitor center first to see if your activity falls under the category of "special use." Special use permit applications are found on the park's website: www.nps.gov/romo.

Service dogs are allowed on Rocky's trails.

HEALTH AND SAFETY

Avalanches

Just after a blizzard has dumped inches of powdery white stuff might seem like the perfect time to go for a ski or snowshoe in the park, but the opposite is true. Avalanches are *more* likely to occur during and just after snowstorms. A number of factors can cause snowpack to become unstable and slide; the best way to learn about them all is to sign up for a formal snow safety course. The **Colorado Mountain School** (800/836-4008, www.coloradomountainschool.com, Dec.-Apr., $360) and the **Rocky Mountain Conservancy's Field Institute** (970/586-0108, www.rmconservancy.org, Feb., $35) both offer classes. The **Colorado Avalanche Information Center** (www.avalanche.state.co.us) is a great resource for learning about snow conditions statewide; consulting with a ranger about park conditions prior to a wilderness outing is wise. Probes, transceivers, shovels, and ski poles can all increase an avalanche victim's chances of survival, but only if properly used. As a basic rule, steer clear of cornices and open slopes in the backcountry, which can deposit loads of potentially deadly snow on an unsuspecting person in a matter of seconds.

Changing Weather

Faster than you can say "changing weather," Rocky can switch from all sunshine and rainbows to a dark and foreboding environment (or the other way around). Always travel with a rain jacket, warm layers, wicking layers, a hat, and an extra pairs of socks. It only takes one hike back to a trailhead in cold sleet to realize that the benefits of being comfortable, warm, and dry far outweigh the burden of carrying a heavier pack. In the spring, weather is highly unpredictable. In the summer, afternoon thunderstorms are common in Rocky. Also, some visitors are surprised to find that the mercury drops between 10 and 20 degrees (or more) on the short drive from the Beaver Meadows Entrance Station to Trail Ridge Road. Lightning can be dangerous anywhere in the park, and especially above the tree line. Snowflakes are a possibility at any time of the year, and the sun—even when obscured by clouds—can translate into nasty sunburns and dehydration. In summary: be aware and be prepared for anything and everything when it comes to weather.

Dehydration

Dehydration is common at high elevations, and can result in unpleasant symptoms such as nausea and headache. Rocky's dry mountain air causes bodies to lose moisture faster than at sea level through breath and sweat. Aim to drink 2-3 liters of water a day, starting several days before you arrive, and consider consuming alcohol and caffeine in moderation or not at all. Keep an extra supply of H20 in your vehicle's emergency kit. Water spigots are located at the visitor centers, and are turned on at high-traffic trailheads and at all of the campsites during the summer season. Some of the park's ranger stations sell bottled water in the summer. Even though your backpack might feel uncomfortably heavy, pack several liters of water per person for longer day hikes, and for extra assurance, consider purchasing a water bottle with a built-in filtration system. Bring a reliable water filtration system or water treatment tablets for overnight trips in the wilderness, and consult with the wilderness offices about specific sources of water along the route that you have chosen.

Elevation

The lowest point in the park is not so low at all at 7,630 feet, and the only place you can go is up. The decrease in oxygen supply at higher elevations can slow down the activities of lowlands visitors for a few days; symptoms like decreased appetite, mild headache, or shortness of breath might appear. Gradually acclimating at lower elevation is recommended when possible, and increased fluid intake is essential. Mild altitude-related symptoms are usually resolved by traveling back down to a lower elevation. Acute mountain sickness (AMS) is a not uncommon and is a more serious condition that can afflict even the most physically fit visitors; pay attention to what your body is telling you.

UV exposure is more intense the higher up you travel; come prepared with sunscreen (which protects against both UVA and UVB rays) and a wide-brimmed hat or cap, and protect your eyes with a good pair of sunglasses.

Falling

Visitors to Rocky tend to worry a little or a lot about bears, but perhaps their attention should be focused elsewhere. Only one death due to a bear attack has been recorded in the park's history, while the leading cause of accidental death in the park is falling. Visitors can fall anywhere or at anytime: while rock climbing, scaling peaks, hiking on established trails, or taking a few short steps off of a trail when nature calls. Always pay close attention to where you are walking, wear sturdy shoes with substantial grip, and consider investing in a set of hiking poles for greater stability. Be aware of areas of exposure before setting out on a hike, and don't tempt fate by taking a selfie on a dangerous precipice.

Falling Trees

Dead or partially-burnt trees that are still standing, called snags, are found in fire-ravaged areas and in other parts of Rocky. At any time, snags can topple without warning; if you are standing nearby, that spells trouble with a capital *T*. While many of Rocky's trees affected by the recent pine beetle epidemic have been cut to the ground, there are still plenty of decaying or dying trees found throughout the park that could fall. Add snow or heavy wind to the mix and such snags might collapse. While evaluating each and every tree in Rocky for toppling potential is unrealistic, for safety, it is prudent to do a thorough visual inspection of trees near your campsite, picnic table, or lunch spot. On trails that travel through fire-ravaged areas, warning signs are often posted.

Giardiasis

Rocky's water might look sparkling and pure, but don't be fooled; there's truly no safe place to take a gulp of untreated H2O in the park. The microscopic parasite *giardia* enters lakes, rivers, and trickling streams through animal and human feces. Ingesting these affected waters can translate into stomach cramping, diarrhea, and other gastrointestinal symptoms that could put an abrupt end to an otherwise happy vacation. With time, giardiasis symptoms can resolve on their own, but sometimes a prescription antibiotic is necessary to completely clear up a nasty bout of the infection. The only way to safely drink water in the park is by using a filtration device, treating it with purification tablets, or by boiling it for five minutes or longer. Otherwise, always explore trails with plenty of water in your pack so that drinking stream or lake water is never a temptation.

removing a fallen tree from a trail

Hypothermia

The stage is set for the potentially deadly condition of hypothermia in a number of ways, and symptoms can creep up on an individual even in moderately chilly weather. Hypothermia occurs when a person's core body temperature drops to 95 degrees or lower. Wet or damp clothes and prolonged exposure to high winds, rain, or snow can be contributing factors. Mild hypothermia presents as shivering, stumbling, and loss of coordination, among other symptoms. Severely hypothermic individuals do not shiver, but have a continued decline in coordination and can show signs of serious mental confusion. To avoid any of these unpleasant scenarios, dress smartly for outdoor pursuits. Choose clothing that wicks moisture away from the body, and always be prepared with insulating layers. If symptoms of mild hypothermia become apparent, remove wet clothing and replace with dry layers, get to a place that is sheltered from the elements, and hydrate. Full-body, skin-to-skin contact with a warm person in a sleeping bag or in thick blankets is recommended for individuals who cannot warm up.

Lightning

Thunderstorms occur with regularity in Rocky on summer afternoons, and are especially dangerous for hikers and sightseers in exposed areas above the tree line. In 2014, two separate lightning strikes in two days resulted in nearly a dozen injuries and two deaths in locations along Trail Ridge Road. Such tragedies can be minimized or prevented by planning hikes for early morning when thunderstorms are less likely to occur, and by never embarking on a hike when thunderheads are present. If you are trekking around above the tree line and a storm hits, look for shelter away from ridge tops, summits, and standalone trees and rocks. In forested areas, crouch down near a cluster of small trees or bushes and wait out a storm until heading back to a trailhead. If lightning is striking near you, and if you cannot get to a safer place, assume the "lightning position": crouch, place your feet next to each other, close your eyes, and cover your ears. Always heed weather warnings from rangers and never hesitate to check in with a visitor center or ranger station about the daily forecast.

Mosquitoes and Ticks

Besides being a nuisance, mosquitoes are potential carriers of West Nile Virus, a serious condition that affects the nervous system. The *Aedes aegypti* mosquito, which carries Zika virus, has not been detected in Rocky. The relatively rare Rocky Mountain spotted fever can be passed along by ticks. Long-sleeve shirts, long pants, socks, and closed-toe shoes offer good protection from both bugs—which are most prevalent in the spring and summer—as will repellents containing DEET. Whether hiking for a few hours or camping overnight, it is wise to disrobe and conduct a visual "tick check" before the end of the day, and to shower if possible. These offensive critters can otherwise latch on to skin and crawl around for hours or days undetected. Pluck any roaming ticks off your body, and if one is partially embedded, remove it delicately with tweezers. Contact your physician with any concerns.

Swift Water

Rocky's rivers and streams are especially full and fast in the spring due to snowmelt. That said, visitors are cautioned about getting too close to raging, white-capped water *any time* of year. At some highly-visited areas in the park—such as the Big Thompson River next to Bear Lake Road and Chasm Falls off of Old Fall River Road—cautionary signs about swift water are posted; however, there are many more unsigned locations that pose safety issues. Should you fall into or purposefully enter the water, potential scenarios include hypothermia, injury, and/or drowning. Some waterways look deceivingly calm. Use good judgment near any body of water and keep children close at all times.

Wildlife

People and wildlife cross paths every day in the park, and the majority of encounters are without incident. To stay safe, creatures should be observed from at least 25 yards away, and never fed, approached, chased, or otherwise taunted. Moose, bighorn sheep, elk, bears, mountain lions, bobcats, and other fauna are all capable of causing harm to humans should the perfect storm of circumstances present themselves. Generally speaking, unless provoked, animals will keep to themselves or scamper off.

BEARS

The park has gone to great lengths to keep humans safe from bears, and vice versa, particularly at campsites. While black bears are fairly docile creatures, they can get aggressive when food is involved, or when a person gets between a mama and her cub(s). Because they are capable of smelling good eats from more than 5 miles away, it is important to be meticulous about food during picnics, at campsites, and during meal or snack time on the

Bear Encounters

Know what to do around bears before you set foot in the park:

- Stay calm if you see a bear. Stop and observe its behavior from a distance. If it huffs, stomps a paw, makes eye contact, or has a cub (or cubs) in tow, leave the area immediately.
- If you are in close proximity to a bear, talk calmly and quietly to alert the bear that you are nearby. If the bear is farther away, talk loudly to indicate you are in the area.
- Do not run, climb a tree, or approach a bear.
- Do not leave food for a bear.
- If a bear does not appear to pose any initial threat, slowly back away and give the bear an escape route.
- If children are present, pick them up.
- If a bear is approaching you aggressively, stand your ground. Stand at your full height, put your arms or backpack up in the air to look larger, and scream and holler. Bang objects together or clap your hands.
- If attacked, do not play dead; fight back.
- If equipped with bear spray, discharge the spray if a bear approaches.
- Report any bear sightings—and sightings of mountain lions or bobcats—to a park visitor center. You will be asked to fill out a short form with the location of the bear sighting and the specific behavior that you observed.

trail. The park requires that food and other scented items—including cosmetics and toiletries—be stored in food storage lockers, in the trunk of a vehicle, or low down inside of a car, never under or on a picnic table or inside a tent. If you are camping and it is time to drain water out of a cooler before refilling with it with fresh ice, the water should be inspected for any major food leaks, like blood from meat or juice from a container that tipped over. If the water is dirty, rangers will recommend that the whole cooler be taken well outside of the campground and dumped on the side of the road so as not to lure bears into the campground. Tableware, stoves, and water containers also need to be stowed away from your campsite. Rangers are diligent about issuing violation notices if the rules aren't complied with (confession time: this author has received more than one such slip for accidentally leaving a camping stove out on a picnic table). Wilderness campers are also required to bring a commercially made bear-proof food container to store their food May 1-October 31. Canisters are recommended, but not required, during the reminder of the year.

When hiking on Rocky's trails, travel in groups of four or more, keep children in between adults, and make regular conversation or sing songs to alert bears and other wildlife of your presence. Do not be shy in asking fellow hikers if you can group up temporarily if you learn of a recent bear sighting along a trail. Be especially watchful for bears when hiking through dense areas of bushes or berry patches. Avoid hiking at dawn and late in the evening. While some travelers are keen to attach "bear bells" onto their packs, purchasing such bells is not necessary; usually the sound of footsteps and voices is enough to keep bears at bay. Products labeled "bear spray" or "pepper spray" can provide additional assurance to hikers and wilderness travelers; the main ingredient of such sprays—capsicum—is an effective deterrent when unleashed into a bear's face at close range. Note that these products can be as harmful to humans as they are to bears. If mishandled or jostled in a backpack, the "safety" latch on the aerosol might slide off accidentally—which once happened to me—leaving the potential for spray to be engaged at the wrong place at the wrong time. I have heard of at least one child inadvertently harmed by bear spray in the park, and surely there are more such stories.

MOUNTAIN LIONS

The chances of seeing a mountain lion in the park are little to none. Though they are out and about—mostly at night—these secretive mammals generally keep to themselves and go undetected by humans. Attacks are rare. In the unlikely event that you encounter a lion, talk in a firm, authoritative voice and slowly back away. Never run or climb a tree. If a lion approaches, fight back with rocks or sticks. Make yourself look as large as possible and pick up children.

Resources

Suggested Reading

BIOGRAPHY

Bird, Isabella. *A Lady's Life in the Rocky Mountains*. Norman, OK: University of Oklahoma Press, 1960. World traveler Isabella Bird was many things—tenacious, self-sufficient, physically strong, and a keen observer of nature. This fascinating account of her journey to the Estes Park area in the late 1800s includes breathtakingly beautiful prose about Rocky's landscape. Bird's nail-biting description of summiting Longs Peak is a memorable one.

Turnbaugh, Kay, and Lee Tillotson. *Rocky Mountain National Park Dining Room Girl: The Summer of 1926 at the Horseshoe Inn*. Nederland, CO: Perigo Press, 2015. Eleanor Parker worked as a dining room girl in Rocky's Horseshoe Inn in the summer of 1926, and engaged in many outdoor pursuits during her off-hours. Compiled in this unique volume are personal journal entries and letters that Parker wrote home to her mother about her experiences in the park.

CHILDREN

Pickering, Patricia P., and Patricia Y. Washburn. *Exploring the Park Together: A Family Guide to Rocky Mountain National Park*. Estes Park, CO: Estes Park Museum Friends & Foundation Press, 2014. Driving tours around Rocky that the whole family will enjoy are the focal point of this locally produced book. Cheerful illustrations and photos, both present-day and historical, combine with interesting text to make this book kid-friendly and fun to read.

FICTION

Yeager, Dorr G. *Bob Flame, Rocky Mountain Ranger*. Estes Park, CO: Rocky Mountain Nature Association, 2010. This work of fiction about a chief ranger in Rocky Mountain National Park is intended for a teen audience, but will be enjoyed by anyone who has dreamed of performing the varied tasks of a park ranger. Originally written in the 1930s and since revised to add supporting materials to the original, unedited text, this tome provides a great snapshot of park history in its earlier years. Author Yeager was a real-life ranger at Yellowstone National Park and Rocky Mountain National Park (RMNP).

HISTORY

Arps, Louisa Ward, and Elinor Eppich Kingery. *High Country Names: Rocky Mountain National Park*. Denver, CO: Colorado Mountain Club, 1966. What started out as an article about the names of Rocky's geographic features was turned into an entire book. This fascinating read is organized in dictionary form and includes old photographs and topographical maps.

Bancroft, Caroline. *Trail Ridge Country: The Romantic History of Estes Park and Grand Lake*. Boulder, CO: Johnson Publishing Company, 1968. Bancroft makes history fun to read about in this colorfully written,

72-page book about how Estes Park and Grand Lake evolved from the mid-1800s until the opening of Trail Ridge Road in 1920.

Buchholtz, C. W. *Rocky Mountain National Park: A History.* Niwot, CO: University Press of Colorado, 1983. Buchholtz spent seven years researching and writing this indispensable guide to the history of Rocky. Clear and concise text paired with fabulous old photographs combine to tell the story of the people and major events that have shaped the park, starting with the Paleo-Indian era.

Butler, William B. *Rocky Mountain National Park Historic Places.* Estes Park, CO: Estes Park Museum Friends & Foundation Press, 2008. This is an outstanding reference book written by the park's first archaeologist. After reading it cover-to-cover, you will come to understand how much humans have impacted the land over the course of its history, from logging to mining to the building of guest lodges.

Drummond, Alexander. *Enos Mills: Citizen of Nature.* Boulder, CO: University Press of Colorado, 1995. Every aspect of Enos Mills's life is dissected in this full-length biography.

Moomaw, Jack C. *Recollections of a Rocky Mountain Ranger.* Estes Park, CO: YMCA of the Rockies, 2001. Originally published in 1963, this fantastic collection of ranger stories includes tales both tragic and humorous.

Pickering, James H. *Estes Park and Rocky Mountain National Park: Then & Now.* Englewood, CO: Westcliffe Publishers, Inc., 2006. Rocky has undergone tremendous change in the last century, which is strikingly evident in the before-and-after pictures in this coffee-table book. The author gathered historical photos of 98 areas in and around the park, and then had them re-photographed in the modern day. Mr. Pickering provides great historical descriptions with each set of photos.

Pickering, James H. (ed.). *The Rocky Mountain National Park Reader.* Salt Lake City, UT: University of Utah Press, 2015. Estes Park Historian Laureate James Pickering has written numerous books and articles about Estes Park and Rocky, and this is one of his best. The anthology includes 33 stories about the park, organized chronologically from 1915 to 2014.

NATURE

Alden, Peter, and John Grassy. *National Audubon Society Field Guide to the Rocky Mountain States.* New York, NY: Alfred A. Knopf, Inc., 1999. This well-respected field guide is a great resource for anyone wanting to become more familiar with the flora, fauna, and landscape features of the Rockies. Like other Audubon guides, this one is richly illustrated with color photographs.

Angel, Leslie. *Butterflies of Rocky Mountain National Park: An Observer's Guide.* Boulder, CO: Johnson Books, 2005. Get to know the butterflies of Rocky with this handy guide. Included are detailed descriptions of butterflies and recommendations for where to spot them.

Brown, Jr., Tom. *Tom Brown's Field Guide: Nature Observation and Tracking.* New York, NY: Berkley Books, 1986. Learn to experience nature through all your senses with tools and ideas introduced in this book. Brown discusses in-depth how to interpret animal tracks, animal signs, and animal highways.

Dahm, David. *Rocky Mountain Wildflowers Pocket Guide.* Windsor, CO: Paragon Press, 1999. This identification guide gets a big thumbs-up for overall usability on the trail; it is lightweight, compact, ring-bound, and organized by flower color. The self-published guide includes every common flower found in Rocky Mountain National Park. Pick up a copy at any of the visitor centers or at Macdonald Bookshop in Estes Park.

Roederer, Scott. *Birding Rocky Mountain National Park*. Boulder, CO: Johnson Books, 2002. Written by an Estes Park resident, this guide includes detailed information about bird species found on the east side of the park and on Trail Ridge Road.

Zwinger, Ann H., and Beatrice E. Willard. *Land Above the Trees: A Guide to American Alpine Tundra*. New York, NY: Harper & Row, 1972. This painstakingly researched book includes rich and colorful descriptions of the alpine tundra. Co-authors Beatrice Willard and Ann H. Zwinger use easy-to-understand language to describe the complex environment that exists above the tree line. The book also contains dozens of line drawings of plants and flowers, as well as a detailed appendix of alpine flora. This was the most definitive book written about the tundra when it was published in 1972.

RECREATION

Carr, Deborah, and Lou Ladrigan. *Backcountry Skiing and Snowshoeing in Grand County, Colorado*. Tabernash, CO: Backcountry Bound, 2003. This guide contains excellent route descriptions and maps for 16 snowshoe/ski outings in the park, as well as several dozen other locations near Rocky. The small, spiral-bound format is easy to pack in a backpack. Available for purchase at the Kawuneeche Valley Visitor Center and stores in Grand Lake.

Foster, Lisa. *Rocky Mountain National Park: The Complete Hiking Guide*. Estes Park, CO: Renaissance Mountaineering, LLC, 2013. Meticulously researched and written by a local resident who hiked every trail, this is the definitive hiking guide to the park and referred to as a "bible" by locals. The volume contains beautiful full-color photographs, all snapped by the author, plus maps and a comprehensive destinations chart in the appendix.

Gillett, Bernard. *Rocky Mountain National Park: The Climber's Guide, Estes Park Valley*. Chapel Hill, NC: Earthbound Sports, Inc., 2001. Comprehensive information about Rocky's Lumpy Ridge climbing area is found in this guide.

Kelly, Mark. *Backcountry Skiing and Ski Mountaineering in Rocky Mountain National Park*. Edgewater, CO: Giterdun Publishing, Ltd., 2013. Backcountry enthusiasts will find this guide incredibly helpful in planning and executing snowy adventures in the park. Even those who have no intention of skiing around Rocky will enjoy perusing the book's many full-color photographs.

The Mountaineers. *Mountaineering: The Freedom of the Hills, 8th Edition*. Seattle, WA: The Mountaineers, 2010. Easy-to-digest information about hiking and rock climbing is found in this 528-page reference manual, which serves as a great companion for anyone planning to climb or do extended hiking in Rocky. Topics include camping, clothing, equipment, knot tying, navigation, climbing fundamentals, snow travel, leadership, and first aid. Simple and effective black-and-white illustrations are abundant throughout the book.

Roach, Gerry. *Rocky Mountain National Park Classic Hikes & Climbs*. Golden, CO: Fulcrum, Inc., 1988. Something of a legend in Colorado, Gerry Roach has climbed more than 2,000 of the state's peaks, and amassed an incredible résumé of climbs worldwide in his lifetime. In this compact volume, Roach describes what is involved in scaling every one of Rocky's named mountaintops. Roach's writing style is at times blunt and to the point; in other instances, enthusiastic and downright funny. Don't be deterred by this book's plain cover, small size, and black-and-white photos; a wealth of information is contained inside.

Rossiter, Richard. *Rocky Mountain National Park: A Comprehensive Guide to Scrambles, Rock Routes, and Ice/Mixed Climbs on the High Peaks*. Boulder, CO: Fixed Pin Publishing, 2015. The organization of climbs in this dense guidebook is superb. The book includes route descriptions, photos, and topographic illustrations.

Schweitzer, Steve. *A Fly Fishing Guide to Rocky Mountain National Park*. Greeley, CO. Pixachrome Publishing, 2011. Everything you need to know about fly-fishing in the park is contained in this book. It features information about more than 150 fishing destinations, hatch charts, maps, and general fishing tips.

Internet Resources

ROCKY MOUNTAIN NATIONAL PARK

Rocky Mountain National Park
www.nps.gov/romo

The official website for Rocky Mountain National Park is chock-full of useful information for first-time and returning travelers. The site is also a vast repository for historical and scientific data about the park, and home to numerous multimedia presentations, reports, webcams, and blogs. Wilderness campsite permits can be downloaded from the site, and the Current Conditions page is updated regularly with trail, weather, and road closure information. Key information about the park is translated into Spanish.

Rocky Mountain Conservancy
www.rmconservancy.org

Rocky Mountain Conservancy is the education and fundraising arm for the park, providing support for a wide variety of activities, including historical preservation and trail maintenance. The conservancy operates nature stores out of the park's visitor centers, with proceeds funneled to park projects. Classes and tours are offered through the nonprofit's Field Institute. Gifts and books are available for purchase on the website, as well as RMNP specialty license plates.

Recreation.gov
www.recreation.gov

Reservations for three of Rocky's campgrounds—Moraine Park, Glacier Basin, and Aspenglen—can be made through this website.

Rocky Mountain Hiking Trails
www.rockymountainhikingtrails.com

This site contains comprehensive information about dozens of hikes in Rocky. Each excursion is described in great detail; trails are searchable by feature, location, and difficulty rating.

ESTES PARK

Visit Estes Park
www.visitestespark.com

The official website for Estes Park is replete with information about the town and Rocky Mountain National Park. Check out this site for information about lodging, activities, restaurants, and events.

GRAND LAKE

Grand Lake Area Chamber of Commerce
www.grandlakechamber.com

On the official website for Grand Lake, get informed about dining options, area accommodations, activities, events, and shopping.

Grand Lake Area Historical Society
www.grandlakehistory.org
This website has a wonderful collection of stories and photos about the people and places of Grand Lake, plus information about local museums.

RECREATION

Colorado Parks & Wildlife
www.cpw.state.co.us
This is one place where you can purchase a Colorado fishing license; a list of agents that sell licenses in-person is also posted on the site. Individuals age 16 and older must have a valid license to fish in Rocky.

Mountain Project
www.mountainproject.com
Climbers will tell you that this website is the best online public forum for rock and ice climbing. Mountain Project features route descriptions and photos for dozens of climbing locations in the park.

U.S. Forest Service
www.fs.usda.gov
Visit this site for information about the Arapaho and Roosevelt National Forests and the Arapaho National Recreation Area (ANRA). Includes important details about camping, boating, fishing, and hiking.

APPS

Hiking Rocky Mountain National Park, TUA Outdoors, LLC. Download to your iPhone or iPad this quick-reference guide to a number of the park's most popular hikes. One of the handiest features is the app's vertical profile graphic, indicating elevation changes for each journey.

REI Co-Op Guide to the National Parks, REI. Even if you do not have a cell phone signal, this app tracks your location within Rocky (and other national parks), which can be especially handy on hikes. In case of a cell phone failure—and to be on the safe side—always carry additional tools for navigation (map and compass and/or a Global Positioning System [GPS] device).

EBOOKS

Photographing Rocky Mountain National Park: The Landscape Photographer's Guide, 2013, Erik Stensland. The premier photographer of RMNP dispenses tips for taking pictures of the most popular places in the park. Included are precise GPS coordinates for where to stand to get the perfect shot.

VIDEOS

The Living Dream: 100 Years of Rocky Mountain National Park, 2015, Nick Mollé Productions. In 90 minutes, Mollé beautifully and expertly tells the story of Rocky, weaving together archival photos, interviews, and video of the park in the present day.

Ski Hidden Valley Estes Park, 2013, Brown-Cow Productions. Lift-served skiing has been a thing of the past since 1991, but Rocky's now-defunct Hidden Valley ski area is still remembered fondly by locals in this 114-minute documentary.

Index

A

B

C

H

IJK

L

List of Maps

Front Map

Discover Rocky Mountain National Park

Bear Lake and the East Side

Longs Peak and Wild Basin

Trail Ridge Road

Kawuneeche Valley

Lumpy Ridge and the Mummy Range

Gateways

Acknowledgments

Many individuals helped to make this book a reality.

I am indebted to numerous park employees and volunteers for sharing specialized information about Rocky. Among them are Michele Simmons, Barry Sweet, Kevin Sturmer, Paul Larson, Barbara King, Larry Gamble, Jeff Maugans, Sam Crane, Corrie Lane, Dar Spearing, and Don Stewart.

I especially thank Kyle Patterson for providing thoughtful guidance throughout the research and writing process. I am so grateful for Marilyn Irwin, who shared her extensive knowledge about the park and cheerfully answered so many random questions along the way.

When I wasn't camping in the woods or reviewing hotels, Richard Bray generously provided a comfortable place to sleep and work.

Thank you Tereza Venn, Mike Neustedter, and Greg Griffith for accompanying me on hikes.

David McQueen gets special recognition for introducing me to Rocky so many years ago, and sharing with me his enthusiasm for hiking, backpacking, fishing, and photography.

I so appreciate the time and energy my team at Avalon Travel put into this book. Thank you Albert Angulo, Holly Birchfield, Elizabeth Hansen, Elizabeth Jang, Kristi Mitsuda, Katie Mock, Kimi Owens, and Sabrina Young.

Additional thanks go out to Dave Lively, Chris Kennedy, Patricia Washburn, Alicia Rochambeau, Jonathan Ley, Luke Terstriep, Jim Gasner, Charles Money, Rachel Balduzzi, John Simmons, Zach Zehr, Brooke Burnham, Samantha Miller, Kent Argow, and Tyler Tworek.

Lastly, I would like to extend heartfelt gratitude to the three most important men in my life. My brother, Tony English, did so much—not the least of which was to look at every chapter of this book in rough draft form and help taste-test doughnuts in Estes Park. From day one, my husband, Eric White, provided unwavering support and wore many hats: hiking companion, computer troubleshooter, photo-taker, proofreader, and general sounding board.

My son, August White, reminded me to slow down on the trails and always look at the park with fresh eyes. Thank you.

Also Available

MAP SYMBOLS

- Expressway
- Primary Road
- Secondary Road
- Unpaved Road
- Feature Trail
- Other Trail
- Ferry
- Pedestrian Walkway
- Stairs

- City/Town
- State Capital
- National Capital
- Point of Interest
- Accommodation
- Restaurant/Bar
- Other Location
- Campground

- Airport
- Airfield
- Mountain
- Unique Natural Feature
- Waterfall
- Park
- Trailhead
- Skiing Area

- Golf Course
- Parking Area
- Archaeological Site
- Church
- Gas Station
- Glacier
- Mangrove
- Reef
- Swamp

CONVERSION TABLES

°C = (°F - 32) / 1.8
°F = (°C x 1.8) + 32
1 inch = 2.54 centimeters (cm)
1 foot = 0.304 meters (m)
1 yard = 0.914 meters
1 mile = 1.6093 kilometers (km)
1 km = 0.6214 miles
1 fathom = 1.8288 m
1 chain = 20.1168 m
1 furlong = 201.168 m
1 acre = 0.4047 hectares
1 sq km = 100 hectares
1 sq mile = 2.59 square km
1 ounce = 28.35 grams
1 pound = 0.4536 kilograms
1 short ton = 0.90718 metric ton
1 short ton = 2,000 pounds
1 long ton = 1.016 metric tons
1 long ton = 2,240 pounds
1 metric ton = 1,000 kilograms
1 quart = 0.94635 liters
1 US gallon = 3.7854 liters
1 Imperial gallon = 4.5459 liters
1 nautical mile = 1.852 km

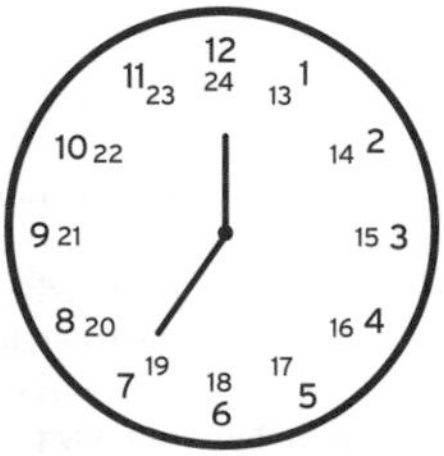

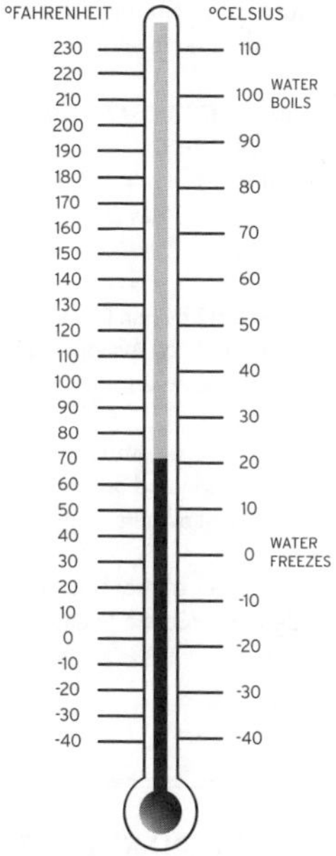

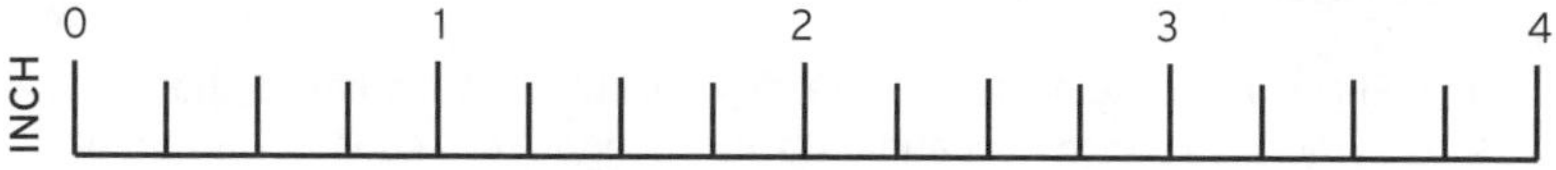

°FAHRENHEIT °CELSIUS
100 WATER BOILS
0 WATER FREEZES

INCH 0 1 2 3 4

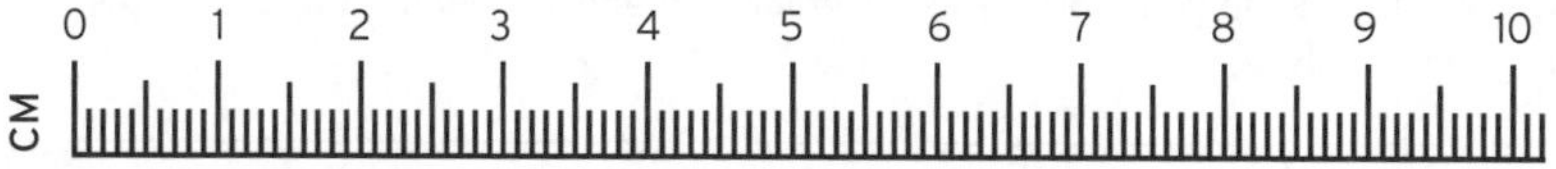

CM 0 1 2 3 4 5 6 7 8 9 10

MOON ROCKY MOUNTAIN NATIONAL PARK
Avalon Travel
An imprint of Perseus Books
A Hachette Book Group company
1700 Fourth Street
Berkeley, CA 94710, USA
www.moon.com

Editors: Sabrina Young, Kristi Mitsuda
Series Manager: Sabrina Young
Copy Editor: Mary Duffy
Production and Graphics Coordinator: Elizabeth Jang
Cover Design: Faceout Studios, Charles Brock
Interior Design: Domini Dragoone
Moon Logo: Tim McGrath
Map Editor: Albert Angulo
Cartographers: Albert Angulo, Brian Shotwell, Moon Street Cartography (Durango, CO)
Proofreader: Elizabeth Hui
Indexer: Greg Jewett

ISBN-13: 978-1-63121-329-8
ISSN: 2475-0832
Printing History
1st Edition — May 2017
5 4 3 2 1

Front cover photo: sunset over Bear Lake © Mike Berenson/Colorado Captures/Getty Images

Back cover photo: large male elk in Rocky Mountain National Park © Nickolay Stanev | Dreamstime.com

All interior photos © Erin English, except the following: page 68 (top) © Don Stewart; page 69 © Tony English; page 89 © Don Stewart; page 94 © Don Stewart; page 112 © Eric White; page 128 © Eric White

Printed in Canada by Friesens

KEEPING CURRENT

If you have a favorite gem you'd like to see included in the next edition, or see anything that needs updating, clarification, or correction, please drop us a line. Send your comments via email to feedback@moon.com, or use the address above.